The Wholehearted Journey

Bringing Qualities of Soul to Everyday Life and Work

written by

Denise Bissonnette

Diversity World
Santa Cruz, California

ISBN 0-9717129-0-5

Printed in the United States of America.

Library of Congress Control Number: 2002113086

Published by:
Diversity World
Santa Cruz, California
www.diversityworld.com

Dedication

I lovingly dedicate this book to my aunts,
Anna Bissonnette and Marion Kenneally,
who have inspired me with their soulful work
as they travel their own wholehearted journeys.

A portion of the proceeds from this book will be donated to Helping Elders At Risk Through Homes (HEARTH) in Boston, Massachusetts. HEARTH was started in 1991, spearheaded by my aunt, Anna Bissonnette, and has provided over 500 homeless and at risk elders with permanent housing throughout the Greater Boston area. For more information about the work done by this powerful non-profit organization, write to 1640 Washington Street, Boston, MA. 02118 or visit www.ceeh.org.

Acknowledgements

Luciano de Crescenzo wisely reminds us, "We are each of us angels with only one wing, and we can only fly embracing each other." The writing and creation of this book would never have happened without the love, support and talents of the people who gave this work wings.

I am blessed to be part of a large family who are a continuing source of wisdom, love and encouragement. Special thanks to Dad, Diane, Debbie, Anna, Marion and Michelle for their generous insights and careful critique in the initial editing of this work. To my brother Tom I am forever grateful for modeling a unique brand of wholeheartedness and authenticity that inspires me daily. I have no idea who I would be without my family, but I do know that what I have written in these pages is a direct result of having been held in their strong and loving embrace.

I am very fortunate to be supported by a wide circle of friends. In particular, I want to thank Jane Robertson who first encouraged me to follow the beat of my own drum, Mark and Louise Griffiths for their always refreshing and insightful input, Lynda Jean Groh for her spiritual reminders and humorous guidance, Roxanne Woodling and Maureen Hamb for monthly doses of love and grounding, and Renee DeMar for her unfailing devotion as a friend. I am grateful to Milt and Anita Wright for their ongoing love and support and to Richard Pimentel for years of priceless mentorship and friendship. To Larry Pitchford and Heather VerWys I offer my heartfelt appreciation for the careful and expert proofing of this work as well as their enthusiastic support as friends. Thank you all for your contributions to this book and for the treasure that you are in my life!

To Sheri McInnis, I could write a separate book of thanks, but suffice it to say that this book and the journey that precipitated it was inspired by her unflinching confidence and belief in me. I will be forever grateful to you, Sheri, for the vision you inspired within me.

A world of thanks goes to Andy Rolphe, graphic designer extraordinaire, who created a beautiful landscape for these words. thank you not only for applying the genius of your craft, but for the gifts of your never-ending patience and kindness at every turn. I pray to write another book, if only for the privilege of working with you again!

I offer heartfelt appreciation and kudos to my dear friend, Rita Wright, for applying her eagle's eye in the apt and incisive editing of these pages. How do I ever thank you, Rita, for being there at the birth of my child, and then again, for the birth of this book? My love and respect for you run deep and wide.

For the hundreds of hours of painstaking and meticulous work in putting together the Source Index of this book, I will forever be grateful to my dear friend, Kendra Webster. You have made this book far richer because of it, just as you have made my life richer through your love and friendship. Thank you, too, for your technical and literary advice as well as your ongoing confidence in me during the writing of this book. You truly were heaven sent!

I would be remiss not to acknowledge the hundreds of great writers, poets, mystics, philosophers and sages who have greatly influenced my life and work. With a humble heart, I bow to the four hundred fellow pilgrims who have illuminated my path with the light of their own. By quoting them in these pages I hope to further spread the light of their wisdom and the beauty of their words.

To my daughter, Jessica Rose, thank you for your unending love and support, for being the first person to hear each poem, and for the great joy you bring into my life. I love being your mother and I thank you for inspiring me to live in color!

Finally, I offer my love and thanks to Rob McInnes, my true companion, who has walked every step of this journey with me. There are no words to adequately express my love and gratitude for your emotional and moral support as well as the love and care you poured into every technical aspect of bringing this book to fruition. Thank you for lending a fine eye and keen ear to the deepening and refinement of this work, always helping me to find my truer voice and a clearer eye. Your fingerprints are on every page of this book, your heart-prints are on every word. I remain wholeheartedly yours.

Table of Contents

Introduction

Welcome to the Wholehearted Journey!

This is a book of poetry, parables and creative ponderings. It is a book of insights gleaned and distilled from the work of hundreds of writers, philosophers and fellow pilgrims throughout the ages. It is full to the brim with important questions and practical suggestions for putting our purposes and principles into practice. It is a call to arms to spirited and soulful living, both in work and in the larger context of our lives. *The Wholehearted Journey* is an invitation to dive deeply into the waters of self-exploration and to come out refreshed and renewed—eager to express our gifts, share our joy and give birth to our dreams. This book is about bringing our whole heart to the altar of every day.

Early in its creation, it struck me that I was writing this book first and foremost for myself, because above all, this writing is a bold and honest expression of how I ache to live. If no one was ever to read this book, the experience of writing it was worth every moment spent in its creation. It has been a wonderful journey: writing and learning from the poetry; ruminating and delighting in the *Reflections* section for each chapter; gathering and selecting quotes for each chapter's theme; and most importantly, putting the suggestions at the end of each chapter into practice in my own life. And while the experience of writing this book has been rich and rewarding, it has also been difficult due to the deep cut of its questions and the discipline required of its tenets.

I began writing this book for the "working person"—a book about ways to bring qualities of soul to the everyday workplace. As I continued writing, however, it became clear to me that the ideas, principles and practices offered in these pages could be relevant to anyone and pertinent to every aspect of life, not just the workplace. For we all work, whether or not we are employed. We all share the important job of living our lives fully, amidst the struggles and strain of daily pressures and challenges that come at us from every direction. So this is written for people who go to a workplace, as well as those who don't. This is for those who continue to search for their true place in the world of work as well as those who are retired and feel in their bones that their "true work" is not yet complete. *The Wholehearted Journey* is for anyone who wants to engage in life and work in a deep and soulful way, bringing their own individual mix of talents, gifts and purposes to every day.

Organization of the Book

Each chapter of *The Wholehearted Journey* consists of four sections:

Poetry: Introducing the central theme of the chapter

Reflections: Offering key insights, parables and anecdotes on the qualities of soul that are derived from the theme

Passages: Focusing on the theme through selected thoughts and comments of great writers and thinkers, present and past

To Ponder and Practice: Posing penetrating questions, suggestions and challenges for integrating the theme and its qualities more fully into everyday life

The Poems

It has only been in the last few years that I discovered the power and the potency of a poem as a way of teaching, expressing and knowing myself. For until then, I, like many, had one of two categories in which to place most poetry: the sticky sweet greeting card version and the kind I feared I could never understand. Like many in our culture, my exposure to poetry was both minimal and cursory. Had I only known the awe and wonder that awaited me through the works of such great poets as Rumi, Rainer Marie Rilke, Elizabeth Browning, Henry David Thoreau, William Blake, Ralph Waldo Emerson, W. S. Merwyn, David Whyte, Mary Oliver, Anne Sexton and Mark Nepo!

As I began reciting poetry in my training sessions and keynote speeches, many people expressed their surprise to find that poetry has the power to touch them, deeply at times, in places they have not visited before. That is the power that poetry can have. It can draw us into the poignancy of our experience and invite us to share aloud the complexities of being human. Poet James Autry says that "Poetry gives you permission to feel." In my experience, it not only allows you to feel but to distill those emotions into their essentials. Writing poetry is a way of seeing and naming where we have been, where we are and where we are going with our lives. It asks, "What do you want to courageously cry about, scream about and sing about?" It is not afraid of its own voice.

I am not a poet's poet—I am not learned in the art nor educated in its history. For me it is simply the voice of my own soul, whispering, singing, crying and celebrating. It is the voice from the deep breaking through the surface waters of my normal expression. A poem is something I receive, not something I craft. It is like a prayer. Once having entered the winds of my own yearning or plea, I am carried on its sails, not the reverse. I never really know where a poem will take me, or upon what distant or foreign shore of meaning I may find myself beached by the end of it. And yet strangely, in the end, they all feel like home. It is with great joy that I share these poems with you as a way of opening each chapter. It is my fond hope that by sharing my poetry, this book might provide a nudge for you to begin, or to continue, writing your own.

Reflections

Each chapter in the book revolves around a unique theme giving rise to yeasty topics relating to life's journey. I use the *Reflections* section of each chapter to delve more deeply into those themes, the characteristics or qualities it summons in us and key ideas or suggestions for weaving those essential qualities into our everyday lives.

As a trainer, I make tremendous use of storytelling as a way of making a teaching point. As such, I have collected myriad fables, parables and stories, many of them originating from various spiritual traditions, which I share in this book to reinforce essential ideas of each chapter. To the best of my ability, I have attempted to name or give credit to the original source of each of these stories. I regret that some have come to me with dubious origins and I only hope that their creators, named and unnamed, will find this book a worthy platform for the voicing of their ideas.

Passages

We exist in a world of words, most of which are used recklessly, without much precision or care. We hear them, speak them, read them and write them with disregard to their potency. Gustave Flaubert said it well in this quote from *Madame Bovary:*

> "Human speech is like a cracked kettle on which we tap crude rhythms for bears to dance to, while we long to make music that will melt the stars."

For as I long as I can remember, I have been enthralled with the world of words. I believe they have the power to startle, surprise and awaken us. Words, employed with precision and care, have the power to melt the ice of our complacency and indifference, to even melt the stars. I have included over 500 such quotations in this book. Their originators use words as the painter wields her brush or the samurai brandishes his sword—with respect and precision, care and attention.

I am elated to gather under one cover a rich and diverse collection of quotations and excerpts from my favorite books. Included in each chapter's section of *Passages* are the inspiring and oft times startling words of writers, mystics, saints, artists, revolutionaries, world leaders and visionaries. I have collected them over the course of several years knowing that I would one day weave these beautiful passages into a linguistic and philosophic composition for and about the everyday pilgrim walking to the beat of their own soul's drum. I offer them here with humble gratitude and unrelenting awe to their originators.

May even just a few of these quotes invoke for you, dear reader, an idea whose time has come. I will never forget the first time I fell under the spell of these words from Mahatma Gandhi: "We must be the change we wish to see in the world." This one line changed my life by bringing me to the realization that I am the *only* person I can change. These twelve words live in me now; they have a place in my being like fresh flowers have a place on the table or a photograph has a place on the mantel. Although there are 25 to 30 quotes in each chapter's *Passages,* perhaps only a few will strike you in a profound way, gravitating towards the mantel of your being. I encourage you to read them with an eye for the ones that speak to you most deeply.

Johann von Goethe once noted, "All wise thoughts have been thought already thousands of times; but to make them truly ours, we must think them over again honestly, till they take root in our personal experience." To that end, I have suggested in the *To Ponder and Practice* section of each chapter that you choose a favorite quote from each chapter's *Passages* and post it where you will see it until it takes root in your own experience.

To Ponder and Practice

Until we put an idea into practice, it does not really belong to us. Only those ideas which we have applied and experienced can ever truly affect our lives in a meaningful way. Thus, every chapter ends with a section called *To Ponder and Practice,* which provides various questions pertaining to the specific theme of the chapter, as well as ideas for nurturing the personal qualities that will enable us to more effectively embrace that theme in daily life.

I recommend that you purchase or designate a personal journal as a companion to this book to record your thoughts and responses to the questions at the end of each chapter. It will be important as you progress through the book to look back at your responses to questions from prior chapters. My hope is that the journal you keep while reading and responding to *The Wholehearted Journey* will remain a treasure that you will return to time and again.

About Questions

Rainer Maria Rilke, though primarily thought of as the finest German poet of the 20th century, wrote prose with equal eloquence. Here is a much-quoted passage from his book, *Letters to a Young Poet:*

> "...have patience with everything that remains unsolved in your heart. Try to love the questions themselves, like locked rooms and like books written in a foreign language. Do not now look for the answers. They cannot now be given to you because you could not live them. It is a question of experiencing everything. At present you need to live the question. Perhaps you will gradually, without even noticing it, find yourself experiencing the answer, some distant day."

Nothing shapes our lives so much as the questions we ask—or refuse to ask. Martin Luther King Jr. suggested, in fact, that the "questions we ask will shape our destiny as clearly as the skeleton shapes the body." The questions we ask serve as a lens on the camera of the mind, telling us what to pay attention to, what to focus on. We are all questioners, but the questions that animate us are profoundly different. Imagine how the nature and quality of our lives might differ according to which set of the following questions most inspires our thoughts and actions.

What will my neighbors think?	*What do I think?*
Who will love me?	*How do I extend my love to others?*
How do I increase my power?	*Who or what shall I serve?*
How can I make more money?	*How am I already wealthy?*
What's my next career move?	*How do I stay true to the journey of my heart?*
How much life insurance do I have for my family?	*What legacy do I want to leave my children?*
How do I avoid heartache?	*What noble challenge has my name on it?*
Where am I going?	*Who am I in the midst of becoming?*
How's my financial portfolio shaping up?	*How am I living in alignment with my highest purposes?*

The everyday questions we ask, like those in the left column, are perfectly legitimate questions—they reflect some of our basic human needs for physical comfort, social acceptance and financial security. But if we ask questions for meaning and purpose pertaining to our worldly needs, exclusive of our spiritual needs, we live a one-sided life. To live wholeheartedly, we must entertain questions that pertain to the inner world as well as the outer world.

Pondering a question is a way of bestowing awareness in our lives. The purpose of the questions provided at the end of each chapter is not necessarily to learn the truth, the whole truth and nothing but the truth. In fact, sometimes a question leads us deeper into doubt and uncertainty, not away from it. Sometimes we are asked a question and the answer appears as if it has simply awaited this invitation to make itself known. Other questions need to percolate or to simply sit in the waters of our being like a teabag, bringing forth flavor over time.

It is not necessary for us to find definitive answers to some of the more elusive, perhaps unanswerable, questions like, "Why am I here?" or "What is the purpose of my life?" We need to ask the big questions, but we may need to be satisfied with small pieces of answers. Even when we are not sure how these pieces fit together, a wholehearted, spirited life requires us to continue facing into the wind and to keep the questions alive.

There is a poetic power in having the right question asked at the right time. My hope is that many questions in this book will give you pause, will stop you in your tracks and cause you to reflect, ponder and ruminate. May your responses to these questions put a brighter light in your eyes or a new song in your step.

About Practices

I believe that we make little progress in our lives merely by attempting to repress or stop what we find harmful, unhealthy or distasteful. Our greatest hope lies in developing what is healthy, wholesome and good, practicing what we cherish, value and love. *The Wholehearted Journey* contains hundreds of quotes and small gems of wisdom from great thinkers throughout time. But the truth is that we can starve while reading a cookbook! Unless we put these ideas to use in our lives, they have no power to bring us real nourishment. The words of Buddha, spoken 2500 years ago, still ring true today:

"However many holy words you read,
However many you speak,
What good will they do you
If you do not act upon them?"

With the multitude of choices and decisions we face on a daily basis, both inside and outside the workplace, how do we know where to begin to take steps that will move us toward our wholeness and joy? Amidst all of the therapies, psychologies and self-help strategies made available to us, how do we discern and select practices that will bring us into balance and rhythm in our lives? I have appreciated this very simple philosophy for improving one's life:

1. Keep doing what works.
2. Stop doing what doesn't work.
3. Start doing what will work.

I like it enough to have reformulated it as the final three questions at the end of each chapter. Taking the time to assess your actions in each of these three areas will give you an opportunity to affirm the good things that you are doing. It will also allow you to identify the habits you have cultivated that are not working toward your highest purposes. Lastly, it will help to bring into focus the new choices you can be making to design the life you want.

Purposes of *The Wholehearted Journey*

The Wholehearted Journey is about bringing qualities of soul to our everyday life and work—with a renewed sense of enthusiasm, purpose and even reverence. That which we regard as sacred, we will naturally treat with the utmost care and devotion. I believe that our lives would love to be treated as sacred—as would our work. Unfortunately, the pace at which most of us live and work prevents this. One of the purposes of this book is to cultivate ways of making a temple of our lives, in and outside of work.

Leonardo Da Vinci advised centuries ago that "Where the spirit does not work with the hand there is no art." His words ring true, whether we work at home or in the world, regardless of industry or position. When our work is vacant of spirit, it will be devoid of vitality, as will our lives outside of work. By making our lives and work more hospitable to the gifts of spirit and to the qualities of soul, however, we are gifted in return in innumerable, very palpable ways. The following nine themes summarize the rewards of traveling the journey of life and work with wholeheartedness, and as such, these are the true purposes of this book.

Renew a sense of purpose and passion

Frederich Nietzsche once said, "When a man has a *why*, he doesn't have to concern himself with *how.*" This is true because of the focusing powers of purpose. When we know why we are doing something, that purpose becomes a horizon within us and our feet find wings. With a renewed sense of purpose, we find meaning and fulfillment in the simplest acts and in the most mundane circumstances. We realize that even when we are in situations that appear unworthy of our time and attention, we can supply the "worthiness" just in the way in which we approach a person, task or deed. This book is an invitation to pursue our purposes and passions, to open our arms and embrace the great "why" that calls to us from the world.

Develop a greater sense of faith in ourselves

The sense of vulnerability that accompanies us on the journey of life in the face of the unknown can leave us feeling overwhelmed, ineffectual and powerless. The insecurity produced by these feelings can cause us to shut our windows and lock our doors, even though a brilliant sun shines brightly around us. Whenever we face change, fear inevitably raises its head as well. Fear of failure. Fear of success. Fear of the unknown. Fear of loss. Fear of fear itself.

There is an art to learning how to flow with the ups and downs of life's challenges and hardships, to be open to the light streaking through the dark shadows of transition. Somewhere deep within us, we know that true security is not the absence of danger but the presence of faith—faith in ourselves and in our ability to survive. On a wholehearted journey we find faith in our ability to make new choices, even as we face adversity and challenges. Although the world cannot guarantee us ongoing employment, for example, we can have faith in our ongoing employability. We all live on faith, because the nature of life is that we are always stepping into the unknown. The issue is what are we putting our faith in. One of the purposes of this book is to shed light on where we have invested our faith and to consider where we want to invest it in the future.

Increase mindfulness and self-awareness

Living happens. Being fully alive, however, takes time and consciousness. For the sake of making a living we often forget to live. Our attention is usually split, in fact, fractured by the many pressures of our lives. We begin sleepwalking through life without noticing that we are not awake to our circumstances, choices and opportunities, much less our needs, desires and longings. Politician and writer Marian Wright Edelman urges us to awaken with this advice, "It is time for every one of us to roll up our sleeves and put ourselves at the top of our commitment list." I don't think she is talking about getting the car in for its 30,000-mile check-up or scheduling a manicure. I think she means attending to our inner lives with as much devotion as we give our outer lives. Indeed, mindfulness is as rare as it is precious.

I remember one of my favorite teachers saying that "one of the greatest tragedies in life is living one's life without ever finding oneself in one's self." Clearly, we have to know ourselves before we can bring ourselves to a job, to relationships or to being in community. There has to be someone "home" before we can harness our powers to affect that which is outside us. As the Hindu sage Ramana Maharshi advises:

> "Wanting to reform the world without discovering one's true self is like trying to cover the world with leather to avoid the pain of walking on stones and thorns. It is much simpler to just wear shoes."

The questions and ideas contained in this book are meant to heighten and enhance the gifts of self-awareness and usher us into more mindful living.

Live more fully in the present

We tend to live in the past or the future; always expecting the coming of some special moment when our life will unfold itself in its full significance. We often approach time as if it is a commodity that belongs to us, as if it is something we can manage, spend or waste at will because there will always be more of it at our disposal. And all the while, our one and precious life continues to flow like water through our fingers.

Our lives are made of a stream of days and it is only here, in the present hours and days of our lives, that we find expression for our gifts, our joys and sorrows, our growth and healing. The only place where we have power is in the present. This book offers myriad choices, gestures and acts to enter each day with a sense of purposefulness and power, even urgency, to live each moment to the utmost.

Take small steps

Friedrich Nietzsche wisely reminds us of the obvious:

> "He who would learn to fly one day must first learn to stand and run and climb and dance; one cannot fly their way into flying."

Nietzsche's words hold real wisdom for us as we travel the winding road of life and work. Being products of a society addicted to immediate gratification, how do we cultivate in ourselves the patience necessary to walk steadily along the journey when all we want to do is fly our way into success? One way to do this is to focus our thoughts and energy in areas where we have direct influence and control, even if in just the next step. By focusing on small steps in the present, we are better able to set aside the anxieties about our futures and preoccupations with the past and the burdens of our regrets. This book suggests a multitude of small steps to take in order to grow, slowly but surely, our greater powers.

Increase our capacity for joy and wonder

Grace, beauty and wonder are carried on the winds of our everyday lives but unless we set our sails to catch those winds, we will never be carried or refreshed by them. We need not strive or search for these qualities; we must cultivate a greater capacity to receive them in and through our most common experiences as suggested by Robert Louis Stevenson in this beautiful passage:

> "The best things are nearest: breath in your nostrils, light in your eyes, flowers at your feet, duties at your hands, the path of right just before you. Do not grasp at the stars, but do life's plain common work as it comes, certain that daily duties and daily bread are the sweetest things in life."

Joy and wonder are not merely incidental to a wholehearted life, they are vital. We can be so achievement oriented that we often fail to see what's before us, thinking that accomplishing things will complete us, when it is experiencing life in all its wonder that leads to the path of true fulfillment and wholeness. Only through wholehearted living will we know how to develop a true sense of belonging in the world as well as the sensibilities to experience its wonders. In and outside of work, we are sure to encounter an everlasting mix of conundrum, enigma, dilemma, paradox, illusion, contradiction and inconvenience. Only by adding an equal mix of curiosity, enthusiasm, awe, wonder and wide-eyed amazement will we concoct a cocktail of life that is not only drinkable but intoxicating in the purest sense. Among other things, this book is a toast to the wholehearted life. May yours bubble with joy!

Shift our focus from reaping to sowing

Many of us wonder where we should be, which position we should be in, and what we should be doing next, while our lives would be better served by shifting our focus to who we are being. We waste time looking for perfect employment, instead of trying to be the perfect employee for the position we hold or using our current positions as the perfect stepping stone to the next job. We continually ask about the meaning of life instead of asking what meaning we should bring *to* life. We can be quick to judge the world around us and to notice what other people should and should not be doing, while we could be taking a little stock of ourselves and of what we are contributing to the world. The measure of our lives is not about what we can scorn, criticize and judge, but about what we can love, appreciate and take into our arms. By shifting our focus from what the world has to offer us to giving of ourselves and being receptive to the gifts of others, we change the world at the end of our fingertips.

American author and minister Robert Fulghum dispels a great myth when he says that "peace is not something you wish for; it's something you make, something you do, something you are and something you give away." I think he is sharing an important basic truth, not just about peace, but about every life-giving quality we yearn for as human beings, including contentment, joy, purpose, forgiveness, compassion and love. Most of what we want in life we must plant in the soil of our own beings. Bringing qualities of soul to the everyday circumstances at home and at work is a way of sowing seeds so that our lives and the lives of those we touch may flower more brilliantly.

Respond to the changes in the world with hope and optimism

The ancient entreaty, "May you live in interesting times," has certainly come true. We have seen more drastic changes in the world of work in the last ten years than we have in all the decades preceding them. Today's world of work is not only full of challenges and surprises, but also every species of colleague, customer and manager, and every variation of work situation, including temping, leasing, outsourcing and project work. Many complain of the "de-jobbing" of the North American workplace, while other economists and futurists tell us that the market is not shrinking but reshuffling, resulting in opportunities that never existed before. So how do we navigate the white waters of today's economic, political and social realties when we were raised with the tools and thinking suited to the serene waters of a world that is gone and may never return?

Circumstances and terms of employment have changed, but what remains stubbornly the same is each person's quest to make his or her way in the world, juggling the needs and demands of practical realities with the deeper yearnings of the human heart. Ralph Waldo Emerson once surmised that, "This time, like all times, is a very good one, if we but know what to do with it." Surely that is as true today as it was in his day.

We are in what futurist John Nesbitt called "the era of parenthesis"—leaving behind the realities of one world without having entered the solid realities of a new time. Each of us is responsible for helping to create the world that our children and grandchildren will inherit. If we want a world that is worthy of our own as well as our children's talents, gifts and potentiality, we must work to shape it. One of the aims of this book is to shake off our fears and anxiety over an uncertain economy, and instead, travel the path of livelihood with renewed hope and optimism. We need to harness our combined brilliance and brazenness and meet our challenges with a sense of usefulness and purpose. By traveling our individual paths wholeheartedly and with qualities of soul, we can rise to the challenges before us so that, in the words of author Jan Phillips," … what we create will be as useful as a hammer, as honest as a prayer, as far-reaching as a bridge and as urgent as a cry."

Give rise to fresh cravings

Artist Abraham Heschel described art as something that introduces us to emotions that we have never cherished before. He says, "Great works produce rather than satisfy needs by giving the world fresh cravings." That is my deepest wish for this body of work—that it rouses in the reader longings, needs and dreams that have lain dormant. That it awakens new cravings. Like thirst of the spirit to pour its purpose into the vessel of a workday—like hunger of the soul to build a place of belonging from the bricks and mortar of one's convictions, talents and ancient longings.

We live as pilgrims, journeying into the unknown of each day in a world that is at once chaotic, confusing and full to the brim with choices. When we find ourselves stranded on islands of fear or doubt, we need to remember that we also have larger continents of wisdom and truth on which to stand. May the poetry, reflections, ponderings, and practices presented in this book take you on small excursions to those larger bodies in the sea of your being. May the ideas offered in these pages usher you into the kind of creative choices, mindfulness and grateful living that will keep your journey alive and vital. May all of our work, individually and collectively, be worthy of the precious investment of our time and talents. As I assert in the last poem of the book:

This is the pilgrim's plea at the
onset of the 21st century:
To bring all that we are and all
that we have
To the joy and the sorrow,
The wonder and the terror,
The known and the unknown
of daily living.

As your journey unfolds, I offer you the East Indian word meaning "the spirit in me honors the spirit in you"—*Namaste.*

I Dedicate this Day

Chapter

Bringing the Sacred into the Everyday

Be both Here *and* There

Be both Here and There

Read the signs of a dispirited life

Read the signs of a dispirited life

Bring the gift of intention

Bring the gift of intention

Take a cue from Brother Lawrence

Take a cue from Brother Lawrence

Dedicate your day

Dedicate your day

Transform habits into rituals

Transform habits into rituals

Reset your perceptual senses

Reset your perceptual senses

Remember how you wish to live

Remember how you wish to live

I Dedicate This Day

With the gift of a dedication
a modest meal becomes a feast, the simplest words, a poem,
a child's carefree sketching, treasured art.

So how about a day like this one?
By rising above my own petty concerns and granting this day a purpose,
can I transform the humble offering of my time, my work and deeds
into something noble, something worthy of another day of precious living?

For I don't want to exist as if in some mindless entanglement
in a meaningless world.
I want to work myself like a silken thread in a web to which I belong.
By dedicating this day, I want to open the door around my heart,
to draw wide the curtain of my being
so that this day may become a window…
a window upon which the bird of purpose may perch and even sing.

Dedicated to the memory of Gandhi, I will walk in peace.
With Mother Teresa in mind, I will look my fellow man in the eye.
Devoted to Anne Frank, I will hold high a steady torch of hope.
Inspired by Dr. King, I might even dare to dream.
Dedicated to Vision, who knows what I might see?
To Listening, who knows what I might hear?
Depending on the purpose I bestow upon it,
this day may become a bridge to friendship, medicine for an old wound,
or an orchard bearing the fruit of my labors.

The day that has not been anointed with purpose
is like a bird with no sky, a fish with no stream, a lantern unlit.
But when I dedicate my day I am an arrow shot from a steady bow.
I am an eagle in spirited flight.
I am a candle whose flame blossoms with light in my own small corner of time.

This day will come and go whether or not I make of it a gift.
I can pray that it goes well…
or I can choose to pray in a medium far more powerful than words,
I can imbue them with a promise.

I choose to dedicate this day.

Reflections

Sometimes I think life is a lot like being a passenger on an airplane. As long as there is no turbulence and the plane is flying smoothly, I often forget that I am even in the air. I become absorbed in a book or in my writing and pay no attention to the forces that are holding the plane up or propelling us forward. I can fly from one side of the country to the other with absolutely no thought of the marvels of aviation that have transported me over mountains, deserts, lakes and plains. I simply get off the plane and hurry to the baggage claim, hoping that my bags have arrived in the same city. Unless, of course, we hit bumpy air.

With even the slightest bit of turbulence, I immediately become white-knuckled, searching the faces of my fellow passengers for clues of just how seriously I should be freaking out. With fear and trepidation, I leave the world of my book and return to the airplane. I remember that we are 35,000 feet in the air and that the small cushion upon which I am seated is supposed to double as a flotation device. I remain acutely aware of my physical surroundings, including the rapid beating of my heart against my chest and the breath as it enters and leaves my lungs. I think about my life and the people I love… I consider all that I may be leaving behind on earth. I am reminded of the tenuous nature of life and the precious gift that it is. In this heightened state of awareness, albeit awakened through terror, I am overwhelmed with my desire to live and not die. In this state, my every breath is a prayer. That is, until the plane levels out again.

I listen for the engines to resume a steady hum and I feel the air beneath us rise up from under the plane like strong arms holding us in the sky. My heart slowly returns to its normal beating. I take a few deep breaths and I look out the window at a world I love and am glad to not have to take leave of—at least not yet. A wave of enormous relief and gratitude rushes through me. I shake my head at my tendency to overreact and I smile in spite of myself. Within a few minutes I allow the plane to rock me back into complete and utter complacency. Amazingly, I can go from a state of deep, earnest prayer back into total absorption in a mystery novel in a few minutes flat. How fickle can I be?

I don't want to live my life like that—half asleep and inattentive to my surroundings, like a passenger on a plane that someone else is flying. I don't want the necessity of turbulence to wake me up and make me pay attention—whether in the form of an illness, a crisis or a challenge. I want to step out of my usual roles and the version of my life that I live on automatic pilot. I desire new ways to become receptive and to stay open to my experiences. Even if these practices only awaken me for a few moments each day, I welcome those moments with a grateful heart.

For I don't want to exist
as if in some mindless entanglement
in a meaningless world.
I want to work myself
like a silken thread
in a web to which I belong.

Because of how much I travel, people can hardly believe that I am such a nervous flyer. For obvious reasons I wish I weren't, but I must admit that flying keeps me pretty humble and prayerful. Some time ago, I started wondering if it weren't for the gift of turbulence, how long could I go without taking stock of the preciousness and tenuousness of life? How long might I live oblivious to the needs of my spirit or the presence of my soul? It was the asking of this question, in part, that put me on the path that led to the writing of this book.

Be both Here *and* There

Unfortunately, I believe that many of us could live for a long time forgetting that we are as Pierre Teilhard de Chardin puts it, "spiritual beings having a human experience, not human beings having a spiritual experience." It is not difficult amidst the chaos and pressures of everyday life to simply ignore the spiritual side of our nature. Financial, physical and social needs keep us connected to the outer world, but the longings of our hearts, souls and imagination are important to a spirited and wholehearted life. We need to stay connected to the inner world as well. Buddhist teacher, Sri Chimnoy, says it beautifully:

> "We must try to synthesize and harmonize the outer life and the inner life. The outer life is like a beautiful flower and the inner life is its fragrance. If there is no fragrance, then we cannot appreciate the flower. Again, if there is no flower, how can there by any fragrance? So the inner life and the outer life must go together."

We can only live disconnected to soul for so long before something happens to awaken us to the spiritual side of our desires and yearnings. It has been professed by sages and prophets throughout the ages that connecting to a sense of the sacred is the deepest need and longing of the human heart. Something in us knows that we are not just here to toil at our work. We are awakened by a mysterious pull or call to remember from whence we came and to what and where are we going.

Joseph Campbell talks about this as "a call to awakening to the hero's journey, always arising from a sacred question." For each of us, this question is different and this awakening can pull and call to us in a thousand ways. It can arise with the birth of a baby or with the death of a loved one. It may be precipitated by a stunning sunset from atop a mountain or by having a near death experience. It may be an accidental encounter with someone or something that shakes us out of complacency. Some awaken to deep questions after being laid off from employment or in the aftermath of a divorce or a painful emotional loss.

Whether through the dark woods of confusion and grief or through the brilliance of beauty, a force as sure as gravity brings us back to our hearts. Questions that have always lived in us arise with fresh urgency. "Why am I here?" "Who am I, really?" "What is my life about?" Without so much as a warning, we find ourselves thrust into a heartfelt spiritual quest. No compass, no map—just the questions that bubble to the surface serving as the "quests we are on." Every spiritual tradition assures us that this happens to everyone. As 13th century Sufi poet Rumi asserts, "Humans long to be alive with soul as the grape desires to turn to wine."

In my workshop entitled, "Cultivating the Spirit to Work," I use the metaphor of a tree for the human spirit. Like the tree, we are rooted in earth and planted in the physical world with our need to survive, to belong and to thrive socially, economically and personally. But also like the tree, we branch toward the sky with arms, hearts and minds belonging to the world of the spirit where purpose, meaning and desires of the soul are primary. Living with the duality of our earthly and spiritual needs requires balance, consciousness and mindfulness. Here is my rendition of an old teaching story on this important subject:

There once lived a king who had a very brilliant servant who served as a personal aide in important matters. The king was always asking questions that he hoped would baffle the servant, but the servant was always able to answer them and thus save his position with the king.

One day the king asked his aide if he could bring him someone who was truly "Here" on earth and not "There" in spirit. The servant brought him a classic workaholic—an ambitious corporate climber, whose entire life was centered on her work, saying, "This person is only in the world to try to make money and to increase her wealth and power in the world. She is definitely Here, but not There."

The king then asked his aide if he could bring him someone who was There in spirit, and not Here on earth. The servant responded by bringing him an ascetic who lived like a hermit on the mountainside and said, "This man completely neglects all aspects of this world, including his body and his own well being. He keeps no connection with anyone or anything in the village and, through daily meditation and prayer, focuses entirely on the world beyond. He is There, but not Here."

"Very good," said the king, "Now bring me someone who is neither Here nor There." The aide thought for a while and then returned presenting him a beggar, saying, "This woman is neither Here nor There, because she lives with envy of everyone else in the world. She refuses to use or give of her own strengths and abilities, even when offered the opportunity. She is not participating in the world except to take and so is not really Here. But she also pays no concern for spiritual matters. Thus, she is in no way There either."

The king was very impressed but he was ready now to up the challenge by asking to be shown someone who was both Here *and* There. The aide did not have to consider long before he brought forth the village baker and his wife. "This man and woman work in the world and tend to their family, but do everything with generosity of heart and purposefulness of mind. Because they do the work of the world and allow their spiritual practices to carry them through both good and bad times, they are a man and woman who are both Here *and* There."

It is important to note that the qualities attributed to the characters in this story have nothing to do with the various postures and positions they inhabited in the world, but with the intent and meaning they gave to those positions. The extent to which we are Here and/or There has little to do with our position in the world and everything to do with the spirit we pour into it.

The notion of being both Here *and* There has long been professed in the world's major religions. Buddha taught that our attachment to things of the world is the cause of our pain and misery and that letting go of our attachment is the path to enlightenment. Jesus also taught a path of nonattachment. He advised, "Be in the world but not of it." Both Buddha and Jesus were active participants in the world without being *of* the world. They both modeled lives in the Here *and* There.

Surely there are times in our lives when we are more Here than There while other events (usually a crisis) catapult us into being more There than Here. Cultivating ways in which we can live both Here and There is essential if we want to live wholehearted lives true to the yearnings of the mind, heart, body and spirit. That is one of the primary purposes of this book—to become aware and attuned to needs and desires of the spirit while living and working in the everyday world.

Read the signs of a dispirited life

It is not uncommon in our culture to compartmentalize the spiritual side of our lives and separate it from the material, earthly aspects of our lives such as making a living, running a business, or responding to the pressures of hearth and home. We have come to believe that the needs of the body, relationships, money, family, community and politics are somehow "unspiritual" and not relevant to issues or qualities of the soul. We divide the world so that part of it is seen exempt from holiness, and as such, our experiences remain compartmentalized. Living with boundaries between our inner and outer worlds, we exist like bonsai trees, beautiful but stunted.

This boundary is unnecessary and detrimental to wholehearted living. By dissolving the borders between our spiritual and worldly needs we can bring fresh vitality and a renewed spirit to every part of our lives. When we show up to any part of our lives with only half of ourselves—namely the analytic, methodical part of our nature solely focused on the outer world—we invite discontent and loneliness. Living true to our dual nature, we must bring the whole self to every part of our lives. It is only through a deep and honest listening to the whole heart that we will respond to our true yearnings and desires—those which are worthy of the investment of our time and energy.

Just as there are physical symptoms of health and illness—blood pressure, heart rate or energy level—we have an inner compass that tells us whether we are moving in the direction of the soulful or dispirited life. There are certain qualities of living that lead us in the direction of a spirited life such as wonder, compassion, purposefulness or hope. Conversely, there are other qualities that lead us in the direction of a dispirited life—like boredom, apathy, resentment or indifference. With the desire to live wholeheartedly, it is important to foster life-affirming habits and qualities, but it is equally important that we stay attentive and vigilant to those habits and qualities that would steal what the French would call our *joie de vivre.*

Contemporary poet and author, David Whyte, warns us of dispirited living in these lines from his poem "Sweet Darkness":

> "You must learn one thing.
> The world was made to be free in.
> Anyone or anything that does not bring you alive
> is too small for you."

How do we know when the life we are living is too small for us, when we have outgrown the job or a relationship, like a plant that has outgrown its container? How do we know when we have fenced corners of our lives from the qualities and gifts of soul which would revitalize and refresh them?

Here are just a few of the signs that would signal a need for attention to the spirit—see if any of these feelings are true for you in corners of your life or work:

- Feeling as if you are not learning or growing in a significant way
- Feeling as if you are not making a difference
- Not feeling particularly appreciated or valued
- Feeling a disconnect between who you are at home and who you are at work
- Having your surroundings cluttered or disorganized

- Feeling unproductive and ineffective
- Not having much physical energy; fatigue
- Feeling as if your senses are dulled
- Feeling a loss of enthusiasm
- Feeling stressed and distracted
- Having little sense of belonging
- Feeling trapped in a habitual, routine existence
- Focusing on the past or on the future
- Feeling bored or apathetic
- Feeling cynical and indifferent
- Feeling discouraged and resistant to change

Throughout the course of our lives we are going to experience highs and lows. We enter rich streams of joy and vitality for some long time, only to find ourselves beached, empty of purpose and direction, at other times. Such is the journey of the human spirit. But noticing when we are beached and that we are beached is critical if we are ever to enter a new stream and belong again to those life-giving waters that carry us to beautiful places within ourselves. It is at those time in our lives when we feel as if we have nothing to give and nothing to receive that we need practices, disciplines or simple daily habits that can reawaken our senses and sensibilities to the sacredness of existence and the preciousness of life.

Bring the gift of intention

The Buddha once said, "Wherever you live is your temple, if you treat it like one." What a lovely aspiration—to treat our own lives as temples. Personally, I am not able to hold the "sacredness of existence" for very long without dropping it headlong into the messy mix of minutia that constitutes much of my day. As I look out at my garden—sure, I see the miracle of creation right in front of me in living color, and my heart skips a beat. As my beloved greets me with a warm hug every morning, my eyes half opened, snuggling into his flannel shirt and feeling the tickle of his beard on my forehead—I feel as if I could melt from the heat of my joy and gratitude. But as I pay the bills, clean out the refrigerator, unpack and repack my bags for the next work trip, coerce my daughter to make a walking path through the jungle of what used to be called her bedroom, somehow my sense of the sacred slips through the hole of my consciousness made larger through the weight of all the things undone and vying for my attention.

When we find ourselves overwhelmed and living on automatic pilot, responding to the world oblivious to intentionality, we live what Henry David Thoreau called, "… lives of quiet desperation." But what if we were to imagine ourselves moving through the day in the awareness that we are encountering the divine through everything we think, say and do? Even as we speak or are spoken to, what if we considered our words as garments of the soul fashioned with heart and intentionality? The truth is that if we brought the gift of intention to everyday tasks, we could not help but become aware of the generosity of our thoughts, the sensitivity of our words and the significance of our actions. We could not help but rise above our own petty concerns and dedicate our days to some higher purpose, something noble and worthy of another day of precious living.

Particularly in times of difficulty, challenge and stress, it is the awareness of our intention (or the ignoring of it) that determines the result of our experience. Whether in a family disagreement, a time of conflict with a customer or in the throes of a hectic day, before we speak and act, by becoming aware of our deepest intention, we can transform our experience into something worthy of our time and energy. In each situation that calls for our engagement, some inner intention will precede our response. The desire to please, an interest to learn, the purpose of change, the fire of love, the heat of anger, the intention to make one's needs known—our intentions color our every deed and action.

For example, if, when planning a trip to visit a loved one, she applies pressure for me to stay with her for an extra week, my response to her will be clearly colored by my intentions. With the intention to honor her request, I will likely respond with love and gratitude for being so welcome in her home—while still asserting my need to depart as I had planned. Alternatively, with the intention to simply affirm clear emotional boundaries, I will likely respond with anger and annoyance for being guilt-tripped—and tell her that my itinerary, as planned, is in the mail. The first response will leave my loved one feeling valued and appreciated, even if she has not gotten her way. The second response will leave her feeling criticized on top of being short-changed. The time I will take in communicating in either situation is not different, but the spirit I communicate with, directed by my intentions, will totally alter the experience for us both.

This is true in all of our actions in the world. We can prepare a meal with love or we can use the same amount of time and energy to prepare it out of a sense of duty and obligation. Guess which soup tastes better? We can weed the garden, clean the bathroom and wash the car out of a sense of duty and distaste—rushing through them half-hearted. Or we can perform the same everyday tasks with a profound sense of gratitude and privilege—mindful that people imprisoned, hospitalized or otherwise unable to perform these tasks would love the opportunity to do them. Guess which duties are performed more completely and with greater joy?

The attitude and spirit we bring to our actions can transform us from moaners to mystics. As Hazrat Inayat Khan writes in his book, *The Inner Life:*

> "A mystic is not born; it is temperament, it is a certain outlook on life, a certain attitude toward life, that makes man a mystic. His chief characteristic is that he knows the meaning of every action, whether it is by intuition or by accident, although to a mystic nothing is an accident. Every action, every condition everything that happens has a meaning and a purpose."

Take a cue from Brother Lawrence

The celebrated 17th century French monk, Brother Lawrence, provided a powerful model of how we can use simple daily activities as spiritual practice—bridging our inner and outer lives through the spirit and intention that we bring to those tasks. His story has inspired millions of readers, me among them.

Little is known about Brother Lawrence's life except that he entered a monastery after years that he spent as a foot soldier. He thought of himself as a clumsy fellow who used to break everything, and apparently, his superiors agreed. Seemingly untalented and having little to offer, he was exiled to the monastery kitchen to wash pots and pans. But Brother Lawrence did not regard his job as a distraction from spiritual life, or as something to be quickly finished so he could get on with his prayers. Instead he decided to use washing, and every other activity, as an opportunity for remembering God, and constantly brought his attention back to this focus. After several years, the results of his practice became so evident that even the abbot of the monastery went to him for advice, and Brother Lawrence was able to make this remarkable statement:

> "The time of business does not with me
> differ from the time of prayer,
> and in the noise and clutter of my kitchen
> while several people are at the same time
> calling for different things,
> I possess God in as great a tranquility
> as if I was upon my knees at the blessed sacrament."

Where better than in the text of our lives are we to look for revelation of the sacred? If we are to discover meaning in our lives, it must be discovered here and now, in the midst of living them. It is easy to enter into the silence and serenity of soul when in the sanctuary, the temple or the mosque, but how about in the office, the parking lot and the laundry room? Like Brother Lawrence who found opportunity to serve God in the noise and clutter of the kitchen, is it possible to bring qualities of the soul and a spirit of ceremony to our everyday lives?

The world's religions tutor us in a variety of methods to knead the vision of the sacred into the dough of everyday life. By employing an endless variety of symbolic acts and objects—ceremonies, sacraments, rites of passage, rituals, liturgies, mantras, dances, chants and vestments—religions around the world have designed ways to remind the faithful to remain true to the sacred possibilities of life. Sufis dance. Buddhists chant. Roman Catholics pray with a rosary. Protestants sing hymns. Hindus gather to receive blessings in temples. Taoists do breathing exercises. Jews wrap themselves in prayer shawls. Native Americans gather at the rising of the sun. Muslims face Mecca when praying. Notice that all employ the simplest of objects and gestures in order to invite a sense of sacred into the physical world.

I have no doubt that a significant part of my decade-long yearning to be a nun was my fascination with and hunger for deeper participation in the rituals and sacraments for which the Catholic Church is famous. I loved placing the lace coverlet over my head before entering the church, genuflecting before entering a pew, dipping my finger in holy water before making the sign of the cross, and kissing particular rosary beads before saying a prayer. I loved every opportunity to show my faith, because the very enacting of these gestures made me *feel* holy.

Ceremony feeds the soul. As spiritual beings, we need the kind of nourishment those rituals and sacraments offer. Even the simplest of gestures carried out in the spirit of ceremony can serve to interrupt the flow of routine time and punctuate our days with brief moments of celebration, thanks or spiritual consciousness. It may be something as simple as lighting candles, playing a particular piece of music or bowing to the sea.

My brother Ed developed a beautiful evening ceremony with his two-year-old daughter, Hannah Joy. Just before bedtime, he takes her outside and they stand together under the moon. He then lifts her high above his head and asks her to choose a star. She reaches with her arm as high as she can, as if to grasp the shining star in her small hands. I cannot help but think that this simple and lovely routine is cultivating a velvet sky within Hannah's soul. It will be studded with sparkling stars, hand-picked of course, throughout her childhood.

A less romantic but equally profound example is the mindfulness that a friend of mine has built into each of her days. As she awakens her first thought is thankfulness for the light of a new day, as she lies down at night her last thought is thankfulness for the dark and the invitation to rest. Regardless of the myriad experiences that will punctuate her day, that she opens and closes her day with a small prayer of thankfulness is enough to carry her with a sense of the miraculous in the midst of the mundane.

Dedicate your day

Dedicating my day, the practice that inspired the poem that opened this chapter, has influenced my life and work tremendously. It is particularly helpful when I find myself anxious before giving a keynote speech or delivering a day of training. Where in one moment I may be concerned with the color of my lipstick, whether or not my slip is showing, and how people are going to receive and perceive me—with the asking of this beautiful question, "To what or whom shall I dedicate this day?" a calm comes over me. My focus moves from petty concerns to the direction of purpose and passion. I remember why I am there and why the people I will be addressing are there. I remember that they do not care what color lipstick I am wearing nor whether or not my slip is showing. The questions of how they receive and perceive me are worthy of neither their time and energy, nor my own. I remember that I am there to share thoughts and ideas with my audience in hope that it will in some way improve the quality of their life or work. It is not a popularity contest and it is not a show.

By dedicating a speech to my dad, you can bet that I only want to put my best foot forward, to be purposeful, clear and deliberate with my words and deeds, to reflect his intelligence and wisdom. Dedicated to my friend, Joan, who died in what seemed the prime of her life, I feel a tremendous sense of urgency to communicate with purpose, passion and my love for life. Once I realized that I was going to dedicate this book to my Aunt Anna and Aunt Marion, the writing of it took on a greater sense of meaning and purpose. Interestingly, I became more rigorous in my editing of it because I did not want fluff in these pages, unworthy of dedication to my aunts. Viewing the decisions and choices about the book within the larger frame of that dedication kept me accountable to higher standards than if I were writing this book simply to advance my career or reputation as a writer.

The wonderful part of dedicating our days or our work is that it is no longer about us or the needs of our egos! Through the setting of our intentions even about simple physical tasks, through ordinary labor we can learn to be in the world in a purposeful, if not sacred manner. Tucking a child in bed, serving an elder his lunch, invoicing a customer, listening to a coworker's complaint, paying the attendant at the gas station, writing an e-mail, picking up the kids from school—each mundane action throughout the day can become another opportunity to act out of our most sincere intentions. It is amazing how easy it is to forget this truth:

With the gift of a dedication
a modest meal becomes a feast,
simple words, a poem.
A child's carefree sketching,
treasured art.

Transform habits into rituals

One of the greatest privileges of human life is that we get to supply its meaning. Meaning does not come to us in finished form, readymade; it must be found, created, received and constructed. We grow our way toward it. The world itself is a pretty neutral place—we give purpose to our lives, not the other way around. As human beings, we have no choice but to be meaning-makers. The fact that we assign different meaning to various events, stimuli and symbols may be the cause of great conflict and misunderstanding in the world, among cultures, within workplaces and within families. But it is this very capability of meaning-making that can enable us to live soulfully and wholeheartedly.

Think about it. If kids reflexively punch us on the arm and say "slug bug" or "punch buggy" when spotting a Volkswagen, what would stop them from giving thanks for life when passing a cemetery or being reminded of the fleeting nature of time when seeing a clock? Our perceptions can be set like the alarm on a clock—but instead of an annoying buzz, we can set off an internal signal of purpose and meaning. When we see the "golden arches" of McDonald's we are immediately set to wondering if we want fries with our burger. Spotting a police car, we immediately check our speed. Why can't we employ those same perceptual senses to alert us to the needs and desires of our souls? What object can serve as a symbol to alert us to practice kindness? What sound can serve to stir the artist within us until we cannot resist entering the dance of creativity? What is the scent of patience? What calendar day could we devote to the act of forgiving ourselves and others—so that one day every year we start with a clean slate?

I believe that a wholehearted life asks only that we look through the eyes of soul and express what it perceives. What is a ritual but a habit made holy? What distinguishes a routine from a ceremony but the spirit with which it is enacted? What is the difference between an act and a sacrament but the spirit poured into the doing? By infusing our routine habits with mindfulness we add the element of soul to our everyday experience.

Our day is but a path we tread, a walk among possibilities—regardless of what we confront upon the road, we have the choice to add meaning and purpose. By imbuing mundane objects or activities with meaning, we allow the living of the day to become symbolic. The living of a day becomes a prayer. Transforming a habit into a ritual helps us to shift from ordinary space and time into sacred space and time.

Pausing to look through the window before washing it changes a chore into an opportunity to view signs of the changing season. Allowing the wind to remind us of the powers of an invisible world of which we are a part transforms a storm into an inspired homily. When walking on a treadmill, we can envision that it is our purposes we are walking toward; when stirring the soup, we can stir the passions that will lead us to our truest purposes. Pausing for an instant in the attitude of worship as we tend the small flowers in the garden makes a ceremony of the weeding. We can use the simple activity of washing our face before bed to symbolize the washing away of cynicism. Through these small but sincere gestures, the day becomes a chalice raised up to creation.

All the habits we have developed up to now are actions we performed regularly, either physically or mentally, until they became second nature. But we had to start sometime to create those habits. It is possible to use that same ability to initiate actions and thoughts that develop the habit of bringing qualities of soul to everyday deeds and tasks. This is not impossible—in fact, it's not even difficult. However, in the course of living our busy lives, adding a pinch of mindfulness here and a tad of the soul's attention there, is not only unusual but rare. The recipe for a wholehearted, soulful life demands attention and mindfulness to the most common of our experiences—seeing through fresh eyes and an inspired mind the objects of every day.

Reset your perceptual lenses

How do we reset our perceptual lenses so that we live in a world where everything swirls with meaning? What message is carried on the autumn wind, in the summer grasses or in the glistening of winter snow? The answer to those questions differs for each of us, as we each provide our own meaning to what we see and perceive and experience. I was recently introduced to a young girl who forever changed for me the meaning of a full moon. Her name is Manja and I was introduced to her via an *NBC Dateline News* program about child labor within the silk industry of India.

The purpose of the program was to expose the prolific use of child labor in an industry to which the United States is a primary customer. They spared us little in the telling (and showing) of the horrors children in India suffer in silk factories. As young as six years old, children are bonded (or sold) into labor by their impoverished families. They are on their feet stirring boiling pots of water filled with silk worms for twelve-hour days, seven days a week. There are no regular breaks. There are no bathrooms. Many children are scalded and burned from having to reach into the water to "test" the cocoons to see if the worms are ready for expulsion.

Both shocked and broken-hearted by what I was hearing and seeing on this program, I sat looking at the screen, riveted and horrified. That's when I saw Manja—an absolutely gorgeous young girl with piercing brown eyes and a smile that could melt the stars. Her voice was soft and sweet, yet strong, as she spoke. I read the English translation of her words as it swept across the screen: "I look to the sky every night for the moon. When I see the moon growing full, I am hopeful, for that is the one day that we are allowed to rest—the day of the full moon." Then she paused and flashed a smile at the interviewer saying, "But one day, I hope to become a doctor."

I am mesmerized by the moon. For me it has always been a symbol of wholeness, wonder and celebration. But hearing Manja's story and knowing how she watches for it every day of the month, how can I ever see it the same again? Now, when standing in the light of a full moon, I can be glad to know that Manja, and other children like her, rested that day and I can remember her in the private temple of my hopes and prayers. I will wonder and worry about how careful she must be with her slender, delicate hands near those boiling pots—careful not to ruin them for the work she dreams of. Most of all, I will be humbled and mindful of how she, in her circumstances, dares to dream so much, while I can fail to have so little faith in my own dreams.

I thought, there is a poem in this… this new full moon. It is not a poem about child labor or about Americans reaping the benefits of such labor in their purchases of Indian products. It will be a poem about a middle-aged, middle-class woman in a hotel in San Francisco whose heart was opened by a destitute, fourteen-year old girl in India and the woman's hope that she will never be the same again as a result. It will be a poem about the moon that we share with all of humanity and the importance of not ignoring the harsh realities experienced by people in all parts of this small globe who sleep under its light. It will be a poem about the power of the human spirit and how a round white ship in the night sky can set us to dreaming of sailing into a new life. The poem is not yet written but it already bears the title, "Manja's Moon."

Remember how you wish to live

Every spiritual tradition suggests regular discipline and continuing practices to cleanse us, steady us and remind us of what is true and what is important. That is the gift of a practice or a discipline—it can serve as a compass on the otherwise stormy seas of regular life. Amidst the daily distractions, clutter and pressures that greet us at home and at work, an honorable practice or a trustworthy discipline can bring us back to the present and remind us to embrace the life we are living with an open heart, creative imagination or any quality of the soul with which we wish to greet the day. The particular gesture or practice is not important, it is the repeating of it and one's dedication to it that lends it power. As Zen teacher and poet, Gary Snyder, writes:

"All of us are apprenticed with the same teacher—reality. It is as hard to get the children herded into the carpool and down the road as it is to chant sutras in the Buddhist hall on a cold morning. One is not better than the other, each can be quite boring, and they both have the virtuous quality of repetition. Repetition and its good results make the very activities of our life into the path."

Spiritual writer and teacher, Wayne Muller, uses the metaphor of planting a garden for understanding the power and purposes of developing a practice. He suggests that we spend a lot of time and money in various forms of self-help and therapies in order to do the vital work of clearing the ground of our lives of its rocks, twigs and weeds. Whether it is dysfunctional relationships, addictions or unhealthy habits, we work to remove those things that will prevent healthy growth. But he asks the next important question, "What if we stop there?" What if we spend all our time preparing the soil, moving rocks, pulling weeds and building fences without considering what we wish to plant in that new ground? What harvest, when it comes, will bring us great joy or nourishment? What seeds, when they blossom, will provide us with delight?

In the same way our various healing methods, psychologies and therapies can help us clear the ground of our past and prepare us to receive a better life, our decision to develop healthy practices is a way of planting and cultivating what we love and value in the garden of our lives. With characteristic simplicity, His Holiness, the Dalai Lama, makes this suggestion in his book, *The Art of Happiness:*

"To be happy, generally speaking, one begins by identifying those factors which lead to happiness and those factors which lead to suffering. Having done this one then sets out gradually eliminating those factors which lead to suffering and cultivating those that lead to happiness. That is the way."

By living mindfully and staying true to a discipline or practice, we plant healthy seeds and strengthen the healthy seeds already in us. Sometimes by working a practice, we find ourselves in new ways through that practice. 13th century Sufi poet, Jelaluddin Rumi, put it beautifully in this verse:

Work. Keep digging your well.
Don't think about getting off work.
Water is there somewhere.
Submit to a daily practice.
Your loyalty to that practice
Is a ring on the door.
Keep knocking, and the joy inside
Will eventually open a window
And look out to see who's there.

I am not suggesting that we all take up yoga, meditate daily or attend daily mass or church services, although such practices may appeal to certain readers. What I am suggesting, however, is that we find some moment in our day when we can turn our attention to our inner lives and perhaps even use ordinary activities and habits as opportunities for developing spiritual discipline and commitment. We develop these practices so that we remember who we are and why we are here. As Wayne Muller wisely reminds us in his wonderful book, *How Then Shall We Live?:*

"The heart of most spiritual practice is simply this:
Remember. Remember who you are.
Remember what you love.
Remember what is sacred. Remember what is true.
Remember that you will die, and this day is a gift.
Remember how you wish to live."

We can trudge, toil and trek through the day and through the week, anxious to get to the weekend again when we can get back to "real" living. Or we can use each circumstance within our day as the sky into which we spread our wings and fly—wings of purpose, love and meaning. Every time we stop at a red light or set out the trash cans, we serve our family, our community and the earth. In each of our roles—as parent, partner, builder, merchant, gardener, artist, teacher, healer, secretary or salesman—with mindfulness and intention we can be messengers of hope, kindness, humility and beauty. When taken by themselves all these things seem small, but I am convinced that life is made up of small things. If these small things were ignored, life would not only be less beautiful, it would be unbearable.

In the end, I don't think what we know or what we believe is half as important as what we do. What we bring to fruition and practice within the living of our lives is what shapes our souls, not the reverse. I am reminded of the statement made by Gandhi near the end of his life. While he was boarding a crowded third-class compartment on an Indian train, some reporters caught up to him and asked him what his message was. As he leaned out of the train door he said, "How I live my life—that is my teaching."

How we live our lives—let that be our teaching, let that be our message. May how we live our lives be our greatest blessing and our truest gift to ourselves and to those we love. May we draw wide the curtain of our beings so that our lives become window sills upon which the bird of purpose may perch and even sing.

Passages

"The true men of soul are those who sit in the midst of his fellow man and rise up and eat and sleep and buy and sell and give and take in the bazaars amongst other people, and who marry and have social intercourse with other folk, and yet are never forgetful of the one who created them."

Kahlil Gibran

"Possession of material riches, without inner peace, is like dying of thirst while bathing in a lake."

Paramahansa Yogananda

Johann Wolfgang Van Goethe

"Knowing is not enough, we must apply.
Willing is not enough, we must do."

"Our own life is the instrument with which we experiment with truth and grace."

Thich Nhat Hanh

"It is good to think well;
it is divine to act well."

Horace Mann

The Bhagavad Gita

"A leaf, a flower, a fruit, or even
water, offered to me in devotion,
I will accept as the loving gift
of a dedicated heart.
Whatever you do,
make it an offering to me."

Walt Whitman

"This is what you should do.
Love the earth and sun and animals.
Despise riches, give alms to everyone that asks.
Stand up for the stupid and crazy. Hate tyrants.
Devote your income and labor to others.
Argue not concerning God.
Have patience and indulgence toward people.
Reexamine all you have been told in school or church or in any book.
Dismiss what insults your very soul,
And your flesh shall become a great poem."

"We are what we repeatedly do.
Excellence, then, is not an act but a habit."

Aristotle

"I flip my little omelet in the frying pan for the love of God."

Brother Lawrence

Hasidic folk saying

"Be master of your will and servant to your conscience."

"The soul's progress does not lie in thinking much, but in loving much."

St. Teresa of Avila

Novalis

"The seat of the soul is there—
where the outer and the inner
worlds meet."

Thomas Merton

"Philosophies impress, ideas abound, but words, no matter how elegant, are cheap in the soul's estimation—doing is understanding—doing is everything."

Hasidic wisdom

"Habit is dangerous. It creeps up surreptitiously like a thief. Invite in only those habits you choose."

"There are glimpses of heaven for us in every act, thought, or word that raises us above ourselves. Like sunlight striking a mirror—the brightness reflects back on us."

Mother Teresa

"Every morning I awaken torn between the desire to save the world and the inclination to savor it. It makes the day hard to plan."

E.B. White

Ella Wheeler Wilcox

"With every deed you are sowing a seed, though the harvest you may not see."

"Don't judge each day by the harvest you reap but by the seeds you plant."

Robert Louis Stevenson

Adrienne Rich

"You must learn to occupy the space you occupy."

"Once when a student complained to my teacher that in his very busy life he did not have time to meditate, the teacher laughed and said, 'Do you have time to breathe? If you are determined, you must simply pay attention.' This is our practice, wherever we are, whatever is happening: to breathe, to be fully present, to see what is true."

Wayne Muller

Sam Keen

"The sacred that many call 'God' is not an object to be known or a problem to be solved by human intelligence, but it is a ground beneath our capacity to understand anything, the totality within which we live, move and experience our being."

"Good actions ennoble us, and we are the sons of our own deeds." Miguel de Cervantes

The Dalai Lama

"Our efforts and practices should be like the flow of a stream—sustained, continuous and balanced."

Morihei Ueshiba

"Heaven is right where you are standing and that is the place to practice your truth."

To Ponder and To Practice

- When was the last time you were awakened to the reality of your mortality and the tenuousness of life?
- What were some of the moments or experiences in your life that awakened deep questions from within you?
- What are the questions that represent the "quests-you-are-on" at this time of your life?
- Peruse the following list of symptoms or qualities that often reflect the need for more attention to one's "inner life" or needs of the spirit. Put a check next to those that you feel from time to time in various parts of your life. Circle those that have begun to feel more chronic than occasional.

Stifled	Fatigued	Lack of belonging	Living in the past
Living in the future	Undervalued	Unappreciated	Disconnected
Dispirited	Unproductive	Ineffective	Disorganized
Stressed	Distracted	On overload	Apathetic
Cynical	Indifferent	Discouraged	Resistant to change
Lonely	Dulled senses	Depressed	Lack of confidence
Cluttered surroundings	Forgetful	Feeling lost	Lack of purpose

  For each of the words you circled, consider a practice that you could plant in the ground of your life that could work to counteract it. For example, if you circled "Disorganized" you might consider asking for help from someone who could help you organize your time, energy or belongings. If you circled "Fatigued," going to bed an hour earlier each night might be in order.

- Using the metaphor from the parable, think back on times in your life when you were living more Here than There, a time when you were more There than Here, and a time when you were most Here *and* There.
- Dedicate each day this week to something or someone very special to you and note how it affects the quality of your days. Note how the days were different depending on to what or to whom you dedicated them.
- Using David Whyte's terms, what area(s) of your life, if any, is feeling too small for you and not bringing you alive?
- What rituals, sacraments or ceremonies did you participate in and particularly enjoy as a child? Which ones do you enjoy today?
- Identify three mundane daily chores or tasks that you find least inspiring at home and at work. Consider how each of them might be transformed into a ritual by imbuing new meaning to them, like Brother Lawrence, turning his omelet in the pan for God.

Practice

- Listed below are qualities, elements and ingredients of a spirited, soulful and wholehearted life. Peruse the list and choose three of the qualities you would most like to cultivate to a greater degree in your personal life and/or in your work.

Wholeness	Mystery	Reverence	Fulfillment
Vision	Questing	Authenticity	Wonder
Wisdom	Joy	Yearning	Solitude
Zeal	Courage	Awe	Free-spiritedness
Purpose	Contentment	Faith	Passion
Tolerance	Generosity	Meaning	Creativity
Enthusiasm	Imagination	Grace	Gratitude
Self-discipline	Optimism	Confidence	Trust
Love	Conviction	Devotion	Tenderness
Health	Integrity	Belonging	Truth
Innocence	Compassion	Spontaneity	Calm
Curiosity	Delight	Humility	Honesty

- Peruse the ideas listed in the Appendix: Everyday Habits as Entrance to Soul, page 344. Look for ideas that could serve as cues or reminders of the qualities you have chosen. Choose habits, routines or objects from the Appendix which will alert or remind you to practice your selected qualities.
- Choose a quote from this chapter's *Passages* which speaks to your desire to live with equal footing in both the outer world and the inner world. Post it in a place where you will see it regularly until it is internalized.
- Given everything you have read in this chapter, what do you want to *keep* doing? What do you want to *stop* doing? What do you want to *start* doing?

Notes

Unlived Dreams and Rising Bread

Chapter

Shaping Fresh Hope from New Dreams

Treat your dreams like sweet peas

Treat your dreams like sweet peas

Open your fists to swing from new branches

Open your fists to swing from new branches

Be careful what you hope for

Be careful what you hope for

Put your imagination to work on your life's behalf

Put your imagination to work on your life's behalf

Hold fast to your ability to dream new dreams

Hold fast to your ability to dream new dreams

Have faith in your discontent

Have faith in your discontent

Let go of the bread to regain the sky

Let go of the bread to regain the sky

Unlived Dreams and Rising Bread

What happened to my plan to return to Spain
and live among the olive trees?
Where is the second, third, and fourth child I dreamed of,
but never gave birth to?
Where is the home I have long longed for?
The one with the porch swing, the fireplace,
the sun pouring through lace curtains as I slip bread into the oven?

There are dreams that come true.
Others die or evolve into new visions.
But some dreams, unlived, refuse to die.
They cling to the heart and
pierce like thorns the bruise of regret.
If dreams are the fruit of our hope and faith,
how do we prune those that are unlived,
in order to make room for new dreams?

I look to the apple tree.
Not every apple makes it to the bushel,
nor from the bushel to the market,
nor from the market to the cart,
nor from the cart to the pie or into the lunch bag.
Yet the apple tree faithfully produces each apple,
in sacred unison with sun and soil and rain,
as if the world depended upon it.
Regardless of drought or violent storm,
regardless of birds making nests in its branches
or small boys making of it a lookout tower,
the apple tree remains true to its nature.
Every autumn it makes new apples.

With every breath
I am capable of fresh faith and new hope
from which infant dreams are born.
Not all of them will make it into the bushel, much less the pie.
But I am human, I am a maker of dreams.
I pray for the courage to live with heart and arms wide open—
like branches pregnant with fruit,
or at least postured towards that possibility.

Spain still lies just west of France,
but the girl it called to is grown.
I have but one natural child,
yet I am blessed with many loved ones
who hold my heart in the palms of their young hands.
And while the home of my dreams is not yet realized,
perhaps one day it will be.
But in the meantime, I am learning to call "home"
anywhere I am that calls me to embody this work I love.
Right here, right now, as I write, or recite, this is home!
And those who pause to read or to listen, you, too, are my family.
I can even feel the sun pouring through my words like lace
as my heart rises and swells, like bread, in the oven of this poem.

Reflections

My heart never fails to rise and swell with the reciting of "Unlived Dreams and Rising Bread." This poem was a tremendous gift to me because it was in the very writing of it that I pruned a few of my own unlived dreams. I decided to put this poem early in the book for one very important reason: everything begins with hope—everything starts with a dream. In the words of Meister Eckhart:

> "When the soul wishes to experience something, she throws an image of the experience out before her and enters into her own image. The power of the soul's dream is its influence in human destiny."

I have been dreaming the dream of this book for years, although my thoughts of what it would be and what it would look like have gone through many incarnations. Even as I write, I am certain that the finished piece will be something I have not yet envisioned. Yet it is the current, working visions of this book that tug at my heart with a gravity I can neither deny nor refuse. The spirit those visions invoke is the axis point of this galaxy of work.

I believe this is so of all true work, that the head and hands of the worker are simply tools in the employ of the one running the show—the spirit. Thus, it is important that we treat our hopes and dreams with utmost care, for they are the winds that stir the soul.

With every breath
we are capable of fresh faith
and fresh hope
from which infant dreams are born.
Not every one will make it
into the bushel, much less the pie.
But we are human.
We are the maker of dreams.

That notwithstanding, not all dreams serve us and move us towards our highest purposes. Dreams that are past their prime are no more food for the soul than apples that have begun to spoil are food for the body. We need to let them fall, having faith in the potential of our spirit to sprout new blossoms that will eventually turn into the fruit of new dreams. Wanting what we cannot have or to be what we cannot be, depletes rather than nourishes the human spirit. Here are some thoughts about harnessing the power of hope and holding fast not only to our ability to dream, but to our ability to dream *new* dreams.

Treat your dreams like sweet peas

Hopes and dreams are a bit like pole beans or sweet peas; they need to be picked in order to keep growing. Before we can be what we are meant to be, we must accept what we are not. Before we can create what we want, we must know what we no longer want. We must prune outlived images of ourselves as well as some of the branches upon which we hang our hopes.

In many ways life is more of a journey from dream to dream and from hope to hope than it is from success to success or destination to destination. We all know that traveling hopefully carries twice the punch of arriving. Once we arrive at any destination, be it vocational, spiritual, mental or emotional, we look for the next destination towards which we will travel. We do not rest on our laurels long. But moving forward for the sake of moving forward doesn't make sense. We need to pay attention to what we are moving towards and be willing to let go of old hopes or dreams that lead us astray. Not unlike the parable of the monkeys and the coconuts.

Open your fists to swing from new branches

There is a great Hindu tale about hunters in India who had a proven way of catching monkeys. A coconut would be hollowed out and a hole made that was just large enough to let a monkey's hand pass through. The coconut was then pinned to the ground and tempting food was placed inside. A monkey would approach, intent on getting hold of the food beneath the coconut, but alas, as soon as it grasped the food in its fist it found itself unable to pull its hand and the food free of the coconut. Imprisoned it would stay, caught by its own unwillingness to open its fist. Sometimes we are no smarter than the monkey—what keeps us back sometimes is our unwillingness to let go of old dreams.

There are dreams that come true.
Others die or evolve into new visions.
But some dreams, unlived,
refuse to die.
They cling to the heart and
pierce like thorns
the bruise of regret.

If dreams are the fruit
of our hope and faith,
how do we prune
those that are unlived,
In order to make room
for new dreams?

I remember what a huge move it was in my own heart when I let go of the dream of having more children. Having come from a large family, I had always imagined having a "whole batch" of kids. That was not to be. And while there was a tremendous sense of loss in letting go of that vision for myself, what came after was an equally tremendous sense of relief! The desire had settled like a heavy weight in my heart and I felt lighter having released it. What I also realized was that I did not have to release my desires to nurture and love; I could instead, direct those emotions and actions to the many other children of family members and friends. Perhaps I could be to them what my Aunt Anna, to whom I have dedicated this book, was to me. She never had children of her own but she was the "aunt of all aunts" to her large brood of nieces of nephews! Opening my fist, I withdrew my hand from the trap of the coconut and found myself swinging on a new branch—I could be an Aunt Anna!

Be careful what you hope for

Writer Mignon McLaughlin once noted, "What you have become is the price you paid to get what you *used* to want." (My emphasis.) What a powerful observation! To know that each of us is where we are due to the desires of our younger selves. We pay a high price for the dedication we invest in our dreams because we only move towards one hope at the expense of all the others we did not choose. It is important that we continually assess and reassess the desires of our hearts so that they are working towards the highest good of the present and future and not the past.

I went to Spain when I was 19 years old and stayed for a year and a half. It was an incredible experience and I fell in love with Andalucia—the snow-capped tips of the Sierra Nevada mountain range, the fields of wild red poppies, the olive trees with their twisting branches holding up the sky. I loved the Moorish castles, the cobblestone villages, the churches harboring the ingenious works of Greco and Goya. I fell in love with the writing of Frederico Garcia Lorca. I came back to California so that I could finish a degree in Linguistics and return to Spain as a better and more qualified teacher of English as a Second Language. I did not say "Adios" to a single friend as I left Spain. I said "Hasta luego," meaning "Until later."

Falling in love with and marrying one of my linguistics professors was the first glitch in that perfect plan. Life snowballed and within a few years it was clear that I was not returning to Spain. Sometimes I think back to the life that I had conjured up in my imagination, and I find it a lovely destination for my daydreams. I have no regrets about waylaying my life among the twisting olive trees and the fields of large red poppies; I discovered a new life waiting for me among the redwoods and the lupine. And I still read Lorca.

We need to remain more loyal to the current gravity of our hearts desires than to our plans and schemes, regardless of how well we have mapped them out. Sometimes we find ourselves stuck in livelihoods that sap rather than tap our creative spirits because what led us to that work were desires that we had outgrown, like loyalty to the family plan, a sense of security, or ties to another individual who once worked there. We see it with relationships as well. What initially drew us into a relationship may no longer be a vital purpose that can keep that relationship alive. Luckily, however, that does not need to be the end of the story, because we can always make new choices springing from the soil of fresh hope.

Put your imagination to work on your life's behalf

Hope is another word for the imagination of the heart. It is an essential part of human life. No matter what one is doing, the imagination is busily working away either towards hope or against despair. If our imagination is not set on the task of building hope, it busies itself weaving a web of inner fears and doubt, blame and excuses. How well you use your imagination can be the difference between hope and despair. For example, someone who has been laid off from a job in the high tech industry can use his imagination to conjure up an image of new work in an organization in which the present staff have little technical expertise. He may even have a hand in designing the job so that it is best suited to his strengths and interests where they will be welcomed and valued, resulting in a new vitality and sense of purpose. However, this same person may use his imagination very differently. What he may imagine, instead, is months of unemployment, hundreds of resumes sent to employers who never respond, endless interviews for jobs for which he will not be hired, resulting in a deep depression and foreclosure on the house. As Leonardo da Vinci so aptly put it, "The faculty of imagination is both the rudder and the bridle of the senses."

I love Wayne Dyer's definition of worry. He says, "It is no more and no less than the total misuse of your own imagination." It makes sense, doesn't it? Since worry is a future-oriented activity, whatever we are worrying about, has not yet happened. The human mind must always make a choice between coloring with the crayon of hope or the crayon of fear—in either case, it sets the imagination to work. We must learn to make the awesome gift of the imagination work on behalf of our dreams by coloring our visions with the lighter and brighter shades of hope rather than the darker shades of fear.

Hold fast to your ability to dream new dreams

Many people are afraid to dream for fear that they will be unrealistic in their desires and end up disillusioned with reality. But we can only be true to ourselves by keeping our dreams alive. If one dream dies, we must search deep inside for the seeds of another. I believe we should heed the warning in the Australian Aboriginal proverb, "Those who lose dreaming are lost."

Throughout the years of my experience working as an employment counselor with people facing myriad problems and multiple barriers, I became convinced that the depth and breadth of their hopes was far more a determining factor in their vocational success than any life circumstance they may have been facing. Without the fire and focus that hope brings, we do not move at all—we simply go in circles. Poet and author, David Whyte, put it this way in the opening lines to his poem, entitled "Sweet Darkness," "When your eyes are tired, the world is tired also. When your vision is gone, no part of the world can find you." When one is low on hope, one is low on possibility.

The capacity to dream new dreams does not mean that our vision is always precise with our hopes clear-cut and straightforward. I remember hearing the analogy of hope with the concept of Russian nesting dolls—one contained within another, like the doll that holds a smaller doll that holds an even smaller one. Attaining one desire does not mean that we will not then find another desire nesting within it. From the viewpoint of the human spirit, hope carries its own implicit reward: it need not be satisfied in order to serve the important purpose of warming the soul or giving direction to our feet. But we must have hope in order to lend power and purpose to our actions. New dreams and a vision for the future are powerful medicine as we stumble, fall and continue to travel through daily life. Fresh and vital hope in the form of wholesome expectations for tomorrow provide meaning for today.

Native American wisdom tells us that vision is essential to life and that we must follow it as the eagle seeks the deepest blue of the sky. Extraordinary American novelist, Barbara Kingsolver, is quite emphatic about the necessity of hope in human life as she writes:

> "The least you can do is figure out what you hope for. And the most you can do is live inside that hope. Not admire it from a distance, but live right it in, right under its roof."

Surely there are multiple reasons why we lose hope and the capacity to dream from time to time. We have all experienced pockets of life that were empty of dreams, when we could not smell or taste or feel very much, when the world appeared in black and white. It is at those times that we must cling to the faith that hope will surface again, in its own sweet time. In those times, we must let those who love us and have not given up hope for us, carry our torch. In better times, we must be ready to carry the torch for others. Maybe we should all have Garth Brooks playing in the background when our vision begins to fade. He sings:

You know a dream is like a river
Ever changin' as it flows
And a dreamer's just a vessel
That must follow where it goes...

...So don't you sit upon the shoreline
And say you're satisfied
Choose to chance the rapids
And dare to dance the tide.

Have faith in your discontent

When we begin to lose hope, we need to restore our faith in our discontent, because that may be the arrow that points us back in the direction of hope. Discontent has many familiar faces—boredom, angst, anxiety, apprehension, or a feeling of emptiness. Discontent is the soul's way of sounding an alarm to remind us of the needs and desires of the spirit! If we were never discontent, we would never move and grow. We would remain complacent and self-satisfied without ever growing new wings or experiencing new dimensions of life. That is why many spiritual disciplines actually refer to divine discontent"—our discontent can be divinely inspired to move our lives along and serve as a catalyst for further blossoming. Thomas Moore alludes to this quality of discontent in his book, *The Original Self.* He writes:

> "Divine discontent is that full, bittersweet, empty feeling which is like incense in a church, announcing the presence of God."

If we were to consider every brave move we have made throughout our lives, I bet we could point to discontent at the source of that movement. Quitting smoking, entering a recovery program, putting an end to a bad relationship, mustering the courage to leave a job in order to pursue a passion, or packing up and moving to a new apartment, town or area of the country—these decisions are motivated not only by a movement towards something, but a movement away from something. In this way, we need to listen more closely to the voice of angst, boredom and displeasure. Discontent is a faithful companion on our walk in life, and it leads us, most assuredly, to our hopes and desires.

We have all had the experience at one time or another of being in a job or a relationship that was going along just fine for a period of time when at some point we notice a gnawing kind of feeling deep in the pit of our stomachs that tells us that "this is not enough." Because we are not always able to point to the source of the discontent, it is difficult to trust that voice that would nudge us along our path. But ignore that voice long enough and it begins to turn up its volume or express itself in more creative ways—like migraines, an ulcer or an addiction to something that provides immediate gratification but never truly satisfies. No amount of chocolate satisfies the desire for a wholehearted life. At some point we realize we are scratching the wrong itch.

The voice of discontent is more of a low, incessant rumble than it is a rallying cry. It does not have the sharp articulation of pain nor the inspiring high notes of hope. It has more the quality of a distant drumbeat than the announcing call of a trumpet. But as Henry David Thoreau so wisely advised, "A man must follow the beat of his own drum, however measured or far away."

While the drumbeat of discontent is essential in waking us up to the areas of our lives which are in need of attention, heeding that call may be exactly what we need to lead us to the more inspiring call of hope. I was a pack and a half a day cigarette smoker for 13 years. Try as I may, I did not believe that I had the ability to quit. I had lots of reasons why I needed to—it was gross, smelly, expensive and, oh yeah, it was killing me and the people around me. But my resolve to quit was not fired up solely by the powers of my discontent—I needed pure, unadulterated hope to rev the engines of my will and determination. The desire to become pregnant and be a mother was the hope that gave me the courage and resolve to overcome my addiction to nicotine. As we assess the greatest sources of our own current discontent, we also need to recognize the itches, daydreams, and yearnings carried on its wings. Surely where there is discontent, there is also hope!

Be willing to let go of the bread to regain the sky

There is a lovely Sufi story that tells of a blackbird who found a large piece of food in the village and lit out into the sky with the food in its beak. A flock of his brothers chased after him and raucously attacked the food, pulling it from his beak. The blackbird finally let go of the last piece and the frenzied flock left him alone. The bird swooped and dived and thought, "I have lost the food but I have regained the peaceful sky!"

I know something of that feeling—regaining a piece of sky—with the redefining in my own mind the concept of "home" and what that means. Working on the road so much of the year, and being a true blue nester, "home" has become my favorite word, as well as my favorite place. So the possibility of bringing a sense of home with me on the road is an enchanting one. Allowing the writing and reciting of my poetry to call me to my inner home has been a joyful discovery. I still long to have a home with a porch swing and a fireplace and place to garden. But that unlived dream does not need to keep me from enjoying a sky of a different shade of blue.

My dear friend and colleague, Joan Fountain, who, like me, traveled a lot as a trainer, shared a suggestion with me a few years before her death. She used to travel with a shawl of a beautiful African fabric that she placed around herself or on her lap on the airplane. It was a blanket of comfort and belonging; I am certain that it must have smelled of home as well. I can't help but wonder if out in the heavens there is one who flies on wings covered in the rich hues of a Kenyan pattern.

Buddhist tradition teaches that to be a good fisherman you must detach yourself from the dream of the fish. This makes whatever is caught or found a treasure. What we envision when we begin is seldom what actually happens. We know this to be true in many aspects of our lives, particularly our career paths. I appreciate the words of Joseph Campbell who said, "If you see your career path laid out perfectly before you, know one thing, it is not yours!" That is because we make the path by walking it. Where the path leads does not matter half as much as the spirit we bring to the walking of it.

The Rolling Stones put it succinctly, "You can't always get what you want, but if you try, you just might find, you get what you need!" How do we put our faith in life's ability to deliver what we need as it opens us to unexpected trails, with all the disappointments and treasures to be found along the way? How do we trust that perhaps our unfulfilled desires are put into our hearts so that our hearts may be stretched beyond their present capacity? In the words of Alan Jones, Dean of Grace Cathedral in San Francisco:

> "Soul-making requires the kind of stretching that comes from the unfulfilled desires of the heart."

Amongst all the giftedness bestowed upon us, we have been given the awesome gift of imagination. We are human—we are the maker of dreams. Let's pray for the courage to live with heart and arms wide open—like branches pregnant with fruit, or at least postured towards that possibility.

Passages

"Though we seem to be sleeping,
there is an inner wakefulness
that directs the dream
and that will eventually
startle us back to the truth
of who we are."

Rumi

"The farthest horizons of our hopes and fears are cobbled by our poems, carved from the rock experiences of our daily lives."

Andre Lorde

Carl Schultz

"I am free when I allow my life to unfold.
As soon as I restrict myself to new outcomes,
I've got shackles on my feet."

Henry David Thoreau

"Dreams are the touchstones of our characters."

"Our reach should exceed our grasp,
or what's a heaven for?"

Robert Browning

"Cherish your visions
and your dreams,
as they are the children
of your soul—
the blueprints of your
ultimate achievements."

Napolean Hill

"Nothing happens unless first a dream."

Carl Sandburg

Simone Weil

"If we go down into ourselves, we find that we possess exactly what we desire."

"A vision without a task is but a dream,
a task without a vision is drudgery,
a vision and a task is the hope of the world."

From a church in Sussex, England, 1730

"You can have anything you want if you want it desperately enough. You must want it with an exuberance that erupts through the skin and joins the energy that created the world."

Sheila Graham

Thomas Merton

"You are your hope. For as is your hope, so is your will. As is your will, so is your deed. As is your deed, so is your destiny."

"All men of action are dreamers."

Hungarian proverb

"Close both eyes to see
with the other eye."

Rumi

Shlomo Breznitz

"Hope takes work: one has to dwell on the situation, think it over, weave possible scenarios and tell oneself stories with happy endings."

Louisa May Alcott

"Far away there in the sunshine are my highest aspirations. I may not reach them, but I can look up and see their beauty, believe in them and try to follow where they lead."

Gloria Steinem

"Hope is a very unruly emotion."

"If one advances
in the directions of his dreams,
And endeavors to live the life
which he has imagined,
He will meet with a success
unexpected in common hours."

Henry David Thoreau

"Do not part with your illusions.
When they are gone you may still exist,
but you have ceased to live."

Mark Twain

Alexander Pope

"Hope springs eternal in the human heart."

"I call intuition 'cosmic fishing'. You feel the nibble, and then you have to hook the fish. What you may catch is a dream."

Buckminster Fuller

Sigmund Freud

"...in the small matters, trust the mind, in the large ones, the heart."

"A very good vision is needed for life and the man has to follow it—as the eagle seeks the deepest blue of the sky."

Chief Crazy Horse

"Sometimes something in us has to die in order for us to know our truths. Perhaps we have to lose our fantasies."

Adrienne Rich

"If you're still hanging onto a dead dream of yesterday, laying flowers on its grave by the hour, you cannot be planting the seeds for a new dream to grow today."

Joyce Chapman

Zadok Rabinowitz

"A man's dreams are an index to his greatness."

"The most pathetic person in the world is someone who has sight, but no vision."

Helen Keller

"Hope is the pillar that holds up the world.
Hope is the dream of a waking man."

Pliny the Elder

"Hope is that thing with feathers
that perches in the soul."

Emily Dickinson

Seneca

"Our plans miscarry because they have no aim. When you don't know what harbor you're aiming for, no wind is the right wind."

"Did the first bird fly because it dreamed of the sky?"

Kent Nerburn

To Ponder and To Practice

- What part of your current life is a result of what you *used* to want? Consider the extent to which you are living on the dreams of the past rather than the present and the future.
- Like the monkey who will not let go of the coconut, thus keeping itself captive, what do you feel yourself holding on to that you would like to let go of? What are a few of your own unlived dreams that you might want to prune in order to make way for new dreams?
- Begin a journal to record your thoughts, feelings, ideas, hopes and aspirations, be they big or little, modest or ambitious, trivial or profound, silly or serious, seemingly idealistic or practical. Find a time and place where you can close the door to the bigger, noisier world and open the door to your silent but speaking heart without the normal filters of the world.
- To dip into the pool of your own hopes and desires, respond to the following prompts with the first thing that comes to mind.
  - I am truly happy when…
  - My version of a "dream job" is…
  - As a child, I always hoped that I would be…
  - If I could accomplish nothing else in my life, I would want to…
  - I know that I am in my element when…
  - I have always dreamed that I would be…
  - If money were no issue, I would probably choose to…
  - I have always longed for…
  - If I had three additional lives to spend in any way I chose, I would choose to…
- Robert Browning advises that "It is not our hopes, but our aspirations, that are our possibilities." To identify your aspirations, begin by drafting a list of your hopes and dreams. Let your imagination run wild. Apply no filter on your brainstorming.

  Once you have drafted the "Master List," put a star next to each item on your list that you are either doing something about or plan to do something about. In other words, which of these goals and desires have you actually made a decision about? This is the difference between hopes and aspirations. And therein, lie your possibilities.

  Make a list of three small steps that you can take this very week that will lead you closer to one of your aspirations. Make and follow a "List of Small Steps" every week.

Practice

- Mark Twain advises us, "You can't depend on your judgement when your imagination is out of focus." Consider how your imagination is coloring your current circumstances. Is it in focus or is it possible that the images you are dealing with are a bit distorted by your imagination?
- Count your blessings this very day for all that you have and as far as all the unlived dreams go, be grateful for the privilege that comes with wanting more.
- Take your dreams seriously. If you want to be a writer, stop telling yourself that you want to be a writer and be a writer instead: start writing. If you want to be an artist, start painting. It gives us a head start when we believe enough in our dreams to act on them.
- Write a speech that beings with the words, "I have a dream…"
- Write the lyrics to your own song or poem entitled, "Imagine."
- Select a quote on the topic of hope from this chapter's *Passages* and post it where you will see it often in order to internalize it.
- Choose a daily habit, routine or symbol to help you remain conscious of letting go of unlived dreams and the power of dreaming new dreams. (e.g. While peeling the potatoes or the carrots, feel yourself peeling away the dead skin of old dreams around your heart. When planting seeds, let a few them stand for your dreams.)
- Given everything you have read in this chapter, what do you want to *keep* doing? What do you want to *stop* doing? What do you want to *start* doing?

Notes

Arriving

Chapter

Embracing the Unknown

Trust the frontier

Trust the frontier

Learn to operate in the dark

Learn to operate in the dark

Journey toward possibility

Journey toward possibility

Allow the search to stir the soul

Allow the search to stir the soul

Be vigilant to the flame of hope

Be vigilant to the flame of hope

Choose the path with heart

Choose the path with heart

Arriving

"Hello! Is anyone there? Can anyone hear me?"

I thought I knew where I was going, but I am not sure any more.
I do not even remember how I came to be on this road.
I am lost and it is dark. The moon is hidden behind the clouds.
Not a single star is shining and I have no wood with which to build a fire.

At times like these, I try not to look at my feet—
those humble faithful servants who carry me each step.
I dare not tell them we are lost, lest they set to stumbling.
Instead, I sing songs of the swallow to give them wings,
I sing songs of the sea to give them sails.
I keep them moving to a merry melody,
fearing that if they stop, they may never start again.

I pass many people along the way.
I smile and wave in a way that assures them
I know just where I am going—as if I am about to arrive,
like Marco Polo into Asia, or Christ into the Holy City.
I do not show them the underside of my terrified heart
nor the holes in the soles of my shoes.

Not that I do not know about arrivals.
I have had many of them, hundreds of them! And departures too.
I have had both in the form of graduations, marriage and divorce,
the birth of a child who had the nerve to grow up.
Employment, unemployment, re-employment and self-employment.
New love, the loss of love and the rebirth of love.
Each beginning holding its own sweetness.
Every ending, its melancholy.
But always, just under the wings of departure,
I could feel the pulse of new arrival like a small heart beating.

I know now that life sways between these two winds.
What the caterpillar considers the end of the world,
the butterfly calls a beginning. And both are true.
Just as winter must die to spring and the night gives way to dawn,
just when we think we are dying, we see that we are being born.
Each moment, each day and year, relinquishing what we have been
in order to surrender to what we will become.

And so we go… these feet and I.
Trusting that the very "going" will lead us, step by step, into some new knowing.
Of one thing I am certain:
As surely as I am making this journey, this journey is making me.
I am being born as I walk.

Ah, the clouds have moved,
and I see by the light of a half-moon
that I am coming upon a bend in the road. This is good.
My feet love an honest bend—
the feeling of rounding one curve as they enter the next.
All the while moving to the merry melodies of the swallow and the sea.

Reflections

I would love to lead a movement to put an end to the ridiculous charade that we all know exactly where we are going. Everyone has holes in their journeying shoes. Everyone's life is a series of arrivals and departures. We all know what it is to be lost.

So why the charade? Wouldn't our individual journeys be that much easier if they were shared? Wouldn't we be less exhausted if we didn't have to feign false confidence? Isn't there beauty and humility in owning one's experience in life? Or am I one of the few out here in the big world whose path is not well marked, whose road is full of unknown twists and turns, and who sings to herself as she enters each new bend?

I can't help but wonder if Marco Polo sang to himself. Moses must have had a few good "top ten" ditties in his repertoire as well. Surely Jesus must have kept a song in his heart as he met with trials and tribulations in his short but powerful thirty-three years. And how his feet, both literally and metaphorically, must have hurt!

Of all of the biblical stories I remember as a child, it was the story of Mary Magdalene washing Christ's feet with her hair that touched me most deeply. Maybe it was the poignancy of carrying out such a humble act, and with her long, beautiful hair, no less. Or maybe, even as a child, I intuited that Jesus's feet must have been so sore from all that walking... all that journeying from town to town, from miracle to miracle, from Bethlehem to Calvary... from earth to heaven and then back again. When I think back on my images of Christ, I do not remember thinking of him as a nester or a homeowner, not even as a tax-paying citizen of a particular county. I think of him as the ultimate pilgrim on a journey to a destination that could not be marked on a map... save for the map of heart, the map of destiny.

Prince Siddhartha was a pilgrim too, leaving the luxuries and privileges of his palace to see the world and discover compassion, to walk on and on in order to find the eight-fold path to enlightenment. It was the journey that made a Buddha.

Then there is the pilgrimage of Mother Teresa, from Bulgaria to India—a walk from one hungry person to the next, in the end, showing the world the power that one person can have in affecting the lives of thousands.

But hey, these folks were in the big league... Jesus of Nazareth, Prince Siddhartha, Moses, Marco Polo, Mother Teresa. We aren't surprised that they were destined to take these harrowing journeys. But how about us everyday folk? How are we supposed to know where to go? Have we had the benefit of a burning bush lately? Where are the fairy godmothers with their magic wands? Where's Merlin when we need him? How are we supposed to find our way through the maze of questions and challenges, such as:

- What should I be when I grow up? And *why* should I grow up?
- What should I be studying?
- What job should I apply for?
- Should I leave the security of a job for something that may not turn out?
- How will I know which path to take?
- How do I follow my bliss when I haven't met it yet?
- How do I "do what I love so that the money will follow," if I don't know what I love?

I guess we are left to wizard ourselves a track through our own rocky circumstances, our ever-winding trail of needs and our longing for answers.

Isn't it amazing how many times in a life we come to the same impasse—stopped like deer in the proverbial headlights of having to choose the next path but not knowing which way to go? Graduating from high school, university or graduate school, we wonder if we can really make good on the future everyone keeps telling us looks so promising. Making a move across the country, the truck has arrived with our belongings, we've unpacked our bags and plugged in the stereo—now what do we do to actually make a new home in a strange environment? Leaving a job that was sucking the very life from our bones—great move—now what do we do? At all these various ages and stages of life, we have the same haunted look in our eyes, the same hungry questions on our lips and the same storm a-brewin' over our worried brows.

And then we make choices. We take a step. Or we don't make a choice and we let life choose for us. Things happen. We experience them. Sometimes we are happy with our choices and sometimes we aren't. When things work out as we had hoped, we keep moving at a steady, self-assured pace or we try to set up camp and rest on our laurels for a while. When we are not happy with our circumstances, our discontent will nudge us slowly but surely back into a decision point. Either way, each step simply takes us to the next one... and to the next one... and to the next one. Meister Eckhart put it this way:

> "There's no stopping place in this life—
> nor is there for any man,
> no matter how far along his path he's gone."

Regardless of the choices we make, sometimes our lives seem to live us, as if they possess their own bizarre momentum. We are carried along. We may set out on a journey of our own making, but in the end, our experience is finally determined by the journey itself. I have come to believe that is how the world gives birth to our souls. We truly are being born as we walk. But like Dorothy in the Wizard of Oz, we long to get back to (or to find) our Kansas, wherever that may be... however long it may take us to arrive. We'll pray at every altar, seek the assistance of career counselors, personal development professionals, therapists, dating services... even commission the services of psychics on the 900 line for a bit of help. The last place we think to look is at the possibility within our own two feet.

But here's the problem. We human beings have this inborn need for self-preservation, for security, for an emergency plan, an escape route, a full money-back guarantee. How then, do we juggle these intrinsic needs with the uncertainty that is inherent in life's journeying? Personally, I find singing to myself very helpful. But beyond that, here are a few core principles and beliefs that may help keep us moving to a merry melody as our feet enter each new bend.

Trust the frontier

I remember reading the quote from Isak Dinesen that "God made the world round so we would never be able to see far down the road." At the time I thought it was because God had an odd sense of humor. Now I believe it's because we are made for the frontier, we were bred for the hinterland. Pioneer blood courses through our veins. We know that we have no control over the events that will take place in our lives. We can affect our futures greatly by the way we respond to these circumstances, but we cannot predict nor control what these circumstances will be. So from the very gate, given the nature of life, we are pioneers, and as such, we not only appreciate the frontier, we need it. Phillippe Diole, the extraordinary diving pioneer, speaks beautifully to this need:

> "Whether one walks, rides a camel, flies or dives deep into the sea, it is for the sole purpose of crossing a frontier beyond which man ceases to feel himself the master, sure of his techniques upheld by his inheritance, backed by the crowd. The more powerless he is, the more his spirit permeates his being. The horizon of the world and the horizon of thought coincide within him. The water, the rocks, and the sand become vital nourishment, and perhaps a poem."

What an incredible concept: the more powerless we feel, the more spirit permeates our being. (I guess that should make many of us feel pretty spiritual about now.)

In reality, I think we have a clear-cut case of a love/hate relationship going on with the unknown. Part of us thrives on the buoyant sensation of anticipation, surprise and possibility; we would never sacrifice that vital part of our experience. Then again, there is that part of us that will hang on to even the tiniest thread of security with everything we've got. But what possible sense of security can we glean from the unknown, stretched like an endless horizon before us?

I think there are a couple of essential capacities that we must cultivate within ourselves in relation to the unknown. The first is learning to navigate in the dark without the benefit of a mapped-out plan or a well-lit path. The other is choosing the path of hope, the one holding the most promise, over the path of fear, the one of least resistance.

Learn to operate in the dark

Everything is unknown until we live it. Agnes de Mille, the famous dancer, reminds us.

> "Living is a form of not being sure, not knowing what's next or how. The moment you know how, you begin to die a little. We artists never know. We guess. We may be wrong. We take leap after leap in the dark."

In "Four Quartets," poet T. S. Eliot, regards the unknown as "the way of dispossession," warning us that we must wait without hope, without love, without faith, lest our hope, love and faith be invested unwisely.

I said to my soul, be still,
and wait without hope
For hope would be hope for the wrong thing;
wait without love,
For love would be love of the wrong thing;
There is yet faith,
But faith and the love and the hope
are all in the waiting,
Wait without thought,
for you are not ready for thought.

To arrive where you are,
to get from where you are not,
You must go by the way
wherein there is no ecstasy.
In order to arrive at what you do not know,
You must go by a way
which is the way of ignorance.
In order to possess what you do not possess,
You must go by the way of dispossession.

Our culture does not cultivate in us much appreciation for the kind of dark that comes with not knowing the next step on the journey, much less a capacity for "the way of dispossession" described by T. S. Eliot. Ours is a culture that loves plans, instructions, remedies and directions. Every time we talk to someone, we can expect an unsolicited map in response. Tell someone that your are experiencing fatigue, and you will be quickly recommended 101 different homeopathic remedies. Share a trouble you are having in a relationship, and you are sure to receive the newest instructions shared on a talk show about dealing with someone from Mars or Venus. Confide in someone a desire for your vocational future, and you will be offered a career plan. (I know people who not only have their present life perfectly mapped out, but their *next* lives as well.) There is always a map of some kind that will show us how to get from where we are to where we wish to be. Ours is a culture that likes directions and faithful guidelines.

But underneath all of our plans and expectations, despite all the professional and personal advice both offered and thrust upon us from everyone in this and the next area code, the next step for each of us is truly unknown and has never been taken by anyone. It is stepping into our own unknown. We know this so well—the being in the dark and stepping inch by inch towards the light of a decision. We know it because it is the only way we know of traveling through the choices that really matter.

I like having a hotel reservation before flying into a city I do not know. I appreciate a good recipe when wanting to transform an eggplant and a chicken into a feast. Occasionally (but only under duress), I've even read the step-by-step directions that came with a new gadget or piece of software. But when it has come to the bigger life choices, like entering (or leaving) a relationship, deciding where to live or whether to stay or leave a place of employment, I personally haven't found prescribed answers of much help. Neither from books nor from talk shows, not even from friends and family. No, it's always the fresh step taken with a deep breath (and fingers crossed behind my back).

I believe Wendell Berry when he suggested:

> "It may be when we no longer know what to do,
> that we have come to our real work.
> When we no longer know which way to go,
> we have begun our real journey."

Maybe the "not knowing" is an essential stage of any journey. Besides, in the same way that a joke is not funny if you know the punch line, maybe our lives would not hold the same level of delight and surprise if there was no mystery. If we always knew where we were going, we would have no capacity or appetite for the magic wrapped in possibility, nor the blossoming of the dark that Wendell Berry speaks about in this gorgeous poem:

> *To Know the Dark*
>
> *To go in the dark with a light*
> *is to know the light.*
> *To know the dark, go dark. Go without sight,*
> *And find that the dark, too, blooms and sings,*
> *And is traveled by dark feet and dark wings.*

Journey toward possibility

"It is not the place we occupy which is important, but the direction in which we move." Such was the wisdom espoused by Oliver Wendell Holmes in the mid-1800s. I remember once complaining to a friend that I had not yet saved or planned for my financial future. She offered me encouragement that has stayed with me. She said, "Denise, you can't undo what you have done or not done. But that's okay, because I see a woman before me who has something no one can take from her—and that is earning power. Better to have no savings but the capacity and power to create a bright future than to have all the money in the world, but no promise." I realized that the place that I occupied at that time was not half as important as the direction in which I was headed.

In the end, all that we can ever do is take the step that is right before us. Regret is not helpful, and worry is worse than regret. We need to honor where we are without judging it in relation to where we still have to go. We do ourselves a great disservice by judging where we are in comparison to some final destination. This is one of the dangers of having a fixed destination in mind: we tend to measure where we are against the imagined landscape of where we are going. So wherever we are—even if we have moved closer—it never feels quite near enough. Turning our gaze, instead, simply to the direction in which we are headed is the most useful gesture we can grant our feet. That and a generous dose of optimism—just enough to put that little bit of spring into our step.

In his book, *Words I Wish I Had Written,* Robert Fulghum quotes Franz Kafka in this passage from Kafka's diaries published after his death at age forty-one. Although he was known for dark and depressing writing, I find this quote luminous with optimism.

> "If we knew we were on the right road, having to leave it would mean endless despair. But we are on a road that only leads to a second one and then to a third one and so forth. And the real highway will not be sighted for a long, long time—perhaps never. So we drift in doubt. But also in an unbelievable diversity. Thus the accomplishment of hopes remains an always unexpected miracle. But in compensation, the miracle remains forever possible."

It makes me think that Kafka, too, loved an honest bend, the thrill of rounding one curve as he entered the next… maybe he, too, moved to the songs of swallows.

Allow the search to stir the soul

> Once upon a time a monk encountered a man who had spent his life looking for beauty and truth.
>
> "Have you found what you are looking for?" he asked.
>
> "No," replied the man.
>
> "Wonderful," the monk responded.
>
> "What do you mean by saying my unfulfilled search is wonderful?" demanded the truth seeker.
>
> The monk replied, "I mean you still have something to look forward to."

Is it the hunt that we love, more than the prey? Is it the very search that stirs the soul? I would think that could only be true if we journey with optimism, but not of the Pollyanna variety. I use the word "optimism" to mean more of a constancy of faith. Faith in our highest purposes, in our ability to survive and in our power to make new choices. Faith in beauty, joy and possibility.

How we view the world certainly depends on our perspective at the moment. When given a choice, life would cast a vote that we choose the lens of optimism. The soul would only wink in agreement. There are those who would argue that constancy of faith or optimism is not a choice we make but the effect of having lived a life full to the brim with good fortune. Either that, or the result of a serious case of naiveté. But it was Helen Keller who said, "No pessimist ever discovered the secrets of the stars or sailed to an uncharted land or opened a new heaven to the human spirit." I find it amazing that this sentiment was born of a woman who was deaf and blind by age two. How else, but through optimism, could she have graduated *cum laude* from Radcliffe College in 1902 and gone on through her writing and teaching to become one of the greatest voices of her century?

Albert Schweitzer mirrors her advice. Here is a man who held an extraordinary mix of education and vocations including theologian, philosopher, medical doctor and musician. He spent most of his life as a missionary in what was then French Equatorial Africa and was awarded the Nobel Peace Prize in 1952. When asked in an interview whether he was a pessimist or an optimist, he answered, "My knowledge is pessimistic, but my willing and my hoping are optimistic—personally, I lean towards the latter." Clearly his search stirred the soul.

Be vigilant to the flame of hope

Have you ever noticed that as soon as we think we have assembled a comfortable life, we find a piece of ourselves that seems out of place? That is because our lives are in process, our bodies are in process, and so are our hopes and dreams. What keeps hope fresh is its stirring from the powerful movement of our wild hearts and the ever-restless soul. What affects our hearts is holy. What we imagine, dream about and yearn for is a sacred vessel carrying hidden truth, truth not yet manifested, but truth just the same. The great poet Keats once said, "I am certain of nothing in this world but the holiness of the heart's affections and the truth of the imagination."

There lives in each of us an exciting, adventurous sense of the possible, a yearning to move forward into the unknown in order to embrace life in all its fullness. This spark is divine and essential to human life. As such, it should be honored and tended with the gift of our awareness, especially when our hopes lie in winter. That is part of every evolutionary process—emergence, birth, blossoming, decay, silence, etc. Hope is not immune from this process.

Not that I do not know
about arrivals.
I have had many of them,
hundreds of them!
And departures too.
Each beginning
holding its own sweetness.
Every ending, its melancholy.
But always,
just under the wings of departure,
I could feel the pulse of new arrival
like a small heart beating.

We must resist our own impatience and discouragement when the clarity of our hopes and dreams is not forthcoming and we have yet to feel the pulse of new arrival. In traveling new paths, we need to be acutely watchful for the insecurity and self-doubt that accompany us—especially when hope sleeps. For those are the feelings that lead us to settle for boundaries rather than horizons.

We've all had the experience of "settling" for something less than we would ever have selected for ourselves in our brighter and clearer moments. Our insecurities urge us to seek reassurance, sanction and identity—through something, anything. How many people have we known who married someone because they feared their true mate would never come along? Or the person who accepts a job they hate because they fear that a better offer will not be forthcoming? How about the people who pursued a graduate degree because it was the next thing they could "belong" to without knowing what they really wanted?

I once met a young Marine on an airplane who was going home for a visit with his family. I asked him how he felt about his time in the military and his response chilled me to the bone, "Well, I guess it's okay, figuring that at the point in my life when I joined, the alternative was putting a noose around my neck. Little did I know that there are all kinds of nooses in life and we hang ourselves one way or another." My response to him at the time was something like, "Good for you. You chose the noose that comes off down the road. At the next juncture in life you will be a very different person who will make a new choice on very different terms—on your terms." He looked at me oddly for a few seconds and then flashed the most incredible smile. Of course, my heart was still too busy breaking in two to fully take in his toothy grin.

Thank heavens I believe there are no mistakes in life, that every choice and circumstance simply brings us to the next place on our journey. But it would be nice if we could just prevent a few of those pitfalls along the way. Keeping hope alive and maintaining a spot of optimism in our hearts is the only deterrent I know for not siding with fear when our choices look bleak. How I would love to meet my grinning Marine ten years down the line. I wouldn't be surprised if he looked at me and said, "Joining up was the best decision of my life. Beacause…." I will leave it to my imaginative readers to conjure your own stories of how and why he might come to feel that way.

And so we go… these feet and I.
Trusting that the very "going"
will lead us, step by step,
into some new knowing.
Of one thing I am certain:
As surely as I am
making this journey,
this journey is making me.
I am being born as I walk.

Like King Arthur's knights in their search for the Holy Grail, our journey is enlivened by the fact that the quest is never over and consists of endless adventures that can enrich us personally and deepen our understanding of life and ourselves. It is the only worthwhile path in today's world.

Around every bend in life lie new opportunities, roads as yet untaken. It is always a time of new beginnings. We know a lot about beginnings, because we have hundreds of them in various forms. And departures too. Like water that grows stagnant when it stops moving, we need a constant flow of change in order to remain healthy and alive. And yet, every decision to launch a new beginning requires from us a leap of faith, an inner act of heroism. Every day of our lives we take these leaps holding on to the invisible ropes of faith. When we face a difficult crossroad we do not have to develop new courage, rather, we simply need to tap into the fortitude we have already developed throughout the course of our lives.

Choose the path with heart

An old pilgrim was making his way to the Himalayan mountains in the bitter cold of winter when it began to rain.

An innkeeper said to him, "How will you ever get there in this kind of weather?"

The old man answered cheerfully, "My heart got there first, so it's easy for the rest of me to follow."

In his wonderful book, *After the Ecstasy, the Laundry,* Jack Kornfield writes about the everchanging journey of the human heart:

> "The unfolding of the human heart is artful and mysterious. We might wish the path were orderly and predictable, but the ways of the heart are a landscape discoverable only in the journey. We cannot capture freedom and place it in time. For the mature spirit, freedom is the journey itself. It is like a labyrinth, a circle, a flower's petal-by-petal opening, or a deepening spiral, a dance around the still point, the center of all things. There are always changing cycles—ups and downs, opening and closing, awakenings to love and freedom, often followed by new and subtle entanglements. In the course of this great spiral, we return to where we started again and again, but each time with a fuller, more open heart."

Perhaps, above all else, this is what the journey of life is about—the unfolding of the human heart. Little wonder then that each of our paths is unique and distinctive. Little wonder that although everyone who has ever lived has journeyed, no one—not a single person—has ever traveled your particular road. Others may have met with similar circumstances or traveled similar roads, but no one has ever felt the dust under your particular feet. It is a good thing that we are pioneers—the territory of the heart is always frontier.

And while the roads we travel are distinctive and individual, there is one piece of advice that I believe holds universal truth. This is an excerpt from Carlos Castaneda, a fellow pilgrim who has penned several rich and inspiring books about the spiritual journey through the voice of his teacher, Don Juan. I am grateful for the opportunity to include this passage as the perfect curve in the bend of this chapter.

> "All paths are the same: they lead nowhere. . . . There are paths going through the bush, or into the bush. In my own life I could I have traversed long, long paths but I am not anywhere. My benefactor's question has meaning now. Does this path have heart? If it does, the path is good; if it doesn't, it is of no use. Both paths lead nowhere; but one has a heart, and the other doesn't. One makes for a joyful journey; as long as you follow it, you are one with it. The other will make you curse your life. One makes you strong, the other weakens you. Choose, always, the path with heart."

May we, as Joseph Campbell suggested, say a hearty "yes" to our adventure. May our hearts point us in the direction of our dreams and highest purposes—may we move, always, to the merry melodies of the swallow and the sea.

Passages

"There is a time for departure
even when there is no certain place to go."

Tennessee Williams

"You are the laboratory and every day is an experiment. Go and find what is new and unexpected."

John Elkes

Sojourner Truth

"I am free when I allow my life to unfold. As soon as I restrict myself to new outcomes, I've got shackles on my feet."

"Make voyages. Attempt them. That's all there is."

Elaine Dundy

"Do not linger to gather flowers to keep them, but walk on, for flowers will keep themselves blooming all your way."

Rabindranath Tagore

Nicaraguan proverb

"Do not follow where the path may lead. Go instead where there is no path and leave a trail."

"If only God would give me a clear sign! Like making a large deposit in my name at a Swiss bank."

Woody Allen

"When we are not sure, we are alive."

Graham Greene

Simon Raven

"Since life is short and the world is wide, the sooner you start exploring it the better. Soon enough the time will come when you are too tired to move further than your front step. Go now."

Antonio Machado

"Walker, there is no path, you make the path as you walk."

"I shall be telling this with a sigh
Somewhere ages and ages hence:
Two roads diverged in a wood, and I—
I took the one less traveled by,
And that has made all the difference."

Robert Frost

Rollo May

"We all stand on the edge of life, each moment comprising the edge. Before us is only possibility."

"Search the darkness, do not run from it....
The moon appears for the night travelers."

Rumi

"All glory comes from daring to begin."

Anonymous

"Faith and doubt both are needed, not as antagonists, but working side by side to take us around the unknown curve."

Lillian Smith

Sam Walter Foss

"In the average man is curled
the hero stuff that rules the world."

"Afoot and light-hearted I take to the open road,
Healthy, free, the world before me."

Walt Whitman

Ralph Waldo Emerson

"What lies beyond us and what lies before us are tiny matters compared to what lies within us."

"Remember, no matter where you go, there you will be."

Mary Engelbreit

"After the final no there comes a yes.
And on that yes the future world depends.
No was the night. Yes is the present sun."

Wallace Stevens

"All beginnings are mysteries, the mystery of creation."

Henri Amiel

Maori proverb

"Turn your face to the sun
and the shadows fall
behind you."

"Faith is a path of heart that enables us to perceive the mysterious meaning of life, live with doubt and paradox, and to be home in a world where the ground of being is always present."

Frederic and Mary Brussant

"If a man wishes to be sure of the road he treads on, he must close his eyes and walk in the dark."

Saint John of the Cross

"Have you ever seen an inchworm crawl up a leaf or a twig and then, clinging to the very end, revolve in the air, feeling for something, to reach something? That's like me. I am trying to find something out there beyond the place on which I have footing."

Albert Ryder

"What saves a man is to take a step. Then another step. It is always the same step, but you have to take it."

Antoine de Saint-Exupery

Robert Frost

"You're searching, Joe, for things that don't exist; I mean beginnings. Ends and beginnings—there are no such things. There are only middles."

"Follow the river and you will arrive at the sea."

French proverb

"To live is to be slowly born."

Antoine de Saint Exupery

To Ponder and To Practice

- List twenty things you wanted along life's journey and have already received.
- Give yourself permission to appreciate where you currently are on life's path instead of where you think you should be. Draw a map of the many places you've been, the positions you've held and points along the evolution of the person you have become so far on the journey.
- Write about your present place on life's journey. What is the terrain? What are the present weather conditions? Where are you coming from? Where are you going? Who are you traveling with? What are you leaving behind and what are you taking with you?
- Do an honest self-assessment about how you are handling your present place on life's journey. For example, are you being stubborn or are you displaying true steadfastness? Are you finding yourself too determined or not determined enough?
- What was one of your most profound experiences of having faith and trusting in something or someone you could not see but believed in anyway? How was that time similar to or different from your present situation?
- Think of someone you know who has totally transformed his or her life in some way. What do you think enabled that person to embrace change and survive the transition that transformation brought?
- Learn to trust your intuition as a loyal friend. Splashing around in the waters of your dreams and desires is an exercise that is refreshing to every other part of your being. Listen to the songs of your intuition and you will hear wisdom that is native to your soul alone. Respond to each of the following prompts with the first thing that comes to mind:
  - In terms of my current vocational circumstances, my intuition tells me to….
  - As unpredictable as life is, with regard to my own destiny, my intuition tells me….
  - If I were to simply follow my intuition about what I need most in my life right now, I would probably….
- Krishnamurti suggested that we are never afraid of the unknown; what we are afraid of is the known coming to an end. How is that true in your life right now?
- At what junctures on your life journey have you chosen the path of least resistance? At what junctures did you apply "constancy of faith" and optimism over the path of least resistance?
- Given where you are now on life's journey, what choices could you make that would be settling for less and what choices could you make that would represent a "path with heart"?

Practice

- Select a quote from this chapter's *Passages* which speaks to you in relation to your present journey and post it where you will see it until it is internalized.
- Choose a daily habit, routine or symbol to help you embrace the unknown with constancy of faith and to choose, always, the path with heart.
- Given everything you have read in this chapter, what do you want to *keep* doing? What do you want to *stop* doing? What do you want to *start* doing?

Notes

Nurture Your Nature

Chapter

Celebrating Your Gifts

Kick the habit of comparison

Kick the habit of comparison

Move the elephant away from the pole

Move the elephant away from the pole

Embrace your limitations and your potential

Embrace your limitations and your potential

Celebrate the differences in our gifts

Celebrate the differences in our gifts

Find the context for your genius

Find the context for your genius

Bring the medicine of what you love

Bring the medicine of what you love

Nurture Your Nature

The acorn worries little about the oak it will become,
the tulip bulb nestles in the dark prepared to see the sun.
For in the nature of these things is destiny's own seed,
the force that spins the planet and hollows the river reed.
We are nature too, we come from dust, we come from stars—
like the oak is in the acorn, Providence is ours.

The swan is not yet graceful while traveling on land,
ah, but when she finds the water, she floats as nature planned.
Watch the fuzzy caterpillar, keep him captive in your hand,
but when destiny is done with him, he'll flutter high above the land.
What makes us think we're different or any less bestowed
with gifts that come embedded, that nurtured, will unfold?

Does the moon know its own phases? Is the sun warmed by its own light?
Is the hawk aware of its gracefulness as it glides in perfect flight?
Does the apple tree yearn to apple, does the grass pray to grow?
Do the dolphins leap self-consciously, are they putting on a show?
Or is it only humankind, so aware of its every move,
too self-conscious to relax, and enter nature's groove?

How do we quiet the persistent mind that insists that a plan we make,
that maps out neatly, step by step, the course our lives will take?
How do we nurture what's in our nature and trust a greater force
to lead us simply by the heart and take a wiser course?
We won't find in books or in tests exactly what to do,
for what is in our hearts to try, is up to me and you.

We trust the force that's in the seed, that directs the night and day,
but when it comes to our own lives, we'd rather steer the way.
While we plan our lives and set our goals can we reserve a place for grace,
and trust that in the greater scheme, we too have been set a place?
To all the powers that we hone, let's add an element of trust
that each of us are acorns too—that there's an oak in each of us.

Reflections

I have an abiding faith that everyone is born to this world gifted. Not with just any gift but something unique to that person that *only* they could bring, and something that the world needs. Creation has breathed into each of us a spark of divinity, and that spark is breathed back through the use of our gifts. All of my work as an employment counselor, a curriculum developer and a trainer, leans on that basic pillar: we have each been given a song and it is the desire of our hearts to sing it. Embedded in our very nature is our gift already enfolded, the oak within the acorn.

If only our gifts came as indelibly inscribed and as apparent as birthmarks. The challenge, however, is in letting our nature be known, first and foremost to ourselves, and then proclaimed and shared with the world. The birds and the bees, the flowers and the trees are not burdened with this challenge. It is as if surrender to their nature is as easy to them as breathing. What if our natural abilities came as easily to us as flying comes to the bird or blossoming comes to the flower? What if the means by which we were to make a living in the world came as naturally to us as making honey comes to the bee as it engages in the larger world of the flower?

John O'Donohue writes of the necessity in human life to be in rhythm with our nature. He says,

> "It is in the depths of your life that you will discover the invisible necessity that has brought you here. When you begin to decipher this, your gift and giftedness come alive. Your heart quickens and the urgency of living rekindles your creativity. If you can awaken this sense of destiny, you come into rhythm with your life. You fall out of rhythm when you renege on your potential and talent, when you settle for the mediocre as a refuge from the call. When you lose rhythm, your life becomes wearyingly deliberate or anonymously automatic.... When you are in rhythm with your nature, nothing destructive can touch you. Providence is at one with you; it minds you and brings you to your new horizons. To be spiritual is to be in rhythm."

Clearly, vocational issues are, at heart, spiritual ones. It is in the not knowing, the experimenting and the discovering that we not only find and celebrate our skills and abilities but our spirits as well. While our lives are much more complex than that of the birds and flowers, we are the lucky ones. For we are not only blessed with inherent skills and abilities, we have the privilege of recognizing and honing them, then making choices about how and when and where we use them. In the quest to uncover and make choices about how to use our talents, we imbue them with humility and intentionality—turning them into true gifts.

We long for ways of working and living that engage the spirit and the gifts of our nature. Work that is in alignment with our natural talents and skills, and that affords the development and blossoming of our gifts is what I refer to as "true livelihood." This means work that is true to your talents, true to your heart, true to your needs and wants, true to your values and ideals. In short, it is based on and sustained by your truth. It is essential to our lives that we mine this gold and bring it into the light. For in the words of Thomas Paine, "Such is the irresistible nature of truth, that all it asks, and all it wants, is the liberty of appearing." It is not about finding "employment," or "getting a job." It is about "vocation"—giving voice to your life through your work. It is about calling—responding to what is calling you and calling back to the world from your depths.

How do we survive those periods of our lives when the only "call" we hear is the one from the landlady reminding us to make the rent?

How do we nurture what is in our nature, surrendering to our truth like birds in flight, while juggling the pressures and responsibilities of making a living? Here are just a few ideas to ponder while you proceed on your heart's path... until you come upon your own piece of sky and surrender to the wings that are yours.

Kick the habit of comparison

We really have only one big job in life and that is to live our lives fully. As ourselves. Not as anyone else, or compared to anyone else. Yet how much of our time is spent comparing ourselves to others, both dead and alive? That comparison is a bandit, a thief of our joy and a roadblock to our growth. Nothing in life is as stressful or as exhausting as trying to be someone different than who we are.

I once heard Mikhail Baryshnikov say in an interview, "I do not try to dance better than anyone else. I only try to dance better than myself." Well, coming from one of the world's finest dancers, that's fine advice, right? If only we, even if in shallower pools of talent, could say the same for ourselves. It is so easy to live, instead, like the crow in Aesop's fable, *The Crow and the Swan.*

> A crow was filled with envy on seeing the beautiful white plumage of a swan and thought it was due to the water in which the swan constantly bathed and swam. So he left the neighborhood of the inns, where he made his living taking bits of meat left from the plates of the diners, and went and lived among the pools and streams. But though he bathed and washed his feathers many times a day, he didn't make them any whiter and at last died of hunger in the bargain.

It has taken me years to learn the lesson of the crow. Why? Because I am the middle sibling between two very beautiful and extraordinarily talented sisters. My older sister, Maria, is stunning in every way and always has been. Aside from being physically beautiful, she is gifted with the ability to learn and master just about anything she sets her mind to. My younger sister, Michelle, is the adorable one, having been the baby of a large brood. She is funny, witty, generous to a fault and pretty much lovable in every way. Now with all that aside, they are both incredible artisans—bringing beauty and artfulness to everything they touch, their homes, their wardrobes, the way they wrap a gift, set a table, or design and whip out a quilt, a banner or a table runner faster than you can say "Eat your heart out, Martha Stewart." Oh, and me? I was the one in the middle who can't draw a circle without using the bottom of a glass.

Tell me I don't know about comparison. But this is not a sad story—this is a great story! Because my sisters are not only perfect, they are also kind. They have shown me (convinced me) over the years that I have my own gifts—some of which have even caused them to feel enviable from time to time. I will never be as elegant as Maria nor as adorable as Michelle. But I get to be Denise—the only Denise in the family. In fact, the only version of *this* Denise in the entire world. I will enjoy my own gifts and not struggle in the difference between their talents and my own.

Incidentally, this new and improved version of my self-confidence (without having to compare myself to my sisters) is a fledgling of a bird, but it will grow with time. My sisters and I look forward to growing older together and celebrating the similarities and the differences in our gifts as we welcome a new generation of women to the family.

We may change our habits but not our nature. When we cease needing to be remarkable, we are free to work according to our own wishes and talents. The rose yearning to be a grasshopper would never bloom. The grasshopper longing to be a tiger would never get off its hind legs. And the tiger, in all of its unmanaged elegance, would never win its prey if dying to be a rose. But we so often find ourselves following other people's dreams, wanting to be like someone else or secretly aspiring to the fortune or fame of people we don't really know. Yet when we compare ourselves to others, we see neither ourselves nor those we look up to. We only experience the tension of comparing. It is impossible to nurture your nature by ignoring it or praying for a nature that is not your own.

Legendary cellist Pablo Casals says in his book, *Joys and Sorrows:*

> "Each second we live in a new and unique moment of the universe, a moment that never was before and will never be again. And what do we teach our children in school? We teach them that two and two makes four, and that Paris is the capital of France. When will we teach them what they are? You are a marvel. You are unique. In all of the world there is no other child exactly like you. In the million years that have passed there has never been another child like you... You have the capacity for anything... we all must work—to make this world worthy of its children."

I adore that passage and the message it carries, but I know full well that we will not be successful in teaching our children what we as adults do not yet know for and about ourselves. When we begin to nurture what is in our nature, without comparing ourselves to others, we will do better than teach children that they are marvels, we will model "marvelousness"!

Move the elephant away from the pole

By force of habit we often allow *who we have been* to determine *who we shall become.* We erect boundaries around our creative imagining, lest they venture too far beyond the boundaries of what we have already achieved. In this way we hold ourselves hostage to our past and rein in our possibilities. Imagination is simply not invited to this party! We become like the elephant who, when tied to a pole by a rope that is two yards long, will learn to live within two yards of the pole. Even when the length of the rope is increased by a mile, the elephant will stay within those two yards.

Perceptions of ourselves can become like a rope of limitations. Expanding the visions of ourselves will only serve to increase the length of the rope, but believing in and moving into that vision is what will move us away from the pole. We need to practice possibility thinking. We don't ordinarily view ourselves standing against a backdrop of infinite possibilities. We are much better at viewing ourselves with our limitations in the foreground. We set our expectations based on the self-imposed boundaries that hide from us our own potential. These expectations can easily become our real limitations.

It is a mistake to draw conclusions about potential ability solely from past experience. No one would look at a healthy infant and say he will never walk or talk simply because he hasn't done so before. While it is important to value what we have already learned to do, it is equally important to recognize that we are still in the process of growing. We all have undiscovered talents.

William James once suggested that most people live in a very restricted circle of their potential being, making very small use of their resources, much like a person who, out of his whole body organism, should get into the habit of using and moving only his fingers. I suppose it is both a curse and a blessing that we are not fully aware of our potential: a curse because so much of our potential is wasted; a blessing because our one small lifetime would seem to us even shorter with the backdrop of our possibilities.

Embrace your limitations and your potential

Everything in the universe has a nature—limitations as well as potentials. Sometimes we are frightened of our capacities because they bring a sense of obligation to use them. But stronger than that fear must be the hope of faithfully making the most of our talents and cultivating the seeds within us.

With equal strength, we must accept our limitations for they are also gifts. Choreographer Leon Danielian was quoted in *Artists Speak* saying, "I don't want a machine in a dancer. The flaws of an individual are sometimes so marvelous." Working with one's limitations is also well known by people who work daily with the things of the world. Making pottery, for example, involves more than telling the clay what to become. The clay presses back on the potter's hands, telling the artisan what it can and cannot do.

Thomas Moore speaks to the importance of responding to our limitations in this passage from his book, *Original Self:*

> "Our neuroses are the raw material out of which an interesting personality may be crafted. They are sometimes dangerous and debilitating but nonetheless valuable. They are the basic stuff of the soul in need of lifelong refinement. Working this annoying and embarrassing material for a lifetime is a realistic work compared with the search for psychological hygiene—ridding ourselves of failure and confusion. Not wallowing in our limitations but creatively dealing with them as resources for a vital life, we arrive not at shallow self-acceptance but at profound love of the soul, which, with its rich mixture of the good and bad, is the starting point of a creative life."

In the ongoing creation and unfolding of livelihood, we must pay attention to the material we are working with, the medium of our lives, accepting with wholeheartedness both our limitations and our potentiality, and with humility, remembering how the towering oak comes from such a tiny, seemingly insignificant nut.

I am reminded of this wonderful passage from the Danish philosopher and theologian Soren Kierkegaard:

> "If I were to wish for anything, I should not wish for wealth and power, but for the passionate sense of potential, for the eye which, ever young and ardent, sees the possible. Pleasure disappoints, possibility never. What is more intoxicating, sparkling and fragrant than the wine of possibility and human potential?"

Celebrate the differences in our gifts

It is so wonderful that every creature on earth has been given what they need, to be what they are. It's just too bad that we humans, with our need to organize and systematize the world, have to muddy the waters. To the extent that we can celebrate our own unique talents, we should be able to celebrate the talents of one another. And with that appreciation for how we are unique, we will also accept how we are different.

The importance of valuing the differences in our giftedness is captured in this classic fable called "The Animal School" written by educator Dr. R. H. Reeves:

Once upon a time, the animals decided they must do something heroic to meet the problems of a "New World," so they organized a school. They adopted an activity curriculum consisting of running, climbing, swimming and flying. To make it easier to administer, all animals took all subjects.

The duck was excellent at swimming, better in fact than his instructor, and made excellent grades in flying, but he was very poor in running. Since he was low in running, he had to stay after school and give up swimming so that he could practice running. This was kept up until his webfeet were badly worn and he was only average in swimming. But average was acceptable in school, so nobody worried about that except the duck.

The rabbit started at the top of the class in running, but had a nervous breakdown because of so much makeup work in swimming.

The squirrel was excellent in climbing until he developed frustrations in the flying class where his teacher made him start from the ground up instead of from the treetop down. He also developed charley horses from over-exertion and he got a C in climbing and a D in running.

The eagle was a problem child and had to be disciplined severely. In climbing class he beat all the others to the top of the tree, but insisted on using his own way of getting there.

At the end of the year, an abnormal eel that could swim exceedingly well and also could run, climb and fly a little had the highest average and was valedictorian.

The prairie dogs stayed out of school and fought the tax levy because the administration would not add digging and burrowing to the curriculum. They apprenticed their children to the badger and later joined the groundhogs and gophers to start a successful private school.

Each of us has had a role in that fable, whether we've played the part of the frustrated duck, the malfunctioning rabbit, the rebellious eagle or the anarchist of a prairie dog. In fact, those of us from large families can probably point to one of each of those characters within our own family!

It's absurd to think of asking rabbits to swim, ducks to run and eagles to cut out all that flying. But is it not equally absurd when we apply the same faulty thinking in the human world, where we are born with distinctive gifts but are asked to operate within the same curriculum within our schools or training centers or within the same job descriptions at work? Rarely does one size ever fit all—whether in clothing or in community.

Have you ever seen the person who had all of the potential in the world to more than exceed the expectations of the job but who could not "fit" the uniformity of the job as required by the employer? In the end, it's not just the employee who loses—the employer loses as well. A world of conforming, average-producing eels is really smooth to administer, but it does not produce the creative, vital results that organizations today need to stay competitive and on the edge. The one-size-fits-all workplace does not invite the intelligence, imagination or passion of its members. Without bringing these qualities, the employees leave their spirits at the door in the morning and attempt to embody them again at the end of the day. I think we call these places "training ground for their competitors," for surely those employees who have "real" gifts to give will find a place where those gifts are valued.

It is essential not only to recognize and value our own unique talents, but to see and acknowledge the talents of those around us. As parents, siblings, neighbors, friends and coworkers, we can help to boost people's confidence and their belief in their own unique abilities by celebrating in each person what we see as their personal brand of genius. Everyone has their own natural abilities—taking the time to recognize and acknowledge those in the people with whom we live and work is one of the finest gifts we have to offer them.

Find the context for your genius

One of the core principles I live by and have leaned on throughout my career as a job developer and as a trainer in the field of employment and training comes from a quote from the incredible Buckminster Fuller. He said, "Everyone, in the right context, is a genius!"

I love that! And I also believe it. In fact, that is one way of posing the great challenge in life—to find the context for our genius. The Buddha taught that "your true job in life is to find your work and then, with all your heart, to give yourself to it." One way to approach that challenge is to look first at your gifts, and then to ask the question, "In what context would these gifts be considered valuable, and in fact, ingenious?"

Martin Luther King once said, "Questions are everything. The questions we ask in life will shape our destiny as clearly as the skeleton shapes the body." I have taught thousands of people in the last fifteen years how to turn the whole employment equation on its head and to look at the world of their possibilities for work with new eyes and a new heart. The essence of the perspective I teach is a simple but essential change in questions.

The traditional question the job seeker asks is something to the effect of, "What does the world need and how do I somehow make myself look and act like what the employer is asking for?" The question I urge people to ask is, "Given my native talents, capabilities and potential, what are the problems I can solve or the benefits I can bring to an organization?" Once a person has a handle on that question, the second question is "Who has that problem and doesn't know it yet?" Or "Who could benefit from my talents in a way they have not yet imagined?" I then provide tools for developing what I call an *employment proposal*. It is a very concise, one-page marketing tool which includes the following elements: what the person has to offer the business and the benefits it will bring; a summary of the skills, abilities and expertise that the person will bring to the job that is being proposed; and the person's employment conditions.

The employment proposal is really nothing more than a cover letter for a job that doesn't yet exist. The cool part is that the person designs the job around her particular needs and desires in the situation and names her own price. Better yet—there are no other job seekers competing for this newly proposed position! I give a thorough review of writing employment proposals in my book *Beyond Traditional Job Development: The Art of Creating Opportunity.*

Can you imagine what a world it would be if we all took more initiative in creating the kind of workplaces and positions that invited and welcomed our giftedness and unique brand of genius? But we have to see it first for ourselves before other people will recognize it for us. There is a myth that perhaps, if we are lucky, we will be "discovered," but I think we have to discover ourselves first.

Bring the medicine of what you love

Jesus once said, "Where your treasure is, there will your heart be also."

What we love, appreciate and are drawn to in life is the gift we bring to the human table. It is our treasure. In native traditions what one loves is thought of as one's "medicine" for the tribe. From that perspective, if we love to laugh, our medicine is humor. If we love to grow flowers, the iris or the lily may be our gift. What a wonderful way to mine the gold in our lives—we need simply to pay attention to what we love. One of my favorite poets, Mary Oliver, expresses this beautifully in the opening lines of her poem entitled, "Wild Geese." She says:

You do not have to be good.
You do not have to walk on your knees
for a hundred miles
across the desert repenting.
You only have to let the soft animal
of your body love what it loves.

Oliver entreats us to trust the gravity of what we love in the same way that the wild geese trust the instincts of their own migration. She suggests that it is through what we love that "the world announces our place in the family of things." Writer Annie Dillard, reinforces this idea through the telling of this story about the connection between what we love and our vocation:

A well-known writer was asked by a university student, "Do you think I could be a writer?"

"Well," said the writer, "I don't know... do you love sentences?"

The writer could see the student's amazement. "Do I love sentences? I am twenty years old and do I love sentences?"

If he had loved sentences, of course he could begin, like the joyful painter who when asked how he came to be a painter replied, "I love the smell of paint."

"All we are," said the Buddha, "is a result of what we have thought." Wayne Muller in his inspiring book, *How Then Shall We Live,* suggests that Buddha might have added: All we are is a result of what we have loved. He writes,

"What we love draws us forward and shapes our destiny. Our love teaches us what to look for, where to aim, where to walk. With our every action, word, relationship and commitment, we slowly and inevitably become what we love."

What we love has tremendous power in our lives. It becomes our center of gravity. I also believe that it is what we are here to teach. When we love something, we feel the truth of it, we touch its deeper nature. There are so many things in the world that we have neither the time nor the ability to love, and thus, we remain ignorant of them. But those things we love, we learn about and we teach. Those who love children show us things about our own that we may have never seen. Those who love music help us to hear the subtle sound of a violin in a song which we never would have recognized. Those who love cooking unlock the succulent secrets of food. (My friend who is an arborist has taught me more about fungal infections of trees than I ever really wanted to know!)

Have you ever noticed that what we love, in essence, becomes our medium for communicating and expressing ourselves in the world? It becomes our native language. For Anne Morrow Lindbergh, it was the sea. For Hemingway, it was the bulls; for Melville, the whale; for Matisse, color and shape. For Georgia O'Keefe it was flowers, for Ansel Adams, the black and white images of mountains and streams. In thinking about the people closest to us, it would not be difficult to quickly identify the language they use in the world—it is simply an extension of what they have loved. It may be the language of the piano, a paintbrush or of poetry—but we all find our medium through our connections of the heart.

How do we nurture
what's in our nature
and trust a greater force
To lead us simply by the heart
and take a wiser course?

We must remember that we grow into selfhood. We cannot force this growth nor engineer it with any amount of analysis or careful career planning. I think we discover (or uncover) our vocations, bit by bit, through the process of living and working and by paying attention to what in this process draws us, moves us and brings us more alive. In that way, learning to pay attention to our own likes, dislikes, longings and yearnings is as essential a life skill as any other that we may ever hone. For how else will we ever come to know and embrace our unique brand of truth or hear our hearts calling to us?

To live wholeheartedly, we must not deny the gravity of what we love but learn to be silently drawn by that irresistible pull. The gifts and talents that are our "medicine" do not have to be added or invented. The seeds are within. All we can do is create the right circumstances for its germination, be faithful to our talents and obey our dreams.

To all the powers that we hone,
let's add an element of trust
That each of us are acorns too—
that there's an oak in each of us.

Passages

"A fish cannot drown in water.
A bird does not fall in air.
Each creature God made
must live in its own true nature."

Mechthild of Magdeburg

"The snow goose need not bathe
to make itself white:
Neither need you do anything
but be yourself."

Lao Tzu

Ramakrishna

"The fabled musk deer searches the world over for the source of the scent which comes from itself."

Elizabeth Browning

"With stammering lips and insufficient sounds, I strive and struggle to deliver right the music of my nature."

"Those who wish to sing always find a song."

Swedish proverb

"An old woman is never old when it comes to the dance she knows."

Ibo proverb

Thornton Wilder

"We can only be said to be alive in those moments when our hearts are conscious of our treasures."

"Oh Man! There is no planet, sun, or star which could hold you, if you but knew what you are!"

Ralph Waldo Emerson

Robert Charles Benchley

"It took me fifteen years to discover that I had no talent for writing, but I couldn't give it up because by that time I was too famous."

"Do what you know best: if you're a runner, run; if you're a bell, ring."

Ignas Berstein

Johann Van Goethe

"We are shaped and fashioned by what we love."

"What are the gifts that we have been given? To deny that we are gifted is, perhaps, to indulge in false humility which allows us to shirk responsibility for the gift. But the gift is a sacred trust… it asks that we develop it. And it asks that we pass it on."

Deena Metzer

"Dwell as near as possible to the channel in which your life flows."

Henry David Thoreau

"We must cultivate our gardens."

Voltaire

Henri Frederic Amiel

"Without passion, man is a mere force and possibility, like the flint which awaits the shock of iron before it can send forth its spark."

"Do not think that your truth can be found by anyone else."

André Gide

"Nature never repeats herself, and the possibilities of one human soul will never be found in another."

Elizabeth Cady Stanton

Seneca

"A happy life is one which is in accordance with its own nature."

"We all have ability. The difference is how we use it."

Stevie Wonder

"Work is a four-letter word. It's up to us to decide whether that four-letter word reads 'drag' or 'love.' Most work is a drag because it doesn't nourish our souls. The key is to trust your heart to move where your talents can flourish. This old world will really spin when work becomes a joyous expression of the soul."

Al Sacharov

"My mother said to me. If you become a soldier, you will become a general; if you become a monk, you will end up as the Pope. Instead, I became a painter and I wound up as Picasso."

Pablo Picasso

"The greatest waste in the world is the difference between what we are and what we could become."

Martin Luther King, Jr.

Kahlil Gibran

"When you work, you fulfill a part of earth's fondest dream assigned to you when that dream was born."

The Talmud

"Every blade of grass has its Angel that bends over it and whispers, 'Grow, grow.'"

"Born into your heart, shaped by your hands, and walked with your own two feet, your life's work is your special gift for mankind."

Larry Boldt

"When love and skill work together, expect a masterpiece."

John Ruskin

"Don't ask yourself what the world needs. Ask yourself what makes you come alive, and go do that, because what the world needs is people who have come alive."

Howard Thurman

To Ponder and To Practice

- Think of someone in your life who seems to be living true to his nature, in alignment with his gifts and abilities. What do you think enabled this person to discover and create a life true to his gifts? How is your life similar to or different from that person's?
- Think of someone you know who is living *outside* the realm of her truest gifts. What do you think might be preventing that person from living in concert with her truest nature? How is your life similar to or different from that person's?
- What is a talent you have that no one at your workplace knows about yet? How could you incorporate it into your work?
- What skill would you really like to develop more fully? Ask two people in your field who you respect for their suggestions on how you might go about doing that.
- What skill or ability do you have that is under-utilized at work but that you can put to use outside of work?
- What personal qualities do you possess that make your presence at work valued and appreciated?
- What would you *most* like to be appreciated for at home? How about at work?
- Make a list of ten ways that you love to spend your time. See if you can incorporate these into your current work situation or your next work opportunity.
- What activities would you engage or participate in if you weren't concerned about whether or not you were good at it?
- Our deepest joy will come from living a life in keeping with our gifts. While our desires are things of the moment, our abilities are permanent and their demands never cease. If you've found yourself bored lately, consider how that boredom may be a cry or a plea from your unused talents.
- It is said that every talent we have will surface in us as a need… like fish need to swim. What skills or abilities do you have that feel more like "needs" at this point than luxuries?
- It is a blessing and a curse that we don't always know our calling—part of our migration is the finding out. What is it you are called to, beneath all your career planning and stated ambition?
- Draft a résumé based on your potentials rather than on your credentials.
- Consider an organization or a business to whom you might write an employment proposal that would provide a great context for your genius. What would you propose?

Practice

- It is said that a spiritual calling contains four elements: a gift, a delight, a need and a discipline. Think about your own work or role in life. Does it contains these four elements? If not, which is missing?
- In the context of Native American wisdom, what medicine do you bring to your tribe?
- Choose a habit or routine that will symbolize your desire and intention to live in alignment with and loyal to the gifts you have been given in life.
- Choose a quote from this chapter's *Passages* that speaks to your desire to bring your finest gifts and talents to life's table—to proclaim your passions and follow your dreams. Post it in a place where you will be reminded of this promise to yourself and to the world.
- Given everything you have read in this chapter, what do you want to *keep* doing? What do you want to *stop* doing? What do you want to *start* doing?

Notes

Chapter 5

Rekindle the Flame

Restoring a Sense of Purpose

Embrace the process of meaning-making

Embrace the process of meaning-making

Build cathedrals

Build cathedrals

Consider the load on your back

Consider the load on your back

Mirror your values while awaiting the arrow of purpose

Mirror your values while awaiting the arrow of purpose

Believe in tiny, invisible forces

Believe in tiny, invisible forces

Rekindle the Flame

I see how you look at me—
searching for that picture of purpose and passion
that I was when I was new on the job.
I have not seen her for a while myself.
Yet, sometimes, deep inside, I can feel some stirring.
Something warm and glowing,
like a small, untended, barely flickering fire in my heart.
And I know, if we could rekindle that flame,
purpose, passion and possibility could be mine again!

But it's not about having a daytimer.
I know we have a new time management system—
complete with the daily calendar, priority stickers,
and varying colored in-boxes.
Those tools can be very helpful, I suppose.
But if you could remind me of the seeds we are sowing,
of the horizon we are heading for,
perhaps I would value my time as the precious resource it is.
Rekindle that flame and my hours will be spent in sacrament, not sacrifice.
The dance of my days will become deliberate again.
But it's not about having a daytimer.

I hate to say it, but it's not about technology either.
I appreciate all the new tools—I've got my pager, the cell phone—
I know that we have just upgraded our software.
Hey, we're networked, we're streamlined, we're happenin'!
But could you remind me how our work with these tools matters?
How our efforts are holy, or even wholesome?
Rekindle that flame and I will play
a simple blade of grass like a fine tuned instrument.
With a simple yellow pad and a No. 2 pencil,
I will write you a report that will drop you to your knees.
But it's not about the tools.

I want to thank you for the investment
you've made in me through training. You know,
Tactics for the Tired
Options for the Overwhelmed
Strategies for the Stressed
Five Steps to Fame and Fortune.
Really, my bag is packed with info—
the walls of my office are lined with training manuals.
If only it were about information.
I am so thirsty for wisdom.
Perhaps if you could remind me
of the truth and testimony of my own experience,
you know, the knowing beneath the note-taking?
Rekindle that flame and I will be teachable again.
I will drink from your learning cup like a desert weary traveler.
But it's really not about information.

I am sure you are wondering how you can help me
tend that barely flickering fire in my heart.
Perhaps if you could remind me
of our collective passion, purpose and possibility!
In a day of valuing diversity,
please focus less on what makes me different
and focus more on what makes me unique!
In the day of the contingent workforce,
please notice what it is about my presence
that is unrepeatable, irreplaceable and worthy of respect.
Really, I just want to be one twig, one branch, in a greater bonfire.

And if all of us offered our work
as kindling for the fire in our individual hearts,
the collective sigh we would sound
at the end of a long day
would resonate like song
that would make the angels weep.
Let's rekindle that flame.

Let's rekindle that flame!

Reflections

If you have ever watched people around a campfire, you have seen what I have seen: how beautiful we are in the fire's glow. How absorbed we are in the dance of the flames. How enthralled we become in the crackling of wood as it surrenders to the fire's heat and becomes a purple ember warming our hands and feet. Even as the smoke burns our eyes with the slightest movement of the breeze, we are drawn to the fire like a babe to its mother's arms. Being close to the elements—fire, wind, night air—we remember Moses before the burning bush and listen for a voice from the heavens. And we wonder if we can carry that fire within us, in our bones and in our hearts, as we pack up for the morning trip back into the city, into the pressure-cooker we call "normal life."

Once back in the throes of daily life, we are taken unawares by the heady scent of a campfire in the sweatshirt thrown carelessly at the bottom of the hamper. And we remember. We fold it carefully, like a ceremonial blanket. We place it amongst the other cottons in the closet, solemnly swearing that we will never wash it again—lest the fire's breath be put out. Then we return to the stove, or the computer, to the story of our lives.

How do we keep ourselves warmed by the fires in our own hearts? How do we carry a flame that lends a glow to every part of our lives? What offerings can we make through our actions that can serve as kindling, as branches, in a greater bonfire?

Here are some ways and means to rekindle the flame, some ideas to serve as fuel for the fires of purpose in our work, at home and in our larger lives.

Embrace the process of meaning-making

Physicist Albert Einstein was once asked, "If you could ask God one question, what would it be?" He answered,

> "I would ask how the universe began, because once I knew that the rest would be simple mathematics. But now, on second thought, I would not ask God how the universe began—I would want to know WHY he started the universe. For once I knew that, I would know the purpose of my own life."

In a different interview, Einstein picked up again on the subject of purpose when he wrote,

> "Strange is our situation here on earth. Each of us comes for a short visit, not knowing why, yet sometimes seeming to divine a purpose."

Like Einstein, the ancients also recognized that cultivating, developing and setting free one's gifts was the essential labor of one's life. Aristotle said that one's purpose is merely a matter of knowing where one's talents and the needs of the world intersect.

I think of purpose as a current in the river our souls, much like blood in our veins. We don't need to create it, we need to let it find us. How do we hear it knocking on the door above the cacophony of pagers, telephones and traffic? How do we hear the voice of purpose calling above the insistent voice in our own heads that chides us into believing that with so much yet undone, we can't afford the luxury of paying attention to purpose or to passion? In response, I hear the words of Albert Schweitzer,

> "I don't know what your destiny will be, but one thing I do know: the only ones among you who will be really happy are those who have sought and found how to serve."

But serve what? Serve whom? Serve when? Purpose alone provides the kind of intelligence of the heart that uncovers our truest passion. When we enter the current of purpose we have available to us a vast range of receptive and connective abilities, intuition, innovation, wisdom, creativity, and sensitivity which enables the essential human process of finding meaning in life. We all aspire to become meaning-makers. The more we want "to give shape to our fate," as Albert Camus put it, "the more the meanings we make or fail to make concern us. But make meaning we must."

I recently heard a most moving story about a man (who I will call Bill) who had been trained as an engineer. Having suffered a traumatic brain injury from a car accident, Bill was looking to reenter the work world. He was participating in a job club support group with other people who were looking for work, and on this particular afternoon they were brainstorming ideas about Bill's vocational opportunities. He listened intently to their ideas until one of the participants suggested that he work at McDonald's. Bill was horrified at the idea and in an angry outburst expressed how offended he was that anyone would suggest that someone who had been trained and experienced as an engineer would work in a fast food restaurant.

A couple of weeks later the group reassembled for another meeting. To their surprise Bill opened the meeting by enthusiastically sharing how he had heard that McDonald's was contributing free food to the rescue workers at Ground Zero in New York City and would continue to feed them until they had recovered every person. With fire in his eyes he exclaimed, "Now that is a company I would be proud to work for!"

What Bill tapped into is what Roy Croft, in his poem entitled "Love," refers to as "taking the lumber of our lives and building not a tavern, but a temple." It is the difference between flipping burgers and feeding the rescue workers. It is in meaning-making that we resolve to not simply lay the stones of our lives in a meaningless row, but to build something beautiful, like a children's clinic, a castle or a cathedral.

Build cathedrals

The spirit with which we approach our work can imbue our work with the kind of glow that heralds the brightness of dawn or the darkness of deep night. The human spirit responds not to what we do, but why we think we are doing it. This classic story of the three stonemasons says it well.

There were once three stonemasons all hard at work when an observer came on site. Moments later the work bell went off signaling the end of the day. The observer addressed the first stonemason saying, "Excuse me, sir, would you mind commenting on what you do for a living?" He turned around, bent and grumbling, sweat pouring off his brow and retorted, "Can't you see I am a stonemason! I have been laying stone all day. But they don't own me anymore! The bell has gone off and I am out of here!" And he shuffled off.

The observer then approached the second stonemason, asking the same question. With a smile on his face and a song in his step, the stonemason responded, "I am a stonemason. As you can see I am laying stone. But if you take a step back you will see that we are building a wall here. We've come pretty far today, too, about three and a half feet. Not bad for a day's work." And the stonemason proudly walked on.

When the observer reached the third stonemason, she was still working and he approached her saying, "Excuse me, but the work bell has gone off and you are free to go." She turned saying, "Oh no, I am not done for the day and you cannot force me to leave!" "Fine," said the observer, "but would you mind commenting on what you do for a living?" The final stonemason beamed saying, "I am a stonemason. As you can see I am laying stone. But if you take a closer look you will see that we are building a wall here. We've come pretty far today, too, about three and a half feet. But if you look even closer, you will see that we are building a cathedral in this place!"

Which of the three stonemasons do you identify with most? Surely we have all felt the sense of duty and obligation of the first stonemason, and in that sense, we work simply to make money. We have all felt the joy of accomplishment of the second stonemason, and in that sense, we are grateful for the opportunity to employ our talents. But it is in the sense of building cathedrals that we understand what the Buddha called *right livelihood*. It is here that our work moves from pastime to priesthood, where we feel that the life we are living is the kind of "splendid torch" that George Bernard Shaw writes about in this celebrated passage:

> "This is the true joy of life, the being used up for a purpose recognized by yourself as a mighty one; being a force of nature instead of a feverish, selfish clod of ailments and grievances, complaining that the world will not devote itself to making you happy. I am of the opinion that my life belongs to the community, as long as I live, it is my privilege to do for it whatever I can. I want to be thoroughly used up when I die, for the harder I work, the more I live. Life is no brief candle to me. It is a sort of splendid torch which I have got hold of for a moment, and I want to make it burn as brightly as possible before handing it on to future generations."

Consider the load on your back

A man once asked a camel whether he preferred going uphill or downhill. The camel responded, "What is important is not the uphill or the downhill—what matters is the load." It is true of human work as well. Unlike the camel, however, it is not the weight of it, but the preciousness of its contents. We are able to endure the most difficult of circumstances depending on the quality of the load on our backs.

Take the person who works two jobs, each of them taxing in different ways, the combination of them allowing him no time for himself. The load is heavy, no doubt, but what he is working for will determine whether or not he feels he is on a downward or upward climb. He could be working to keep a roof over his children's head, to save enough money to earn a college degree, or to sponsor his brother from his native land. This person's journey is significantly different than that of the person who is a workaholic, never refusing additional work because she is in a fast-paced profession that demands 200%. It is the person's purposes, not just the circumstances, that determine the spirit with which they bear a heavy load.

French philosopher, Albert Camus, poses a question regarding the meaning of life that I think we should apply to work. He says,

> "Judging whether life is or is not worth living amounts to answering the fundamental question of philosophy. All the rest—whether or not the world has three dimensions, whether the mind has nine or twelve categories—comes afterward. These are games; one must first answer."

We must ask ourselves first and foremost whether or not our work is worth doing. Where, how, for whom, and under what conditions we do it, comes afterwards. But first we must answer, "Why?" When our gut response is that the work we are doing is not worthy of our time and talent, no fiddling around with the terms of employment is going to satisfy the spirit. When our gut response is that our work is indeed worth the precious investment of our days, we will happily find a way to do it.

Mother Teresa, whose lifelong dedication to serving the poor earned her a Nobel Prize and a reputation as one of the great saints of the 20th century, saved thousands of lives and inspired millions more. Beginning in 1948 when she felt called to serve the poorest of the poor, she left the security of her convent and lived and worked in the slums of Calcutta. There she tended the sick, fed the hungry, and ministered to the dying. Her life was a whirlwind of loving service, and for years she stopped only to pray and to sleep three hours a night.

By the time of her death in 1997, she had established centers in Calcutta for the sick, dying, mentally disturbed, lepers and abandoned children, as well as hundreds of other centers around the world staffed by thousands of followers. She was clear that the task was not only to offer food and medicine but above all, to offer love. "God loves the world through us," she exclaimed, and she regarded herself as "a pencil in the hand of God writing a love letter to the world."

Beyond the movement she created, Mother Teresa was said to have *personally* tended to tens of thousands of individuals throughout her lifetime. When asked how she could possibly carry that kind of load and handle that kind of burden, she replied with shining eyes, "I see my Lord in each of their faces." She also said, "If I never picked up the first person, I'd never have picked up 42,000. So I think, one at a time." If in her heart she was out to save the masses, she may have given up decades before. But her "one person at a time" philosophy enabled her to reach out to thousands.

Check the load on your back. Are you carrying a burden worth your precious time and energy? Is it the kind of work you care about? Does it hold meaning and purpose for you?

Mirror your values while awaiting the arrow of purpose

I have been asked by many people in my workshops who has most inspired me, who my heroes are. I recently sat down and drafted a list. My list included: Jesus of Nazareth, Mahatma Gandhi, Helen Keller, Albert Schweitzer, Viktor Frankl, Anne Frank, Martin Luther King Jr., Buckminster Fuller, Maya Angelou, Jimmy Carter, Nelson Mandela, Cesar Chavez and Mother Teresa. Among other things, everyone on my list was gifted with something extraordinary—concentrated focus on their purpose.

Focus in human life works like it does in the world of light—without focus you have a floodlight, dispersed and diffused; with focus, it takes on the power of a laser beam, able to speed rockets to the moon or to cut through diamonds. With focus, we can lead a country into economic independence, put an end to racial apartheid or inspire a nation into a civil rights movement. As in the words of Margaret Mead,

> "Do not ever doubt that the world can be changed by the efforts of a single human being, for that is the only thing that ever has."

If only we knew our purposes. I don't know about you, dear reader, but at times my purposes have about as much concentrated light as the flicker of a Bic lighter while I can only dream of wielding the glow of Luke Skywalker's light sabre. At those times we must rest assured that the flaming arrow of purposefulness is ready in the bow, if we could but make our hearts the target.

Writer, psychiatrist and survivor of a Nazi concentration camp, Viktor Frankl, suggests that we detect rather than invent our mission in life. He says,

> "Everyone has his own specific vocation or mission in life... therein he cannot be replaced, nor can his life be repeated. Thus, everyone's task is as unique as is his specific opportunity to implement it."

This mission, however, is not always easy to detect. In the meantime, we must work to simply live what we believe in, be it ambassadors for peace, carriers of enthusiasm or models of courage. Even when we are not living according to some well-written, deeply thought-out personal mission statement, it is enough to know what we stand for, and to know that our lives reflect, in big or little ways, our values and convictions. As Golda Meir, the Prime Minister of Israel from 1969 to 1974 once admitted,

> "I can honestly say that I was never affected by the question of the success of an undertaking. If I felt it was the right thing to do, I was for it, regardless of the possible outcome. That is how I choose to live and to lead."

At the end of the day, we are alone with the beating of our hearts. There can be no lasting joy in our hearts if the things we believe in are different from the things we do.

Believe in tiny, invisible forces

In a letter from William James to Mrs. Henry Whitman in 1899, he wrote,

> "I am done with great things and big things and great institutions and big success. And I am for those tiny, invisible, molecular moral forces that work from individual to individual through the crannies of the world like so many rootlets or like capillaries oozing of water yet which, if you give them time, will rend the hardest monuments of man's pride."

We do not need to achieve huge, visible heroic acts in order to live a life of purpose. We need to believe in the forces of the tiny, of the invisible, even in the seemingly insignificant corners of our lives. Does it matter that we smile with gratitude at the waitress or that we compliment the janitor for a job well done? Does it matter that we take the time to calm the irate customer, to ease the burden of the nursing assistant or to treat the telephone solicitor as a person worthy of dignity and respect? Does it matter, in the big picture, if we work day in and day out to provide a world for our loved ones that is not only safe, but touched by the magic of comfort and love? Personally, I am not interested in any picture, big or small, that does not value such tiny purposes as all-important. In my mind, that is the big picture!

We all live somewhere between nothing and everything, and to reenact, along the way, the smallest gesture of valuing life is to pour a little soul into the vessel of the world. How do we let faith in our purposes warm our desires and melt our cynicism? How do we pour tiny drops of love into the ordinary and the extraordinary moments of our working day? How do we gently blow on the smallest embers of our hearts until they rise and take fire? In the awesome words of Pierre Teilhard de Chardin:

> "Some day after mastering the winds,
> the waves, the tides and gravity,
> we shall harness for God the energies of love, and then,
> for the second time in the history of the world,
> man will have discovered fire."

Can we rekindle *that* flame?

Passages

"If I could only remember that the days
were not bricks to be laid row on row,
to be built into a solid house where one
might dwell in safety and peace; but only
food for the fires of the heart."

Edmund Wilson

"The coal that has been an
ember is easily kindled."

Uruguay saying

Henry David Thoreau

"Live your life as though every act were
to become a universal law."

"Do not try to satisfy your vanity
by teaching a great many things.
Awaken people's curiosity.
It is enough to open minds;
do not overload them.
Put there just a spark.
If there is some good, inflammable stuff,
it will catch fire."

Anatole France

"Yesterday is ashes;
tomorrow is wood.
Only today does the fire
burn brightly."

Eskimo saying

Henry David Thoreau

"It is not enough to be a hardworking person.
We must consider what are we working at."

Father James Kellar

"A candle loses nothing by lighting
another candle."

"When you do something,
you should burn yourself completely,
like a good bonfire,
leaving no trace of yourself."

Suzuki Roshi

"I choose to inhabit my days,
to allow my living to open me,
to make me less afraid, more accessible,
to loosen my heart until it becomes
a wand, a torch, a promise."

Dawna Markova

Reggie Leach

"Success is not the result of
spontaneous combustion.
You must set yourself on fire."

"May I become at all times
Both now and forever
A protector for those without protection
A guide for those who have lost their way
A ship for those with oceans to cross
A sanctuary for those in danger
A lamp for those without light
A place of refuge for those who lack shelter
And a servant to all in need."

The Dalai Lama

"Happiness comes of the capacity to feel deeply, to enjoy simply, to think freely and to risk life, and, of course, to be needed."

Storm Jameson

"To the dull mind all nature is leaden.
To the illumined mind the whole world burns and sparkles with light."

Ralph Waldo Emerson

"You should be a lantern for yourself.
Draw close to the light within you
and seek no other shelter."

Buddhist wisdom

"Every bird always knows where to make her nest. And if she knows how and where to make her nest, this means that she knows her purpose in life. And why does man, who is the wisest among all creatures, not know that which any bird knows, that is, his purpose in life?"

Chinese wisdom

Patanjali

"When you are inspired by some great purpose, some extraordinary project, all of your thoughts break their bonds, your mind transcends limitations, your consciousness expands in every direction, and you find yourself in a new great and wonderful world. Dormant forces, faculties, and talents come alive, and you discover yourself to be a greater person by far than you ever dreamed yourself to be."

"Here's a test to find whether your mission on earth is finished: If you're alive, it isn't."

Richard Bach

"Make of yourself a light."

The Buddha

To Ponder and To Practice

- Respond to the following prompts to begin uncovering some of your life and work purposes:
  - In my life I feel called to…
  - In exchange for taking up space on this planet, I plan to…
  - One of the things I would like my life to stand for is…
  - No matter what else happens in my life, I am going to…
- Summarize in writing *"what seeds you are sowing, what horizon you are headed for"* in your life and/or in your work. Work with it until it takes on the feel of your own personal Mission Statement.
- Identify three things you could be doing in your life or work to contribute to or participate in your larger purposes.
- What is *"holy and/or wholesome"* about the work you do and the efforts of the organization you work for? How about in your home life?
- What is it about your own presence at work that you feel is *"unrepeatable, irreplaceable and worthy of respect?"* How about in your home life?
- Think back to the last time you felt the satisfaction of being *"one twig, one branch, in a greater bonfire?"* What are the similarities and differences between those circumstances and where you are currently?
- What part of your day feels more like sacrifice than sacrament? What could you do to change that part of your day so that it feels more like an integral part of your larger purposes?
- Why did you take the job you are in today? Are the needs and desires that led you to take this position still relevant to you? How have they changed?
- Identify three specific goals, purposes or practices at work that you consider to be *"kindling for the fire in your heart."* Commit to those purposes with renewed conviction.
- It is said that "Back of every noble life there are principles that fashioned it." What are three of the primary principles that have fashioned your life thus far? What additional principles would you like to use to fashion your life for the future?

Practice

- St. Francis of Assisi taught that our purposes should seek roots as well as branches. He said that if our purposes are only about us, they have no branches, but if they are only about the rest of the world, they have no roots. Think about your own life. Do you pay attention to your individual purposes to the extent that you pay attention to your purposes for others? Which is out of whack? How could you bring more balance to the two?
- Kindle your spirit by refusing to associate with people who would like to see it extinguished. Resolve to be with people whose purposes and principles you respect.
- What are a few of the things that you would regret never having done if your life ended tomorrow? Plan to do them. Start them now.
- Select a quote on the topic of purposefulness from this chapter's *Passages* and post it where you will see it often in order to internalize it.
- Choose a daily habit, routine or symbol to help you remain conscious of living true to your purposes. (e.g. Use the occurrence of passing a construction site as a reminder to consider what you are building with the lumber of your life.)
- Given everything you have read in this chapter, what do you want to *keep* doing? What do you want to *stop* doing? What do you want to *start* doing?

Notes

The Masquerade

Chapter

Befriending Yourself and Others

Don't be a stranger

Don't be a stranger

Befriend yourself

Befriend yourself

Be careful of what you think you *aren't*

Be careful of what you think you aren't

Be careful what you pretend to be

Be careful what you pretend to be

Don't be defined by the roles you play

Don't be defined by the roles you play

Dare to act out of character

Dare to act out of character

Let the witch have her ride

Let the witch have her ride

Live in the question "Who am I?"

Live in the question "Who am I?"

The Masquerade

If only we could meet in the early hours
when the lines around our eyes cut a deep horizon…
before we paint the rosy face…
If only we could meet in the insecure hours,
before we don the coat of confidence we like to wear out in the world…
If only we could meet in our sorrow and our sadness,
as well as our celebration…
We would no longer need the words
"rival," "competitor" or "enemy,"
but we would find a thousand new variations of the words
"brother," "comrade," "friend."

If only we could see each other as we see ourselves
caught in the crosslight between
utter despair and true innocence…
If only we felt as lovable in our tiredness as we do our joy…
We would find hundreds of new ways
to use our hands in shaping the beauty of the world
because we would no longer need them for holding up the masks.

If only we could release the armor that lays so heavy upon our hearts,
we could, for the first time, know what it is
to love and work in true community.

Fear led us into this masquerade…
May faith, in ourselves, and in each other, lead us out.

Reflections

William Shakespeare tells us that the world is a stage and all of us actors. No kidding. Personally, I hate being part of the Masquerade, and yet I know, like everyone else, I cannot resist it. That is because we do not always recognize the boundaries between "the play" and our own authenticity. It is so much a part of our reality that we often do not know what is a mask and what is our true face. We are not clear when we are merely on stage and when we are on true ground. As long as that is true, even if we wanted to shed the masks and put down the various scripts that we read from one relationship to the next, we remain powerless to do so. Until we can distinguish what is real from what is not, what is put on for our own or others' purposes from what is an authentic expression, we are puppets rather than puppeteers.

So much of what we refer to as "socialization" is, among other things, a turning away from ourselves and our own self-awareness, turning down the volume of our own voices in order to tune into and join the larger chorus of the culture. Those few who have been successful at remaining true to themselves, even in the face of cultural, family and social pressures to conform, are often considered "eccentric." While we may find comfort in counting ourselves among those who are "normal," we can't help but admire those who refuse to conform and envy how comfortable they look in their own skin.

It is interesting to note that the word "personality" is derived from the Greek word *persona,* meaning mask. Our personality is a construct we use to experience the world, but it is not the essential part of us. It is the clothing that the soul wears. Carl Jung described the persona as the facilitator of our relationship with the outer world, while the soul is the facilitator of our relationship with the inner world. I think he was correct in saying, "We meet ourselves time and again in a thousand disguises on the path of life."

Where is that more true than in the workplace where we find ourselves playing multiple roles, all in the course of a day? Those roles may include being a supervisor, a subordinate, a coworker, an employee, a customer, a competitor, a vendor and/or a contractor. Depending on the role we are playing, we meet ourselves, once again, in a disguise befitting that role. That is fine as long as we can remember who we are behind the masks and beyond those roles.

Like the Wizard of Oz, we may not be what we pretend to be, but at least there should be *someone* standing behind the curtain. I think that by exploring the multiplicity of who we are, we become more fully who we are. We simply cannot bring the best to our work nor enjoy the finest that life has to offer if no one is home. By keeping ourselves at bay, silent and unseen from even ourselves, we may try and indeed succeed at becoming what the world needs and wants us to be. But in the end, we will have relinquished the only true gift we have to give the world, and that is ourselves.

Arthur Schopenhauer warns that, "We forfeit three-fourths of ourselves in order to be like other people." On the other side of it, by participating in "The Masquerade," we also miss out on the gifts of other people as they, too, forfeit themselves to fit a mold. Here are a few ideas that, if taken seriously, could help us grow the faith necessary to lead ourselves out of "The Masquerade" and into the domain of true authenticity.

Don't be a stranger

I remember sitting at the departure gate of the Las Vegas airport on October 17, 1989, awaiting a flight back to San Jose, California. As usual, the gate was jam-packed with people anxious to get home. Few of us looked one another in the eye, everyone keeping to themselves, reading their books or tending to their children. And then, from the television screen on the ceiling, we heard that an earthquake registering 8.9 on the Richter Scale had hit the Bay Area. There was no power in the area and all the telephone lines were down. There would be no flights in or out of the San Jose airport.

There we sat in stunned silence, most of us having no way to communicate with our families, leaving it to our imaginations to conjure up pictures of devastation and loss. As the hours passed the silence broke and we began to connect with one another, not as silent passengers awaiting a flight, but as fellow human beings sharing a crisis. We began passing photos of our children and telling stories. We laughed, we cried and we prayed. We were no longer strangers to each other; we had become kin in a few short hours. When we did arrive in San Jose eighteen hours later, an airplane of people embraced one another, wishing one another and our families well.

Now when I sit at departure gates at various airports I look at the faces of the people around me. I think back to the Las Vegas airport, knowing that I am in the company of my kin. We may be blanketed in complacency and self-absorption, but all it takes is a crisis, be it an act of Mother Nature, terrorism, or a disturbed human being, and we shed our separateness in a heartbeat. September 11, 2001 was a more recent reminder of this profound truth.

If only we could meet each other
in the early hours
when the lines around our eyes
cut a deep horizon...
before we paint the rosy face...
If only we could meet
in the insecure hours,
before we don the coat of confidence
we like to wear out in the world...
If only we could meet in our sorrow
and our sadness,
as well as our celebration...
We would not longer
have use of the words
"rival," "competitor" or "enemy,"
But we would find thousands
of new variations on the words
"brother," "comrade," "friend."

Contemporary writer and humorist, Leo Rosten, has some great advice for seeing beyond the masks of roles, titles and the facades of social interaction. He advises,

> "You can understand and relate to most people better if you look at them—no matter how old or impressive they may be—as if they are children. For most of us never really grow up or mature all that much—we simply grow taller. Oh, to be sure, we laugh less and play less and wear uncomfortable disguises like adults, but beneath the costume is the child we always are, whose needs are simple, whose daily life is still best described by fairy tales."

I took Rosten's advice recently while on an airport bus. I looked at each person's face searching for the face of the child they once were. It was great! There they were—very tall, overgrown children! I was surprised at how easy it was. I wonder if anyone was curious as to why I was sitting there with such a delighted grin on my face.

Befriend yourself

An important step in ending "The Masquerade" is having faith in ourselves. By definition, this faith requires intimacy, self-knowledge and self-awareness. Anne Morrow Lindbergh in *Gift from the Sea* suggests,

> "When one is a stranger to oneself, then one is estranged from others... Only when one is connected to one's core is one truly connected to others."

It is impossible to appreciate the complexity of others if we are not able to love ourselves, being privy to our own faults, flaws and frailties. The following story from Anthony de Mello's book, *Taking Flight,* speaks to the essentialness of self-knowledge:

> A great religious persecution broke out in the land, and the three Pillars of religion—Scripture, Worship and Charity—appeared before God to express their fear that if religion was stamped out, they would cease to exist.
>
> "Not to worry," said the Lord, "I plan to send One to earth who is greater than all of you." "By what is this Great One called?"
>
> "Self-knowledge," said God. "It will do even greater things than any of you have done, because with its power, each of your own powers are enhanced. Without it, your powers are dulled."

Clearly, self-knowledge is essential, yet most popular books, seminars and programs that fall under the category of "self-improvement" deal with our *outer person*—the self that we show the world in the mask of emotions, habits and personality. Once in a while we will come by a book or a program which will help us delve into the world of our *inner person* where our secret hopes and fears dwell, where our self-image and our picture of who and what we think we are lives. Intimacy and self-knowledge of ourselves on both these levels is important. Rarely, however, do we find assistance in looking seriously at our *deepest person*—the one that is connected to our divine nature, the one that houses the soul and the spirit.

Our *deepest person* is the self that we are often strangers to and would benefit most from befriending. The more we are able to relate to ourselves as spiritual beings, the better we will be able to relate to one another on the level of our values, convictions and purposes rather than on the level of our personal agendas, our personality conflicts and our politics. When we cultivate a love for our own souls, we are more apt to extend beyond ourselves to include the world and practice more than an abstract tolerance for one another despite our differences.

While we know an awful lot about many things, we sure can be in the dark about ourselves. We are a culture infatuated with knowledge, but seek little of it when it comes to our own lives, our values and priorities, our principles and convictions, our likes and dislikes, our fears and our hopes. Not that awareness of some of these aspects of our being doesn't show up around our edges, but even when it does, it is more like an uninvited dandelion than a cultivated rose. Strangely, while it is the longing of our hearts to be who and what we are, we have not matched that longing with the discipline to find out who and what that is. I agree with Jack Kornfield who writes in his book, *A Path with Heart,*

> "Who am I? When we begin to answer this question, we are filled with images and ideals—the negative images of ourselves that we wish to change and perfect and the positive images of some great spiritual potential. Yet the spiritual path is not so much about changing ourselves as it is about listening to the fundamentals of our being."

Dawna Markova reinforces the importance of self-exploration by making a wonderful suggestion in her inspiring book, *I Will Not Die An Unlived Life:*

> "We need courage and time to reorder our priorities and consider internal exploration as important as our career and outward success. We need to practice the art of stripping away false notions about who we think we are so we can deal with what is real, and release anything that is deadening to our spirits. We have to learn to reconnect with ourselves so that we can stand for something that is greater than ourselves."

Be careful of what you think you aren't

Jesuit priest and renowned storyteller Anthony de Mello often began his spiritual conferences with the following tale:

> A man found an eagle's egg and put it in the nest of a barnyard hen. The eaglet hatched with the brood of chicks and grew up with them.
>
> All his life the eagle did what the barnyard chicks did, thinking he was a barnyard chicken. He scratched the earth for worms and insects. He clucked and cackled and thrashed his wings to fly a few feet into the air.
>
> Years passed and the eagle grew old. One day he saw a magnificent bird above him in the cloudless sky. It glided in graceful majesty among the powerful wind currents, with scarcely a beat of its strong golden wings.
>
> The old eagle looked up in awe. "Who's that?" he asked.
>
> "That's the eagle, the king of the birds," said his neighbor. "He belongs to the sky. We belong to the earth—we're chickens." So the eagle lived and died a chicken, for that is what he thought he was.

Initially, I wished for an uplifting ending for this tale, something on par with "The Ugly Duckling." In that classic fable, as soon as the criticized, misunderstood, maltreated duckling discovers he is a swan, his identity crisis is resolved and justice prevails. The difference between these two tales, however, is profound. The eagle didn't even notice he was different, and as a result, experienced no real discontent. Dying a chicken was not his tragedy; the tragedy was his failure to discover his own greatness.

Am I likening us to barnyard chickens? No. But I do believe that we spend far too much time on the ground, unaware of the heights to which we can soar. Perhaps it is not what we are that holds us back, but what we think we aren't! By settling into the roles and scripts of our daily work lives, we can forget who we are and what we can aspire to.

I will never forget the time that someone in one of my workshops complimented me saying, "Your training was great, but your work as a poet moved me most deeply. Thank you." Being new to the world of writing and reciting poetry, I was not prepared to accept this gentleman's praise. Instead, I shuffled my nervous feet and blushed saying, "Well, I'm not a real poet… I just love the world of words." At which point he responded in a direct manner, "Excuse me, but I find it hard to not be offended. I have just told you that your poetry deeply moves me, and now you are telling me that what moves me is not really poetry at all. Shouldn't your listeners be the judge of that?"

I was dumbfounded. To me, the word "poet" is one of the most beautiful words in the English language; a word with which I would never have identified myself. But that day I realized that if I was going to continue bringing my poetry to my training sessions, I needed to accept at least part of my identity as a poet. I still blush as I write, obviously not born in a poet's nest.

I have known this feeling before. One of my business partners, Richard Pimentel, is one of the most gifted and talented conference speakers I have ever had the privilege of hearing. He is funny, poignant and profound all at the same time. He has been a great mentor in my life, and I am also proud to call him a beloved friend. Rich and I used to deliver training sessions together as a team, until we began delivering our own material to distinct audiences. Rich is a great trainer, but he is a fantastic keynote speaker. I began delivering mostly two day training sessions while Rich was busy doing keynote speeches at large conferences. Then something strange began to happen; we were getting requests for *me* to do keynote speeches. I would respond saying, "I'm sorry, but I am a trainer, not a keynoter." Thinking that I had to have the kind of presence and charisma that Rich exudes, I felt totally out of my league. Until I did the first one. And then the second. And a third. And, by gosh, by the fourth keynote, well, I started to like it!

We undoubtedly grow into new roles and identities, as long as we do not hold ourselves back by identifying more with what we *have been* than what we will become. One of my favorite sayings from the Native American tradition is the question, "Why do we pray for the wings of a swallow when we have been given the wings of an eagle?" I think this popular passage by Marianne Williamson sums it up well:

> "Our deepest fear is not that we are inadequate. Our deepest fear is that we are powerful beyond measure. It is our light, not our darkness, that most frightens us. We ask ourselves, who am I to be brilliant, gorgeous, talented, and fabulous? Actually, who are you not to be? You are a child of God. Your playing small does not serve the world. There is nothing enlightened about shrinking so that other people won't feel insecure around you. We were born to make manifest the glory of God that is within us. We have to shine our light brightly so that others can shine too."

As a child I was taught that humbleness was a virtue, while vanity, if not a full-fledged sin, was most unattractive in the eyes of God. It was important to be modest and never boastful or arrogant. Seems reasonable enough, right? But I also remember feeling conflicted and somewhat confused when wanting desperately to parade my newest acrobatic trick or dance step in front of the family, yet at the same time, not wanting to appear as if I was "showing off." It was difficult to draw the lines between wholesome self-respect and self-conceit. Could I be proud of my new handstand and not appear arrogant? Could I perform the new jazz steps and not be full of myself? Whenever the question arose, I would quickly err on the side of humility rather than run the risk of appearing boastful, conceited or, God forbid, "stuck up."

I can't help but wonder how many proverbial cartwheels go unturned and how many songs go unsung because we learned the lesson of humility so well as children. How do we unlearn the kind of humility that would have us hide our beautiful light under a bushel rather than allow ourselves to shine brightly as Williamson suggests? I don't know the answer to that question but I have no doubt that recognizing and claiming our own gifts is not unrelated to our seeing and affirming the gifts of others. Maybe when we see one another's light, our own shines too - like candles that glow twice as bright when reflected in a mirror.

Be careful what you pretend to be

When I hear the expression "a wolf in sheep's clothing" I immediately think of someone who is manipulative and creates a facade in order to take advantage of others. But notice, the lessons of Aesop's fable go much further:

A wolf resolved to disguise himself in order that he might prey upon a flock of sheep without fear of detection: so he clothed himself in a sheepskin and slipped in among the sheep when they were out at pasture. He completely deceived the shepherd, and when the flock was penned for the night, he was shut in with them. But that very night as it happened, the shepherd, requiring a supply of mutton for the table, laid his hands on the wolf, mistaking him for a sheep, and finished him off with his knife on the spot.

We must be careful of what we pretend to be. I love this advice offered by Marion Woodman in her book, *Coming Home to Myself:* "Don't worry about being true to yourself until you know to what voice you are being true."

Kurt Vonnegut, Jr. cautions us, "We are what we pretend to be, so we must be careful about what we pretend to be." Whether we pretend to be experts, clowns or someone on a mission, at some point, we will believe ourselves and become what we have pretended. Rarely, though, do we pretend to be something bigger or more honorable than what we really are.

A lot of our pretending is more about covering up what we don't want other people to see than it is about conjuring up new and splendid ways to be in the world. For example, have you ever seen the person who oversold herself in the interview and then had to somehow live up to the impossible image she projected? Have you ever been in those shoes? Not fun. As Ken Kesey put it, "The trouble with people who pretend to be superheroes is what to do in between phone booths."

Don't allow the role you are in to define you

Professional roles and jobs carry their own myths, scripts, costumes and parts. The barmaid is brassy, the librarian is straight-laced, the actor is temperamental and the artist is unemployed. Lawyers wear wing tips, bikers have tattoos and small town waitresses have big hair. Secretaries don't need to pursue a college education. Computer programmers are unemotional and analytical. A good social worker or counselor does not get too involved in the life of a client.

These are myths... based on generalizations that happen to be true, for some people. That does not mean that they are true for you. Why not decide to be the classiest cocktail waitress this side of the Mississippi? You can be sexy and be a librarian, too. Why not sport a tattoo under a silk suit? Show them just how touchy-feely a programmer can be! Pursue your dream of being a writer even as you spend your day answering phones. Sam Keen writes,

> "To remain vibrant throughout a lifetime we must always be inventing ourselves, weaving new themes into our life-narratives, remembering our past, revisioning our future, re-authoring the myth by which we live."

Don't be satisfied with the myth surrounding your job or your vocation. Your job is an empty, abstract shell—you give it definition, not the reverse. We need to be less hesitant to inhabit our positions with our distinct brand of spirit and personality.

It's always surprising and delightful to meet the person inside the role they are playing at the moment. For example, when the doctor lets down enough to admit that she is also uncomfortable when she's the one sitting on the table covered with paper, or the flight attendant engages in a real conversation with you about the book you are reading. Or, the cashier at the dry cleaner wants to know where you got your jacket. These seemingly insignificant small encounters are what connect us as community. That is, in part, why I am letting my Microsoft Word program have a heyday with my grammar… nearly the entire document is underlined in green on the computer screen. Mind you, it's not that I don't know grammar. It's just that I prefer to write a book that is written in *my* voice, fragmented sentences and all. I don't want to merely give you ideas, words and paragraphs; I want to give you me.

Dare to act out of character

We often behave not according to our true feelings or emotions, but out of "habit" to the person we are used to portraying to the world. We'd like the people around us to have a certain image or picture of who we are, and we work hard at living up to the reputation we've earned for ourselves. Whether we've decided that we want to be perceived as silly, smart, sexy, or saintly, we pay a price by sticking to the script. We pay the price of vitality, spontaneity, and authenticity.

What if we allowed air time for the entire cast of characters, emotions, perceptions and voices that inhabit the theaters of our minds—to be as crazy, unseemly or inconsistent to our character as they may appear? (You would see in me the witch, the queen, the saint and the sinner, the wise one as well as the innocent—sometimes all in the same day, depending on the day of the month you choose.) But I am very good at being "Denise," thus my rough edges are softened, my soft edges are squared off. I appear as a mostly sane and rational person, other than my propensity for joyous outbursts.

Several years ago I learned to ride a motorcycle. It was such a wild and exhilarating experience; I loved it! What was strange was other people's reactions. It reminded of me of when I used to smoke cigarettes and people would say, "But Denise, you don't look like a smoker!" To be honest, part of the thrill of riding a motorcycle was that it was outside my view of myself. Being the same year that I divorced, I think it was important for me to inhabit my own life again in some particular way that was my own; albeit on the seat of a Suzuki 450. There is a thrill in crossing the borders surrounding our character. I think a part of us longs to be not only a pilgrim, but a fugitive. Mark Nepo, in *The Book of Awakening,* put it this way:

> "There is a conspiracy to put a consistent face before the world, to cover up the glorious inconsistency of our native and untamed world of emotions and desires. The character we develop domesticates the world and leaves no wilderness to play in. There are many territories of imagination and many strange regions of emotion that we may not enter without throwing our sanity into question. Until we are willing to cross some borders we are likely to remain rational, banal, boring and bored."

Let the witch have her ride

Do you remember how fun it was to dress up for Halloween? What a blast! You could be whatever or whomever you wanted to be—for just a night! The scarier, the stranger, the more outrageous, the better! For just an evening, you could be as bizarre as you like, without anyone lifting an eyebrow. For just one evening, you could appear wild, ludicrous, ferocious and/or as perfect and magical as your little heart desired.

I grew up in one of those households in which you pieced your costume together with whatever you could find in the forty-five minutes between dinner and dusk on Halloween night. As a result, I was usually a hobo, a gypsy, an old woman or an Indian, all of which would be politically incorrect by today's standards. (This was the day before "Halloween stores" or when mothers, like one of my sisters, hand sewed and beaded a costume from scratch, beginning in July!) Anyway, I pretty much punted through every Halloween. Well, one recent Halloween I went all out and dressed up as kind of a vampy, modern day witch. I got into it. It was so cool being wicked, I could hardly stand it! I could barely sleep that night, the smile on my face was so wide. I awoke to a black tattered dress and a pointed hat at my bedside. I remember making a solemn promise to myself, "That witch will fly again!"

It was a profound and wonderful experience to let the witchy part of me see the light of day. Having been closeted for decades, (my daughter might beg to differ), I found it exhilarating and freeing. I no longer view Halloween so much as a day of masquerading, but as a day of *un*masquerading. Not that I am a witch; it's just that I am part witch, too.

I saw this happen for my daughter, too. From ages three through seven my daughter wore the same costume—she was a fairy-princess-angel-ballerina-bride, all rolled up into one! I knew that my child was growing up the year she put her tu-tu, angel wings, fairy wand, wedding veil, and princess crown away and announced, "Mom, I want to be Darth Vader for Halloween." Enter stage left, right in the middle of an adorable childhood—the dark side.

There is something so powerful about getting to be someone else. In a few of my workshops I have participants demonstrate situations in a 2–5 minute scenario in which they are to break as many of the rules and guidelines that we've covered on a given topic as they can. It is not only hysterical to see what people come up with and just how "into it" they get, but I find it a great way for participants to actually meet one another on a different level. When play-acting, we shed our masks in order to put another mask on. In the spaces between those two masks, we see hints of one another's true faces.

Just for fun, imagine the face you would wear if we held a day of the "Un-masquerade" at the family Thanksgiving meal, at the neighborhood barbecue, or at the yearly performance review. What if we declared this next year as "The Year of True Faces." Perhaps… just perhaps,

We would find hundreds of new
ways to use our hands
in shaping the beauty of the world
Because we would no longer need
them for holding up the masks.

Live in the question "Who am I?"

The recurring theme of this chapter is the importance of becoming aware of the various masks we wear and distinguishing those masks from our true selves—from a sense of spirit or soul. Clearly, when we over-identify with our positions, personalities and roles we too often neglect our search for the mystery that we are part of. The deepening of our relationship to that mystery is essential to our souls. Without the quest for spirit or soul, we live on the surface, we exist superficially. Our egos and personalities, inevitably constricting, need to be modified by a spiritual perspective. We need a strong sense of self, but we also need a strong sense of spirit—that which helps us transcend our social and psychological conditioning and experience ourselves as being encompassed within a cosmos we perceive as sacred or holy.

Our assignment, should we decide to accept this mission, is to explore the heights of our spirit, our beauty, and our power, and to transcend whatever addictions, habits, obsessions and false identities that have held us captive. Our assignment, should we decide to accept it, is to live in the question posed in this wonderful teaching story:

A woman in a coma was dying. She suddenly had a feeling that she was taken up to heaven and stood before the Divine.

"Who are you?" a voice called to her.

"I am the wife of the mayor," she replied.

"I did not ask whose wife you are, but who you are."

"I am the mother of four children."

"I did not ask whose mother you are, but who you are."

"I am a school teacher."

"I did not ask what your profession is, but who you are."

And so it went. No matter what she replied, she did not seem to give a satisfactory answer to the question, "Who are you?"

"I'm a Christian."

"I did not ask what your religion is, but who you are."

"I am the one who went to church every day and always helped the poor and needy."

"I did not ask what you did, but who you are."

She evidently failed the examination, for she was sent back to earth. When she recovered from her coma, she was determined to find out who she was. And that made all the difference in her new lease on life.

The mystery of identity, "Who am I?" is one of humankind's central spiritual questions. Are we this body of flesh and bone? Is consciousness merely a product of our nervous system, our thoughts and feelings? Are we our genetic heritage and ancestors' patterns or is our essential nature more fundamentally spiritual? Are we a spark of the Divine? Such is the inquiry of mystics and sages.

I hope that I am more able to live in the question of "Who Am I?" than when I first heard this story almost twenty years ago. Yet, as I reread it, I know that there is not an answer that will one day occur to me. The question itself is a journey because "who we are" is always in the process of changing, developing and evolving. We are always in the process of becoming. The quest for our truest response to the question of who we are, still, is a worthwhile venture. May we continue that journey with a whole heart and happy feet.

Passages

"There is nothing with which every man is so afraid as getting to know how enormously much he is capable of doing and becoming."

Soren Kierkegaard

"I've always had this thing of "him" and "me"; "He" goes on stage, "he's" famous, and then there's me—just a kid from Liverpool."

Paul McCartney

"People travel to wonder at the height of mountains, at the huge waves of the sea, at the long courses of rivers, at the vast compass of the ocean, at the circular motion of the stars, and they pass themselves by without wondering."

St. Augustine

Sam Keen

"Consciousness is like a lantern on a dark night illuminating everything within a circle. When it's carried from one place to another some new obscurity surrounds the circle of clarity. What we know about ourselves is in continual dialogue with darkness. Self-knowledge and ignorance are linked because of the selective structure of the human mind. In focusing attention on one thing we ignore another."

Leonard Cohen

"Ring the bells that still can ring,
Forget your perfect offering.
There is a crack in everything.
That's how the light gets in."

W. E. B. DuBois

"Herein lies the tragedy of the age: not that there are good men… not that there are wicked men… but that men know so little about each other."

"Self-esteem isn't everything—it's just that there's nothing without it."

Gloria Steinem

"The world is a looking glass and gives back to every man the reflection of his own face."

William Makepeace Thackeray

Blaise Pascal

"Look for the truth; it wants to be found."

"Each person must decide for himself who and what he will become or there will be no real joy in his identity."

Sam Keen

Anthony de Mello

"Live your life as you see fit. That's not selfish. Selfish is to demand that others live their lives as you see fit."

"Look within.
Within is the fountain of good,
and wilt ever bubble up,
if thou wilt ever dig."

Marcus Aurelius

Leo Tolstoy
"If you could only know who you are, all your troubles would seem utterly unnecessary and trivial."

"Make it thy business to know thyself, which is the most difficult lesson in the world."

Miquel de Cervantes

"God gave us the consciousness of mankind as a whole, as well as our consciousness as individuals; with the help of these two things, as with two wings we can fly higher and come closer to God and to understand the truth."

Guiseppe Mazzini

Alphonse Karr
"Every man has three characters—that which he exhibits, that which he has, and that which he thinks he has."

"If we had no faults we wouldn't take so much pleasure in noting those of others."

Francois Duc de la Rochefoucand

"It is easier to sail many thousands of miles through cold and storm and cannibals than it is to explore the private sea, the Atlantic and Pacific Ocean of one's own being."

Henry David Thoreau

e. e. cummings
"To be nobody-but-yourself in a world which is doing its best, night and day, to make you everybody else—means to fight the hardest battle which any human being can fight; and never stop fighting."

"The curious paradox is that when I accept myself just as I am, then I can change." Carl Rogers

"This above all, to thine own self be true,
And it must follow, as the night the day,
Thou canst not then be false to any man."

Hamlet, Shakespeare

"It is the chiefest point of happiness that a man is willing to be what he is."
Desiderius Erasmus

Epictetus
"O God, while I stay on this earth I want to be that which I am."

"You are truth from head to brow.
Now what else would you like to know?"

Rumi

To Ponder and To Practice

- Make a list of ten words or phrases that describe you best. They might be functions, feelings, activities or affiliations (e.g., public servant, student, jokester, resourceful, choir member, etc.). Rank the ten phrases in the order of their importance to you.
- Think back to moments of your life when you felt that you were at your best. Where were you and what were you doing? How can you be there again, not in that situation, but within yourself?
- If you were to die tomorrow, how do you think you would be remembered by your friends? Your family? Your colleagues and co-workers?
- In what ways do you think you are conforming to the myths surrounding your particular position, vocation or role in life? In what ways do you see yourself living outside those myths?
- Think about the masks you wear at home, at work and out into the world. Draft a list of the qualities and scripts you play, and for each one, consider what wearing that persona costs you in the long run. For example, it is nice to appear "sweet" but what that may cost is the ability to speak up for yourself or to rock the proverbial boat.
- What is one way you could cross the borders around your character, to shed light on an aspect of your being that you keep hidden?
- What is one thing that you *pretend to be* that you would just as soon give up?
- Like the eaglet raised with the chickens, how might you be holding yourself back due to what you think you *are not?*
- Think about one of your favorite Halloween costumes. What was particularly fun about wearing that costume? Next Halloween, observe the unmasquerading of the people around you.
- There is a Hindu proverb that says, "There is nothing noble in being superior to some other person. True nobility comes from being superior to your previous self." What one thing could you begin doing which would make you feel superior to your present self?
- Muriel Rukeyser writes, "The universe is made of stories, not atoms." Who in your work place knows nothing of your story with whom you would like to share it? Whose story do you know absolutely nothing about? Make an opportunity to share stories with someone in your workplace.

- What is the most common stereotype people have about you? How do you think you might be promoting that image?
- What do you think the people you work with should know about your "personal work culture" in order to work more effectively with you?
- Look for the child in the people around you today. Look again and see if you can see the old person they will become. Try it with the person in the mirror first.
- If you, like the woman in the coma, were being asked, "Who are you?" what response bubbles up from your depths?
- Select a quote on the topic of self-knowledge from this chapter's *Passages* and post it where you will see it often in order to internalize it.
- Choose a daily habit, routine or symbol to help you remain conscious of the masks that you wear or of the mask that you want to remove. (e.g. When looking in the mirror in the morning while brushing your teeth or applying make-up, look to really see the person who is under the mask of your face.)
- Given everything you have read in this chapter, what do you want to *keep* doing? What do you want to *stop* doing? What do you want to *start* doing?

Notes

Chapter 7

New Wings

Moving Through Fear

Befriend the dragon

Befriend the dragon

Feed your courage with the aid of an inner mentor

Feed your courage with the aid of an inner mentor

Dip into your "belly faith"

Dip into your "belly faith"

Soar on wings of choice

Soar on wings of choice

Be among the movable

Be among the movable

Take the hundredth blow

Take the hundredth blow

New Wings

You say that you're not ready, don't put you to the test,
you're like a bird with fragile wings, clinging to the nest.
We tell you that your future holds possibility,
because we see in you what you can't see, your true ability.

Well it's not in leaps and not in bounds that you will try your wings,
you'll lift them gently from your sides by risking little things.
Starting exactly where you are, moving one step at a time,
learning to move slowly to the beat of your own heart's rhyme.

Honoring who you've been, and how it's led to who you are,
bowing to every lesson, that's brought you where you are.
You only grow by growing and you only move by moving,
but with the faith of each small act, you will continue proving:

Your destiny is in your hands, not bound by luck or chance,
it's in the choices that you make, in every circumstance.
So move one foot and then the other, and with each ardent stride
you'll make a habit of your courage, and with it come new pride.

The day will come when, with surprise, you'll glide on eagle's wings—
you'll make new nests in future trees with what the morrow brings.
But you'll look back to where you are, you'll shake your head and sigh,
as you hear again that still, small voice, gently urging, "Fly!"

Reflections

The theme introduced in this poem is as old as the hills. It is at the heart of every great story, every hero's journey and every person's life: nesting, not flying, needing to fly, not wanting to fly, flying, nesting, not flying, needing to fly… etc.

William James asserted that "It is only by risking ourselves from one hour to another that we live at all." The astonishing Helen Keller put it even more bluntly:

> "Security is only superstition.
> It does not exist in nature,
> nor do children of man as a whole experience it.
> Avoiding danger is no safer in the long run
> than outright exposure to it.
> Life is either a daring adventure
> or nothing at all."

It is only when we risk ourselves and dare to experiment with our own lives that we grow and change. Life is the experience of feathering one nest after another, and just as it gets comfortable and warm, we are required to try our new and fragile wings. We would prefer to cling to the nest but fly we must, because our very futures depend upon it.

Fortunately, we are all avid risk-takers and expert learners. We know this for two solid reasons:

1. *All* of life is the exercise of risk as we daily travel headlong into a future we cannot control.
2. This is, by its very nature, a lessons-based world. Everything we know, we had to grow into, through learning, risking, erring and then coming to understanding.

This is how we learned to walk and talk and ride a bike. This is how we learned to relate to adults, to make friends on the playground, how to act at the supper table and how to cheat on spelling tests… we had to grow into this learning. Psychologists estimate that we take about 35 risks a day; be they big risks, little risks, or medium-sized risks. That is how we live in the midst of the unknown… by groping in the dark and taking our best shot.

Although life requires persistent learning and risk-taking, each step in the direction of change and growth brings fresh feelings of fear, anxiety, or at the very least, disorientation. We have seen and experienced this disorientation time and again—at times with angst, at other times with glee.

I'll never forget watching my precious niece, Hannah Joy, move through the disorientation of taking her first steps. My brother crouched down about five feet from her, extended his long arms, and in his deep, loving voice, beckoned "Come to Daddy." Barely steady on her feet, she raised her right arm high above her head as if holding a baton, puffed up her little chest, and with all the majesty a one-year-old could muster, marched as if in a parade for two or three, maybe four grand steps, before falling into my brother's arms. Everyone in the room applauded and cheered, and hence, another crawler-turned-walker was born.

What I witnessed that day fit the definition that Soren Kierkegaard once gave to the anxiety that accompanies change. He called it "the dizziness of freedom." When even the tiniest feet find wings. Every fresh experience carries this dizziness that we must move through. Every time we reach beyond what is familiar, there is the necessity to acclimate to what is new, to surrender to the disorientation. This is the womb of all learning, and we, its babes. We needn't be afraid of it or give it too much power. We simply have to keep leaning into the learning. We have been doing this since before our own first steps and will continue to do so until our last breath.

Well it's not in leaps
and not in bounds
that you will try your wings,
You'll lift them gently
from your sides
by risking little things.
Starting exactly where you are,
moving one step at a time,
Learning to move slowly
to the beat of
your own heart's rhyme.

Learning to move slowly to the beat of your own heart's rhyme.... Unfamiliar ground always lies ahead of us. How do we learn to greet it as an inviting landscape rather than as a threatening precipice? Here are a few ideas that may help us lift our wings ever so gently from our sides—to unfetter our hearts and our spirits.

Befriend the dragon

Our minds love to create imaginary problems. We have all learned the art of recreational worrying. There are no limits to what our thoughts can conjure up when given a lack of information about any given situation and the time to wander freely. As Mark Twain put it, "My life has been filled with terrible misfortunes... most of which never happened."

When my daughter was young we lived just a few houses from the seaside cliffs of the Pacific Ocean. When she would go out to play with the neighborhood children, my imagination would work overtime. Even though she was forbidden to cross the street to the ocean and never showed any inclination to disobey this order, my mind would conjure images of her standing at the edge of the cliffs and falling headlong into the rocky edges of the deep, cold sea. With that thought, I would literally go weak at the knees and feel my stomach tighten into a knot. A couple of times this image caused me to leap from my chair and out the door—only to find her sitting on the bunny hutch with her best friend, silhouetted against a rosy sky.

The fact that my fear always appeared with the same image and sensation did not dull it—it always seemed new and real, with the jagged edges of premonition. Without much effort, I can recreate the same fear, almost to the point of losing the contents of my stomach. Where the fear came from I do not know, but it is amazing that I did not keep my daughter locked indoors to calm my fears. I wonder as I write, how many other "terrible misfortunes" have filled my life without ever having happened? How do we train our imaginations to stop scaring us to death and start inspiring us to new life?

The journeys of our lives are greatly affected by our fears. When they go unexamined and unidentified, we are not traveling as the conscious pilgrims our lives deserve. It is more like we are sleep-walking, believing the images created in our minds as if they were real. I remember a psychology professor who likened us to artists who paint pictures of monsters and then flee in terror. We paint our thoughts with fantasies of pain and disaster and then recoil in horror. When we look carefully, however, we recognize that the monsters are not real, and in that recognition we are safe. It's like the story of the fellow who was afraid of a dragon:

A man went to see a psychiatrist and said that every night he was visited by a twelve foot dragon with three heads. The man was a nervous wreck, could not sleep at all, and was on the verge of total collapse. He had even thought of suicide.

"I think I can help you," said the psychiatrist, "but I must warn you that it will take a year or two and will cost three thousand dollars."

"Three thousand dollars!" the man exclaimed. "Forget it! I think I'll just go home and make friends with the dragon!"

When we stop to think about the myriad ways our fears exact a price on our lives, facing, naming and even befriending them may be our best option. But before we can befriend the dragon, the dragon must identify itself. We need to know its name. I find it helpful in the face of fear to ask myself, "What is it I am really afraid of?" This is a liberating question. John O'Donohue in his book, *Anam Cara,* describes fear as a kind of fog, because it tends to spread everywhere and falsify the shape of everything. But when you pin it down with the question, "What are you?" it shrinks back to a proportion that we are able to engage. When we know what is frightening us, we take back its power. Fear multiplies in anonymity; it does not want a name. When you name your fear, it shrinks.

Susan Jeffers, in *Feel the Fear and Do It Anyway,* describes three levels of human fear. She says the first level is fear of the event itself (i.e.: earthquakes, poverty, illness, divorce or unemployment). But, she asserts, that is not what we are really afraid of. The second level of fear is *emotions*—how those events will make us feel. So what we are really wanting to avoid are feelings like pain, humiliation, loneliness, embarrassment or loss of pride. But, she says, that's not really what we are afraid of either. The third level and the core of our fear is that overwhelmed by those feelings we won't be able to handle it. She suggests that at the core of every fear is the loss of control. I love this way of seeing things. We can effectively deal with fear by asking ourselves how we can gain a sense of control in the situation. An increased sense of control eclipses fear.

During a difficult period of my life when I was feeling a bit eclipsed by fear, I read a beautiful book written by Dawna Markova entitled *No Enemies Within.* Through the exercises in this book, I came to befriend my fear in new ways. While we often treat fear as something to hide from, avoid or ignore, Markova entreats her readers to recognize fear as an important messenger, to respect it for the wisdom that it holds and to listen to its voice. Sometimes as a shout, other times as a plea, fear is always voicing something important to us. Here are a few excerpts from her book:

> "Fear shows us where our boundaries are... It lets us see where we've been and lets us know the places we want to avoid... It points the direction like an internal compass... We must learn to use fear as the useful tool it can be, not as a master... Fear is meant to be tapped into and drawn upon like a rich and loyal resource."

Markova is not suggesting that we allow our fears to control or stifle us, but that we allow fear to be a faithful guide on our life's journey. During that trying time in my life, I came to trust that my fear had something worthwhile to say, that it was worth listening to. The surprise that came on the wings of that courage was that, being willing to listen to my fear, I was also able to hear the new comforting voice of my own inner faith. The dragon was tamed.

Not only can we tame our fear by identifying it, sometimes we can even use it! It is possible to ride on the back of the dragon because fear contains energy that can be harnessed and employed in positive ways. Just before giving a speech in front of a large crowd, my body feels electric with fear. Where I used to fight this feeling, now I use it to improve my work. I translate this energy into excitement and enthusiasm. My fear now is that if I stop feeling fear, I will lose my edge. I recently read that this is true for swimmers and runners poised on the starting blocks—the jitters they experience add to their explosive leap toward their goal. As they say in Outward Bound programs, "The idea is not to get rid of the butterflies in your stomach, but to get them to fly in formation!" That kind of energetic fear drives us courageously forward, straight toward the thing we're afraid of. It can help us deal with reality, rather than avoid it.

It is a truth of the heart that what we resist persists. What we avoid makes us frightened, hard and inflexible. It is an equal truth that what we embrace becomes transformed. This is especially true of fear. A playful statement made by Emerson makes the point well: "When a dog is chasing after you, whistle for him." Who knows? He and the dragon just may become friends.

Feed your courage with the aid of an inner mentor

A rose only becomes beautiful and blesses others when it opens up and blooms. Its greatest tragedy is to stay in a tightly closed bud, never fulfilling its potential. Without the warmth and light of the generous sun, the rose would stay tight in its bud. In a similar way, without the warmth and light of hope, we too might never bloom. The world provides the imagination with plenty of images that would color our minds with shades of dread and fear. How beautiful then that we have been given the gift of consciousness whereby we can choose different colors—shades of hope and strength.

We can feed our souls with images of people whom we admire and respect—heroes who give us working images of different types of lives. We don't have to be limited to the image of one spiritual hero. We can each construct our own inspirational collage. We might incorporate Georgia O' Keefe's reverence for beauty, Nelson Mandela's political courage, Helen Keller's enthusiasm for life, Ralph Nader or Jimmy Carter's passionate commitment to social issues, and Mother Teresa's simple kindness and compassion. You might add a touch of charisma with the likes of Tina Turner and the velvety smooth grace of Maya Angelou.

I have been blessed with parents who model for me qualities I long to cultivate in similar fashion—my mother's penchant for laughter and lightheartedness as she whistles and hums through the activities of her day, my father's strong work ethic and his kind and gentle wisdom. From my step mom, Diane, I learn the gift of thoughtfulness and sensitivity. My mother-in-law Felicia models for me an abiding faith in God and an extraordinary penchant for loving, while my mother-in-law Shirley is the very embodiment of generosity in its every form.

No one person needs to be the model of all that we wish to cultivate in ourselves, but each person we love is modeling something precious which can affirm and encourage our faith in what we can become. They can become our inner mentors. The collaged images we hold of them in our hearts and minds can feed our faith and hope in the face of discouragement or despair.

Dip into the "belly faith" of the everyday hero

Have you ever had it happen that when you mustered the courage to face what you feared most, a reservoir of strength and power arose from within you? This is not only common, it's typical. I believe this is true, in part, because of what New Zealand mountaineer Sir Edmund Hillary suggested: "It's not the mountain that we conquer but ourselves." Through courageous action, even in small steps, we find our faith.

Japanese martial artists tell us that courageous action is centered in the "hara," the belly; but if there is no faith in your heart, it's hard to spark the fire of courage in your belly. We know that genuine security does not come from the absence of danger; it comes from the presence of faith. This faith is born in the heart and sustained by a spirit of trust in our own ability to respond in the best way we can to whatever life passes our way. It's the kind of faith that Victor Hugo eludes to in this beautiful short verse:

Be like the bird, pausing in his flight
On limb too slight,
Feels it give way, yet sings,
Knowing he has wings.

While we often associate faith with religious or spiritual convictions, we must also have faith in ourselves—in our own survival mechanisms, in our gifts, our vitality and in the will of our own spirits. We should be cognizant of what we never would have achieved, learned or earned if it weren't for faith in ourselves, in the wise faith that opened rather than narrowed our choices. That is what faith does—it encourages us to question, to explore and to inquire, rather than to blindly follow the path of least resistance.

A favorite exercise I use in one of my workshops is called New Beginnings. I ask everyone to consider risks they have taken in their lives when the outcomes of their actions were truly uncertain. This is how philosopher Soren Kierkegaard defined heroism. He said that heroism does not lie in great achievements but in the moment when we take the step—not knowing what the outcome will be. According to this definition, we all walk the path of the everyday hero. When asked to identify five to ten times when they relied on faith in themselves in order to move forward in their lives, my workshop participants never fail to amaze themselves and each other. Examples of the kinds of things people have shared include:

- Leaving an abusive relationship
- Going back to school
- Moving to a new city (state, country)
- Getting married
- Going into recovery from an addiction
- Adopting a child
- Changing professions
- Joining Weight Watchers
- Writing a manuscript and submitting it to publishers
- Learning to scuba dive
- Buying a house
- Facing a history of sexual abuse

What this exercise never fails to bring home is that we all live courageous lives—we each walk the road of the everyday hero. We all live on "belly faith" because we have no other choice. If we could rely on certainty, we would. But because we do not have control of our futures, we simply invest our faith in one outcome or another. As one workshop participant put it, "It's never a matter of having faith or not, it's about where we are putting our faith." We may have faith in our failure or we may have faith in our success. An important question we need to continually ask ourselves is, "Where are we putting our faith?"

In the meantime, we should also take deep bows as we pass the mirror; bowing to the one in us who knows well the meaning of "belly faith":

Honoring who you've been,
and how it's led to who you are,
Bowing to every lesson,
that's brought you where you are.

You only grow by growing and
you only move by moving,
But with the faith of each small act,
you will continue proving...

Soar on wings of choice

Many people live their lives with their fingers crossed, throw their fates to the wind or make wishes as they throw pennies in a fountain. (Okay, I've been known to throw a few pennies myself.) Others keep a rabbit's foot in their right front pocket. But as the old saying goes, "Depend on the rabbit's foot if you will, but remember: it didn't work for the rabbit."

As human beings we were not consulted about many factors that have shaped our destinies, like where, when or to whom we would be born. But we have been given tremendous freedom and creativity to go beyond those givens—to forge new relationships, and to learn and develop our skills in our own distinctive ways. We can transcend the circumstances of our birth and our upbringing rather than be limited by them. We have been gifted with a power immensely more potent than luck, stargazing or wishing—the power of choice. One of the strongest factors in our growth lies in our ability and willingness to make choices. Philosophers throughout time have referred to the power of choice as the very essence of what it is to be human.

Your destiny is in your hands,
not bound by luck or chance,
It's in the choices that you make,
in every circumstance.
So move one foot and then the other,
and with each ardent stride
You'll make a habit of your courage,
and with it come new pride.

It behooves us to pay attention to the extent to which destiny really is in our hands... and how we continually shape it by the choices we make and don't make, by the decisions we consider and fail to consider.

Sometimes it's not the choices we make that get us in trouble; the true culprit is the way in which we make them. For example, there are those who live by the "hopeful method," choosing the most appealing option while keeping their fingers crossed and hoping everything works out well. Then there are those who use the "safe method," choosing the option which presents the least amount of risk. Some prefer the "whatever you say method," allowing other people to make the decisions for them. The "non-deciding method" is always convenient when you dislike your alternatives. I always liked the "go for it method," the one where you don't bother looking before leaping, hoping that the net will miraculously appear.

Obviously, each of these ways of making choices brings risk—just different variations of risk. Few of us make choices that spring from a calm and serene place inside us where we have identified our goals in the situation and our various options, then considered, in turn, how each option brings us closer to our real goals. This is too neat and logical a map to reflect the chaotic territory of our lives. So we make our choices using some variation and or combination of the methods described above, and in the end, we follow our gut instinct.

As I look back on my own life, it is astounding to me to think about the choices I have made that drastically affected the rest of my life. The one that amuses me most is how I chose to leave San Diego to attend the University of California in Santa Cruz in 1975. This is where I then met the man I would marry and with whom I would have a child, and where, even after our divorce, we would remain and nurture our daughter into adulthood. This is where I began my work as a job developer, which in turn led to my present livelihood which I treasure deeply. This one move, this one decision, had such a profound influence on the rest of my life.

So guess how I made that fateful decision to attend UC Santa Cruz which snowballed into so many profound life experiences? After being accepted to several schools, I decided that I would attend the first school that responded with dormitory information. (Imagine the power I put in the hands of some innocent file clerk in the Student Housing Office.) No trumpets sounded when I received the dormitory survey form from UCSC. The winds of fate had blown and I had not experienced even the hint of a breeze.

It's pretty awesome, and also disconcerting, to realize that the way we approach choices, make decisions and take risks has as much to do with our destiny as anything else. Here is an entry from my journal which broaches this important phenomenon with a series of seemingly benign questions about how we approach everyday life.

Participation

How do you get into the water?
Do you jump in, dive in,
or do you tiptoe in, bit by bit,
feeling the cool water
from head to toe
and every space in between
for fear of the one big splash?

How do you awaken in the morning?
Bright-eyed, wide-eyed
or do you peer out of your dark cave,
inching slowly towards the brightness
of a new day?

How do you order food
at a restaurant?
Immediate and certain
or forever wavering,
your mouth watering
for every item on the menu?

How do you enter love?
Do you fall fast and furious
into the heart's deep caverns
or do you climb down
that mountain cautiously,
finding proper foothold
every step of the way?

How will you find your true work?
Will you dive in, awaken to it,
place your order and fall in
or will you tiptoe in,
consider a million and one choices
and inch slowly, step by step?

Life is lived choice by choice—
all the while offering
her sweet waters, a sunrise,
daily bread, the wonders of love
and the dignity of work.
How we choose to participate
is not what matters.
Dive in, crawl in, jump in
or inch your way,
but what life demands
is our participation.

Choose.

Be among the movable

There is a great Arabian proverb, "All mankind is divided into three classes: those that are immovable, those that are movable and those that move." I am sure that if we were to stop and think about it, each of us could identify people we have known who would fit into each of these categories. The tougher question, of course, would be, "Which category do we, ourselves, fit into?"

In which areas of our lives do we find ourselves immovable? In which areas of our lives do we find ourselves moving? This is where we are deserving of applause even if it is with baby steps that we go forward. For as Todd Siler said in his book, *Think Like a Genius,* "A pawn in a chess game moves only in small straightforward steps, but with these steps it can become a queen, who can move in any direction she chooses." Baby steps eventually turn into a stride—the stride into a full-fledged strut!

I want to be one of those people who move. Even when I am unsure. Even when standing still feels better and would be the more comfortable choice. I want to move, even if not gracefully or gallantly. I want to follow the advice of Martin Luther King Jr., "If you can't run, walk. If you can't walk, crawl. But by all means, keep moving." In some aspects of my life, I remain movable—in my work and in my ever-evolving relationships with friends, family members and business associates. I almost feel a built-in flexibility in these areas of my life. But there are other areas of my life in which I feel rather immovable, like in my taste in clothing, hair style and jewelry (much to my sisters' chagrin); in my political affiliations; my eating, exercising and communication patterns; and clearly in the physical risks I am willing to take and not take. I don't want to be immovable in these areas; I just don't feel particularly moved to move.

If we waited to be moved to move, we might wait forever. We need to continually remind ourselves that whatever we hope to do with ease and comfort, we must learn first to do with courage and diligence. It hardly matters what we call our mission, whether it's ourselves or others we set out to help, or if it's fear, doubt or excitement that leads us to action. What matters is that, whatever our fear, we make our way to the edge of the cliff, and looking beyond, dare to jump. For that is the action that calls forth wings. They do not sprout until we have left the ground. In the words of Johann Wolfgang von Goethe:

> *Until one is committed, there is hesitancy,*
> *the chance to draw back,*
> *always ineffectiveness....*
> *The moment one definitely commits oneself,*
> *then Providence moves too.*
> *All sorts of things occur to help one*
> *that would never otherwise have occurred....*
> *Boldness has genius, power, and magic in it.*
> *Begin it now.*

Take the hundredth blow

Risk-taking is a skill that, like any other, needs practice, then practice and then some more practice. It is like the lesson of the stonecutter. She hammers away at the rock a hundred times without making a dent. Then, on the hundred-and-first blow, the rock splits into two. It's not that the one blow split it, but the combined effect of them all. We have to hang tough, because one day, if we're practicing the right concepts, the rock will split—and courage will show its shining face.

We learn to manage risk by planning and measuring it in small, acceptable increments. We develop our risk muscle by being responsible in tiny and doable matters. By drawing our own conclusions about smaller daily choices, we begin to understand through "belly faith" the larger, more significant ones. What more natural way do we know to grow?

So if I can walk a mile longer than my usual stroll along the ocean, perhaps I can make that call or send that e-mail to a potential new customer. And if I can make that call, why can't I accept that offer to make a keynote speech to a new audience? And if I make that speech, what is stopping me from writing the book to that audience that it is outside of my usual purview? And if I am really writing a book to perfect strangers, what is keeping me from speaking my truth to the ones who are dearest to me? The courage mustered for one risk seeds the courage for another.

I find comfort in the words of Krishnamurti who said that the only courage that matters is the kind that will get you from moment to moment. I love knowing that while I may never find the courage that gets me from month to month or from year to year, I can always muster enough to get me from moment to moment. That I can do. And then, of course,

The day will come
when, with surprise,
you'll glide on eagle's wings
You'll make new nests
in future trees
with what the morrow brings.
But you'll look back
to where you are,
you'll shake your head and sigh,
As you hear again that still,
small voice, gently urging, "Fly!"

Passages

Dorothy Gilman

"It is in the daily choices we make that we sit with the gods and design ourselves."

"And then the day came when the risk to remain tight in a bud was more painful than the risk to bloom."

Anaïs Nin

"When I dare to be powerful—to use my strength in the service of my vision, then it becomes less and less important whether I am afraid."

Andre Lorde

"I've been absolutely terrified every moment of my life and I've never let it keep me from doing a single thing I wanted to do."

Georgia O'Keefe

"We must travel in the direction of our fear."

John Berryman

"Birds make great sky-circles
Of their freedom.
How do they learn it?
They fall, and falling,
They're given wings."

Jelaluddin Rumi

Basil King

"Be bold, and mighty forces will come to your aid."

Zimbabwean Proverb

"If you can walk, you can dance.
If you can talk, you can sing."

"Life is like playing the violin in public and learning the instrument as you go on."

Samuel Butler

"Courage is the price that life exacts for granting peace. The soul knows it not, knows no release for little things; knows not the livid loneliness of fear, nor mountain heights where bitter joy can hear the sound of wings."

Amelia Earhart

Ernest Hemingway

"Courage is grace under pressure."

George Woodberry

"The willingness to take risks is our grasp of faith."

"There are people who shape their lives by fear of death, and others who shape their lives by the joy of life."

Charles Handy

"There is no security in life, there is only opportunity."

Mark Twain

"Seek the ways of eagles, not the wren."

Omaha saying

Anonymous

"Throughout history, the most common debilitating human ailment has been cold feet."

"In the poetics of growth it is important to appreciate how life, with its endless possibilities and ever-changing nature, remains so faithful to us. Returning that faithfulness in the form of acceptance of risk, we engage more deeply in life and we open the door to growth."

John O'Donohue

"To dare is to lose one's footing momentarily. To not dare is to lose oneself."

Soren Kierkegaard

"The most drastic and usually the most effective remedy for fear is direct action."

William Burnham

Plato

"We can easily forgive a child who is afraid of the dark; the real tragedy of life is when adults are afraid of the light."

William Ward

"Man, like a bridge, was designed to carry the load of the moment, not the combined weight of a year all at once."

Michel de Montaigne

"He who fears he will suffer, already suffers from his fear."

"Little by little the bird weaves its nest."

Cherokee proverb

"We learn to fly not by becoming fearless, but by the daily practice of courage."

Sam Keen

"He who is outside the door already has the most difficult part of the journey behind him."

Dutch proverb

Chinese proverb

"The man who removes a mountain begins by taking away small stones."

To Ponder and To Practice

- Who is one of the most courageous people you have ever known? How would you like your life to more closely reflect the qualities of that person?
- Draft a list of every job you have ever held. Consider how you made each choice of accepting and then leaving each position. Look for the thread(s) of reason of how and why you chose those particular paths. Is there a pattern? If so, do you like the pattern? If not, how would you like to change it? Would you like to choose a new pattern? If so, choose it based on your deepest values and the longing of spirit. Your soul's joy may be your reward.
- We all live on faith, whether we put it in our failure or in our success. Where do you find yourself putting your faith these days?
- One of the rules of caution is not to be too cautious. In what areas of your life do you tend to play it safe? In what area of your life might it be wise to throw just a bit of caution to the wind?
- Consider some of the risks you have taken in your life which you are glad you took. Consider some of the risks you have taken that you are not so glad about. How are your present circumstances different or similar to these past situations?
- Rainer Marie Rilke advised us that "Our deepest fears are like dragons guarding our deepest treasure." What treasure do you think your current fears are guarding?
- Life is a river that keeps running, whether or not you make decisions, it will make them for you. What decisions have you been putting off which life may just make for you unless you take control?
- What do you love more than you fear? How can you motivate yourself more by what you love than by what you fear?
- We must always give up something in order to get something. You can't fill a cup without emptying it first. You can't even move to a new place in the room without giving up the space you occupy. Sacrifice is a basic concept of our universe. What are some of the sacrifices you are willing to make in order to make necessary changes in your life?

Practice

- In the face of new challenges, it is important to keep the flame of hope and faith burning. What are three small things you can do to keep that flame burning? (For example, reread a book you love, listen to music that takes you back to a great time in your life, rent a few of the movies that you find inspiring or spend time with people who encourage you.)
- From what sources do you take your idealized image of yourself? In forming your own collage of a spiritual hero, which people in your life model for you the qualities you aspire to?
- Choose a favorite quote from this chapter's *Passages* and post it where you will read it often and internalize it as you work to foster courage in your life and work.
- Choose a daily habit, routine or symbol to remind you of your desire to practice courage and take small steps in the face of fear. (e.g., Use being in line or waiting in traffic as a reminder that life is lived moving one inch (person or mile) at a time, or let birds in flight remind you to try your own wings.)
- Given everything you have read in this chapter, what do you want to *keep* doing? What do you want to *stop* doing? What do you want to *start* doing?

Notes

Lessons from the Apple Tree

Chapter 8

Accepting Change

Take the unknown one piece at a time

Take the unknown one piece at a time

Learn from the earth how to transition with grace

Learn from the earth how to transition with grace

Accept your seasons

Accept your seasons

Find comfort in the constancy of change

Find comfort in the constancy of change

Allow darkness to be a gift

Allow darkness to be a gift

Cultivate patience for cycles

Cultivate patience for cycles

Be as the flower in your blossoming

Be as the flower in your blossoming

Lessons from the Apple Tree: Part I

I am in love with an apple tree.
She is a miracle to me.
I am in awe of her cycle:
from bareness to blossoms,
to bright green branches heavily laden
with sweet, red, round fruit.

I just want to sit under her all day,
to lean against her trunk
and learn from her how to trust my own nature.

I want to learn to accept the bareness,
the emptiness, and winter of my days.
To let cold, wind and rain,
sorrow and disappointment,
do their vital work
to soften, deepen and nourish me.

I want to lean even closer and learn from her
how to delight in the newness of spring,
to be willing to sprout again,
to have faith
in the slightest nub of green
protruding from the bark of my own uncertainty.

She teaches me to surrender
to the slow but sacred process of flowering—
all hopes and dreams and yearnings
turning to petals and filling the air
with the sweet fragrance of blossoms.

I want to learn from her to trust my nature,
to let the blossoms turn to fruit—
though small, bitter and inedible at first,
with patience and daily turning to the sun,
to trust the process of ripening—
of turning from green to pink to red,
holding and nurturing the smallest of my gifts
until they ripen and become food.

I lean closer and learn the lesson of the autumn—
how to enter the harvest with arms wide open.
Generous and grateful—
accepting that not all of the fruit of my labors
will be noticed and appreciated—
to let the unpicked fruit fall from the branches,
and return to the earth,
full of seed for future trees.

I lay down in the grass and look up at my teacher.
She is a miracle to me.
Ironically, I want to give her
the shiniest, the reddest of apples.

Lessons from the Apple Tree: Part II

Every day the two legged creature comes out to look at me.
She sits in the shade of my branches and leans against my trunk.
I want her to gather my fruit and bake a pie.
I want the scent of cinnamon and apple to waft from her kitchen window.
But I suspect that I am the first apple tree she has ever really known.
She is far more enthralled with my process
than she is with the possibility of my fruit.

She just looks at me in wide-eyed amazement.
She delighted in my blossoms last spring, but I'll tell ya,
she has this thing for my apples.
Don't get me wrong,
any tree on God's green earth would love to be in my roots—
to be admired and doted upon through human eyes.
But I am dumbfounded because it appears to me
as if she does not even know what she is, as if she is blind to her own gifts.
There is so much I would say to her, if I could.
If my branches were a choir and my fruit were a song,
this is what I would sing:

To be a tree, a river or a mountain is a wondrous thing. Ah, but to be human!
All of creation looks back on you in your resplendent giftedness.

You, with your holy hands, your nimble fingers and branching arms
that rise and fall at will, arms that can gather, and carry and embrace.
You, with your wild feet and those blessed legs
that can sit as if rooted, in one moment,
and then in the next, stand, run, walk,
and then fold again, and be still in the forest,
glen or meadow of your own choosing.

You, with your miracle senses—
Eyes that can see in any direction
with the slightest movement of your head from your impossibly limber trunk—
Ears that hear the bird, the cricket, the thundering sky
and your ability to sense the inaudible.
A soft body that feels the down of feathers,
the hardness of ground, the solid of rock and the fullness of air.
The ability to taste the bitter, the sweet, the pungent,
and to taste with your heart, salt from another's tears.

Ah, to be human, with the privilege of consciousness—
– To choose or refuse your own flowering,
– To reflect or neglect your genius,
– To nurture and bless, or ignore and repress your nature.

And amidst all of this blessedness,
you turn to me,
a simple apple tree,
as if I was some kind of garden angel,
a keeper of a some succulent secret.

Please, Human, rise!
Gather my fruit with your holy hands,
set your wild feet in the direction of the kitchen
and bake a miracle pie!

Feast on my fruit by employing your own
and together we will set our larger world to blossoming!

Reflections

"Just when summer gets perfectly fresh nights and soft casual breezes, it ends. Life is like that too. Just when we get it right, it starts to change. Just when the job gets easy and we get a sense of what we're doing, they ask us to retire. The children grow up and get reasonable and they leave home. That's life on the edge of autumn. And that's beautiful—if we have the humility for it."

Writer and poet Joan Chittister hits the nail on the head in her passage above. Just when life is sweet and we are moving on calm waters we can be assured of one thing—there is an unexpected rapid just around the corner. Whether or not we were cut out for white water rafting, endure the tides of change we must. Life requires it. Humility would help, no doubt. But so would patience, trust and courage. No wonder we are called the "unfinished animal"... it is life itself that must have its way with us in order for us to bring forth the fruits of our spirits. Our seasons and cycles are no less dramatic than that of the apple tree... they are just less predictable.

Imagine a world in which nothing has to change. The body does not age, the state of relationships is forever constant, and one is never faced with new decisions. You make one career choice; you have one nest in which to make a home and one person with whom you will ever share your heart. For some, this would be a lovely existence with all of its calm and certainty. A nice respite from the storms of life. And yet, with all of that being true, it would not be living—for by definition, change is the stuff of life. Growth is the only evidence that we are alive. When we stop growing and our lives stop changing, we can be certain of one thing only, we are dead.

All of life is creation, every moment is new birth. Self, circumstance and time are the medium, the raw materials we work with in creating something of our lives. Rollo May said, "We all stand on the edge of life, each moment comprising the edge. Before us is only possibility." What a beautiful word—possibility. It dances off the tongue, doesn't it? But then again, it depends on what is possible. It is possible that we will know perfect peace and prosperity. It is also possible that we will face dreaded difficulties and despair. The crux of the matter is, we never know. Says English novelist, George Eliot, "The world is full of hopeful analogies, and handsome, dubious eggs, called possibilities."

I believe that to the extent that we love life, we love change. We just don't know we love it. We love that we live on the edge of possibility in terms of what is still possible for us to be and know and learn... to do and experience and give. We wouldn't even consider surrendering the seasons or the shifts of sun and moon. We wouldn't have our children cease to grow. We would not deny ourselves the adventure of growing into the next stage of our lives, enjoying the fruition of seeds we have already sown. We may be inconvenienced and uncomfortable with the affects of change, but we court her all the while as a welcome companion.

Take the unknown one piece at a time

As human beings we were engineered for self-preservation, but we were also made for growth and discovery. Thus, one of the great paradoxes of human life is—how do we live with "the unknown"? The unknown is part of the air we breathe, yet we devise lovely illusions of safety and security that serve as a veil to cover our sensibilities, filtering out it's smallest particles. Still, we know that to live is to be slowly born. We rarely know the direction of our journey until we have almost arrived. As it says in the Talmud, "Would that life were like the shadow cast by a wall or a stone, but it is like the shadow of a bird in flight."

The element of change is as present in our relationships as it is in our careers. Life is like a puzzle, except that we do not get to see the finished picture on the cover of the box. We are just given little pieces, one at a time, in the form of experiences and insights, and we piece them together as they come. Writer and poet, Edith Wharton, described life as "... just a perpetual piecing together of broken bits."

But while we feel a constant current of change washing over us as we attempt to place pieces of our lives together, the truth is that we are not victims of change, we are the very source of it. Look at our lives, how they move and shift: once we were young, now we are older. Friends and family have come and gone. Social circles have evolved, jobs have changed, and we may have moved our homes many times. Even our bodies change. The molecules making up the cells in our body are completely replaced every seven years, which means that we literally do not have the same body we had seven years ago. Psychologically too, there is a sense in which we are not the same person we were. Our mind learns new things and forgets other things; our heart opens and closes. The luster of things we once loved may have faded; what we most value, may not last. What will arise to take its place as we walk the path of life we do not know.

We embrace the unknown one piece at a time, finding a place within us to fit the new day, yet another change in the workplace, developments in our relationships, a fresh crop of white in our hair, and ever-ripening questions in the garden of our hearts. As we face these changes, we, too, change. An essential issue, however, is whether or not we *grow* from these changes.

Learn from the earth how to transition with grace

Like the apple tree, we are rooted in a world of change—growth, on the other hand, is optional. William Bridges, the author of several remarkable books on change management, reminds us that while change is external, transition is internal. This distinction is critical. For example, we may become legally married in a fifteen-minute ceremony, but it takes time to grow into the role of husband or wife. Being promoted to supervisor can happen in a day, on record, with new business cards bearing a new title. But becoming a supervisor requires the time to slowly grow into new roles, responsibilities and relationships. Change often comes with an event, but the accompanying transition by which we grow is not an event, it is a process.

It is only by learning to transition with grace that we find ourselves enriched rather than toppled by life's unrelenting changes. Embracing change with the elegance of an apple tree is possible, even for us, when we open to new ways of learning, thinking, and being. The apple tree speaks to me of these ways, but so does the rushing river, the phases of the moon, and fields of wheat. Nature is an astounding teacher, unceasingly parading its wisdom about transition, if we could but pay attention. We learn tenacity from the grass breaking through the cracks in the sidewalk, courage from the tree that stands alone, limitations from the ant which crawls on the ground and freedom from the eagle. William Shakespeare said it beautifully in *As You Like It,*

> "And this our life, exempt from public haunt,
> finds tongues in trees, books in the running brooks,
> sermons in stones, and good in everything.
> I would not change it."

I believe that if we were to listen deeply, among the lessons we would hear in such sermons, there would be these.

Accept your seasons

One of the toughest parts of transition is leaving what we have known, letting go and surrendering to what is not yet born. Yet throughout life we have to let go of what is no longer useful, what no longer fits. Be it the beloved Levi's that we will never get back into, the bond with a friend that has faded over time or an innocence to which we can never return. We must accept that as we grow, part of the life we have known or the person we have been is dying away as well as being born anew. Like the snake sheds its skin, or the baby bird leaves the shell of its egg behind, the nature of being is a constant shedding away of what is no longer essential. Can we learn from the apple tree how to let go as a necessary process rather than cling and hold to that which we cannot keep?

I want to learn
to accept the bareness,
the emptiness
and the winter of my days
to let cold, wind and rain,
sorrow and disappointment,
do their vital work
to soften, deepen and nourish me.

Nothing escapes the cycle of birth and death, letting go and welcoming the new. All living things emerge, spark new life, fall apart, die, and emerge in new ways. Our desire to be immune from this reality does not make it so. We will never know the bounty of the harvest without having first experienced the bareness of winter, the patience of spring, and the greening of summer. Even within a given a year, we, like the apple tree, shed and re-flower.

We may feel confused and alone, but through the bitter cold of such winters we may learn how to warm ourselves and seek shelter in the company of those we love. As we cultivate new hope and give birth to new dreams, we revel in the glory of spring and experience a personal kind of Easter—a resurrection of vision. Our dreams will be transformed by our experiences, and some will take wing like birds on the wind. When we find our confidence and hit our stride with the fruit of our labors in autumn, we will find that our successes are only ripe for a time before they, too, fall away and re-enter the earth of our being. Winter will follow, and then spring—and we will continually astound ourselves with our capacity to grow, to change, to feel loss, to hope again, to stretch and bloom, to risk yet again. In the words of Robert Bly,

> "We did not come to remain whole.
> We came to lose our leaves like the trees
> The trees that are broken
> And start again, drawing up from the great roots."

Find comfort in the constancy of change

Life is laced with many ambiguities and too few certainties, but we can always find comfort and pleasure in what is certain and never changing. We can find solace in those things which carry and manifest truth which is immune to change.

That the light of dawn follows night is a daily display of constancy rooted in change. There is truth in the very shifting and changing of things in which we can find solace and comfort: the truth of rain and rainbows, the truth of the moon in its phases, the truth of the tides and the sea. I love that with all of the world's great changes in information technology, the natural world grows as wonderfully today as it did in the past. The earth has no need to adopt new or startling methods in order to continue its exquisite pageantry.

She teaches me to surrender
to the slow but sacred
process of flowering—
all hopes and dreams and yearnings
turning to petals, filling the air
with the sweet fragrance of blossoms.

Change may be constant, but there is a beautiful and dependable sense of truth and constancy in change as well. Trusting this constancy, I know even when I am downhearted, that my spirit waits like the sun behind clouds. I know in the midst of my daughter's adolescent turmoil that she will blossom into adulthood in her own sweet time. I know while in the grips of fear and scarcity of consciousness that new opportunities will arise, and I will be able to keep a roof over my head. I, too, can move one step at a time into my own confidence. I give thanks daily for this inner knowing and the gifts of nature there to remind me.

Allow darkness to be a gift

As the apple tree in winter cannot envision itself laden with pink blossoms, while in the midst of transition, we cannot imagine ourselves with the bloom of confidence or petals of self-assurance. And yet, the tree surrenders to a process it can't see. We call it spring. What a powerful lesson for human life. Moving through the dark into blossoming. German poet, Johann Wolfgang Von Goethe, was once quoted as saying "Learn to trust yourself and you will know how to live." Trusting ourselves, even in the dark… even when we feel lost, we learn how to live with the grace of nature.

I want to lean even closer
and learn from her
how to delight
in the newness of spring,
to be willing to sprout again,
and to have faith
in the slightest nub of green
protruding from the bark
of my uncertainty.

Writer and poet David Whyte speaks beautifully of the gifts that "lostness" and uncertainty bring into our lives as a necessary precursor to awareness. He gives the example of being lost in the wilderness when suddenly everything comes to life—from tracks on the ground, to the trees and the direction of the sun. He warns us, "Be careful if you have not been lost in your relationship for a while, because you could be asleep." It is true vocationally as well. While in the dark about work, everything can come alive to us—our needs, our desires, our values and our choices. Darkness can be a gift, if we let it be.

Cultivate patience for cycles

May Sarton writes of the need for us to be patient and have faith, even in the midst of transition. She says,

> "It does not astonish or make us angry that it takes a whole year to bring into the house three great white peonies and two pale blue iris. It seems altogether right and appropriate that these glories are earned with long patience and faith… and also that it is altogether right and appropriate that they cannot last. Yet in our human relations we are outraged when the supreme moments, the moments of flowering, must be waited for… and then cannot last. We reach a summit, and then have to go down again."

Modern psychology pushes the idea that we are constantly developing creatures, but I think it is giving us more credit than we perhaps deserve. To some extent I think we are more like other trees or flowers in that we are seasonal beings, perennial in our nature. We have our summers of sunny pleasure, and winters of discontent. We experience springtimes of renewal and autumns of necessary decay.

The way that we experience our flowering this year is not necessarily more developed than it was last year, anymore than the blossoms on the apple tree this year are more beautiful or fragrant than they were last spring. The gifts we have to bring to the world this year need not be bigger, better or more brilliant than what we offered last year or the year before. Perhaps, in fact, we will harvest little fruit in the coming season.

I lean closer and learn
the lesson of the autumn—
how to enter the harvest
with arms wide open.
Generous and grateful—
accepting that not all
of the fruit of my labors
will be noticed and appreciated—
to let the unpicked fruit fall
from the branches,
return to the earth,
full of seed for future trees.

It would be nice if we accepted ourselves as essentially rhythmic and musical rather than forever moving from one stage to another stage, or from one step to another step on an ever-increasing ladder. In some ways I was more resilient and flexible in my youth than I am now. My "development" does not always reflect growth. Sometimes it reflects deeper patterns of stubbornness or rigidity. And sometimes I just return to places and stages in life where I have been before. As the ancients used to say, our emotions are in orbit, like the planets. Patterns that define us return again and again, and in these returns we find our substance and our continuity, our original nature and our identity.

Thomas Moore reinforces this idea when he says in his book, *Original Self:*

> "We might know ourselves better and be closer to our nature by honoring our cycles rather than by running away from them in sentimental philosophies of growth. I don't grow, I am. I don't change, I merely manifest differently the prime material with which I am born. Perhaps if we got off the demanding belt of change and growth, we might relax into the circumambulations of life that turn us over and over, polishing the arcane stone of our most essential selves, revealing more and more of who and what we are."

With similar thinking, Anaïs Nin suggests that embracing our cyclic nature will bring a serenity to our spirits. She writes,

> "We do not grow absolutely, chronologically. We grow sometimes in one dimension, and not in another, unevenly. We grow partially. We are relative. We are mature in one realm, childish in another. The past, the present, and future mingle and pull us backward, forward, or fix us in the present. We are made up of layers, cells, constellations. Once we know this, peace of mind circles us because we are always growing."

How do we accept the necessary cycles that human life requires without judging ourselves in the process? Wouldn't it be nice if we had the similar patience for ourselves that we have for a garden? At the end of the year it lies quiet and dormant. No butterflies are fluttering and no bees are buzzing. Nothing protrudes from the dark, hard earth. When we feel tired and dormant, perhaps even apprehensive about the next period of life, how do we treat ourselves as the master gardener would, knowing that with patience and care, our own fruition will be forthcoming? We are always in the making, like the beloved fruit on the apple tree... or a rose in its bud.

Be as the flower in your blossoming

When my daughter was a little girl, I loved making up bedtime stories that wove in the morals and lessons that I suspected she needed to hear given the particular trials and tribulations of her day. One day she came home from pre-school in tears because some of her friends at school already knew how to tie their shoes and ride a bike and climb quickly to the top of the monkey bars—none of which she could yet do. Her frustration and impatience inspired this bedtime story with which I have chosen to end this chapter's *Reflections*. (By the way, until she was about the age of ten, my daughter, Jessica Rose, went by the name of Rosie.)

Once upon a springtime there lived a mother rose bush who had given bud to at least a dozen daughter roses. One of the youngest roses just happened to grow in great proximity to some of her sisters whose petals were already opening in lovely, fragrant folds while hers remained tightly folded in a bud. How she longed to open and greet the blue sky, to be the playground for the small garden critters who had wings. She longed for the day when Rosie, the little girl who lived in the house, would come out and bury her soft nose right in the heart of her petals. She just knew the child would sway and swoon with the sweetness of her fragrance. She just knew that her own beauty would set the child to dreaming beautiful things about when she would grow up to be a woman and blossom herself. But the little rose could not wait. She pushed and prayed to open her petals; she dug deep down into her stem and tried to muster from her very roots the strength to force her petals open.

The mother bush began to notice that the leaves on her youngest rose had begun to droop a little, and her thorns seemed to be growing extra sharp. Concerned, she asked her baby rose how she was doing. The little rose poured out her heart to the mother bush crying, "I can't stand it. All my sister roses are in blossom and filling the air with their fragrance. They're using up all your color and scent before I get to bloom even a little. My petals don't work." As she pouted her leaves drooped even lower.

The mother bush rustled with a smile (as bushes do when they are tickled) and responded in a soft voice, "My Darling Rose, you are growing just as you should. At each moment of your blossoming, you are as open as you can be. If you were to force your petals open, they would tear and show the strain. They would lose their velvety finish and you would diminish their sweet scent. A rose must learn to be patient and open when the world is ready for her to open, no later, no sooner."

In characteristic impatience, the young rose burst out, "But how does she know when the world is ready for her, Mama? How does she know when it is too late or too soon? I want to blossom perfectly!"

"You must trust the timing of your own petals, my dear. Just as the humans must trust their heart and follow their feet, roses must trust their nature and follow their petals. Have no concern about being perfect, care only about offering your own beauty to the world. Let your own beauty and your own brilliance carry you."

The young rose did not know how she would muster the patience to do as the mother bush suggested. That night she watched the stars, twinkling so confidently in their courses. She listened to the wind as it rustled the leaves in the tree above her—it sounded like music and it put her to sleep.

Awakening with the first light of the sun, the young rose heard a long sigh from one of her sisters as the older rose watched the first of her petals break lose from the stem and fall gracefully to the ground. All the roses held their breath for a moment, in silent ceremony. For this too, they knew, is part of being a rose.

Suddenly the youngest rose was not overly anxious to blossom. She was happy to be a bud, happy to let her petals open when they were ready. Happy to let her beauty carry her into the world. The blue sky would have to wait, as would the winged creatures. Even the child, Rosie, would have to wait for her to open, just as the child would have to wait for her own blossoming—to tie her shoes, to ride a bike, to climb the monkey bars…

I have watched my daughter blossom into a beautiful young woman. But even now she is impatient to know and do and be that which is before her time. She is not unlike her mother, and I suspect that her mother is not unlike those who are reading this book. We are impatient. We want to blossom already. If only we could live with the wisdom of the flowers, letting our own beauty and brilliance stem from patience, from trusting our own petals to open in their own sweet time.

Life continually requires us to practice the trust that comes with a faith in our own readiness. How do we know when it is time to go or to leave? When do we know when we have enough of grief and when it is time to move on? How do we know when we are prepared to jump into our lives with both feet, risking what we have not risked before? These are questions of readiness, and like the rose bush, we must trust our greater nature to give us the nudge of readiness, be it in the form of newly found exhilaration, unbearable boredom or the faintest whisper of hope on the wind. When we find ourselves struggling over and over with some aspect of our lives, perhaps we are working against the grain, and what we need is patience, not greater effort. Maybe what we need to do with our impatience and frustration is what I found myself inspired to do last autumn—to fall under the spell of an earth creature who has so much to teach…

I am in love with an apple tree.
She is a miracle to me.
I am in awe of her cycle:
from bareness to blossoms,
to bright green branches heavily
laden with sweet, red, round fruit.

I just want to sit under her all day,
to lean against her trunk
and learn from her
how to trust my own nature.

It's amazing how, when we are postured to listen, nature speaks back.

Passages

"The seed that is to grow
must lose itself as seed;
and they that creep
may graduate through
chrysalis to wings.
Wilt thou then, O mortal,
cling to husks which
falsely seem to you the self?"

Wu Ming Fu

"Everything is gestation, then bringing forth."

Rainer Marie Rilke

"Wherever there is chaos, there is wonderful thinking. Chaos is a gift."

Septima Clark

"I want to learn from the fish how to surface and dive, from the flower how to open and accept, from the stone how to crack and let light in, and from the birds that wings are more useful at times than brains."

Mark Nepo

"A change in the weather is enough to renew the world and ourselves."

Marcel Proust

"Transformation, innovation, evolution—these are the natural response to crisis. Our pathology is our opportunity. Armed with a more sophisticated understanding of how change occurs, we know that the very forces that have brought us to planetary brinkmanship carry in them the seeds of renewal."

Marilyn Ferguson

Charles C. West

"We turn to God for help when our foundations are shaking, only to learn that it is God who is shaking them."

"Sad soul, take comfort, not forgetting that sunrise never failed us yet."

Celia Layton Thaxter

"The grand show is eternal.
It is always sunrise somewhere;
the dew is never all dried up at once;
a shower is forever falling; vapor is ever rising.
Eternal sunrise, eternal dawn and gloaming,
on sea and continents and islands,
each in its turn, as the round earth rolls."

John Muir

"Empires rise and fall like the abdomen of God. It's just the universe breathing."

Wes Scoop Nisker

Henry David Thoreau

"Change, individuation, metamorphosis, all of these point to growth itself (not the grown thing) as the great underlying reality in nature."

"Life is a slow process of becoming, a combination of states we have to go through. Where people fail is that they wish to elect a state and remain in it, this is a kind of death."

Anaïs Nin

"There is always new life trying to emerge in each of us. Too often we ignore the signs of resurrection and cling to parts of life that have died for us."

Joan Chittister

"To live is to be marked. To live is to change, to acquire the words of a story, and that is the only celebration we mortals really know."

Barbara Kingsolver

Anatole France

"All changes, even the most longed for, have their melancholy; for what we leave behind is a part of ourselves; we must die to one life before we can enter into another."

"Change is the elixir of the human circumstance, and acceptance of challenge is the way of our kind. We are bad-weathered animals, disaster's fairest children. For the soundest of evolutionary reasons man appears at his best when times are worst."

Robert Ardrey

Ray Kroc

"When you're green, you're growing; when you're ripe, you rot."

"All birth is unwilling."

Pearl S. Buck

Pierre Teilhard de Chardin

"All progress is inevitably accompanied
by strife and shock...
Evolution never happens
without work and suffering.
It is not enough to let oneself
be borne passively along by it;
man must collaborate in the event."

"I have crossed over the backs of Sojourner Truth, Harriet Tubman, Fannie Lou Hamer and Madam C. J. Walker. Because of them I can now live the dream. I am the seed of the free and I know it. I intend to bear great fruit."

Oprah Winfrey

"Keep on sowing your seed, for you never know which will grow; perhaps it all will."

Ecclesiastes 11:6

Ursula LeGuin

"The only thing that makes life possible is permanent, intolerable uncertainty: not knowing what comes next."

Rabindranath Tagore

"When old words die out on the tongue,
new melodies break forth from the heart;
and where the old tracks are lost,
new country is revealed with its wonders."

To Ponder and To Practice

- The apple tree must let go of its old fruit and leaves each autumn in order to prepare for its blossoming in spring. Identify one aspect of your way of being in the world that has outlived its usefulness—a way of thinking or feeling, of speaking or relating. Be willing to let go of this aspect of your being and create a ritual that marks the event.
- Think about some of the most difficult transitions you've experienced in life. What helped you survive those times? When did you know you were on the other side?
- Make a list of the various transitions that you are experiencing at this time in your life. Add to that list transitions that you expect to be faced with in years to come. Refer to this list when responding to the questions below.
- During times of transition, it is helpful to focus time and energy in areas where we have control. In other words, resign as "General Manager of the Universe" and take the job of managing your own time and energy more seriously.
- Like the apple tree experiences a predictable cycle for its growth and fruition, this is often true of human transitions as well, such as the cycles of grief identified by Elizabeth Kubler-Ross. Consider what stage of transition you are in now. Are you towards the beginning, the middle or the end?
- Take comfort in knowing that just about any change or transition that we can possibly go through has been experienced by many before us. Reach out to people who may have been through what you are experiencing, and allow them the privilege of sharing what they learned.
- Have you ever known the person who is newly married or the new retiree who is having difficulty adjusting to their circumstances because it wasn't as they expected? The source of their discontent may have more to do with their expectations than the actual situation they are in. It could be their pictures that need changing, not their circumstances. Take stock of how your expectations may be helping or hindering you in your current transition.
- Taking the advice of William Bridges, an expert in managing transition, discern what you can do with your losses which accompany the transition you are going through. Begin by drafting a list of your losses. Using the four steps outlined in his book, *JobShift,* consider which of these losses are those that you can retain (you don't have to lose your old friends); those that you can replace (like your income if it has been dropped); those that you can rebuild (like a sense of your vocational security); and those that you can relinquish (like the idea that your employer would be as loyal to you as you were to them).
- While in the grips of uncertainty, it is easy to lose sight of how far you have already gone along the road of transition. Draft a list of all the steps you are proud to already have taken in your current situation and find a way to celebrate the distance you have come.

Practice

- In what area of your life right now are you like the rose who wants to push its blossoming? What can you do to reorient yourself towards "readiness" and cultivate patience in this area of your life?
- If it is true that "To everything there is a season and a time for every purpose under Heaven," consider how this particular point in time is a rite of passage for you with its own timely purpose. What is it too late for? What is it too soon for? What do you feel ripe for?
- What is the harvest of your current season of life? Is it achievement, confidence, perspective, wisdom, serenity? How are you challenged to grow or awaken in this season of your life?
- Select a quote on transition from this chapter's *Passages* and post it where you will read it often until it is internalized.
- Choose a daily habit, routine, or symbol to remind you to keep faith, hope, and patience during transition and to trust your nature as your life carries you from season to season. (e.g., Plant a tree in your garden or a potted plant in your home and measure its growth along with your own.)
- Given everything you have read in this chapter, what do you want to *keep* doing? What do you want to *stop* doing? What do you want to *start* doing?

Notes

Meadowlarks

Chapter

Renewing the Joy of Giving

Sing for the joy of singing

Sing for the joy of singing

Allow "added value" to spring from the heart

Allow "added value" to spring from the heart

Make a habit of generosity

Make a habit of generosity

Practice "royal giving"

Practice "royal giving"

Consider the spirit of the gift

Consider the spirit of the gift

Be someone's Sister Ann Marita

Be someone's Sister Ann Marita

Meadowlarks

If I go the extra mile and burn the midnight oil,
who will count the time, the hours that I toil?
If as a gardener I sow seeds for which I am not paid,
who will stop and notice the difference one small flower's made?
If as a nurse I tend to the needs of a mother at her child's bed,
who will track that kind of mileage on the daily road I tread?

The asking of these questions does injustice to the gift,
it takes away from the purpose, from the heart that it may lift.
For why does the meadowlark sing, but for the joy of its own song?
Why does the sun keep setting in colored ribbons long?
Every creature has a gift, for the joy of its own soul,
the expression of it natural, for which there is no toll.

The world may notice, or it may not, the gifts that we may give,
but the true gift is to ourselves and the way in which we live.
So fold the napkin with panache! Paint the walls with strokes of cheer!
Park the car so carefully! Find a nickel in the small boy's ear!
Add a note of thanks to the invoice—bow to the folks in line,
every gesture matters, no kindness is benign!

Let us be as meadowlarks, thrilled to have a voice,
let us use our daily work as the meadow of our choice!
But do it first, for yourself, without the need for glory,
for the only joy for which the soul has time, is the truth of your own story!

Reflections

Most of us grew up hearing, "Get a good job." And we assumed that "good" jobs lasted. We heard, "Give the job your best." And we assumed that promotions and entrée to a logical career path would follow. We heard, "Be loyal." And we assumed that the loyalty of the employer would be returned. We heard it, lots of us did it, and then we woke up from the proverbial American dream.

And just as we were rubbing the sleep from our eyes we began to hear the new party line: "The only job security in the 21st century work world is to be more valuable tomorrow than you are today." "Be responsible for your own continuous learning." "Develop entire skill sets, not job competencies." "In today's market, everyone is self-employed." "Go that extra mile, where there is no traffic."

We hear this advice—and we even believe it. But something is missing that we had as children. Is it faith? Is it hope? I think it might be spirit. To some extent, we are dispirited.

The new party line, with its utilitarian undertone, rings hollow to that part of us that knows that life is sacred and that time is our most precious resource. We want to be inspired again. We want a chance at one of life's powerful experiences, to make something whole from the pieces of our lives. Sigmund Freud taught that work can serve more of our basic human needs than any other activity we engage in throughout our lives. Unfortunately, many of us have forgotten the basic human yearning for meaningful labor.

Sing for the joy of singing

See if you can relate to the man in this classic story.

There was once man who died and found himself in a beautiful place. He was surrounded by every conceivable comfort. A white-jacketed man came to him and said, "You may have anything you choose—any food—any pleasure—any kind of entertainment. Relax. Enjoy. Everything is free!"

The man was delighted, and for days he partied hard, he feasted, he sampled every delicacy and dove headlong into experiences he had only dreamed of on earth. But one day he grew bored with all of it. He went to the attendant and said, "This is a great place. I've really enjoyed myself. I'm ready now to pitch in. I need something to do. What kind of work can you give me?"

The attendant sadly shook his head and replied, "I'm sorry sir. That's the one thing we can't do for you. There is no work here for humans. You are not allowed to give here, you can only receive."

The man was flabbergasted. He responded, "That's a fine thing. You are telling me I cannot participate in anything, I can't build anything, I can't plan anything, I can't improve or create anything? I might as well be in hell!"

The attendant said softly, "And just where, Sir, do you think you are?"

For why does the meadowlark sing,
but for the joy of its own song?
Why does the sun
keep setting in colored ribbons long?

Every creature has a gift,
for the joy of its own soul,
the expression of it natural,
for which there is no toll.

That includes us. The man was in heaven, as long it was a holiday. But we were not engineered for a permanent holiday. Every gift we have to give and every talent we have to share will eventually surface in us as a need. The problem-solver needs problems to solve; the writer cannot keep from writing, and as the carpenter must breathe, she must build. Poet Marge Piercy expresses this beautifully in this stanza from her poem, "Broken Vessels":

> *Greek amphoras and Hopi vases*
> *are put in museums,*
> *but you know*
> *they were made to be used!*
> *The water pitcher cries for water to carry!*
> *Why would we think*
> *the human being cries any less*
> *for work that is real?*

The analogy of the unlit lamp is a good one. Its function is to shed light—it is still a lamp when unlit—but when it's lit, it lives its true life. When we employ our skills and embrace our capabilities we are living our true lives. As Kahlil Gibran reminds us in his beautiful book, *The Prophet,* about giving and receiving,

> "I would give, but only to the deserving.
> The trees in your orchard say not so,
> nor the flocks in your pastures.
> They give that they may live,
> for to withhold is to perish."

A question that deserves our consideration is, "What are the gifts with which we have been bestowed, that to withhold, would cause us to perish?" Can you imagine if Robin Williams was forced to withhold his humor, if Tiger Williams was never to golf again, or Sarah McLaughlin was asked to give up singing? It's not that they would not have wonderful lives, but they would not have full lives in the truest sense of the word. In the same way that we cannot take flight from the bird without adversely affecting it's birdhood, to withhold our natural gifts, and not share them, would adversely affect our humanity.

Our employment is not always the vessel containing our finest gifts. We must resist the temptation to mistake our skills and competencies with our truest gifts. I am blessed with the ability to articulate and express my thoughts and ideas in front of a large group. I have been told that I am a natural public speaker. But that is not my true gift. The true gift that I have to offer my audiences is my joy, my enthusiasm and the power of my belief in the ideas I express. The skills and competencies we use to express those gifts are important, but it's the spirit with which we employ them that carries the real treasure. And the best part is that the gift that is shared always returns to its source—the giver. As Kahlil Gibran put it, "The scent always remains on the hand that gives the rose."

Allow "added value" to spring from the heart

It is a popular business maxim, that the only job security to be found in today's market is to be more talented and valuable tomorrow than you are today. If that is true, from where will all that "added value" flow? Probably from the places within us that rush like a river anyway… be it through our ability to listen, our technical savvy, our customer relations skills or our attention to detail. Whatever our individual songs may be, when we sing them generously and wholeheartedly, watch what happens—"added value" beyond our wildest imagining.

The kind of giving I am talking about isn't the kind that is done with intent of getting back. The tree grows with no one's consent and no one's applause. The flower doesn't dream of the bee. It blossoms and the bee comes. The primary reward of practicing generosity and giving 100% even when we know 80% will do, is the joy we feel in the giving.

In one of my earlier publications, *30 Ways to Shine as a New Employee,* I suggest myriad ways of going the extra mile on the job. The intent behind these suggestions is not primarily to help new employees to impress people nor to stand out from the crowd. The intent is to help new employees discover ways of adding their own signature to the job, to bring spirit and joy to what they do, and in so doing, to inhabit the position with renewed pride and individuality. Some examples include:

- Volunteering to do something that falls between the cracks (like taking notes in the meeting and e-mailing them to everyone who was present);
- Bringing hobbies, interests, or specials gifts to the table in a way that adds to the capacities of the organization (like the person who is fluent in sign language and offers to teach her co-workers twelve basic signs so that anyone in that place of business can greet a customer who is deaf); or
- Looking for creative ways to save money, make money or expand the services offered by the organization (like the assistant manager at a hardware store who suggests that he extend delivery services to prime customers, or the office assistant at a medical clinic who has a gift with children and offers to set up a play area for the patients' little ones).

The following quote which opens the chapter in *30 Ways to Shine* in which these suggestions are offered is one of my all time favorites by Martin Luther King, Jr.:

> "If a man is called to be a street sweeper,
> let him sweep the streets
> as Beethoven composed music
> or Michelangelo painted,
> so that all the host of heaven and earth
> pause to say,
> there is a street sweeper who did his job well."

Our gifts are blessings, but until they are given, they are not gifts. If we are open, our gifts will choose us as much as we choose them. But the question often arises, what if, unlike the street sweeper, we have not heard the call? How do we recognize our true gifts? To begin, we must listen and learn from our every experience of true joy and true purpose—those moments when we feel most in our element, when we are showing our truest colors. Perhaps if we were able to quiet ourselves from the clamor and pressure of the culture, we could better hear the intimate whisperings of what we are to do. That voice will tell us whether we are to organize a book club, start a garden project, write letters to the governor, read to ailing elders, or plant a fig tree. We must listen for the voice of our gifts so that they might be given.

Make a habit of generosity

I will never forget a wonderful story that I heard years ago in a Sunday service at a Unity Temple which speaks to the gift of generosity. It went something like this:

There once lived a woman who was envied by many for the beautiful and valuable jewels that she had been bequeathed from her late father. Many came to look at, hold and admire them. She treasured her jewels not so much for their value, but for their beauty and the fact that they were a gift from her father whom she had dearly loved.

One day a stranger came through town. He was the kind of fellow who was always on the make, always looking for the next innocent who would be an easy mark. He heard about the woman and her beautiful jewels and decided that she would be his next victim.

He knocked on her door and asked to see the jewels. She invited him in and happily displayed them on a table. She watched as he slipped one jewel into his jacket pocket while commenting to her about another that glimmered in his hand. She looked at the man and said, "I would like you to have the jewel that you slipped into your coat pocket. May it bring you the joy that it has brought me." The man was shocked, a bit embarrassed, but accepted the woman's gift and left.

The next day he approached her door and said, "If you would so easily part with one jewel, why not give me the rest? You have a nice house and plenty to eat and I have nothing." The woman paused and thought about the man's words and his weighty request. She looked at him with resolve and responded, "Yes, you may have the rest of my jewels." She quickly fetched the velvet pouch in which she kept them and placed it in the man's hands. Again, she wished him well, hoping that the jewels would bring him joy and prosperity. As she closed the door her very heart sparkled like a jewel.

Weeks later the same man appeared at her door, looking as if he had not slept a wink since they parted. He looked at the woman longingly and pleaded with her, "What I really want from you, dear woman, is not your jewels. What I want is that quality in you that allowed you to give these jewels to me." He retrieved the velvet pouch from his pocket, set it on the woman's table, and departed.

I suspect that the man's recognition of the woman's generous spirit was the beginning of his realizing his own riches. It is so amazingly and wondrously true that the greatest gift of giving comes to the one who has made the offering. Cultivating the habit of generosity is a powerful way to give deeply to our own lives.

We often think of generosity as a feeling, but I think it is also a choice. The more we make the choice, the more we experience the feeling. When we make the choice often enough, it becomes a habit. There is a saying that some habits are worth being fanatical about. I think generosity would count as one of those habits.

It is a wonderful, mystical law of nature that the things we crave most in life—happiness, freedom and peace of mind—are attained by giving them to someone else. What we often want from other people we will receive by giving it first. When you long for love and attention, offering yours to someone else is a great first step. When you want the customer to be open-minded and responsive to the product, begin by being open-minded and responsive to their needs, wants, and concerns. Strangely, it is when we feel the neediest that we will benefit the most from giving to another.

One of my favorite exercises from a curriculum I published years ago is called "Food from the Soul" which suggests various ways of keeping up one's spirits in the midst of a job search. One of those suggestions is to reach out to other people; to find ways of making yourself useful or necessary to others who are in need. I truly believe that when we find ourselves downhearted and out of sorts, it is possible that we are too self-absorbed and need to change our focus from getting to giving. Giving blood at the Red Cross, volunteering at a soup kitchen or preparing a meal with love for the family could be just what the doctor ordered! Here are some other ideas taken from that list:

- Make a homeless person a bag lunch.
- Give someone who is laid up in bed a foot rub or a back rub.
- Read to children in a hospital.
- Campaign for a cause you care about.
- Offer to shovel the walk or rake the leaves of an elderly person in your neighborhood.
- Organize a donation for a woman's shelter.
- Take part in the nearest Habitat for Humanity.
- Become a hospice volunteer.
- Find a way to make each person in your home feel appreciated.

What we find by taking part in such efforts is that service is not only an expression of awakening, but also a means to awakening. The Nobel Prize-winning, Indian poet Rabindranath Tagore summarized the practice in two lines:

> "I awoke and saw that life was service.
> I acted and, behold, service was joy."

Another Nobel Prize winner, Albert Schweitzer, who devoted his life to treating the poor and sick of Africa, agreed and warned:

> "The only ones among you who will be truly happy
> are those who have sought and found how to serve."

We are not necessarily called to do world-shaking deeds, but we are called to do what we can with as much wisdom, awareness and love as we can. Listen to the advice extolled in these beautiful and poignant words of the Christian mystic, St. Teresa of Avila, in her poem as quoted by Andrew Harvey in his book, *Teachings of the Christian Mystics:*

> *Christ has no body now on earth but yours,*
> *No hands but yours, no feet but yours,*
> *no eyes but yours.*
> *Yours are the feet*
> *with which he is to go about doing good;*
> *Yours are the hands*
> *with which he is to bless men now.*

Practice "royal giving"

In his remarkable book, *A Path with Heart,* Jack Kornfield talks about three kinds of generosity: *tentative giving* in which we are hesitant to give lest we lose out, but then we find it feels good; *brotherly or sisterly giving* in which we share in what we have, experiencing the joy in doing so; and, *royal giving* in which we simply delight in the welfare and happiness of all beings, and give the best of what we have. We never consider scarcity and our hearts are abundant like queens and kings. I believe that each of us has generous impulses and a great capacity for royal giving; we just need to follow through on those impulses. The first step is to recognize that we have gifts to give and to believe that what we have to offer, even as solitary individuals, matters.

A profound example of the power of one person to make a difference is encapsulated in the story of Buckminster Fuller. As a young man he fell to the lowest point of his life. Tormented by doubts and depression, he stood on a bridge and agonized about whether or not to throw himself to his death. He knew that if he killed himself, his pain would end. But he asked himself what would happen if he lived. He wondered what would make life worth living and what could give his life sufficient meaning and value to be worth facing his difficulties and despair. As he tells it, in a flash, the answer came to him. He would devote his life to the challenge of finding out just how much good one person can do.

Some sixty years later, Buckminster Fuller, known to the world as Bucky, died of natural causes. During those six decades he had patented over two thousand inventions, written twenty-five books, and achieved an international reputation as one of the century's greatest inventors, designers and thinkers. Through the practice of royal giving I believe that Buckminster Fuller discovered that his one solitary life was worth living, and that indeed, there is a lot of good that one person can do.

In the true spirit of "royal giving," Emily Dickinson writes:

If I can stop one Heart from breaking
I shall not live in vain.
If I can ease one Life the Aching
Or cool one Pain
Or help one fainting Robin
Unto his Nest again
I shall not live in Vain.

Consider the spirit of the gift

Living in a very competitive culture, I think we hold back our gifts and talents until we deem them good enough, big enough or significant enough to somehow count. But to count for what? Everything we have to offer the world and to each other matters. We do not have to wait until our gifts are potent and comprehensive enough to solve all the world's problems. As Wayne Muller writes in his beautiful book *How Then Shall We Live?*:

> "Every gift is a drop of water on a stone; every kindness, every flash of color or melody helps us remain hopeful and in balance. Each of us knows some part of the secret, and each of us holds our small portion of the world's light... We each have something to offer. If we compare our gift with those who served in the concentration camps or those working with lepers, our gift may seem quite small and insignificant. But however large or small, dramatic or simple, if we ignore or suppress our offering, something deep and vital within us will wither and die."

It is imperative that we acknowledge and honor what we have to offer in the various contexts of our lives. How many times have I put off being in touch with a long distance friend or relative because I could not find the time to write the long and detailed letter I intended while a quick note would have sufficed? How long did I put off meeting my elderly neighbor, fearing that I could not be to her what I had been to my previous neighbor, when all the while a quick visit and a bouquet of daisies would have thrilled her to the bone? Why am I afraid to drop a quarter in the can of the Salvation Army solicitor when I do not have a dollar? We must be aware of the extent to which we simply fail to give because we deem the gift too small.

I recently experienced a profound example of "royal giving" which brought home to me the importance of not judging the size of the gift, but the spirit of the giving. It was on a Sunday when I was being trained to be an usher at the church that I attend. I had arrived early and found only one other person in the church parking lot. He was a homeless man who regularly attends services. He approached me at my car, asking for spare change. I was a bit taken aback at first and then, finding myself in the shadow of a holy temple, reached into my purse to retrieve some coins. I fumbled nervously into my wallet only to find that the only money I had was a five dollar bill. I handed it to the man and when he saw that it was a five dollar bill, he lit up. He smiled widely and extended his arms in gratitude, wanting to embrace. With a quick glance I took in the disheveled beard, the matted and oily hair, the toothless grin, and the soiled clothing. As I returned the embrace I found myself holding my breath, avoiding the offensive smell that would surely emanate from this man. We parted without a word and I hurried into the church.

A little while later as I stood at the door welcoming people, I noticed the homeless man enter among the flow of the congregation and take a seat in a row by himself near the back of the church. Later in the service we came to the time of offerings. One of the functions of the usher is to pass the velvet pouch for donations from the congregation. Before heading down the rows, I looked into my purse and realized that I had given my only bill to the homeless man. Looking over at him in his torn and soiled jacket, I felt glad in my heart that I had given it to him.

As I proceeded to pass the pouch from row to row, starting at the front of the church, I grew apprehensive as I drew closer to the homeless man, knowing that he would have little or nothing to give, but not wanting to offend him by passing him by. Finally, as I got closer to his row I just threw him a glance with the question in my eyes. He nodded and put out his hand to take the pouch. I watched his hands fumble through the lining of his torn jacket pocket. He appeared unsuccessful in his search when suddenly his eyes sparkled and he smiled a wide, toothless grin. Out of his pocket emerged the five dollar bill. He crinkled the bill into a ball and placed it into the pouch. He never looked directly at me nor took in the fact that I was the person who had given them the five dollars.

I couldn't believe it. This man had been begging in the parking lot for money with which to make an offering at church. Dispossessed of worldly goods and resources, he gave what little he had—the small fortune he had come into only half an hour before.

At the end of the service I saw the homeless man standing alone as the other congregants gathered their things, chatted with one another and hugged. I found myself drawn to him like a magnet and grabbed him in an emotional embrace. I am fairly certain that he had no idea why this person who had embraced him so tenuously in the parking lot was so eager to hug him now. It wasn't until I was driving home that I realized that in that embrace, it hadn't even occurred to me to hold my breath.

What is the value of a five dollar bill? It seemed a generous amount at the time I gave it away… but I had given it in the spirit of embarrassment and discomfort. But it was all the money in the world to the man who gave it in the spirit of generosity and joy. The worth of the bill had not changed, but the value of the gift had just increased a hundred fold.

It is impossible that we have nothing to give, regardless of the context or circumstance in which we find ourselves. Perhaps we are unsure of our gifts, or are afraid to share them, but we are never without them. Or perhaps we are waiting for the right opportunity. Anthony de Mello speaks to this in his book, *More One Minute Nonsense*. He writes:

> A young man eagerly described what he dreamed of doing for the poor.
>
> Said the Master, "When do you propose to make your dream come true?"
>
> "As soon as the opportunity arrives."
>
> "Opportunity never arrives." said the Master, "It is here."

Be someone's Sister Ann Marita

There is no doubt that when we work with a generosity of spirit, we make a difference in peoples' lives in ways which we cannot even imagine. I know, because I was lucky enough to enjoy the gifts of one such person, a very special teacher, Sister Ann Marita.

I loved her to my core. She was beautiful and good and kind. I remember thinking of her as the Virgin Mary incarnate. She was as pretty as Sally Field in the "Singing Nun" and as gifted and spirited as young Maria in "The Sound of Music." (Both shows were big hits while Sister Ann Marita was my teacher, thus my strong associations between her and those characters.)

I do not have many memories of her, but those that I have are vividly clear. One was her showing me the various shapes of snowflakes against her black habit on the playground. Another memory is putting my arms around her as she wept after John Kennedy was shot. The third and most important memory was when I was standing on the pea green steps on the last day of school of first grade, and Sister Ann Marita looked at me, and in front of the whole class said, "And there's Denise, who at the beginning of the year couldn't figure out the difference between letters with the squiggles at the bottom (f, g, j, q, y,) and now reads and writes with a perfect alphabet!" I was so proud, I swear I burst those ugly gold buttons right off my uniform!

It may seem odd, but I cherished that handful of memories over the years as if they were as significant to my upbringing as any other. A couple of years into my relationship with my mate, Rob (and ten times through my accounting of the same three memories of Sister Ann Marita), he asked me whether or not I had ever tried to contact her, to tell her what she had meant to me. I explained that she had left Kankakee, where I grew up, the summer after first grade. I was crushed. I inquired at the rectory as to how I could be in touch with her but was told that Sister Ann Marita had other children to teach in a new place and that there was no forwarding address.

Well, Rob, being both inquisitive and persistent, decided that anyone who had been a nun could not be that hard to find. He wrote to the school I attended and they sent his letter to the Mother House of the Sisters of Loretta in Denver, Colorado. They later forwarded his letter to her directly. He found Sister Ann Marita!

Rob was thrilled to have found her but began to worry that perhaps she would not remember me. After all, this was thirty years after her one short year with me, and I was one of forty students in the class! She called him at his home (in Canada) and inquired as to who this friend was who was searching for her. He told her, and with the mention of the name "Bissonnette" she paused briefly and then responded, "Let's see, there was Andy, and Mary, Tommy and Eddie, then Denise. Then there was another one, a younger one, but I never got to teach her." Imagine... after 30 years, she remembered the names and the sibling line-up of my entire family! My instincts as a child were right on... this was someone very special.

Mary Ann (a.k.a. Sister Ann Marita) had left the convent and married Dave Van Etten, an ex-Jesuit priest, whom she met on the streets of San Francisco in the late sixties. (As we came to find out, we had lived about fifteen miles from each other for over a decade.) When we reconnected by phone I asked her if she had any children. Her enthusiastic reply was, "Yep, about two hundred of them!" You see, she continued to lavish her gifts and her generous heart in the Head Start day care program that she and her husband have run in their home for the past many years. On my first visit to their home I walked in to see a bulletin board that covered an entire wall of the kitchen, every inch of it covered with the photographs, new and old, of the 200 children they have cared for over the years. Among the garden of faces on the kitchen wall, are the faces of the two beautiful Van Etten children, one of them about twenty-one years of age, the spitting image of Sister Ann Marita thirty years ago.

It was exciting for Mary Ann to learn that she had touched one of her students in such a profound way. There is no way she knew at the time how her caring and loving ways were helping to mold the heart of a six year old. For me, it is simply thrilling that a photograph of me and my daughter are now among the collage of faces on her kitchen wall. And not only did I learn to use all those letters with the squiggles at the bottom, but I make my living with them.

The world may notice, or it may not,
the gifts we have to give,
but the true gift is to ourselves
and the way in which we live.

Perhaps many of the gifts we have to give are like seeds, not necessarily impressive when we offer them, but potent with power in what they will become. And through the sharing of what we have to offer, we are changed in the process, we flower. The miracle is not just the gift; the miracle is in the offering. The wonder of it, of course, is that we never know whose Sister Ann Marita we may be!

Passages

Rumi

"You say that you can't create something original? Don't worry about it. Make a cup of clay so your brother can drink."

"The more you have,
the more you are occupied,
the less you give.
But the less you have,
the more free you are."

Mother Teresa

"We receive the light, then we impart it.
Thus we repair the world."

Kabbalah

"Do all the good you can,
By all the means you can,
In all the ways you can,
In all the places you can,
At all the times you can,
To all the people you can,
As long as ever you can."

John Wesley

"Twenty years from now you will be more disappointed by the things you did not do than those you did do. So throw off the bowlines. Sail away from the safe harbor. Catch the trade winds in your sails. Explore. Dream. Discover. Give yourself away to the sea of life."

Mark Twain

Ralph Waldo Emerson

"The only gift is a portion of yourself.
The poet brings a poem;
the shepherd his lamb…
the girl a handkerchief of her own sewing."

"Let me light the lamp," says the star, "and never debate if it will help to remove the darkness."

Rabindranath Tagore

"The world needs all of our power and love and energy and each of us has something to give. The trick is to find it and use it, to find it and give it away, so there will always be more. We can be lights for each other, and through each other's illuminations we will see the way. Each of us is a seed, a silent promise, and it is always spring."

Merle Shain

Vincent Van Gogh

"I have walked this earth for thirty years and, out of gratitude, want to leave some souvenir."

Charles Dickens

"No one is useless who lightens the burden of another."

"Any man who strives to do his best—
Whether his work be great or small—
Is considered to be doing
The work of a lion."

Buddhist teaching

"To laugh often and much;
to win the respect of intelligent people
and the affection of children;
to earn the appreciation of honest criticism
and endure the betrayal of false friends;
to appreciate beauty and find the best in others;
to leave the world a bit better whether by a
healthy child, a garden patch, a redeemed social
condition; to know even one life has breathed
easier because you have lived—
this is to have succeeded."

Ralph Waldo Emerson

Boris Pasternak

"It isn't the earthquake that controls the advent of a different life, but storms of generosity."

André Gide

"Complete possession is proved only by giving. All you are unable to give possesses you."

"Life engenders life.
Energy engenders energy.
It is by only spending oneself
That one becomes rich."

Sarah Bernhardt

"Everybody can be great because anybody can serve. You don't have to have a college degree to serve. You don't have to make your subject and verb agree to serve. You don't have to know about Plato and Aristotle… (or) Einstein's Theory of Relativity… (or) the Second Theory of Thermodynamics to serve. You only need a heart full of grace. A soul generated by love."

Martin Luther King, Jr.

"Make yourself necessary to someone."

Ralph Waldo Emerson

"The fragrance always remains in the hand that gives the rose."

Kahlil Gibran

"I have spent my days stringing and unstringing my instrument, while the song I came to sing remains unsung to this day."

Rabindranath Tagore

"It is one of the most beautiful compensations of this life that no man can sincerely try to help another without helping himself."

Ralph Waldo Emerson

To Ponder and To Practice

- Who is one of the most generous, giving people you have ever known? How would you like your life to more closely reflect that person's life?
- What was one of your most joyous experiences of giving to someone or something?
- What was one of the most memorable gifts you have ever received?
- Draft a list of those people in your life who have given to you in the most profound ways.
- Like the brilliant and prolific artist Vincent Van Gogh once said, "I have walked this earth for thirty years and, out of gratitude, want to leave some souvenir," what souvenir would you like to leave this earth? What small steps could you take towards the fashioning of that gift?
- In what small ways can you give a little more of yourself at work or at home, whether it be a thoughtful act, a helpful idea, a word of appreciation, a lift over a rough spot, a sense of understanding, or a timely suggestion? Devise and follow through on a plan to share these small gifts.
- Ralph Waldo Emerson made a jewel of a suggestion, "Make yourself necessary to someone." Offer to do something for someone in your life who cannot ask for what they need. Enjoy the privilege and blessing of having made yourself necessary to another person.
- What preciousness do you find yourself holding back from the world, at work or outside work? How can you enjoy the fruit of that gift by giving it away?
- What is one way you could go the extra mile at work or in your community which would put to work one of your natural gifts or inclinations?
- One way to begin practicing generosity, even in the smallest of ways, is to do good works quietly, without drawing any attention to the giving. "So whenever you give alms," urged Jesus, "do not sound a trumpet before you, as the hypocrites do." Bestow one act of generosity upon another and do it in secret!
- Some people are a lot better at giving than they are at receiving, but we need to be able to do both, equally. Think about what you allow yourself to receive. What do people offer you that you have a hard time receiving? Make a point of being on the receiving end of someone else's generosity this week.
- We do not have to look far to witness royal giving—the world is full of unsung heroes. You probably know some of them yourself: the people who quietly work extra hours at schools or hospitals, visit the sick, serve meals to the homeless, or staff volunteer organizations. Make a point of noticing and acknowledging your community's or organization's unsung heroes!

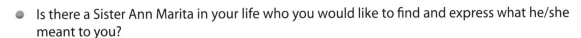

Practice

- Is there a Sister Ann Marita in your life who you would like to find and express what he/she meant to you?
- Choose a favorite quote from this chapter's *Passages* that can be a helpful reminder of the importance of generosity in your life.
- Choose a daily habit, routine or symbol to remind you of your desire to practice "royal giving" (e.g. a tree giving shade, birds freely sharing their song or the ocean continually giving itself in waves upon the shore).
- Choose another daily habit, routine or symbol which will help you increase your ability to receive (e.g., watching the earth receive the rain, a nursing baby at its mother's breast, or awakening with the awareness of receiving yet another day of precious life).
- Given everything you have read in this chapter, what do you want to *keep* doing? What do you want to *stop* doing? What do you want to *start* doing?

Notes

Chapter 12

The Puppeteer

Pulling Your Own Strings

Claim your power

Claim your power

Choose to respond rather than react

Choose to respond rather than react

Live the prayer of St. Francis

Live the prayer of St. Francis

Sweep your own front steps

Sweep your own front steps

Embrace the world before working to change it

Embrace the world before working to change it

Be a believer in seeds

Be a believer in seeds

The Puppeteer: An Ode to Work

How can anything be such a curse and a blessing?
Ah, Work, you are a two-sided coin, a double-edged sword.
How can I love and hate you so much in exactly the same breath?

Half the time I think of you as a prison.
The walls of my particular cell are covered
with mortgage payments, electric bills, insurance premiums.
The only view from my cell is the hopeful vision
of my daughter some day graduating from college.
Ah, but I dream of my escape!
The only thing I would leave behind
are the tracks of my happy-go-lucky feet
in the dust of your prison yard.
Sometimes, I would be willing to risk everything,
including my own security, to jump your high fence.

And yet, you are an altar
upon which I can give a little, just a little,
to a world that daily opens its wide arms saying,
"Here, take me! I was made, in part, just for you!"

Well, forgive me if I am not thinking about altars on Monday morning.
Don't you think I would like to greet Mondays
with as much gusto as I do Fridays?
After all, they are a seventh of my days,
fourteen-point-two percent of this temporary, fleeting existence I call my life!
Don't you think I would like to arise daily saying,
"This is the day the Lord has made, let us be glad and rejoice"?
I don't want to go into the office!
Don't you think I'd like to go into my garden and watch it grow?

And yet, you may be the greatest cultivator of the garden that is my life!
It is in your dark, fertile soil that I have seeded and grown
some of my finest qualities, attributes and skills!
It is through you that I have learned to stand in a row
like wheat or corn and be food for the world!
It is through you that I have learned to grow wild and untamed
like wisteria in springtime—
allowing the wind to carry my seed to yonder pot!

And so I vacillate
between the burden that you are in my life
and the blessings that you offer.

Hah! But I know the truth!
You're just a puppet on the floor in front of me!
You don't even have the ears to hear this melodrama.
You are waiting for me to pick you up
and let you dangle like a hanged man,
or to wrap your strings around my nimble fingers and set you to dance!
If you had eyes with which to see and a voice with which to speak,
you would look back on me and say,

> "You, my dear, are the two-sided one.
> You carry the curse and the blessing.
> For I am just a puppet, my name is Work.
> I do your bidding.
> You are the puppeteer.
> You are the puppeteer!"

Reflections

I bet I am not the only person who vacillates between the burden of work and the blessings that it offers. Surely we have all felt the angst that comes with work, bemoaned the demands that it makes on our lives and longed for the freedom of not having to succumb to its daily pressures. As one young participant in one of my workshops once put it, "Work is tough... that's why they have to pay us to do it! If work was all about fun and fulfillment we'd have to buy tickets to it."

I bet I am also not the only one who forgets from time to time that I hold the strings! And while I did not create all of the circumstances in which I find myself, I am the one who chooses how I will respond or not respond to those circumstances. I appreciate the observation of Gloria Steinem, "We're all born into this mess. We're not responsible for it. We're only responsible for every day we let it go on without changing things."

Claim your power

At times it seems as if we live in a random universe composed of accidental and haphazard events that produce miscellaneous experiences. Our shifts from success to failure, from joy to despair, from good fortune to bad, appear chaotic and unpredictable. We use words like "fate", "luck", "destiny", and "jinx" to make sense of the variety of experiences that seem to just happen to us. We refuse to notice how it is with our own actions and inactions that we weave the tapestry of our lives, how our daily responses to circumstances ultimately shape our experiences and our destinies.

But there does exist in the universe the simple but unavoidable law of cause and effect. If we plant an apple tree, we don't get cherries. If we act out of scarcity and greed, we don't produce a life of abundance and generosity. As we meet the day with a hopeful or a desperate heart, the world responds accordingly. We hold the strings. We are the puppeteers. Like artists, we paint the landscape of our lives using the palette that holds the colors of our thoughts, values, actions and feelings. As one anonymous writer put it:

> "Watch your thoughts; they become words.
> Watch your words; they become actions.
> Watch your actions; they become habits.
> Watch your habits; they become character.
> Watch your character; it becomes your destiny."

We are heirs to the results of our own actions, of the intentions we bring to every moment. What we habitually think, feel and act directs the course of our lives. In these three domains, we each hold the power to shape and reshape destiny in every new moment. This power derives from our ability to change perspective, to manage our thoughts and feelings, to learn by carefully observing the consequences of our own actions.

In Tibetan Buddhism there are four principles that are referred to as "mind-changers." They are:

1. Life is inconceivably precious.
2. Life is short and death is certain.
3. Life contains inevitable difficulties.
4. Our ethical choices mold our lives.

It seems that most of the world has less problem with the first three principles than with the fourth. I have met many people who resist the idea that they are more puppeteers than puppets—that they participate in the ongoing creation of the world. They believe that they are simply meant to face the challenges given them and that destiny and providence are stronger forces than what they contribute as human beings. To people of this thinking, I would relate the following teaching story:

Goldberg had the loveliest garden in town and each time the rabbi passed by he would call out to him, "Your garden is a thing of beauty. The Lord and you are partners!"

"Thank you, Rabbi," Goldberg would respond with a bow.

This went on for days and weeks and months. At least twice a day the rabbi on his way to and from the synagogue, would call out, "The Lord and you are partners!" until Goldberg began to be annoyed at what the rabbi evidently meant as a compliment.

So the next time the rabbi said, "The Lord and you are partners," Goldberg replied, "I am sure that is true, Rabbi. But you should have seen this garden when the Lord had it all on his own!"

Choose to respond rather than react

Clearly we do not have much say in the hand that we are dealt in life but we have tremendous say in how we play out that hand. This is as true in every small situation we encounter as it is in the bigger picture of our life. How we respond to our circumstances has more do with the quality of our lives than the circumstances in which we find ourselves. Here is a beautiful and touching story from the Zen tradition about the power of our reactions and responses to the world in creating our experience.

A big, tough samurai once went to see a little monk. "Monk," he said, in a voice accustomed to instant obedience, "teach me about heaven and hell."

The monk looked up at this mighty warrior and replied with utter disdain, "Teach you about heaven and hell? I couldn't teach you about anything! You're dirty. You smell. Your blade is rusty. You're a disgrace, an embarrassment to the samurai class. Get out of my sight. I can't stand you."

The samurai was furious. He shook, got red in the face and was speechless with rage. He pulled his sword and raised it above him, preparing to slay the monk.

"That's hell," said the monk softly.

The samurai was overwhelmed. The compassion and surrender of this little man who offered his life to give this teaching to show him hell! He slowly put down his sword, filled with gratitude, and suddenly became peaceful.

"And that is heaven," said the monk softly.

What a powerful sword, we might think, holding dual power—to both brandish destruction or to wield peace. But the samurai's sword was neutral. It held no power except in how it was wielded. What made the difference between heaven and hell were the samurai's thoughts, feelings, and reactions to the teacher. And so it is with us and how we respond to bothersome coworkers, difficult customers, an impossible boss or our teenaged children. It really isn't our circumstances that make our lives difficult, but our responses to them. We give people power by how we react to them. In a sense, we become victims of our own emotional responses.

We are not unlike the man in the classic Sufi story who was riding along the path when something startled his donkey. All of a sudden, the donkey was galloping at breakneck speed. Some of the man's friends seeing him speeding past cried out, "Where are you going so fast?" "Don't ask me," he shouted back, "Ask my donkey!" Our emotional responses sometimes get in the way of and usurp our better and more rational sensibilities and we find ourselves riding on the back of an unreined donkey. Gaining control of the donkey requires refocusing our attention.

I will never forget hearing the story about Leonardo da Vinci when he was working on what would become one of his finest masterpieces, "The Last Supper." He was in the midst of an emotional conflict with one of the men who created the scaffolding on which he worked. He found himself so full of anger and hatred that, try as he may, he could not bring himself to paint the face of Christ. It was not until he put his brushes down and sought out the person with whom he needed to find peace that he could return to his painting and render the beauty and compassion that lined the face of Jesus.

On a more personal note, I was once hired on contract by a consulting and training company. I packed up my Volkswagen Bug and moved 1200 miles for this, my first opportunity to be a real trainer! I was overly eager to impress and nearly worked myself to death. My employers enjoyed my enthusiastic contributions and readily accepted any overtime I would like to donate to the cause. They made money, hand over fist, with what I was bringing into their firm—never considering to cut me in on the profits, much less extending any kindness, courtesy or appreciation. I felt bullied in many ways and cowered in their presence. I would return to an empty apartment at night, in a city of people I did not know, too tired to weep but dying inside.

A couple of months later while I was traveling and training in another city, I met two men, Milt Wright and Rich Pimentel, who would change my life. They were starting a new company of their own—offering training to job developers. Having delivered workshops on job development for the previous six months, I was very anxious to find out what other people were doing. I called my employer and requested the opportunity to stay another day and attend their workshop. His response was, "If you do not return immediately, you are fired. You will return to an empty desk. It's up to you."

It was so strange. Here I had cowered at anything and everything this person had said to me over the last several months while working myself to the bone. But in this moment, he sounded stupid, ignorant and selfish. I had to keep from laughing through the phone. Once I regained my composure, I responded with incredible calm, "Be careful what you say. I will be staying an extra night and attending the workshop. If you fire me, you will lose the most lucrative contract of your firm." When I hung up the phone, I did some sort of crazy dance and howled to a moon that had not yet risen. I was free! It didn't matter whether or not I was returning to an empty desk, I had returned to myself! I was no longer a puppet.

As it turns out, I was fired. Shortly after, I joined forces with Milt and Richard and became a partner in our own training firm. Those mean ol' bullies lost not only one good employee but also their most profitable contract.

You may be wondering what this story has to do with the samurai's sword or the guy on the donkey. Well, I had lost what is referred to in martial arts as "my center." For months I responded to my circumstances with fear and trepidation, giving not only my power away but my dignity as well. I was a passenger on the back of my fear. By the time I knew to get off the darn thing, I found myself holding a sword. I could have had myself a good hearty laugh and told my employer where to put his cell phone; I could have gone for the throat. But I didn't. With calm and resolve, I asked him to choose carefully. I was not in a match. My sword was not drawn. Freedom was mine on terms I could live with.

Live the prayer of St. Francis

We cannot tell what may happen *to* us in the strange medley of life. But we can decide what happens *in* us... how we take it, what we will do with it... and that is what really counts in the end. It's not where we work—it's what's working in us. It's not where we live—it's what's living in us. Have you ever experienced a time in your life when you were repeatedly dissatisfied in job after job or in relationship after relationship? Is this just a run of bad luck? I doubt it. Discontent is like a weed inside us that, never having been identified and extracted by its roots, will repeatedly erupt in the soil of any and all circumstances.

Did you ever hear of the guy who searched the world over for the perfect bride? He met many fine women, but none of them was just right. One would be very intelligent but not quite attractive enough. Another would be very attractive but not quite talented enough. Another would be very talented but not very easy-going. The one who was easy-going was not interesting enough, etc. Finally, in the autumn of his life, he found the perfect woman! He was thrilled, until she broke the news to him as gently as she could, "Sorry, but I'm still looking for the perfect man."

We've all lived this story to some degree at different times in our lives. Buddhist tradition teaches us that we will not know contentment at work when we find the "right job" and have what we want but when we want we have. We must take responsibility for the job we are in and bring our own contentment to it. Then again, as Erica Jong, with tongue in cheek, reminds us, "Take your life in your own hands and what happens? A terrible thing: no one to blame."

I think the story of Gandhi's life speaks beautifully to the power of a person to create the circumstances they wish to see, rather than seek to find them in the world.

Gandhi started his career as a timid, rather ineffective lawyer, too shy to hold his own in court. That all began to change when he worked in South Africa and was exposed to the horrors of racial discrimination. At one point he was thrown violently off a train when he attempted to sit in a whites-only carriage. He began his life's work of social reform, first in South Africa and then in his native India.

Gandhi could easily have become an angry, embittered man and an apostle of violence. Instead, he became an apostle of peace and forged a new revolutionary movement that combined social action with spiritual values. Instead of regarding his opponents as inhuman enemies, he viewed them as potential friends; instead of slandering them, he relied on satyagraha (meaning holding fast to truth), instead of crushing them physically, he sought to uplift them morally. With these ethical weapons he drew millions of Indians into a social movement of such moral force that it shook the mighty British Empire, won India its freedom and inspired similar leaders and movements around the world. Gandhi embodied the powerful words of St. Francis of Assisi:

> "Where there is hate, let me bring Love—
> Where there is offense, let me bring Pardon—
> Where there is discord, let me bring Union—
> Where there is error, let me bring Truth—
> Where there is doubt, let me bring Faith—
> Where there is darkness, let me bring Light—

> Where there is sadness, let me bring Joy—
> Because it is in giving oneself that one receives;
> It is in forgetting oneself that one is found…"

Sweep your own front steps

In his book, *A Calendar of Wisdom,* Leo Tolstoy suggests that we would think a man insane who, instead of covering his house with a roof and putting windows in his window frames, goes out in stormy weather, and scolds the wind, the rain and the clouds. Each of us does the same when we scold and blame the depravity of other people instead of fighting the faults that exist within ourselves. It is possible to battle our own demons, just as it is possible to make a roof and windows for our house. We cannot remake the world to our liking, just as we cannot order the weather to change and the clouds to disappear.

In our heart of hearts we know that any job can be made great. It is the worker, not the work, that counts. Any home can be a happy home, depending on those who live in it. It's true in relationships as well. And while it is clearly not easy to find happiness in ourselves, it is impossible to find it anywhere else. If we are dissatisfied with our lives, the real source of our angst should be, first, with ourselves. It's that old "you will reap what you sow" thing. Rumi has, as always, a more poetic way of saying it: "Whoever acts with respect will get respect. Whoever, brings sweetness will be served almond cake." Would you like yours warmed up and *a la mode?*

I am so happy to recollect this little story, although I regret not knowing its origins.

> A man, who all of his life had been a sincere spiritual seeker, was now old, looking back on his life. He sat with his friends on a park bench telling his story: "When I was young I was fiery—I wanted to awaken everyone. I prayed to God to give me strength to change the world. In mid-life I awoke one day and realized my life was half over and I had changed no one. So I prayed to God to give me the strength to change those close around me.
>
> Alas, now I am old and my prayer is simpler. 'Lord,' I ask, 'please give me the strength to at least change myself.'"

Mother Teresa tells her own version of this story by suggesting that if we want to clean up the world, we should begin by sweeping our own front steps. I think she and the man in the story are kindred spirits.

Embrace the world before working to change it

We are challenged to love the world and our lives as they are. If we do not love our lives, how can we expect to change them or to give something enduring to them? It is true of our work as well. If we cannot embrace the challenges and inconveniences of the position or circumstances we are in, we should probably look to change our circumstances.

It drives me crazy when I hear people say that they are not in their "dream job." I think the term "dream job" is appropriately named—it exists in our dreams. Every job has its mix of good and bad, fun and not so fun, enjoyable and frustrating. I don't mean to say that there aren't industries or positions that play more to our strengths, interests and talents than others. For sure, we must seek livelihoods that are "true" to us in these ways. But once in them, it is only a matter of time before the weeds start cropping up among the lovely flowers.

When I am delivering workshops in the social service sector, I plead with my participants to consider the extent to which they are able to fully embrace all of their work, good and bad, pleasant and unpleasant, joyful and frustrating. To the extent that they are unable to accept the difficulties of the position, I strongly encourage them to consider taking their talents elsewhere, where they can wholeheartedly inhabit their work. There is too much work needed to be done in the world of social services and too little money coming down the pike to have people inhabit their positions halfheartedly. I can only imagine that the corporate plea would be similar to its own employees: accept the entirety of your position, not just the part that suits your fancy.

Anyone who has been in a long-term relationship knows about this kind of acceptance. In relationships we have to embrace all that the person brings to the table, the pleasant and the not so pleasant. To be embraced and accepted in this way has to be one of the loveliest experiences in life. How perfect that it is a gift that we can give to someone else.

Be a believer in seeds

I remember once hearing a story that tells of the laws of the harvest in a rather unique way. Here is my rendition:

Once upon a time there was a woman who happened into a charming little store, the shelves stocked full of wonderful things. There was beauty in bulk, joy in abundance. There were bags and bags of passion and purposefulness. There were huge containers of peace and contentment and a glorious display of wonderment and awe.

As she perused the store, her eyes dancing with delight at the choices that lay before her, the shopkeeper approached the woman saying, "Welcome to my shop. Everything is free. Take your time choosing that which you most want, and let me know the quantity in which you want it. Here is some paper upon which to write your list."

The woman was shocked! Everything was free! What a shopping spree she embarked upon! She requested a little peace and a lot of joy, a tad of optimism and a generous sampling of contentment. She included a measure of purposefulness and a nice juicy helping of enthusiasm. (She added a pound of passion just for fun.)

She brought her list to the shopkeeper who nodded and smiled as he read her list and then turned to take something from a huge cabinet of drawers. When he was finished, he placed several small packets on the counter in front of her. "There's everything on your list, Ma'am," he said.

The woman was shocked. They were packets of seeds! Seeds of Joy. Seeds of Purposefulness. Seeds of Wonder. "This is a rip-off," she exclaimed, "I expected the real thing!"

The woman stomped out of the shop, never noticing the sign on the door, "The Shop of God: Seeds Within."

May we aspire to join the circle of people who are working to both embrace and better the world, starting with our own small corners, be they at work, at home or in our communities. May we sow our seeds with hope, faith and constancy of purpose. In the daily act of living may we wrap the strings of our circumstances around our nimble fingers and set ourselves to dancing, never forgetting that we are the puppeteers of our own lives.

Passages

Ram Dass

"As you look at many people's lives, you see that their suffering is in a way gratifying, for they are comfortable in it. They make their lives a living hell, but a familiar one."

"I don't like work—no one does. What I like is what is in work; the chance to find yourself."

Joseph Conrad

"I do not ask of God that He should change anything in events themselves, but that He should change me in regard to things, so that I might have the power to create my own universe, to govern my dreams, instead of enduring them."

Gerard de Nerval

"Though we travel the world over
to find the beautiful,
we must carry it with us
or find it not."

Anonymous

"We either make ourselves miserable,
or we make ourselves strong.
The amount of work is the same."

Carlos Castaneda

Johann Wolfgang von Goethe

"It is not doing the thing we like to do, but liking the thing we have to do that makes life blessed."

Thich Nhat Hanh

"Happiness tends to drop in unexpectedly when you are working on something meaningful."

Ralph Waldo Emerson

"Shallow people believe in luck and circumstances. Strong people believe in cause and effect."

"It will never rain roses.
When we want to have more roses,
we must plant more trees."

George Eliot

"Your living is determined not so much by what life brings to you as by the attitude you bring to life; not so much by what happens to you as by the way your mind looks at what happens. Circumstances and situations do color life, but you have been given the mind to choose what the color shall be."

John Homer Miller

David Whyte

"We cannot sleepwalk into the life we want to live. We must choose it."

"A thankful person is thankful under all circumstances. A complaining soul complains even if he lives in paradise."

Anonymous

"God doesn't make orange juice; God makes oranges."

Jesse Jackson

George Bernard Shaw

"The people who get on in this world are the people who get up and look for the circumstances they want, and, if they can't find them, make them."

"Natural wisdom seems to suggest that the way you are toward your life is the way that your life will be toward you."

Golda Meir

Aldous Huxley

"There is only one corner of the universe you can be certain of improving, and that's your own self."

Ralph Waldo Emerson

"People seem not to see that their opinion of the world is also a confession of character."

Henry David Thoreau

"However mean your life is,
meet it and live it;
do not shun it or call it hard names.
It is not so bad as you are. It looks poorest when you are richest.
The fault-finder will find faults even in paradise.
Love your life…."

To Ponder and To Practice

- Reflect on a time or a circumstance in your life when you felt more like a puppet than the puppeteer. Now think of a time when you pulled your own strings. What was similar or different in those two circumstances than your present situation?
- In what areas of your life do you find yourself playing more the part of the puppet than the puppeteer? What are just a few of the most obvious strings in your life or work which you could wrap around your nimble fingers and set to dance?
- Think of a person who truly appears to the puppeteer of her own life. What do you think is the source of that person's ability to take responsibility in her circumstances? How would you like your life to reflect more of that quality?
- Think about the sum of your attitudes and actions at work in the last month or so. What message are you sending out loud and clear?
- We are always an ambassador for someone or something, whether it be for peace, conflict, acceptance or criticism. What do you think other people would say you are an ambassador for these days at work? How about at home?
- What are a few currently neglected aspects of your circumstances that you could consider embracing as part and parcel of the position you are in?
- What was one of your most recent experiences of riding a startled donkey? What emotion took you for a real ride?
- Circle three of the following which you would like more of at home or at work.

Direction	Respect	Stamina	Community	Gratitude
Discipline	Commitment	Tenderness	Acceptance	Humor
Well-being	Peace	Effectiveness	Fun	Balance

  Think about how you are spending your time at work and at home that supports these qualities. What are a few small things you could begin doing in order to bring more of those qualities into your life?

- Circle three of the following which you would like less of at home or at work.

Worry	Anxiety	Paper work	Anger	E-mail
Procrastination	Noise	Silence	Interruptions	Junk
Clutter	Gossiping	Conflict	Pressure	Stress

  What are a few things you could begin doing which would help you decrease the elements you circled?

Practice

- John Irving suggests that "Good habits are worth being fanatical about." Can you think of one good habit you could cultivate that would be worthy of being fanatical about? What's the first step in fostering this habit?
- Choose a quote from this chapter's *Passages* that speaks to you and post it someplace where you will read it often and internalize it as you work to foster increased responsibility in response to the circumstances in your life and work.
- If you could practice any quality in the coming days, what would it be (e.g., wild, proud, focused, strong, determined, easy-going, patient, etc.)? Consider how you could develop a reputation for that quality among your co-workers. Choose a symbol, a ritual or a habit that will remind you to practice this quality.
- Given everything you have read in this chapter, what do you want to *keep* doing? What do you want to *stop* doing? What do you want to *start* doing?

Notes

The Beauty of Today

Chapter

Seizing the Day

Live knowing you will die

Live knowing you will die

Choose important over urgent

Choose important over urgent

Seize the present day

Seize the present day

Think moment to moment

Think moment to moment

First move, then enjoy the ride of momentum

First move, then enjoy the ride of momentum

Finish each day and be done with it

Finish each day and be done with it

The Beauty of Today

The beauty of today is that it has not happened yet;
it is awash with possibility, it does not know regret.
A new life begins today, as I face the world anew,
and set out like a pilgrim on a path not tried but true.
Mistakes I made the day before belong now to the past;
I meet the present fresh again, like the sun that dawns at last.
I have the power to become the person I long to be
if I use the wand of choice that has been given me.

I am king and I am queen of a kingdom called "today,"
for I can rule how I act, how I work and how I play.
In the great adventure that is life, in the awesome act of living,
I alone can choose today just what I will be giving.

I needn't run a marathon, but I could go round the block,
I won't become an engineer, but I could reset my clock.
I will not earn a million; I doubt that I'll be rich,
but I can earn enough today to keep me from a ditch.
I probably won't be winning a perfect parent's prize,
but I bet I could do one small thing to put joy in my child's eyes.
I will not single-handedly bring about world peace,
but I could see to it that the wars in my house are brought to a halt and cease.
I'll never be an angel, and I won't become a priest,
but I could find the time it takes to give a blessing for each feast.

For today I bring my truth to what I do and say,
I can even live with merriment at least for just a day!
I don't know if I have the strength to get me through this year,
but thankfully I have the strength to deal with what is here.

That is all that life asks of me, to muster hope that carries through
from one sunrise... until it sets, and enough to greet the moon.
So my designs are on today, tomorrow I cannot taste;
the night will come again rapidly, I have no time to waste.
For tomorrow is not promised; what will come, we cannot say,
that a day like this may not come again brings an urgency today.
To live mindful of each moment, to live with thanks and heartfelt praise
for that gift we call "possibility" that comes wrapped in each new day.

Reflections

> "I'm late! I'm late! For a very important date.
> No time to say hello! Good-bye!
> I'm late! I'm late! I'm late!"
>
> The Mad Hatter, from *Alice in Wonderland*

These well-known lines from Lewis Carroll bespeak our generation's relationship to time—we're late, we're late—even for dates that aren't that important—we're late! At least that's the popular notion.

Perhaps this "time-starved" perspective springs from our preoccupation with all that we are not able to do and accomplish in the course of an average day, relative to all we could be doing. There is always something calling to us which we have not been able to address. There always will be. Not because we don't have time, but because we do not always use it in the employ of our best purposes.

How grateful we should be that there is no cosmic timekeeper keeping track of how we idle away hour upon hour, week after week, year after year, while simultaneously singing our woes about not having enough time. In the amusing words of Susan Ertz, "Millions long for immortality, who do not know what to do with themselves on a rainy afternoon." I think the idea of time management is a misnomer; it is the management of our goals and our choices that would give us a new perspective on time, not the other way around.

There are a lot of things we do not have in life, but time is not one of them. Time is the puddle we wade in. It is the raw medium of our lives. We must come to terms with the fact that we are creating our lives through and with the use of this precious resource. Whether we use time well or not, it passes; like a river that continues to flow, whether or not we travel with its currents.

We have twenty-four hours a day with which to work and to play—the future depends on what each of us does with those hours.

While we are blessed with the precious gift of time and the free will to use it as we will, there is one minor drawback: it is limited and we don't get to know how much of it is left. It is when we face the fact that our bodies are temporary quarters, and our very existence here on earth is transient, that our lives take on true meaning.

How do we bring a sense of urgency to our days, a reverence for life to the mundane realities of an everyday job—particularly when we are in work circumstances that may not seem "worthy" of our time and talents? How do we make choices for the wise use of our time when there is more to be done than we can possibly accomplish?

In the deepest marrow of my bones, I believe that if we were determined to embody the following principles, our lives would change dramatically. Even in those moments or corners of our work that seem unworthy of our time and talents, we would begin to bring fresh "worthiness." None of these ideas is novel or difficult but they do require something rare and powerful—conscious decisions. Decisions to move, to act, to persist, and to carry on. Decisions to focus our attention and to invest our power in the present. Consider which of these ideas, if acted upon, would improve the way you employ time to your highest purposes.

Live knowing you will die

Woody Allen once jested, "If I survive this life without dying, I'll be very surprised." While we all know that we will not be getting out of here alive, we rarely live congruent with that knowing. In the Hindu writing the Bhagavad-Gita, the question is asked, "Of all the world's wonders, what is the most wonderful?" The answer is simple and direct:"That no man, though he sees others dying all around him, believes that he himself will die."

It seems that death is something that we expect to postpone until we have received our fair share of what life has to offer us—until we are ready to go, on our own terms. From that perspective, believing that we will live as long as we wish, we can afford to waste time; we can spend precious days, months, even years engaged in mindless activity and fruitless relationships. We can arrange our career, our friends, and our possessions just the way we like. We can work for decades on our psychology, our spirituality and our finances until we are perfectly content with our lives. Then, finally ready to begin our lives in earnest, we can gather up the fruits of our labor and be rewarded with a happy and fulfilling life, free to enjoy for many years the harvest of all our good work.

Awareness and acceptance of death can be a powerful wake-up call. Death dispels the most potent illusion about life—that it belongs to us, and that we have all the time we need to arrange it the way we want. In many ways it is a gift that our life is limited, impermanent. We hold it more dear because this is so. In the face of death, we would not fear embarrassment or humiliation nor would we care very much about fame, fortune or popularity. What we would care a lot about are things like integrity, sincerity, dignity and love. Death would put a different face on what we consider to be our obligations, our responsibilities and our priorities.

With an ever-present awareness of death (or even occasional awareness), I doubt that we would give much attention to the ways in which we have been harmed or hurt by others, but we would give twice as much attention to those who have touched us with kindness and love. With a sense of our own impermanence I doubt that we would allow ourselves to stay in unproductive relationships, but we would jump at the chance to work at those relationships that matter. With an appreciation of the fragility of life, I doubt that we would care much about career progress, but we would care more about our career purposes. If we had a sense of having little time left, we would find that we have none to waste. Every conversation, every action, every choice would be full to the brim with meaning and value. Indeed, given a choice between doing what is important and what is urgent—the decision would be clear.

> *Gather ye rosebuds while ye may,*
> *Old time is still a-flying.*
> *And this same flower that smiles today*
> *Tomorrow will be dying.*
>
> *Robert Herrick*

Choose important over urgent

Johann Van Goethe lends this wise counsel, "Things which matter most must never be at the mercy of things which matter least." Stephen Covey offers a simple but profound time management matrix in his classic book, *The 7 Habits of Highly Effective People,* which picks up where Goethe left off. He categorizes the way we use our time into four types of activities:

- Those that are important and urgent, such as crises, pressing problems, and deadlines, often resulting in stress, burnout, crisis management, and putting out fires
- Those that are important but not urgent, such as relationship building, planning, recreation, recognizing new opportunities, often resulting in a greater sense of balance, control, and self-discipline

– Those that are not important but urgent, such as interruptions, meetings, e-mail, entertainment, often resulting in short term focus, feeling victimized and out of control

– Those that are not important and not urgent, such as trivia, phone calls, time wasters, and entertainment

Covey suggests that 90% of our time is spent in the first and third categories (both urgent, regardless of importance) with 10% in the fourth category, not urgent and not important. His book reinforces the idea that happy, effective people spend more time in the second category, focusing on areas of our life which are important, but because they are not urgent, rarely receive our focus or investment.

If you think about it, we say "yes" or "no" to things daily, usually many times a day. Having a strong sense of what is important and deserving of our focus and energy would empower us with wisdom to make those judgments more effectively. The essence of effective time and life management is to organize and execute around our own balanced priorities. Covey asks a great question:

If you were to fault yourself in one of three areas, which would it be:

1. the inability to prioritize;
2. the inability or desire to organize around those priorities; or
3. the lack of discipline to execute around them, to stay with your priorities and organization?

Rather than prioritize what's on our schedules, we need to schedule our priorities!

Seize the present day

The beauty of today
is that it has not happened yet;
It is awash with possibility,
it does not know regret.
A new life begins today,
as I face the world anew,
And set out like a pilgrim
on a path not tried but true.

John O'Donohue urges us to consider the gift that a day brings when he writes:

> "Days are where we live. This is the rhythm that shapes our lives. Our lives take the form of each new day that is given to us. A day is precious because it is essentially the microcosm of your whole life. Each new day offers possibilities and promises that were never seen before. To engage with honor the full possibility of life is to engage in a worthy way the possibility of each new day. And each day is different."

If we wish to change or better our lives, even in small ways, our hopes and visions must enter the practice of our days. A day is a sacred place because it is the vessel into which we pour our lives. How do we approach the day not as a cage, but as a window, a meadow or entrance to a holy temple?

This little parable, credited in various places with Sufi, Buddhist and Christian origins, expresses well the need to seize the day:

A wise man was asked what was the most important time, person and thing in life. He answered, "The most important time is the present time, because at this time a person

> has power over himself. The most important person is the one with whom you deal at present, because there is no guarantee that you will ever be able to deal with any other person in the world. The most important thing is to love this person, because everyone is sent into this world with the sole purpose of loving other people."

Seize the day. This day—without letting yesterday or tomorrow use up too much of the present.

Mistakes I made the day before
belong now to the past.
I meet the present fresh again,
like the sun that dawns at last.
I have the power to become
the person I long to be
If I use the wand of choice
that has been given me.

The present is the only place of true power in our lives, but there are two thieves who typically steal that power, the past and the future. Regrets about yesterday and worries about tomorrow steal the thunder of the present—but only if we let them. When we find ourselves regretting all that we have not done, or what we did and wish we hadn't, these words from Martin Luther King should bring us comfort: "The time is always right to do what is right."

Whatever we choose to do in any given moment, we need to give our best to that activity and not waste time and energy worrying about all the things we are not doing. Doing one thing at a time and doing it entirely, can then lead us to the next moment of discernment when we can make new choices. Five words, passed on through the ages and out the mouths of sages, sum it up sweetly, "Let us be here, now."

Think moment to moment

Since we cannot rewrite history nor live in the future, our only real duty is in how we live each day—one day at a time. But even that is too large a chunk of time for the human brain. There is a long time between our mornings and our evenings, and there are many stopping places in between. Bringing attention to how we live moment to moment and hour to hour is really more within our realm of possibility. I can wake up feeling lazy and drift in a fog all morning, but I can still resolve to move out into the light of my productivity by afternoon. And even at the end of an afternoon when I have failed to get done what I hoped to accomplish, I can still look towards evening for a spot of time to use in a way that will allow me to greet the moon with a grin.

For today, I bring my truth
to what I do and say,
I can even live with merriment
at least for just a day!
I don't know if I have the strength
to get me through this year,
but thankfully I have the strength
to deal with what is here.

I am reminded of the advice given me by my roommate in college. It was during my first semester when my literature class was assigned *Moby Dick*. We had one week to read it. Not having been much of a reader up to that point in my life, I was stunned. Here was a 1000 page book—(small print and no pictures!) and I was supposed to somehow plow my way through while juggling the assignments of five other courses. My roommate found me despairing, tears streaming down my face and she said, "Denise, get me a razor blade." I admitted that it wasn't really all that bad, at which point she smiled and explained that she needed the razor to cut the binding of my book. She proceeded to cut the book into seven smaller pieces. Handing me one of them, she asked, "Do you think you could finish one of those in a night, even given the rest of what you have to do?" I picked it up and thumbed through the 150 or so pages and replied, "Yeah, no problem." "Okay," she finished, "just do one of those every night for the next seven nights and you've got Melville cooked!" I still have my copy of Moby Dick held together by a thick rubber band as a reminder that the book of life is meant to be read page by page, chapter by chapter.

It is so easy to become overwhelmed with the pressures coming at us from all sides. It takes discipline to train the mind to direct its attention to those areas in which we actually have control, to concentrate on those areas of our lives which are within our direct influence. Swimming in the wider waters of concerns where we have no control makes for tired arms and no real progress. We feel as if we are dogs paddling through our days. By making small choices within our smaller areas of control, we swim the river of time with sure and solid strokes. The great part is that every time we use one moment well, we have increased our power to use the next moment even better. As Alice Walker notes, "Every small, positive change we can make in ourselves repays us in confidence in the future."

First move, then enjoy the ride of momentum

Madeleine Kunin wisely reminds us, "Inaction, contrary to its reputation for being a refuge, is neither safe nor comfortable." When we want to change, to move one step closer to our goals, we need to do something. We need not waste time and energy worrying about doing the right thing or the best thing; we most likely need to just do something. It is strange how when we are not moving, we are clueless to what our next step should be. But as soon as you take one step, the next step seems a little more logical and at times, even obvious.

There is truth in the Native American adage, "We do not walk on our legs, but on our will." Unfortunately we are often too self-conscious about how we come across, to simply move out on the wild wave of sheer will. We would rather wait until we can ride the surer wave of our confidence of talents tried and true. But in the waiting, we move no closer to those talents and time continues to roll in on life's shores. The wise sage, Yoda, from the movie "Star Wars" put it succinctly, "There is no try… there is only do." Showing up and doing what we can do in the manner in which we can do it is where we will find the magic of momentum.

I believe there are laws of the universe that cannot be cheated and these laws apply in every area of our lives. One of these is the law of inertia. The dictionary defines inertia as, "the tendency of all objects and matter in the universe to stay still, or, if moving, to go on moving in the same direction."

Think about the last time you had to push a car. Do you remember mustering every ounce of strength you could from your arms and legs as the voice inside your head muttered, "You're not going to be able to move this thing." And then an amazing thing happened. The car budged, just a little, and you suddenly felt like the little red engine from the storybook as you said, "I think I can. I think I can." The second inch was slightly easier, but then you thought, "Can I keep this up? I think I can. I think I can." By the time you moved it a yard, all doubts had fled. "I can do this! I *am* the Little Engine that Could!"

Soon you pushed just hard enough to keep the car rolling as you trotted along behind it, tooting your own invisible horn.

The day-to-day grind of life and work can feel like pushing a car. Your car doesn't begin to roll the moment you begin to push, and it doesn't stop rolling the moment you quit. The inertia that is your enemy at first becomes your ally in the end. Momentum is a wonderful thing. Unfortunately, it never comes cheaply.

Ray Kroc, the man behind the McDonald's enterprise, is famous for sharing two small words of advice based on his experience. They are "Press on." He went on to say that "Nothing in the world can take the place of persistence. Nothing." Surely we have all experienced times in our lives when we persisted in doing something that we could have just as easily given up on. No doubt we were happy and proud to have done so. Persistence feels so good played backwards, doesn't it?

Being persistent requires resolve to some greater purpose than what is seen or experienced in the moment. I believe persistence is a gift of the spirit that is always available to us when we plug into that purpose drawing us forward. It brings its own reward. In the words of Ralph Waldo Emerson, "That which we persist in doing becomes easier not because the nature of the task has changed, but our ability has increased." Procrastinating may steal our power but persistence recovers it. We may be wise to remember the words of poet Margaret Sangster:

It isn't the thing you do, Dear.
It is the thing you leave undone
which gives you a bit of a heartache
At the setting of the sun.

Finish each day and be done with it

At the end of each day, rest in the knowledge that you did what you could with what you had at that time. Surely the day will have allowed for a few blunders or a few choice absurdities to creep in. So what? Today is ending and tomorrow is a new day. Resolve to begin it in a spirit of sincerity and serenity.

That is what is so sweet about time. We are forever being given new opportunities to be and do what we have never been or done before. It's like entering a dark room. If we go into a darkened room and turn on the light, it doesn't matter if the room has been dark for a day, a week, or 10,000 years—we turn on the light and it is illuminated. It doesn't matter how long we've been making the same mistakes or limiting ourselves in any way, as soon as we act differently, we are different. Everything we do illumines the next step before us. No action needs to be thought of as an empty one.

That is all that life asks of me,
to muster hope that carries through
from one sunrise... until it sets,
and enough to greet the moon.
So my designs are on today,
tomorrow I cannot taste;
the night will come again rapidly,
I have no time to waste.

Passages

"Until one is committed, there is hesitancy, the chance to draw back. The moment one definitely commits oneself, then Providence moves, too. All sorts of things occur to help one that would never otherwise have occurred. Boldness has genius, power and magic in it. Begin it now."

Johann Wolfgang von Goethe

"Life is a coin. We can spend it any way we want. But we only get to spend it once."

Miquel de Cervantes

Zen proverb

"Sit, walk or run, but don't wobble."

"Give us grace, O God,
to dare to the deed
which we know cries to be done.
Let us not hesitate
because of convenience
or ease, or our own lives."

W. E. B. DuBois

"This is not a day for asking questions,
not a day on any calendar.
This day is conscious of itself.
This day is a lover, bread, and gentleness,
more manifest than saying can say."

Rumi

Emily Dickinson

"That it will never come again
is what makes life so sweet."

"Seize every minute of your time.
The days fly by—
Ere long you too will grow old.
If you believe me or not,
See there, in the courtyard,
How the frost, glitters white and cold and cruel
On the grass that once was green."

Tzu Yeh

"Each day that I live I say to myself:
the visible world is mine, use it,
change it, but be quick, for the
night comes too fast and nothing
is every entirely finished, nothing."

Gore Vidal

Johann Wolfgang Von Goethe

"Nothing is worth more than this day."

"Carpe diem, quam minimum
Credula a postero.
Seize the day, and put the least possible trust
in tomorrow."

Horace

"Oh bolting time, rough pony of my days,
Halt by the hedgerow of my life to graze."

Vita Sackville-West

"My last defense
is the present tense."

Gwendolyn Brooks

"Life isn't a matter of milestones,
but of moments."

Rose Kennedy

"Time is infinitely more precious than money,
and there is nothing common between them.
You cannot accumulate time;
you cannot borrow time;
you can never tell how much
you have left in the bank.
Time is life."

Israel Davidson

"Each small task of everyday is
part of the total harmony of
the universe."

St. Theresa of Lisieux

Stephen Vincent Benet

"Life is not lost by dying;
life is lost minute by minute,
day by dragging day,
in all the thousand uncaring ways."

Henry Wadsworth Longfellow

"Do not delay—
The golden moments fly!"

"All the gold in the world cannot buy a dying man one more breath—so what does that make today worth?"

Og Mandino

"Each day is a droplet of water
filling the chalice of our legacy."

Wayne Muller

"Live in the present.
Do the things that need to be done.
Do all the good you can each day.
The future will unfold."

Peace Pilgrim

"Do you love life?
Then do not squander time,
For that's the stuff life is made of."

Benjamin Franklin

To Ponder and To Practice

- Take the time to enjoy one accomplishment today without rushing on to the next task waiting to be done. Pause long enough to celebrate.
- Choose a daily activity that will remind you that life is impermanent and that, in fact, you could die today. It could be as mundane as turning on the faucet, brushing your teeth, watering the flowers, turning out the lights at night, or closing a book.
- Consider planning your own memorial. Who would you want to see there? What would you want said about you by whom? What would you like to have read, sung or on display? What would you like to be remembered for?
- What do you like/dislike about the first half of your day? What can you add or subtract from the first half of your day to increase your productivity and joy? Answer the same for the second half of your day.
- There is a saying in business, "What gets measured, gets done." We are more likely to follow through on things for which we are accountable. Make appointments with yourself for those activities which will feed your spirit, whether it be reading, walking, playing laser tag or sitting in a garden. Make them priorities as if they were doctor appointments or business meetings.
- Somerset Maugham once commented that "The unfortunate thing about this world is that good habits are so much easier to give up than bad ones." What is one good habit you've enjoyed in your life that you gave up at some point but would like to start again?
- Just for the heck of it, try being pleasant and optimistic every morning until ten o'clock and then just see if the rest of the day doesn't take care of itself.
- Time is the ultimate gift that we can give to our work, to ourselves and to one another. The fact that our time is limited makes it that much greater a gift. Think of someone who could use the gift of your time right now and devise some wonderful way in which to deliver that gift. (For example, washing someone's car, writing a letter, lending an ear to someone who is troubled, reading to a sick friend, holding a surprise celebration for someone at work.)
- Decisions are different from goals or dreams because they require an actual investment of our time and energy. What two decisions could you make about the use of your time that could dramatically impact your day? (For example, setting aside time to schedule your priorities or eating lunch with co-workers so you can get to know them better.)
- Leo Tolstoy warns, "The most dangerous temptation is the temptation to prepare to live, instead of living. The future does not belong to us." What do you need to stop putting off until the future?

- Select a quote on the topic of "being in the moment" and "seizing the day" from this chapter's *Passages* and post it where you will see it until it is internalized.
- Choose a daily habit, routine or symbol to help you remain conscious of the precious gift of time (e.g., pay attention to the life cycle of growing things in your yard or use the routine of getting dressed in the morning to signify "putting on" a brand new day of fresh living).
- Given everything you have read in this chapter, what do you want to *keep* doing? What do you want to *stop* doing? What do you want to *start* doing?

Notes

Chapter

The Journey To Belong

Employing Your Inner Compass

Select carefully that to which you belong

Select carefully that to which you belong

Establish an inner house of belonging

Establish an inner house of belonging

Rest in the warm pockets of the world

Rest in the warm pockets of the world

Find belonging in your longing

Find belonging in your longing

Develop an internal Jiminy Cricket

Develop an internal Jiminy Cricket!

Embrace life as a journey of becoming

Embrace life as a journey of becoming

A Cradle of Wings

A Cradle of Wings

The Journey To Belong

When I was six, I had a very important decision to make:
Would I grow up to be a nurse, a teacher or a nun?
Well, I couldn't stand the sight of blood and I didn't like the smell of chalk,
and I mean, who wouldn't want to be holy?
Plus I knew that if I joined the convent,
they would give me some beautiful name, like Sister Mary Catherine.
They would tell me how to sit and where to stand,
and when I would lie down at night,
I would know that I had a place of special belonging in the world.

When I was sixteen, and way past the idea of being a nun,
I had a different decision to make.
When I graduated from high school, would I go to a big time university
or attend a local community college and work?
Maybe I should just travel the world over.
Well, in thinking about it, I chose the university, figuring
that for that much time and money, surely they would shape me
into something of real value in the labor market.
I could just imagine a plaque with my name on it for my desk or on my door.
I knew that they would tell me how to sit and where to stand,
and when I would lie down at night,
I would have a place of valuable belonging in the world.

By the time I was twenty-six the choices got harder.
Now that I was a seasoned professional in the world,
Could I handle the responsibilities of being a wife and mother too?
In thinking about adding these roles
to my ever-increasing list of adult identities,
I thought that when I would lie down at night,
other than being totally exhausted,
I would know exactly where I stood,
and for the first time, I would have a place of deep belonging in the world.

At thirty-six, I faced another crossroad.
Should I continue as an independent contractor and trainer
or would it be better to work with individuals close up again, one on one?
As I considered my options, I realized that having been published,
I had a place of standing in my field.
Why then, I remember thinking, when I lay down at night,
do I continue to wonder if I will ever
feel a place of true belonging in the world?

Well, it is now almost a decade later,
and I refuse to wait until I am sixty to know, in my bones,
that the only choices that really matter
are those that affect my wholeness and my joy, and not my résumé.
The truth is that I do not want anyone to tell me how to sit,
because I would rather dance!
I do not want someone to tell me where to stand.
I am not some ornament on the mantel of the world;
I am a vital living element in an ever-changing universe.
I do not want to lie down at night wondering
if I will ever have a place of belonging in the world.
I want to change my question to
"Do I have a place in me for the world?"
I want my belonging to be in my longing
to be worthy of this world and to love it fully.

Now I wonder, if I had become a nun,
would my journey have led me to exactly this same place?
After all, a career path is only as fruitful as it is able to lead us back to ourselves,
to who we are, to why we are here.
The particular choices we make matter little.
But the traveling, ah, the traveling is everything!

Reflections

It was a healing and somewhat enlightening experience to follow the steps of my own sojourn of meaning-making in writing the poem "The Journey to Belong." I was amazed to find that at the core of many of my major life choices was the desire to simply belong. It wasn't about being a nun or getting a degree or having a career or being a wife and mother or owning my own company. To some great extent, I have been pulled by the gravity of my own need to connect, to be attached, to find a place of belonging somewhere—in something or with someone.

Perhaps there lives in all of us a longing to feel complete, to be whole, to know in our bones the joy of *being* enough and *having* enough. Like being hungry and having bread… being lonely and having love… being gifted and having work that invites those gifts. The need to belong is an ancient ache… ancient in terms of mankind, ancient in term of our own lives.

Select carefully that to which you belong

If only we were not so careless in our belonging. Wanting to connect and be connected, we will attach our hearts, our loyalties, our very identities, to things that can never provide true belonging. Like to relationships—be they marital, parental or bonds of friendship. Like to groups—be they religious, political or related to a social cause. Like to systems—be they medical, economic or employment-related.

I will never forget working with people who had been laid off from the Mare Island Naval Base in Vallejo, California in the early 1990s. It was as astonishing as it was heart wrenching to look into the faces of a crowd of talented and capable people who, having faced this sudden unemployment, felt broken, wounded and demeaned. The term "displaced workers" was not sufficient in describing the havoc this event was playing in their lives. They looked and spoke as if their very hearts and souls had been displaced. Many of them had come to attach their sense of belonging and their very identities not just to the work, but to the base and to the naval community at large. I was hired to help them find new employment, to identify and market their skills to the outside, civilian world. But it was clear that first they had to grieve their loss before they could invest themselves in new hope. They had to *belong to themselves again* before they would be capable of moving forward in their lives.

This is a common story in nearly every corporation or workplace. You do not have to look long before finding many disheartened people who, having invested the loyalty and innocence of their belonging to their work, found themselves treated as cogs on a wheel. Worse yet, the wheels they had been cogs on, were being discarded, replaced or outsourced. Their energies and talents were employed and used, but their hearts and souls were never really invited to the party.

The heart of the matter is that we should never belong fully to anything outside ourselves, be it a role, a cause or a system. We need to find the balance between giving to and working toward roles and causes without forfeiting or surrendering the very ground we stand on. But the tendency to attach ourselves to roles, causes and systems is great when we are afraid of belonging to our own lives.

That to which we attach our belonging should be deserving of our love and our loyalty. It should be worthy of our devotion and dignity. It should be deserving of our recommitment to core principles, primary values and native longings. These qualities and properties are the sum and substance of our inner world which will never betray us. These are the bricks and mortar of the house where our real belonging dwells. When we return to this place in our being where these essential elements are held precious, we are like Dorothy in the *Wizard of Oz* awaking from her dream, her heart full of song, chanting, "There's no place like home, there's no place like home."

Establish an inner house of belonging

We need to belong to ourselves before we can find true belonging in the world. When we connect to that deep source within us, we do not find ourselves vulnerable to circumstances in the world. Affected, yes, perhaps even deeply, but not torn asunder. This is the place of solid ground. This is our true home. This is where we can be free of the need to scrape affirmation, respect and significance from things and people outside ourselves. When we operate from our own solid ground we are less prone to involving ourselves in the power games, mind games, manipulations and seductions of the outer world. From here we see the forest because we are not of the trees. The house of our own belonging provides a place within us from which we can engage with others in a way that is real, authentic and wholesome. It is our own holy ground.

It is no easy feat to recognize and move into our own house of belonging while living and operating within the larger world. While this is the never-ending saga of our lives, we are not clueless in the sojourn. We live a bit like Hansel and Gretel, leaving bread crumbs every step of the way to find our way back home. They are crumbs of longing, of losses and of loyalties. If we were to follow them, they would lead us back to the cozy cottage in the sunlit meadow of our own belonging. It sits just outside the forest of our self-ignorance and our infatuation with the outside world. It is not made of bricks and mortar, nor straw and clay. It is a home built bit by bit of our life experiences, sensations, visions, sorrows, joys, memories, alliances, loyalties, relationships, secrets, truths and longings. The foundation of this house is built on the values, convictions and the principles we live by.

Rest in the warm pockets of the world where your belonging lies

Like swimming in a cool lake in summer and entering warm pockets of water that surprise and delight us, life has its warm pockets of belonging. Most of our experience in life is cool, the waters of our experience meant to awaken, refresh and revitalize our instincts and impulses for continuous growth. But we need those blessed and rare moments of warm waters to keep us diving in. We need those places where we are at home, where we feel accepted and encouraged, where we do not have to explain ourselves. Where we feel somehow known and understood. We all harbor myriad places, events, and sensations that stir those feelings of belonging in us. Here are some obvious places to look:

The sights, sounds and sensations of childhood

The child in all of us remembers how to belong in the world in a carefree way, and certain memories trigger those golden feelings. For me, the scent of long green summer grasses, autumn leaves, the loud roar of motor boats on a river, April lilacs and bluebells, the crunching snow under my feet, a cup of cocoa on a winter morning. There's nothing like the taste of Twinkies, Fritos, and grape Kool-aid for a real hit of childhood bliss. Catching toads, spitting watermelon seeds, the thrill of a summer carnival in the shopping center parking lot, readying for the Christmas pageant with a tinfoil halo, the smell of paste on construction paper. These sights, sounds and sensations have the power to send me into a nostalgic reverie where I have the heart and sensibilities of a child again, where my belonging in the world is fresh and new and unquestioned. What are some of yours?

Places of belonging

I feel at home in the Midwest because of my Illinois upbringing. I felt wonderfully at home in Granada, Spain, where I lived for a year and a half when I was younger. Oddly, after having the privilege of doing a lot of work throughout Canada for the past twelve years, I feel pretty much at home anywhere there, as much as I do in most of the United States.

Every summer for the last ten years, I have retreated with my family to a cabin in Lake of the Woods, Ontario. The sights and sounds of the Canadian wilderness now fill me with a joy that stems not just from delight, but from the comfort that comes with familiarity. It has become "home" to me so that there is a feeling of belonging in the call of the loon, in the rocking sensation of the boat and the sound of lapping water against the boat as we fish. The colorful moss on the rocks and trees on the surrounding small islands, the song of the white-throated sparrow, even the nearby town that has become our summer village—all of this provides a warm pocket of belonging for me now. The best part is that there is now a place within me, when I am far from the lake, that I can call up from inside and restore a sense of calm that being at the cabin invites.

But of all the places I have ever lived or spent time, I feel most at home in the Santa Cruz redwood forest. Actually, among the redwoods, it feels more like I have died and gone to heaven. Where do you feel at home in the world?

Memories and life experiences

Life is lived from experience to experience; it is the stuff our lives are made of. Often the lessons, truths and sometimes faulty assumptions we take from these experiences is what we cling to, not the experiences themselves. The significance we give these experiences becomes yet another important aspect of our belonging in the world because we come to understand ourselves and our lives in the context of those experiences. Memory is potent. It does something to us. It makes us who we are. It gives us depth. To a great degree, how we remember, what we remember, and why we remember, forms a personal map of our individuality. In this process of remembering, we unconsciously cast an overlay of meaning. John O'Donohue, tells us in *Anam Cara,*

> "Meaning is the sister of experience, and to discern the meaning of what has happened to you is one of the essential ways of finding your inner belonging and discovering the sheltering presence of soul. Every human heart seeks meaning; for it is in meaning that our deepest shelter lies."

We are always sowing new experiences, but as we harvest the meaning from them we give shape and fashion to our values and perspectives, to our very identities. We often tie much of our identities to key experiences of our lives. For example, we describe ourselves in terms like: navy brat, adult children of alcoholics, ex-hippies, recovering Catholics (Baptists, Methodists, etc.), the eldest of six kids, the black sheep of the family, the star of the team, a two-time loser in marriage, the first person in the family to graduate from college or the bread winner in a relationship. Describing ourselves in terms like these reflect that we are identifying with the experience as part of who we are. We are belonging to the event or the circumstances and the meaning it carried for us at the time.

It is neither right nor wrong that we do this, it is just part of our nature. But we must be cognizant of what we are identifying with and the meaning it continues to carry into our lives. Hopefully the experiences we identify with embolden our sensibilities and our personal power rather than deplete them. I have noticed that many people are more apt to take their identity more from the shape of their wounds than from where they have found joy or love. But whether we call ourselves Republican or Democrat, father or mother, survivor or victim, lover or friend, weak or strong, the naming of who we are will set the course of our lives, determine what we love, how we live and what gifts we bring to the world. What are some of the memories and life experiences which have shaped your identity?

In the company of loved ones

There are relationships that provide us a home in special ways and bring with them particular feelings of belonging. There are people in our lives who bring us to places within ourselves that we do not otherwise visit except in their company. It is as if they hold the only key to particular places in our hearts, be they rooms of hilarity, deep secrets, philosophical conversation, memories from certain periods of our lives or shared interests.

Family

Family relationships can bring a tremendous source of belonging to our lives. I love being with my siblings for this very reason. Although we are all so very different, we share some very basic Bissonnette traits and characteristics, which other people refer to as "quirks," albeit with affection. Among other things, we have a shared inheritance of memories, experiences and family folklore. I do not know how accurate a picture we really hold of one another or the extent to which we are relating out of old patterns and perceptions. Like all families, we enjoy our own particular mix of dysfunction. But this I know—I am completely at home in their loving eyes. I have no doubt that my brothers and sisters provide one of the most powerful sources of belonging I will ever know. And yet, I am not sure that I am ever happier than when I am in the company of my nieces and nephews and the other children in my life whom I embrace as such. It is in this role that I am in my true glory; my only job as their aunt is to adore them, and this I do quite readily.

Friendships

In considering relationships that bring us a profound sense of belonging, we should look deeply and with great appreciation to the people we call our friends. As I consider my own friends and imagine myself alone in a room with each of them, I can feel a different face emerge from underneath my skin, a different mode of my being, a distinctive hue of my spirit. Perhaps that is one of friendship's finest gifts—the way each one, like a private sun, urges us to new and distinctive flowering. The result of a life, then, invested in deep and enduring relationships, is a garden.

A true companion

One of the great experiences of life is to be in love. It's romantic and exhilarating and exciting, no doubt. But finding the person with whom you feel truly mated, with whom you somehow survive thick and thin and rich and poor—that is a horse of a different color. The one who knows you inside and out and accepts you; the one who sees your brilliance and your beauty, and does not need to pretend that you have no flaws and frailties because you are loved wholly. And when you find such a person along your life path, you know you have found treasure. You are ready to set up camp right then and right there, forever.

But your love for one another is too real to let your lives revolve around one another. So you enjoy the year or two looking deeply into each other's eyes, and then you rise to your feet and ready yourselves for the continuous journey of your unfolding. Except this time it's different, this time there is someone by your side. In such a connection between two people, there is a sense of belonging that is hard to match in any other way.

There are many things about my mate, Rob, that I love and appreciate. But one of the things that tipped me off to knowing that I had found my own true companion was when I realized that he had brought me to love my own name. I have never really liked my name, but when Rob says, "Denise Marie," it sounds so beautiful. He makes me want to live up to the beauty and tenderness with which he speaks it. The amazing part of it is, I don't feel like I have to work to be the woman he loves… I just get to be me and somehow, miraculously, I find that I am enough. If there is a clearer definition of what it means to be at home with or to belong with someone, I would like to know what it is.

In the company of loved ones we come home again to places within us that will never be foreign, could never be foreign regardless of how much time passes, because they have come to shape and fashion us. These are the people we describe as easy to be with, with whom it feels natural and in whose company we can unwind and let our hair down. People who invite us to be ourselves. In a world in which we often feel adrift and ungrounded, these relationships are priceless because they provide anchor, or at least a temporary beach to rest our weary bones. Who are those people in your life?

Natural talents

Have you ever noticed how at home in the world the rabbit looks in the tall grass of summer or how the squirrel exudes belongingness as it leaps from branch to branch? There is such a sense of peace in the natural world as we witness each creature being so totally itself in its habitat. I think we humans are also at home in the world when we are responding to our natural habitat with the gifts and abilities that we were given. This is what they were getting at in the movie, "The Legend of Bagger Vance." The search for the young golfer's "swing" was not about a golf stroke, but about finding one's stream in life in which every stroke is taken from a soulful and natural place—the place that is our nature, our home.

I am at home (and in my swing) when I am teaching and training, or delivering a keynote speech. I am at home when I am writing or reciting my poetry. I am at home on the tennis court, in a Scrabble game, playing euchre or deeply engulfed in my latest art project. I am at home in the kitchen, preparing a meal or baking a pie. I am at home in my garden.

The ways in which it is possible for us to engage and participate in the world are seemingly endless. Our natural talents and abilities can provide us with a sense of belonging through the choices we make in participating in the world, not only on Saturday afternoon, but through a lifetime. What are some of those activities which engage you deeply in the world?

Village and community

In today's global economy and with all the wonders of modern technology, the world may seem to be getting smaller on some levels, but to our personal human psyches, the world is still a pretty big place. All of human history points to our inclination to belong to a village. While we are growing in our capacity to value diversity and embrace differences, we are no less tribal in our bones than our descendants who lived in caves. And so we find our own caves, we develop our own tribes, we seek out our own territory that will be our village. We tend to frequent the same places in our communities, day in and day out, that bring us a sense of home in the world. Regardless of how large a city we live in, we all find our "village"—even if it's a strip mall with our own corner market, video store, dry cleaner and pizza parlor.

I live in a town of about 50,000 people. Relatively speaking, Santa Cruz is not that big. And yet, within Santa Cruz, I have marked my territory within particular bookstores and coffee shops. I have favorite parking spots downtown, certain places I always sit at church and certain cashiers I go to at my grocery store. I even have a favorite ATM I like to use at the bank. I have my regular restaurants and places I like to sit at those restaurants. There is a particular stretch along the ocean that is "my walk." There is a grand old cypress tree at the edge of the sea, whose lap I love to sit on and who I lovingly refer to as "Father Tree."

In the aftermath of the 1989 Loma Prieta earthquake, I was devastated with the damage that downtown Santa Cruz sustained. I remember grieving the loss of "my village." That was before I understood the meaning of village and community. Once the old stores and establishments set up in temporary tents, it was amazing to enter the "big top" and recognize faces, to sense the reminiscent style of a place and how they set up their merchandise; I couldn't believe it—the "spirit" of these places was still alive! I learned that a village is not made up of bricks and mortar; it is made of the fiber of relationships and the endurable threads of community.

In the wake of the attacks on the World Trade Center and the Pentagon, many people in the United States gained an acute awareness of what it means to be American. The images of firefighters and rescue workers laboring for days on end, people lined up for hours to donate blood to the local Red Cross and local school children holding bake sales and setting up lemonade stands to earn money to send to the families of the victims, gave the people of the United States a strong sense of community and village. What places do you frequent which constitute your village?

Nesting and what makes home, home

The human species is a nesting species. We like to stake out our territory and set up camp. Even if it is temporary. We need to belong, in some form or fashion, to the place where we rest our heads. For many, that feeling of belonging may be in the home itself, in the trees we've planted in the yard and the annoying but familiar creaking of the back door. For others who have not had the advantage of having a house to make home, we still find ways to nest.

I met a lovely, elderly woman in my community who is homeless. She approached me in a bakery and asked for a ride to the Community Center where they were hosting a Thanksgiving feast for the homeless. I could base another book on the contents of that fifteen minute conversation, but I will simply share this one penetrating insight that was one of the gifts from that experience.

Ida told me she had been an actress in her day, and a fine one at that. She had come from a wealthy family and had enjoyed an affluent upbringing in the hills of Carmel, California, forty minutes south of Santa Cruz. "In fact," she said with enthusiasm, "for my 18th birthday, my father, who was quite a famous politician, gave me a ring with diamonds all around it, like a flower." Her eyes danced as she set her hand atop my arm to proudly display her ring. All but one of the diamonds was missing." All I have to do is look down at my hand," she said, "and I remember who I am and where I came from." Ida carries her sense of home around her finger, despite where she lays her head.

I carry my sense of home differently. I have lived in many houses in the past twenty years and I have been able to make each one feel like home by finding a place to set my "treasures" that make any house my home. Christmas lights strung around the windows and mantels of each room (yes, all year long), and places for my collections of birds, eggs, nests, angels and a potpourri of Native American art quickly make me feel nested again. It is strange (and perhaps not healthy but still stubbornly true) that until my physical environment is in order (and by that I do not mean organized, but decorated), I cannot rest or relax inside. What about your environment tells you that you are "home"?

Pockets of belonging within ourselves

In the chilly waters of our lives, each of us has our own warm pockets of places, talents, memories, people, sensations and experiences that call up feelings of home, the song of belonging from our souls. Taken together, they provide a kind of temple of our own belonging in this massive universe. These are gifts of the outside world, because they are things we can touch the ground of, see photographs of, read old letters about, smell, sense, visit and embrace. They are strings to which we lovingly attach ourselves to this spiraling globe. But they are not the only strings. There are other threads which draw us into the fabric of this universe that have no outward manifestation. They are invisible, save to the eye of the heart and the vision of the soul. They are the silken threads of our desires and our longings.

Find belonging in your longing

Perhaps there is great treasure buried within each of us that must be sought with tools of diligence, solitude and contemplation. But one of the greatest treasures of our lives does not hide in secluded corners or in dusty hidden chests within our being. It comes right out in the open and makes itself known like hunger or thirst, we know it by the name of "longing."

Our longing is a pathway home to ourselves. It carries our vitality, our truth and the opportunity for our renewal. It carries the creative juice and urgency that stirs our passion and awakens our native talents. Longing is a threshold to the native home inside us.

"The Journey to Belong," the poem that begins this chapter, is really an ode to the journey of my longings. Obviously this poem is an extremely abbreviated version of that journey, highlighting a few of its primary points along the way: my ten-year longing to be a nun and to belong to God; my longing to go to college and somehow qualify myself for independence in the world; my longing to be a wife and mother, and to love and be loved in the most complete way I knew possible; my longing to choose and hone my work so that I could give the best of my gifts, and in turn, reap the rewards of that work. The points that I did not highlight in the journey include some of those in which my original desires and longings led to conflicting loyalties. (Who would want to muddle an otherwise nice flowing poem with some of the grittier points of life?) Here's a fairly benign example:

I was very steadfast in my longing to be loyal to the people of the company of which I have been a part for several years. This longing steered my professional choices for more than a decade. The journey I undertook with my partners had been rich professionally and personally. One of the results of following the longing to be loyal to them and to the company, however, was not being loyal to myself in other ways, and abdicating some of my own basic needs and desires in order to "stay the course." Fortunately, I found the courage to step out on my own and to follow the beat of my own drum… this book being the first result of that move. The longing to be loyal to my partners has not ceased, but the longing to be loyal to myself and to my own life has a stronger pull.

Clearly, we have conflicting loyalties in our longings, and hence, difficult choices we must make along the way. It is so important, however, that we recognize the forces that are leading our course and to know what we are being loyal to. Because many of our choices are based on our basic longings and our desire to belong, it is easy to get off track and to take ourselves where we never meant to go. For example, the woman who is loyal to her abusive husband, the teenager who is loyal to the gang or the person who is loyal to a profession long after the work has ceased to feed his spirit. It is essential that we chart our journey with sound values, principles and convictions that can help us make good and healthy choices—choices that follow the current of our longings and feed into the river of our souls.

Develop an internal Jiminy Cricket

We need to develop a conscience as faithful and persistent as little Jiminy Cricket, Pinnochio's friend, to remind us: "Always let your conscience be your guide."

Stephen Covey, in his book, *The Seven Habits of Highly Effective People,* suggests that we each have a center, though we do not recognize it as such. Nor do we recognize the all-encompassing effects of that center on every aspect of our lives. Some of the factors that we ultimately allow to affect the sum and substance of our lives include:

- Our relationship with our spouse or partner
- Our family and our desire to care for them
- The need and desire to earn and spend money
- The pressures and demands of work
- Owning and maintaining possessions
- Affiliation with a church or a religious group
- Obsession with ourselves, our own pain and pleasure

These elements are important and deserve our serious devotion and attention. But we must be wary of letting them become *the center* of our lives. These are circumstances that are beyond our control and can change without our consent. A spouse can leave us, we can fail to get the promotion, the church can undergo massive changes conflicting with our faith, the house can go into foreclosure, the kids grow up, our hair turns gray… I am beginning to sound like a country and western song, but you catch my drift.

Life is chock full of the unknown which blows two ways—ways we like it and ways we don't. We don't get to choose which way the winds of change will blow. But we can tolerate change, any change, if there is a changeless core inside of us. The key to coping with the storms of life is having a changeless sense of who we are, what we are about and what we value. We must navigate our path of belonging with the stuff that is constant and grounding, regardless of circumstances. We need an inner core that provides us with a sense of power and security, serving as a compass with which to make important decisions and choices in our lives. At the center of our lives should be the dwelling place of the treasure no one can steal: a sense of self-worth, emotional maturity, self-esteem, a perspective on life, a healthy sense of balance, discernment, and a sense of wholeness.

What if we were to belong first to our integrity and our sense of fairness, to our dignity and our self-determination? What if we, at our core, belonged to joy and wonderment and a deep, abiding faith in the ways of Spirit? What if we belonged, in some serious sense, to our values and principles? I, for one, know that my life would change dramatically if I could attach my sense of belonging and my loyalties to these deeper currents of longing. What this requires, of course, is living with mindfulness and wholehearted discernment. Revolutionary economist, E. F. Schumacher, spoke of the need for our careful discernment in his book, *Good Work*. He writes:

> "You are put into this life with the task of learning to distinguish between that which is really real and really important and permanent and of true value on the one hand, and things trivial, amusing, ephemeral, and of no value on the other hand."

One immediate result of living from a core of principles and values to which we pledge our deepest loyalties would be a completely different perspective on goals and the meaning of them in our lives. We would realize in a meaningful way that life is not about having or obtaining or arriving or finishing or earning or marrying or achieving. The whole purpose of life is about our *becoming.*

Embrace life as a journey of "becoming"

We live in a goal-oriented culture that would ask not only that we articulate our final destination, but the goals and objectives, strategies and schedules we plan to follow in order to get there. These goals should be specific and measurable, attainable and realistic with very clear-cut timelines. Conventional wisdom tells us that if we fail to plan, we should plan to fail.

I would not argue with the principle that everything is created twice—we have to have vision of something before we can create it. In fact, I would argue that the more ambitious the goal and the clearer the vision, the greater the likelihood that we will actually achieve it. That's because when we have a horizon that we can taste and feel and see, we are granted one of the most powerful forces in human life, the power of focus.

What we may have lost sight of, however, is that goals are a means to an end, not the ultimate purpose of our lives. They are simply a tool to concentrate our focus and move us in a direction. The only reason we really pursue goals is to cause ourselves to expand and grow. Achieving goals by themselves will never make us happy in the long term; it's who we become, as we overcome the obstacles necessary to achieve our goals, that in the end gives us the deepest and most long-lasting sense of fulfillment.

Haven't we all experienced the distinct lack of fulfillment that comes with having achieved a goal that had, up until that point, worked wonderfully well as a kind of gravity, but, soon after arrival, proved a disappointing destination? Whether it was a college degree or a painting or the final performance of a play or a long-awaited promotion or arriving at the top of a mountain… the getting there was the whole point. And then what?! We rest on our laurels for a few minutes before we are busy looking outward for the next horizon that has enough juice in it to stir our souls and move our feet. We can't settle into the destination for long, because our real home in life is in the traveling, in the growing and becoming.

Freeman Dyson reminds us "the universe is infinite in every direction." What matters is our manner of traveling within the galaxy that is each of our lives. What we are really seeking is the rapture of being alive and taking comfort and sustenance from the spots along the way that provide a sense of true belonging. In the words of the great writer James Michener, "For this is the journey that man makes: to find himself. If they fail on this, it doesn't matter what else they find."

Perhaps we would serve ourselves (and the world) better if we began to ask, "Who do I want to become?" rather than, "What do I want to do for a living?" or "What is my next goal on the journey?" If we approached life as a mystery that is meant to be lived rather than a problem to be solved, maybe we would feel less lost.

I presently have that "no clear destination" sense about my own livelihood. It is frightening in some moments and exhilarating in others. The fear is that if I am not working toward something specific, I may just venture off on some weird path and awaken, like Dante, in the middle of a dark wood. The exhilarating part is the hope and faith that if I continue to follow my feet and lean into the current of my native intuitions and longings, I will enter a river of joy, the likes of which I could never have imagined. The biggest piece of the puzzle is not where I will end up, but who I will become in the process. Any destination I choose for myself now can only be envisioned with the image I have of myself at present. As Shakespeare said, "We know what we are and what we are not. What we do not know is who or what we will become." That is what this journey is all about.

A Cradle of Wings

I once had a dream—a marvelous dream—of being at the top of a lovely mountain overlooking a horizon lined with hills of rolling green. Out of nowhere, I was swept up into the wings of a huge white dove. Sensations of both terror and thrill soared through me as I was swooped high above the ground in a cloud of billowing white. I grasped helplessly at the air, searching in vain for something to hold on to in the stark white plumage. As my panic began to rise, a warm realization happened over me, a recognition that I was safe… that I was being held in the wings of Spirit, in the downy folds of the Holy Spirit. I was more than safe. I was being cradled and carried in a feathery bed of belonging.

I will be forever grateful for the experience of that dream, for that completeness of belonging, if even in a dream, because it was *my* dream and those were *my* feelings, and now that potentiality of experience lives in me. Something tells me that I can travel the world over and I will not fully find that Cradle of Wings in my human experience. But that's okay, because in my day-to-day life, I can be blessed with glimpses of its shadow and whispers from its wings.

I do not want to lie down
at night wondering
if I will ever have a place
of belonging in the world.
I want to change my question to
"Do I have a place in me
for the world?"
I want my belonging
to be in my longing
to be worthy of this world
and to love it fully.

Now the *Great Belonging* I experienced in my dream shows up in the smaller belongings of my life in the faces of those I love, on a walk in the redwoods, in the sprouting of the first bulb from the winter ground and on the wings of a poem that alights on the white page. It is here, in these small experiences that I find a place inside myself for the world. It is here that I find myself loving it fully and in those moments I do not question that I am worthy, because I belong to these small comforts and joys as I belong to my own life. To what do you belong?

Passages

"We shall not cease from exploration
And the end of all our exploring
Will be to arrive where we started
And know the place for the first time."

T. S. Eliot

"The journey is my home."

Muriel Rukeyser

"And the world cannot be discovered
by a journey of miles,
no matter how long,
but only by a spiritual journey,
a journey of one inch,
very arduous and humbling
and joyful,
by which we arrive
at the ground of our feet,
and learn to be home."

Wendell Berry

"Don't compromise yourself.
You are all you've got."

Janis Joplin

"It's good to have an end to journey towards,
but it is the journey that matters in the end."

Ursula K. LeGuin

"Any road is bound to arrive
somewhere if you follow it
far enough."

Patricia Wentworth

Glenn Clark

"If you wish to travel far and fast, travel light,
take off all your envies, jealousies, unforgiveness,
selfishness and fears."

"We have to stumble through so much dirt and
humbug before we reach home.
And we have no one to guide us.
Our only guide is our homesickness."

Hermann Hesse

"Through fear of knowing who
we really are and what we want,
we sidestep our own destiny
which leaves us hungry in a
famine of our own making."

John O'Donohue

Rudolf Steiner

"He who would know the world,
seek first within his being's depths;
he who would truly know himself,
develop interest in the world."

"Whether drifting through life on a boat
or climbing toward old age leading a horse,
each day is a journey
and the journey itself is home."

Basho

"The afternoon knows what the
morning never suspected."

Swedish proverb

"Live your life each day
as you would climb a mountain.
An occasional glance toward the summit
keeps the goal in mind, but many beautiful
scenes are to be observed from each new
vantage point. Climb slowly, steadily, enjoying
each passing moment; and the view from
the summit will serve as a fitting climax for
the journey."

Harold B. Melchart

"Be brave enough to live life creatively.
The creative is the place
where no one else has ever been.
You have to leave the city of your comfort
and go into the wilderness of your intuition.
You can't get there by bus,
only by hard work and risk
and by not quite knowing what you're doing.
What you'll discover will be wonderful.
What you'll discover will be yourself."

Alan Alda

Christian Morgenstern

"Home is not where you
live but where they
understand you."

Anaïs Nin

"There are few human beings
who receive the truth,
complete and staggering,
by instant illuminations.
Most of them acquire it fragment by fragment,
on a small scale, by successive developments,
cellularly, like a laborious mosaic."

"Life is painting a picture, not doing a sum."

Oliver Wendell Holmes, Jr.

Joanna Field

"I began to have an idea of my life,
not as the slow shaping of achievement
to fit my preconceived purposes.
But as the gradual discovery and growth
of a purpose which I did not know."

"The seeker, however, must seek—and this
is the core of his difficulty. He cannot know
what he is looking for until he finds it."

William Segal

"The only journey is the one within."

Rainer Maria Rilke

James Michener

"Life is like a good book.
The further you get into it,
the more sense it begins to
make."

"There are no wrong turns… only wrong
thinking about the turns our lives have taken."

Zen saying

"Like it or not, we grow like onions grow,
layer upon layer, or like a tree ring upon ring.
Outward from it's core."

Carl Rogers

To Ponder and To Practice

- List the last five positions you've held or roles you have played in your life. What have you learned through these various experiences? How have you been shaped by these positions or roles? What new qualities or attributes do you think your present position or role is developing in you?
- Given the nature of life's twisting and turning path, there are no wrong turns, only unexpected paths. What was the last unexpected path you took on your journey? Did that experience strengthen or weaken your trust in life's journey? How did that path lead you closer or deeper into your own sense of belonging in the world?
- Construct a map marking the distances traveled and the varied destinations visited on your own "journey to belong."
- Create a "Book of Belonging" by filling a blank book or journal with thoughts, images, photos and pictures from magazines of images, words and symbols that invoke in you the feelings of belonging, of being at home in the world. (This book could be an incredible treasure to pass on to a loved one some day.)
- When you were a child, what did you think your life would look like as an adult? How is your life different than you expected? Are there any expectations you have continued to carry that may be getting in the way of your ability to fully embrace where you are now?
- What core beliefs, values or principles do you feel make up your own inner house of belonging?
- In what circumstances do you feel most at home in the world? With whom do you feel most at home in the world? Where are the places of your own deep sense of belonging?
- What choices have you made in your life that have led you to discover that, like Dorothy, you are wearing the red slippers that will carry you home?
- Think about some of the key experiences in your life that have come to define you. Does your identifying with these experiences embolden your sense of personal power or deplete it?
- Author Zora Neale Hurston once noted that "There are years of our lives that ask questions and years of our lives that answer." Which phase are you currently in—the questioning period or one that is providing answers?
- Select a quote on the topic of belonging from this chapter's *Passages* and post it where you will see it until it is internalized.

Practice

- Choose a daily habit, routine or symbol to help you remain conscious of your values and convictions—of your internal Jiminy Cricket.
- Given everything you have read in this chapter, what do you want to *keep* doing? What do you want to *stop* doing? What do you want to *start* doing?

Notes

Chapter 13

On Second Thought

Harnessing Perspective

Choose abundance over scarcity

Choose abundance over scarcity

Harness the power of perspective

Harness the power of perspective

Make the connection between thoughts and words

Make the connection between thoughts and words

Remember the Rabbi's Gift

Remember the Rabbi's Gift

Know when to change the channel

Know when to change the channel

Expand the size of the fishbowl

Expand the size of the fishbowl

Rediscover your riches

Rediscover your riches

Take another point of view

Take another point of view

On Second Thought

"Two men in prison looked through bars, one saw mud, the other saw stars."
The poet speaks in one bare line,
of the power and command of the human mind.

So, dear mind, I ask you, why do you look to the ground?
Why is the muddy, the ugly, mundane, usually the first to be found?
When beauty, goodness, and even truth are also there to be seen,
why in cynical judgment do you gravitate and lean?

"Ah," says the mind, "if at first it seems in a web of doubt I'm caught,
don't forget I am capable of a second more hopeful thought.
If at first blush to the gutter, I cast a casual glance,
with just a nudge I'll lift my gaze, if you give me a second chance.
That's the marvel of being human and gifted with a brain;
prompt me to look to the very same thing and I'll perceive it fresh again.

Are you really going crazy, or do you have lots of questions?
Is your co-worker really insane, or could you ponder her suggestions?
Do you see a lonely weed or is it a lovely flower?
What is coming, a foreboding storm or a needed springtime shower?
That's the splendor of a second thought, of entertaining a wider view,
it'll give you an opportunity to see the world anew.

Is your work a drudgery, nine to five, it's all a duty,
or will you entreat me to look again, to unveil the unseen beauty?
It all depends on how I'm used, if you stop at my first thought
and believe my fear and crankiness of which, at times, I'm fraught.
But what if you remember, that isn't my full story
and you freed me to think a brand new thought—that is my finest glory!

There may be some who ignore the mud and solely see the stars,
but both are there for us to see in this wild world of ours.
So if I look down in dark complaint and begrudgingly slug through the day,
lift my eyes—and I promise you, I'll spot you the Milky Way!"

Reflections

"The mind is its own place, and in itself can make a heaven of Hell, a hell of Heaven." In this simple statement 17th century English poet John Milton summed up a basic truth; all of our experiences in life are colored by our thoughts. This classic teaching story instructs in the implications of this basic truth:

> Once there was a lady who was sitting on her porch as a stranger passed by. "Good morning," he greeted her as he tipped his hat. "What a beautiful day! I am new in town and quite excited about my prospects. I understand this town is just brimming with possibility for someone like me."
>
> The woman responded gaily, "I see a future so bright for you that it hurts my eyes to even look your way! Welcome to our fine city!" And he walked on.
>
> Moments later another young man passed by her porch. "Good morning," he said as he tipped his hat. "Boy it's hot today. And the mosquitoes are bitin', too! I am new in town. I'm a bit worried because I understand there are lots of people here competing in a very limited job market."
>
> The woman responded in a concerned tone, "I'm afraid you're right, young man. I see a troubled future ahead for you. Don't forget where I live, if you ever need a bit of charity. Good luck!" And he walked on.
>
> A moment later the woman's husband opened the screen door and commented to his wife, "Pick a lane, dear. There you are telling one young whippersnapper that everything is comin' up roses and in the next breath you're all pity and gloom."
>
> His wife, in all her wisdom, responded, "That's because, my dear, I am absolutely certain that each of those young men will find exactly what he expects to find."

As the woman in the story is saying, cynicism tends to be a self-fulfilling prophecy. Because it likes to blame and complain, cynicism ignores the key that would unlock the ball and chain attached to our minds. Everything seen through the eyes of the cynic proves itself true, thus the thought pattern remains solidly in place. In like manner, optimism is also a self-fulfilling prophecy. The world seen through the eyes of the optimist proves itself equally true. We may think that everything we experience is to some extent a reflection of our minds—like looking through a kind of mirror which receives accurate impressions of reality. But the human mind, with all of its attitudes and perceptions, is the principal element of creation—the creator of the reality we see.

It should give us pause to realize the extent to which we author the story of our lives each day and each moment, not just in the choices we make and the actions we take, but in the way we think. Like the two newcomers in the story, whether we experience scarcity or abundance has more to do with us than it does the outside world.

Choose abundance over scarcity

There is so much about our culture and our upbringing that is reflective of our minds' bent toward the scarcity mentality, none more so than in the area of employment. The scarcity mentality professes that there is not enough opportunity to go around and that we had better fight to get our small piece of the pie. From this perspective, we are all in competition with each other; it is a dog eat dog world—survival of the fittest.

I am of the strong belief that there is more opportunity for any given member of any community than they could possibly take advantage of in one short lifetime. Our job is to live our lives fully and to hire ourselves the right employer, to put our gifts to work in our own unique way. From this perspective, our world is affected by our choices and actions, by the opportunities we create or do not create. I am not competing with anyone because there is only one me and the same is equally true for everyone else.

I heard a great example of someone who lives in the abundance mentality. Currently a motivational speaker, he had been a physically active ex-marine who had been severely burned in a fire—disfiguring his face and losing most of his fingers. Once recovered from the deep depression of this tragedy, this man re-entered the world by running for mayor. He won. Then he decided to take up flying. One day, he was forced to make an emergency landing, and the crash left him paralyzed from the waist down. In speaking about his life he says, tongue in cheek, "Before my accidents, there were 10,000 things I could do. Now there are only 9,000."

What a great story in a day in age when perfectly talented and healthy individuals complain of having too much competition in a limited job market. How many possible work opportunities would it take for us to believe in abundance? 12,000? 15,000? Especially since we can only work one, maybe two at a time? It's all a matter of perspective.

Harness the power of perspective

"Oh, to be seventy again!" Such were the words of Oliver Wendell Holmes, expressed in his 87th year while watching a pretty girl walk by. How's that for changing perspective as we bemoan the advent of another year?

Try this thought on for size. It is from Douglas Adams in the *Hitchhiker's Guide to the Galaxy:*

> "Far out in the uncharted backwaters of the unfashionable end of the Western Spiral arm of the Galaxy lies a small unregarded yellow sun. Orbiting this at a distance of roughly ninety-eight million miles is an utterly insignificant little blue-green planet whose ape descended life forms are so amazingly primitive that they still think digital watches are a pretty neat idea."

When we change how we are looking at something (namely, our perspective), we change everything! It's not unlike hiking in the wilderness. It is so easy to get lost while you are traveling through a forest, especially if you are off the beaten path. To avoid becoming disoriented, it helps if every once in a while you climb to the top of a hill in order to get your bearings. From that higher vantage point, you can better survey the landscape of the entire forest, without being confused by the individual trees. Based on the perspective of a wider point of view, you can do a better job of figuring out where you are and how you can get to where you want to go.

Albert Einstein warns, "The problems we face cannot be solved at the same level of thinking we used to create them." Indeed, in order to get a useful grip on a problematic life situation, we need to be able to step back from it and rise above it, to widen the view, expand our awareness, and shift from the framework in which we are presently thinking about it. To be able to do this, we have to lift ourselves out of the ruts of our minds and let go of our usual way of seeing things. Instead of going around and around in the same struggle, we free up our minds to new possibilities. This is what it means to harness the power of perspective.

What is the use of having an imagination if we don't use it to pull ourselves out of our perceived misery and into some more pleasant illusion? I think that's why we were gifted with an imagination. "Okay," thought the Creator, "it's tough on Earth... I have made it plenty inconvenient, frustrating and troublesome, all for their highest good, of course. But why don't I throw in Imagination—that way they can pull themselves out of their own misery on a moment's notice. Yeah, that's what I'll do—I'll give them the gift of perspective."

Make the connection between thoughts and words

> Change your language and you change your thoughts.
> Change your thoughts and you change your feelings.
> Change your feelings and you change your experience.

Have you ever noticed that someone whose glass is "half-empty" may have exactly the same of amount of water as someone whose glass is half-full? Yet the person with the half-empty glass feels deprived while the other feels blessed. People who would say "I have failed three times" might tend to think of themselves as losers, while people who "haven't yet found a way to succeed" think of themselves as winners in the making.

That's the marvel of being human
and gifted with a brain;
Prompt me to look to the very same
thing and I'll perceive it fresh again.
Are you really going crazy,
or do you have lots of questions?
Is your co-worker really insane,
or could you ponder her suggestions?
Do you see a lonely weed
or is it a lovely flower?
What is coming, a foreboding storm
or a needed springtime shower?
That's the splendor
of a second thought,
of entertaining a wider view,
I'll give you an opportunity
to see the world anew.

As we speak, thus do we think, and vice versa. The particular words we use to talk about our situation tell us how to think and feel about it. Whether we got those words from our families or came up with them on our own, the stories we speak closely reflect the way we think and feel about our situation. Together, these control our instinctive responses to the events that come our way.

I am writing this chapter from a cabin in Lake of the Woods, Ontario, Canada. It is relatively early in the summer and the water in the lake is very, very cold! I have been trying to rethink my response to the water as I dip into it by saying aloud, "Refreeeeshing..." rather than, "Holy Iceberg, it's freezing!" I have found that the words I use actually influence how my body responds to the temperature of the water.

My dear friend and fellow trainer, Nora Gerber, once passed on a great example of this language-feeling connection. She says that when something goes wrong, like locking keys in the car or missing a turn-off on the freeway, instead of allowing a few choice words to flow from her mouth, she stops and says, "Oh well." It cracks me up every time I remember to do this because the difference in my emotions when I use the "choicer" words or when I say "oh well" is so very dramatic. Try it.

Taken from one of my earlier publications, *30 Ways to Shine as a New Employee,* here are a few other examples of how our language changes our experience. This is from an exercise in which two people are in exactly the same circumstances, but are saying different things to themselves about those circumstances:

I am so confused!	I have a lot of questions right now.
I am making so many mistakes!	I am learning a lot right now.
These people are insane.	How do I maintain my serenity in this environment?
This job is so boring.	I am going to have to be very creative to enjoy this job.

The point of the exercise is not to convince people to become "positive thinkers"—to imagine that they will automatically apply their most positive bent in any given situation. I mean for the two points of view to actually be coming from the same person; the left hand-side being their first thought, the right hand-side being their second thought. It is one of the glories of being gifted with a mind; we do not have to stop at our first thought. The mind is like a train that has the capability of suddenly switching tracks.

"Ah," says the mind,
"if at first it seems
in a web of doubt I'm caught,
don't forget I am capable
of a second more hopeful thought.
If at first blush to the gutter
I cast a casual glance
With just a nudge,
I'll lift my gaze,
if you give me a second chance."

Remember the Rabbi's Gift

We live in a world that is neutral to our experience. It is up to us to decide each day what meaning we shall bring and where we will apply our focus. Will we notice the way the sun is playing on the river, the formations of the clouds and the scent of fresh cut lawn lacing the air, or we will focus instead on the humidity and the annoyance of the mosquitoes? Look for beauty and you will find beauty. Look for problems and you will find plenty of trouble everywhere. It seems an abiding truth that the way we are in relation to the world is the way the world is in relation to us.

We accept that when our eyesight is poor, the world becomes a blur, or when our hearing is damaged, a dull silence replaces what could be music or the voice of a loved one. In a similar way, when our thoughts are impaired, negative or diminished, we will never discover anything rich or beautiful about the world we live in. If our thoughts are allowed to be impoverished or dulled, the world we perceive will be dull as well. Change the eye that sees and you change the world that is seen, as Lao Tzu reminds us in this short and powerful parable.

> Once upon a time a man whose ax was missing suspected his neighbor's son. The boy walked like a thief, looked like a thief, and spoke like a thief. But the man found his ax while digging in the valley, and the next time he saw his neighbor's son, the boy walked, looked and spoke like any other child.

It is a commonly held belief that beauty is in the eye of the beholder. But rarely does it occur to us that wisdom, ugliness, holiness—any judgment we would make about the world and other people—these too, are in the eye of the beholder. Inside ourselves or outside, we never have to change what we see, only the way we see it. How do we keep ourselves ever aware of the fact that the eyes are not responsible when it's the mind that does the seeing?

The following story has shown up in many books and texts, always attributed to a different spiritual tradition. It remains one of my all-time favorites. I have written it in my own style, but borrowed the basic story from the version that M. Scott Peck includes in his book, *The Road Less Traveled.*

There was once an abbot of a dwindling Christian order with only five monks left, all over seventy years old. The abbot heard that his trusted friend, an old rabbi, was to be on a hermitage in the forest near the order's decaying house. The abbot was hopeful that the wise rabbi could give him some advice on how to revitalize his order. They met and embraced and talked about deep things way into the night by the light of a fire. They commiserated on the lack of spiritual awareness left in the world, as the rabbi had experienced similar apathy in his own temple. The rabbi was sorry that he had no advice to give his friend. As morning approached and the abbot was about to take his leave, the rabbi said, "I wish I had some advice to give you, my friend, but I do not. The only thing I can tell you is that the Wise and Holy One lives amongst you."

The abbot was perplexed by his friend's comment but when he returned, he shared this comment with the other four aged monks. They each wondered who the Wise and Holy One was and they began to view one another through new eyes.

Could it be Brother Andrew? But he is always so pensive and quiet. And yet, he does have a gift for listening. Could it be Brother Thomas? But he is always acting like a clown. But then, his laughter and humor does have a healing affect. Could it be Brother Edward? But he is always so competitive and opinionated. But then again, he is almost always right. They even began to look in the mirror wondering, "Could it be me?" They began to treat themselves and each other as if each were potentially wise and holy.

Villagers who happened to be hiking near the monastery were attracted by the extraordinary love and respect that emanated from the order of monks. More and more people came to play and pray. Some began to talk to the monks. As time went on, a steady stream of spiritual seekers asked to join the order and it began to flourish once again.

This all came to pass because of the rabbi's gift.

The Rabbi could not have bestowed a more beautiful, powerful or enduring gift—the gift of new eyes and a new mind. This is a gift we can give ourselves with attention to our thinking.

Know when to change the channel

Psychologists estimate that we typically think as many as 50,000 thoughts a day. Thoughts run non-stop through our minds like programs on a radio station, sometimes in the background and sometimes blaring so loudly we can't ignore them. Sometimes our thoughts play the blues, and sometimes they put a happy bounce in our step. I love the metaphor that Vietnamese poet and author Thich Nhat Hanh uses to describe the human mind. He writes:

> "A human being is like a television set with millions of channels. If we turn on sorrow, we are sorrow. If we turn on a smile, we are the smile. We cannot let one channel dominate us. We have the seed of everything in us and we have to seize the situation at hand, to recover our power. We need to change the channel once in a while!"

Aside from the fact that we often forget to change the channel, even from the seediest of programs, what is even more profound is to consider what Deepak Chopra suggests when he says:

> "Your body is a 3-D projection of your state of mind. Your slightest shift of mood is picked up by every cell, which means that you do not think with your brain alone—all fifty million cells in your body actively share your thoughts."

It is amazing and scary to think that our bodies are like sophisticated holographic images that are programmed by our thoughts. From that perspective, it makes sense why we get sick when we are stressed and why we look so refreshed when we are happy. As the anonymous writer says so eloquently:

> "Remember that as you think, so you travel.
> As you love, you attract.
> You are today where your thoughts have brought you;
> you will be tomorrow where your thoughts take you.
> You cannot escape the result of your thoughts;
> but you can endure and learn, accept and be glad.
> You will realize the vision of your heart,
> not the ideal wish.
> You will gravitate toward that
> which you secretly most love.
> Into your hands will be placed
> the exact result of your thoughts;
> you will receive that which you earn; no more, no less.
> Whatever your present environment may be,
> you will fall.
> Remain or rise with your thoughts,
> your vision—your ideal."

Expand the size of the fishbowl

Like the earth growing what is planted in it, we always draw to us that which we have planted in our minds. The perspective we hold can put us in a positive state of mind or a negative one, in scarcity or abundance, in darkness or in light. Our ordinary habits of thought can be helpful and serve us well, or they can be hurtful and weaken our mental resources. As the following story reminds us, how we use our minds can readily increase or diminish our powers in the world.

Once upon a time there was king who had a son who walked with a humped back. The king brought in experts of every kind to help his son to stand straighter. They tried Reiki, Swedish Massage, Rolfing, Deep Tissue Work, Hypnotherapy, Herbology, Aromatherapy... people trained in every possible therapy were coming out of the woodwork! But alas, none of their suggestions worked.

One day a wise old woman was passing through the town and she saw the boy playing in the Village Square. She asked to see the king and shared with him one final suggestion: to build a statue of his son with a perfectly straight back and place it right in the middle of the square where his son preferred to play. The king figured that they had nothing to lose, and so, commissioned the building of the statue.

Time passed and each day the boy looked upon the statue of himself with a straight back, and each day, he stood just a little bit taller himself. Not even a full summer had gone by when the boy himself stood as straight as his own statue.

For better or worse, our daily thoughts have tremendous power in affecting what we feel and experience throughout the day. Wouldn't it be great if we could think thoughts that cheer and nourish us rather than those that weaken and diminish our spirit—the kind that make us stand straight and proud rather than thoughts that have us laid up like couch potatoes at the end of the day? You know, vitamins-for-the-soul kinds of thoughts rather than junk food thoughts? Thoughts that set you dancing to your heart's song instead of thoughts that wrap you up in a cloud of dark foreboding.

The way the goldfish grows to the size of its environment is a good metaphor for the human mind. A goldfish in a bowl in a child's bedroom may only be two inches long, but placed in a natural pond, will grow to the size of small dog. The advantage we have over goldfish is that we get to choose the size of our bowls. We can either enhance or diminish our potential by our belief systems. We remain limited only by our self-imposed bowl size. The trick to achieving majestic heights is, I believe, to limit ourselves only to the expectation of greatness.

My friend Sheri has such a strong belief in me that when I am in her presence, I can almost feel myself growing. Growing in heart, in confidence, and in power. Her expectations of me and what I will achieve are nothing less than fantastic. As I write these lines I am reminded that this book is in part due to Sheri's prompting to follow my dream and to respond to my gifts and my calling with unadulterated confidence and joy. Everyone needs a Sheri in their life, someone who holds up a statue of you with a straight back and broad smile. Everyone needs that guardian angel sans wings. Likewise, each of us should serve that purpose for someone else.

Rediscover your riches

Here is a wonderful story about the power of perspective which I have adapted from a Sufi tale shared in the wonderful book, *Stories of the Heart, Stories of the Spirit,* written by Christina Feldman and Jack Kornfield:

> Once upon a time a couple who were having marital problems visited a wise sage for advice. They were surprised at what he suggested. He told them to round up a few goats, a few cows, some chickens and a dog and bring them into their home to live. With his guarantee that this would solve their problem, they agreed.
>
> Well, everything was going fine until the goats starting chewing on the furniture, the cows took up half the living room, the dog began howling deep into the night and the chickens shed their feathers everywhere. The couple put up with it for a week, but finally reached their limits! They returned to the sage complaining of the noise, mess and commotion the animals caused. He simply smiled saying, "I suggest, then, that you get rid of them at once! Come and see me again in a few days."
>
> The couple did as they were told and returned a few days later. As he had expected, the sage watched the couple approach arm in arm, giddy with joy. They expressed that they had never known such peace or serenity and that they were taking advantage of their newly-discovered joy and intimacy with one another. The sage just smile and nodded, as wise sages do.

Can you imagine how happy we would be if we were to lose everything we have right now—our health, our relationships, our belongings—

and then somehow get it all back? We would be ecstatic. We would sit like kings and queens, aware of our abundance and good fortune. I suggest that we need not lose everything first in order to appreciate all that we have. We only need to employ the magical powers of perspective.

Take another point of view

I have a few tricks that help me gain perspective in any situation pretty quickly. When I am stressed or up in arms about something, I think about some of the people I have known and loved who have passed away. I stop to consider what they would say about my situation from where they are now. Somehow, I am always convinced that what is so serious to me in the moment looks pretty insignificant from the other side.

At other times I gain perspective by thinking about my friend, Joel, who is serving a ten-year prison sentence. Once, while I was traveling, my flight was canceled and I knew that I was going to be stuck in an airport for an extra five or six hours. I wanted to scream. And then, somehow, I thought about Joel and found myself wondering what he would do with five hours if he were there, free and out of prison, in the airport. Suddenly, I saw everything differently. Hey, there's a phone—I can call anyone I want and talk for as long as I want without anyone watching me or listening in. Hey, there's a snack bar where you can order anything you want, and it's not prison fare! And there's a bookstore —a glorious bookstore with hundreds, no, thousands of books that you can pick up and skim through, perhaps even buy and read! And look at all these people—young and old, men and women, people of every walk of life—and not in striped uniforms! What a feast for the eyes!

It occurred to me later that I should suggest to airport personnel that when they have to cancel a flight they say over the intercom," We are sorry to inform you that your flight has been canceled. However, we are pleased to remind you that, since you are not in prison, you may use the next five hours of your freedom in any way you please."

It's amazing how a crisis or an illness can later bring the enduring gift of perspective to a family. Our family knows this well after experiencing the terror and strife that resulted from our youngest sibling, Guy, being diagnosed with leukemia at sixteen years old. Guy was just your typical teenager who fought with his older brother, swam on the swim team and struggled with his paper route. Weeks into an unabating cold and sore throat accompanied by unaccounted for and excessive bruising on his legs, my step-mom took Guy to the doctor for a physical. One look at him and the doctor knew that not only did Guy have leukemia, but that it was probably already advanced. And it was.

Guy suffered through years of the physical, mental and emotional traumas that accompany the process of radiation and chemotherapy. By the grace of God and medical advances in cancer-fighting drugs, I am elated to say that my little freckled brother with the bald head is now a handsome, happy second-grade schoolteacher with a full head of hair! Unfortunately, many of the friends he made on the pediatrics cancer ward were not so lucky.

This painful experience brought a gift to our family. It is reflected in the words that leap to mind when someone in the family faces a new challenge, be it vocational, financial, or marital in nature. We will barely have waded into the waters of conversation about the newest problem when someone will pipe up with, "Well, it's not leukemia!" We paid a high price for the gift of this perspective but it works like a charm every time!

Sometimes it helps to consider a difficult situation from three different perspectives. For example, viewing things from the perspective of the optimist, the pessimist and then the pragmatist. Or asking what is funny, what is tragic and what is just fine about the situation. If the situation involves other people, taking on the perspective of each person and considering the individual points of view can be helpful. Another great idea is to write down the names of ten teachers in your life. These could include classroom teachers, neighbors, a parent or a friend whom you highly respect. Some of your teachers may be qualities or characteristics like love, patience or discernment. When facing a challenge or burdened with a concern, entertain the input you would most likely receive from each of those teachers.

A powerful way to maintain or regain proper perspective in the midst of daily turmoil or overwhelm is to simply take a mental walk through a cancer ward, a homeless ghetto, or a children's hospital, and then re-ask yourself, "And what is bothering me?" For weeks after the bombing of the World Trade Center in New York as people commiserated about the events of that week and how their lives were affected, I heard people comment, "But I cannot complain given what other people have suffered." It is amazing how rich and beautiful our lives begin to look when viewed with the reality of a tragedy in the background.

When we choose not to focus on what is missing in our lives but are grateful for the abundance that is present, the wasteland of illusion falls away and we experience heaven on earth. In that spirit, I will close this chapter's *Reflections* with a beautiful passage from 13th century Persian poet Muslih-Ud-Din-Saadi, quoted in Aaron Zerah's book, *The Soul's Almanac,* saying:

> "I never complain about my fate. Once, I did not have shoes and I complained to God. I went into church with a heavy heart and in the church I saw a man without both feet. So I thanked God that he had given me both feet, and that my only problem was that they were unshod."

Passages

"Two men in prison looked through bars,
one saw mud, the other stars."

Frederick Langbridge

"We are what we think.
All that we are arises with
our thoughts. With our
thoughts, we make the world."

Buddha

"We are responsible for the world in which we find ourselves, if only because we are the only sentient force which can change it."

James Baldwin

"A thought might touch the
edge of our life with light."

John Trowbridge

"Think lovely thoughts."

Peter Pan

"Tell me what you pay
attention to and I will tell
you who you are."

Jose Ortega y Gasset

"The human mind is a miracle.
Once it accepts a new idea
or learns something new,
it never returns
to its original dimensions.
It is limitless."

Leo Buscaglia

Marcel Proust

"The secret to discovery lies not in seeing new landscapes, but in having new eyes."

"We build ourselves with our thoughts.
We climb upon the visions of ourselves."

Orison Swett Marden

"Don't seek truth.
Just drop your illusions."

Zen saying

Anthony de Mello

"Wakefulness is a state of non-illusion,
where you see things not as you are,
but as they are. This is a state we rarely know."

"It is time to come to your senses. You are to live and to learn and to laugh. You are to learn and to listen to the cursed radio music of life and to revere the spirit behind it and to laugh at its distortions. So there you are. More will not be asked of you."

Herman Hesse

"We are more luminous than the moon, as beautiful as stars—why do we tolerate our muddy existence?"

Rumi

"The greatest thoughts come directly from the heart!"

The Dalai Lama

"We should believe that the goodness which exists in us, and in this world, will be fulfilled. This is the major condition to make it happen."

Leo Tolstoy

William Blake

"The man who never alters his opinion is like standing water, and breeds reptiles of the mind."

John Ruskin

"All great thoughts are living thoughts, and they can grow and be changed. And they change and grow as a tree, and not at as a cloud."

"Every thought a person dwells upon, whether he expresses it or not, either damages or improves his life."

Lucy Mallory

"Few people think more than two or three times a year. I have made an international reputation for myself by thinking once or twice a week."

George Bernard Shaw

"The mind is like a river; upon its waters thoughts float through in a constant procession every conscious moment. You stand on a bridge over it and can stop and turn back any thought that comes along. The art of contentment is to let no thought pass that is going to disturb you."

Leo Tolstoy

Tanis Helliwell

"There is no sense setting positive goals if we're undermining ourselves with negative self-talk. It's like planting weeds in our own garden."

"Every man takes the limits of his field of vision for the limits of the world."

Arthur Schopenhauer

"I never cease being dumbfounded by the unbelievable things people believe."

Leo Rosten

Seneca

"Every man prefers belief to the exercise of judgment."

"The man who never in his mind and thought traveled to heaven is no artist."

William Blake

"Life does not consist mainly, or even largely, of facts and happenings. It consists mainly of the storm of thoughts that are forever blowing through one's mind."

Mark Twain

To Ponder and To Practice

- Who is one of the most positive people you have ever known? What factors do you attribute to that person's ability to see the world through eyes that support his/her positive worldview?
- Go on a fast from negative thinking for a day—if you like the results, try it for a week. If you dare to go where no person has gone before, try it for a month!
- When was the last time you consciously took control of your thought process in a trying situation? What enabled you to do that?
- Charles Pierce says, "The essence of belief is the establishment of a habit." Draft a list of some of your most primary beliefs. Consider what habits you have established based on these beliefs. Which of these beliefs would you like to put more into practice through the establishment of a habit?
- Notice the difference between talking to yourself and "listening to yourself talk." We have the choice between feeding ourselves nourishing thoughts or listening to ourselves ramble with the same old jive. Notice the difference between them and then make a choice.
- Like the boy who walked with a humped back, what is a limitation of your own that you would like to slowly but surely think yourself out of?
- Are you more apt to employ scarcity or abundance consciousness in your own life and work?
- Try looking at everyone around you as a "wise and holy one" and see if you don't begin to perceive them differently.
- What channel of your mind have your thoughts been tuning into lately? Do you have other channels you can turn to? Which ones?
- What are a few helpful vantage points that will bring the gift of perspective when you are troubled or stressed?
- Write down the names of seven of your greatest teachers or people whom you highly respect. Think about the input each of these people might give you on a current situation that you are finding challenging.
- Thinking about a current challenge that you are experiencing, try looking at the situation from the following points of view: an optimist, a pessimist, a humorist, a pragmatist, a spiritual teacher, an alien, a young child, a person on his/her deathbed. How does the situation and your possible responses to it change as a result of the shift in perspective?

Practice

- Real contentment is not so much a result of circumstances or change of events but of the contents of our minds and hearts. If your mind were a container that could only hold five thoughts, which five would you choose?
- It is as important to know what one should not think about as what one should think about. What has had your focus lately that is not worthy of your precious time? What one thing can you do to direct your attention to more worthy matters and purposes?
- It has been said that the most powerful thing we can do to change the world is to change our own beliefs about the nature of life, people and reality to something more positive… and begin to act accordingly. What is one positive belief you can begin to act on?
- Choose a favorite quote from this chapter's *Passages* to post where you can read it frequently as a reminder to use the power of your mind to your life's advantage.
- Choose a daily habit or routine that can symbolize your intention to live with a trust in abundance and to lessen your scarcity thinking (e. g., using sunlight or rain as a symbol of abundance as they give equally and generously to whatever is in their path).
- Given everything you have read in this chapter, what do you want to *keep* doing? What do you want to *stop* doing? What do you want to *start* doing?

Notes

Chapter

At the Feet of the World

Becoming More Teachable

Don't make history repeat itself

Don't make history repeat itself

Recognize your teachers

Recognize your teachers

Embrace the gifts of your shortcomings

Embrace the gifts of your shortcomings

Eat the coconut and drink its milk

Eat the coconut and drink its milk

Employ "the last of the human freedoms"

Employ "the last of the human freedoms"

Try the Matisse method

Try the Matisse method

Remember the four magic words

Remember the four magic words

Read your own circumstances

Read your own circumstances

At the Feet of the World

Life is a brilliant teacher. The world is the ultimate classroom.
If only we would show up for the lessons.
Luckily, the world is patient.
It will repeat its lessons as many times as it takes
for even the most stubborn of students to grasp.
Students like us. Lessons like these:

> Tell the truth. Be kind. Play fair.
> Give thanks. Share. Listen with your heart.
> Love fiercely. Seize the day.

You know, simple stuff like that.

If only we could sit at the feet of the world and learn.

The world is quite responsive to our varying learning styles,
employing a multitude of instructional tools and methods.
Take its teachers, for example.
They come in every shape, size and situation:
noisy neighbors, crazy customers, ailing elders,
ornery children, talkative taxi drivers,
gossiping co-workers, meddling in-laws…
Life will use absolutely anyone in our presence to deliver instruction.

If only we could sit at the feet of all who could teach us and learn.

Life specializes in experiential learning.
It spares no expense in conjuring up the perfect circumstances
as personal tutorials in important subjects like
patience, coping and the art of flexibility
using flat tires, cancelled flights, toothaches,
tangled Christmas tree lights, spilled milk, lost keys,
gum under our shoes and overdrawn checking accounts—
oh, and let's not forget the common cold, the flu,
and the occasional computer virus.

If only we could sit at the feet of all our circumstances and learn.

What an amazing curriculum the world has devised,
giving equal time to the counsel of our trials and tribulations
as to the truths told in our hours of triumph.
Life loves a nice juicy error or an all-out, ass-kicking blunder
to anchor us in deep learning.
And yet, on the high winds of our kite-flying joy,
it will scribe its message across the heavens.

If only we could sit at the feet of every experience and learn.

Even as we resist its lessons, refuse its counsel
and declare ourselves the master of our own lives,
life will find a way to break the shell around our hearts wide open.
It will astound or confound us, startle or surprise us,
shake and awaken us to the very core.
With sudden unemployment or an unexpected promotion,
by way of divorce or a reconciliation,
through an illness or through healing,
on the wings of a miracle birth or the loss of a loved one,
we will find ourselves humbled, ungrounded, unsure.
At a loss for words, with eyes wide open,
with hands unclasped and our hearts soft, tender and teachable again.
There we will be, sitting at the feet of our own lives,
unable to do anything but learn.

In every situation, there is a lesson.
At any moment, even now, there is a teacher like a hovering angel.
Let's not run, hide or look away.

Let's sit at the feet of this world and learn!

Reflections

As human beings we struggle in an imperfect world where suffering and grace both abound. Life is at once frightful, beautiful, bitter and astonishing. Opportunities for growth, never ceasing, inconvenience ever present. It is as if being human requires us to stand up to life experiences, one after the other, each one altering us in some way—like rocks being smoothed over time by the unceasing waves of the sea.

And though we go through periods when we would love to hit the pause button on those waves, I doubt that we would change this aspect of life, even if we could. Like the legend about a man who was given the ultimate punishment, a life without any suffering, writer H. G. Wells poses, "What on earth would a man do with himself if something did not stand in his way?" It is, in part, dealing with the struggles in life that make it so very precious. A perfect, finished world would have no need for us. Tragedy, injustice, pain and inconvenience provide the tasks that give human life purpose. William Blake expresses this beautifully in the following poem:

Joy and Woe are woven fine
A Clothing for the Soul divine
Under every grief and pine
Runs a joy with silken twine
It is right it should be so
Man was made for Joy and Woe
And when this we rightly know
Thru the world we safely go.

Life requires an ongoing willingness to learn. Even when the learning is not fun. Even when the learning is painful, embarrassing or humbling. If we were more teachable, more willing to sit at the feet of the world and learn, and less resistant to it lessons, our lives would change dramatically. While this simple wisdom has been espoused throughout the ages, it is difficult to put into practice. Falling on our faces is one way to sit at the feet of the world, but here are a few other suggestions to open us to the gifts of our struggles, while still standing.

Don't make history repeat itself

I have heard it said that the problem is not that there are problems—the problem is expecting otherwise and thinking that having problems is a problem. To some extent, we can always expect to experience familiar trouble and repeated problems, to continually encounter both life-affirming and defeating themes that are embedded in our souls. How often do we have to be presented with the same lesson before we finally get it, like the fool with the blistered ears?

A fool was walking down the street with blisters on both of his ears, when a friend asked him what had happened to cause the blisters.

"My wife left her iron on, and when the phone rang I picked up the iron by mistake."

"Yes, but what about the other ear?"

"The damned fool called back!"

There is only one thing more painful than learning from experience, and that is not learning from experience. If we don't like the lesson the first time, we can be pretty much guaranteed we won't like it the second time! History must repeat itself because we pay such little attention to it the first time. As celebrated poet Edna St. Vincent Millay put so succinctly, "It is not true that life is one damn thing after another—it is one damn thing, over and over!"

Why are we so hard headed? Why are we so stubborn? We are like the child who must keep repeating the same grade or the employee who never lasts more than a few months at any job. Or the supervisor who is being sued, yet again. Or the person who ends up in still another dysfunctional relationship.

Luckily, the world is patient.
It will repeat the lessons
as many times as it takes
for even the most stubborn
of students to grasp.

Thomas Moore urges us to not only learn from our mistakes but to value them as something essential. In his book, *Original Self,* he writes:

> "Of course, however bright or dim we are, we will still make mistakes. If I kept a diary of all the bad decisions I have made in my life, it would be too thick to carry. But as in most things, it may take a bundle of mistakes to arrive at something sublime, just as it takes a thousand flowers to produce a few drops of perfume."

We all wrestle with the problems, gifts and wounds that life has presented to us. To some degree, these themes, both good and bad, are probably an important part of growing and expanding the human soul. Perhaps with our conscious intent to make *fresh* mistakes, rather than repeat the same mistakes, through the living of a life we will each arrive at that *something sublime.* Perhaps with a willingness to make new mistakes rather than repeating the same lessons over again, we will find ourselves living a journey that is wholehearted.

Recognize your teachers

What would our lives be like if we were truly teachable from moment to moment? What if we were able to let the chair teach us about being still, to learn from the window how to let light in, and from the door how to open with the slightest prompting? What if we learned tolerance from racists and bigots, and hope from the stories of holocaust survivors? We have seen in the United States how profound lessons of courage, resolve, and unity have resulted from the actions of those who would try to tear us apart through acts of terrorism. Abhorrent, loathsome teacher—amazing lessons!

So many of our most powerful teachers show up in disguise. Even those who threaten, intimidate or drive us the most crazy… what else could they be but our teachers? If they weren't our teachers, they wouldn't have so much of our attention. A work situation that is challenging or difficult can be great in teaching us how to communicate, to solve problems, to prioritize, and to grow out of our limitations. These are the kind of teachers we give nasty names to, but they are teachers just the same.

The world is quite responsive
to varying learning styles,
employing a multitude
of instructional tools and methods.
Take its teachers, for example.
They come in every shape,
size and situation.

Unfortunately, we are not always astute at recognizing our teachers, much less the lessons they bring. In fact, sometimes we miss the lesson because we are too busy reinforcing our own deeply ingrained habits.

I remember when a friend of mine, who I will call Ann, was going through a very difficult period with her boss for whom she felt undying loyalty and affection. They had worked together for many years, and he had provided moral support for her when she had gone through a challenging time in her personal life. When problems arose with her boss, Ann was enthusiastic to support him in a like manner. It began with financial troubles in which she would go weeks without pay, and never say a word. Then he began not showing up and missing appointments, and she covered for him, working overtime almost daily. Months into this situation, his problems with alcohol became more and more apparent, and he fell into a deep depression and would not show up for work at all. Still, Ann stood by him, much to the detriment of her own financial situation, professional reputation, and personal sense of power.

Through these many months I encouraged her on several occasions to leave the situation. I assured her that she had gone more than the extra mile but that enough was enough. It was very painful to watch Ann flounder emotionally as she struggled to maintain her own self-esteem and integrity while being the friend she wished to be to her employer. For six months my "friendly advice" to jump ship seemed to be falling on deaf ears so, I decided to go for the big one—guilt! I told her that her decision to not act was not just affecting her, but her daughter as well, as she had to watch her mom struggle day in and day out with the challenges of the situation. I suggested that she needed to act for her daughter's sake. I will never forget my friend looking at me and, in the sincerest way, saying, "I know that everything in life has a purpose and is happening to teach me something. I believe that my work situation is trying to teach me patience."

I was stunned. "Patience?" I asked. I actually burst out laughing because my friend is by far and away the most overly patient person I have ever known. Tenderly, I took her hand, looked her right in the eye and said, "Ann, I doubt very much that life is trying to teach you patience. I am pretty certain that what life is asking from you right now is assertiveness! Life is asking you to cut the patience thing already!" I could visibly see the affect of this realization as it washed over her—Hallelujah—she believed me! She smiled from ear to ear and shook her head saying, "Wow, that never occurred to me." She resigned from her job a few days later, and I am happy to report that her boss got the professional help he needed to get back on his own two feet.

It is much easier to see other people's "life lessons" than it is to see our own. How often do we miss the real sermon hidden in our life experiences because we are so busy repeating the lesson with which we are more at home and comfortable—which is to say—aren't really lessons at all? How much of what we consider to be "our lessons" are just ingrained habits which we justify by reading our circumstances in a way that supports them? Maybe that is why we need loved ones so badly, because sometimes they can see what we can't see.

Embrace the gifts of your shortcomings

Perhaps the most interesting camouflage for one of life's greatest teachers is the gift of our own flaws and failings. We trust someone we shouldn't and we learn discernment. We play it too safe for too long and we learn to surrender and take a risk. We strut our stuff with heads held high only to trip over our own arrogance, landing face down in a puddle of humility. What a great twist—if we don't learn from the world, we eventually learn from our own shortcomings. In fact, as this story from the Zen tradition expresses, it is our failings that can lead to the path of wisdom.

After a long, hard climb up the mountains, the spiritual seekers finally found themselves in front of the great teacher. Bowing deeply, they asked the question that had been burning inside them for so long: "How do we become wise?"

There was a long pause until the teacher emerged from meditation. Finally the reply came: "Good choices."

"But teacher, how do we make good choices?"

"From experience," responded the wise one.

"And how do we get experience?"

"Bad choices," smiled the teacher.

That story is a wonderful reminder that all of our experience is valuable—even that which is riddled with mistakes. Our lives were not meant to be lived perfectly, but with humility and the ability to learn and grow.

I remember making a very bad choice as a teenager which has affected the rest of my life in a very positive way. I had been invited to a concert (the Eagles!) by someone who had been a friend of mine for a couple of years. He was a very nice person, he had not dated much, and his asking me to the concert was a big deal. He was as thrilled that I accepted his invitation, as I was thrilled to be invited. The problem arose when a few days before the concert I received a much more attractive invitation to go camping for three days with a group of people with whom I really wanted to spend time and rarely had the occasion. I knew in my heart of hearts that I should I go to the concert, but I gave in to my own selfish desires to go camping. The weekend was fun, but my friend never forgave me. He was crushed. When I realized the extent of his hurt weeks later, I regretted my decision horribly. I would have given anything to relive that weekend and make a different choice. But we don't get to live backwards—we have to move forward, reaping the lessons from our bad choices. The silver lining in this story is that in every situation since, having to choose between "the right choice" and "a more appealing choice"—the decision is made without a second thought. What a great lesson to have learned early in my life. (Still, I get that guilty twinge every time I hear anything off the *Hotel California* album, and I have a feeling my would-have-been-date probably avoids that album too.)

Life's challenges are not supposed to paralyze us; they are supposed to help us discover ourselves. Once we have overcome a difficulty, it blesses us in ways we would otherwise never have experienced. Author Caren Boldman writes about the "witnessing" aspect of overcoming adversity:

> "In meeting a challenge, we become witnesses to our ability to go where we haven't gone before, do what we've never done before, and arrive at a new place in our lives. Indeed, once witnessed, the courage, fortitude, self-trust, and even the humility that helped carry us through can never be unwitnessed."

Who would we be without the gifts of the challenges we have overcome, without the blessings brought on the wings of our shortcomings?

Eat the coconut and drink its milk

Unfortunately, life doesn't measure out our troubles in fair increments and say, "This year your father was ill so I'll wait until next year to have you hate your boss and a couple years down the line for the ulcer to develop." Life just rolls on its way with disregard to our particular circumstance. It is our job not to be bowled over by it. Or better yet, to roll with the punches and, one way or another, come out standing taller.

Did you ever hear about the woman who was walking along as a monkey threw a coconut from a tree and hit her on the head? She rubbed her head, picked the coconut up off the ground, cut it open, ate its meat and drank it's milk. The moral of the story is clear—if you are going to get hit in the head by a coconut, you might as well have it for lunch.

Life loves a nice juicy error
or an all-out, ass-kicking blunder
to anchor us in deep learning.
And yet, on the high winds
of our kite-flying joy,
it will scribe its message
across the heavens.
If only we could sit at the feet
of every experience and learn.

How do we adopt an attitude of opportunity in the face of our trials and tribulations? What if once we perceived a problem, we were able to look at it again in terms of our desires in the situation? Rather than arguing about the issues going on in our lives, what if we sank deeper into the opportunities that lie beneath them, changing the subject of our conversation from our concerns to possible solutions? We deplete our energies by hanging out in the question, "Why is this happening?" but we refocus our energies when we change the question to, *"How do we proceed from here?"*

Learning to ask the right questions in the face of adversity is essential because it enables us to discern the difference between what feels like a problem and what avails us to deep learning. Sometimes one shows up looking like the other. And sometimes, both are true.

- *Have I really been laid off? Yes, and now you are free to create the position that employs your passion and your purposes as well as your gifts.*
- *Am I really alone again? Yes, and now you may learn how to live by yourself and discern the difference between loneliness and solitude.*
- *Do I really have to file bankruptcy? Yes, and once on the other side of it, you may discover the riches in your life that no one can ever take from you.*

Is this the coconut that hit me on the head? Yes, and it may also be your lunch.

Employ "the last of the human freedoms"

I have suffered from migraines since I was twelve-years-old. I use the word "suffer" consciously… with over three decades of migraines under my belt, I have not yet found a way to do anything but suffer through them. But I have learned something invaluable. While in the throes of the headache, I have found ways to *ride* the pain without *becoming* the pain. I have discovered ways of concentrating my awareness on those aspects of my being which are not in pain… like my toes or my hands, my thoughts and my feelings. It is very easy to slip into the migraine as the totality of my existence. But even while my head throbs with pain, I have discovered that I can smell the lilac at my bedside, feel the cool satin of a pillowcase, or listen to the laughter of children outside the window. In those small investments of my awareness, I anchor myself in something other than the pain, even as it washes over me.

Learning to focus our attention on parts of our lives other than what we are struggling with at the moment is key to being able to sit at the feet of world. How do we find comfort in the solace of family, even as we feel estranged from a workplace? Is it possible to lean on the support of friends while suffering a family crisis? Can we pay attention to the numerous blessings of the physical body even while riding out the storm of depression? Poet and author Mark Nepo writes beautifully of hope in the midst of adversity in this passage from *The Book of Awakening.*

> "There is a wonderful Nigerian proverb that states, "No matter how dark, the hand always knows the way to the mouth." What a great way to remind us that no matter how awful our circumstances are, we have inner reflexes, impulses and natural gifts that will keep working for us. Even in our lostness or loneliness, our lungs will continue to fill with air. Even in our despair or disappointment, the moon will rise and stars will shine, even if behind the clouds. It makes no difference how horribly we have blown it, how tangled a web we have woven, or how hopeless the outlook; there will always be rich reserves available to us from the bounty of a generous world."

It is said that tragedy, heartbreak, and illness can greatly concentrate the mind. No kidding. The value, of course, is not in the misfortune, but in the light that misfortune can shed upon our lives. Misfortune can refocus our attention to the things that really matter in life. When we have been ill, a respite from pain is a welcomed blessing. When we have lost a loved one, our appreciation of those remaining becomes acute. In the midst of struggle, we would be wise to anchor ourselves in that which has become that much more precious to us due in part to our angst... like friends who are with us in our grief, physical health in the midst of emotional turmoil, or the gift of imagination when we are physically incapacitated.

A most poignant and catalytic example of facing adversity with courage and grace is the amazing story of the great Viktor Frankl. Frankl was a psychiatrist trained in the determinist thinking of Freud, holding to the precept that what happens to us as children largely determines who we become as adults. He was also a Jew and imprisoned in the death camps of Nazi Germany. He suffered the ghastly horrors of physical torture as well as the mental torment of not knowing each day if he would die in a gas oven by the end of it. The worst of it is that he suffered all of this carrying the weight of grief and despair of having lost his parents, his brother and his wife in the camps.

It was here, under conditions that would drive most of us into madness, that Frankl became aware of what he later called "the last of the human freedoms"—the power to choose one's response to one's circumstances. By gathering within himself that which could not be taken, his personal inner freedom, Frankl maintained his dignity in the midst of horrendous atrocities. He would imagine himself lecturing to his students or writing of his experiences. He abandoned his deterministic views and began formulating what he later called "logotherapy," the philosophy that man's greatest challenge and responsibility is to find one's unique meaning and mission in life. Frankl became an inspiration to those around him, even to some of the guards. He helped others find meaning in their suffering and dignity in their prison existence.

Frankl's book, *Man's Search for Meaning,* is one of the best books I have ever read. Among other things, I realized that I do not have to find myself in the deathly grips of a concentration camp to exercise "the last of the human freedoms." My power to choose my response in the midst of circumstances comes in handy even in more mundane circumstances like running late for an appointment in the middle of rush hour traffic or burning dinner an hour before the guests arrive. Obviously, in the midst of the turmoil that comes with unexpected unemployment, an illness, or the death of a loved one, it could be nothing less than grace, alighting upon the human heart, that whispers softly in our ears, "Remember the last of your human freedoms."

Try the Matisse method

When I think back to the lowest points in my life, I remember believing that my life would never be the same again. And I was right; it wasn't. But what was to be different was not "life"—but my heart in relation to it. Ultimately, regardless of the circumstances that assault us, we have the power and the choice to move beyond the pain of that experience. We can choose to remain stuck in our sense of loss, to remain wounded by it, or to consciously grow our way through the pain and into our healing. Struck by a blow, we can wallow endlessly in our grief, or we can give grief its place, gather what lessons we can glean from the experience, and strike out once again on our journey. The shell around our hearts will harden or soften. Either way, we are never the same. That is what "being alive" means, living each moment into new changes, into new wholeheartedness.

I can easily identify experiences that have hardened my heart and those that have softened it. I realize now that even with an experience long past, I still have a choice about how I will let it affect me. Wrongs done to us cannot be changed, but how they affect our present and future is largely within our power to determine.

One of the most extraordinary examples of someone who sat at the feet of his struggles and rose above them is the awesome Henri Matisse. He had been a celebrated painter before developing arthritis which spread throughout his arms and hands, disabling him from painting. Rather than being conquered by his condition, Matisse worked with his hands to discover other capabilities, one of which was to cut paper. Today Matisse's most celebrated works are those of his incredible paper cuts. Circumstances that robbed him of one gift also opened him to new treasure, both for himself and for the world.

The same circumstances that can break our hearts can open them. Within every story and circumstance, there is the person in the story. The word "person" comes from the Latin *personare,* which means "sounding through." We can allow our experiences to sound through us without *becoming* those experiences. We are changed, yes, by our experiences, but we need not be defined by them. This is the point of healing: once we have lived the story and survived to tell the tale, we can leave the story behind. I will never forget the first time I saw these words written in a bathroom stall: *Pain is inevitable. Suffering is optional.* It may take a lifetime to achieve, but I am determined to live the wisdom of those words.

In every situation,
there is a lesson.
At any moment, even now,
there is a teacher
like a hovering angel.

Remember the four magic words

Long ago a very miserable and troubled king called together a forum of the wisest people of the kingdom. He asked them to invent a motto, a few magic words that would help him in time of trial and distress. He insisted that it be brief enough to engrave on a ring so that he could have it always before his eyes. It must be appropriate to every situation, and as useful in days of joy and prosperity as in days of sorrow and adversity. It must be a motto wise and true and endlessly enduring, words by which a man could be guided all his life, in every circumstance, no matter what happened.

The wise people thought and thought, and finally came to the king with their magic words. They were words for every change or chance of fortune, declared the wise men... words to fit every situation, good or bad... words to ease the heart and mind in every circumstance. And the words they gave the king to engrave on his ring were:

This, too, shall pass.

Century after century this legend has survived. Whether or not the motto was invented for a troubled king, no one really knows—nor is it in the least important. But this much is for sure, the words are wise and true and endlessly enduring. They have proven their power over and over again through the centuries, to uncounted numbers of men and women, every land and every conceivable situation.

Personally, those four magic words gave me strength while I was in the thirtieth hour of labor during the birth of my child. Those four magic words gave me courage while helping my young step-brother make it through a spinal tap while in the beginning throes of learning that he had leukemia. Then again, those four magic words have catapulted me into awareness and gratitude when in the midst of the most joyous times—while walking in the redwoods, swimming in the lake, or rocking my newborn niece to sleep—because, those precious times, too, shall pass.

Poets and philosophers have toyed and played with these words for centuries. Shakespeare put it, "Come what come may; Time and hour runs through the darkest day." Poet William Cowper added his own touch with:

> "Beware of the desperate steps; the darkest day—lived till tomorrow, will have passed away."

Perhaps the most widely known and celebrated of the poems inspired by these words came from 19th century American poet Paul Hamilton Hayne:

"This, Too, Shall Pass Away."

Art thou in misery, brother? Then I pray
Be comforted. Thy grief shall pass away.
Art thou elated? Ah, be not too gay;
Temper thy joy: this, too, shall pass away.
Art thou in danger? Still, let reason sway,
And cling to hope: this, too, shall pass away.

Tempted thou art? In all thy anguish lay
One truth to heart: this, too, shall pass away.
Do rays of loftier glory round thee play?
Kinglike art thou? This, too, shall pass away!
Whate'er thou art,
where'er thy footsteps stray,
Heed those wise words:
This, too, shall pass away.

Whatever we are experiencing in this moment, this hour, this season of our life, it is in the state of passing. We must take heart and hope, draw courage and strength from this knowing, seize the moment for all that it is worth—before it passes and is gone.

Read your own circumstances

We know that people learn differently and at their own pace. This is true in learning to read, to write, to speak another language, and to run a computer program. What is harder to accept is that the same is true for "life learning." Learning to love, learning to fail, learning humility or patience, learning to live knowing we will die, learning to give for the sake of giving, learning how to rise time and again after we fall. This kind of learning only comes when we need it, no matter how old or young, no matter how many times we have to start over. And we cannot force other people's learning in any of these areas either, as painful and frustrating as it is to watch loved ones grapple with a particular lesson that we may have learned for ourselves long ago.

I appreciate this advice from Morihei Ueshiba, the founder of Aikido, a Japanese martial art:

> "Depending on the circumstances
> You should be solid as a diamond;
> Flexible as a willow;
> Smooth flowing like water;
> Or, empty as space.
> The important thing is to pay attention
> And read your own circumstances."

I think we need to realize that the only circumstances we can read are our own. We each learn at our own pace and in our own ways. Being responsible for ourselves is a daunting enough task without presuming to be responsible for other people's lessons. There are times when I am as solid as a rock, even when I should be as flexible as a willow. But other people's wisdom about what I should be doing or how I should be acting will not smooth me like the waters of my experience. When I am inflexible, life will bend me one way or another.

Even as we resist its lessons,
refuse its counsel
and declare ourselves
the master of our own lives,
life will find a way to break
the shell around our hearts wide open.
It will astound or confound us,
startle or surprise us,
shake and awaken us to the very core.

Socrates believed that, "If all our misfortunes were laid in one common heap whence everyone must take an equal portion, most people would be contented to take their own and depart." Sometimes I wonder about that, especially when I am under the weight of my own portion. But deep inside I know that it is true. We each have our own lessons to learn and our demons with which to do battle, and at each point in our journey we are uniquely qualified to face those challenges. I would probably choose my own heap of troubles because I am the one who needs those lessons, and those are the troubles for which I have prepared myself, consciously or unconsciously.

Even when life presents several of us with the same circumstance, we will each respond in a way that is in concert with the ripeness of our learning. The Dalai Lama tells the story of a discordant community of monks who one night prayed deeply for a word of counsel or advice from God to bring peace to their monastery. Each one heard one word, but each heard a *different* word. The event is immortalized in this poem:

> The one who wanted to die heard, "Live."
> The one who wanted to live heard, "Die."
> The one who wanted to take heard, "Give."
> The one who wanted to give heard, "Keep."
> The one who was always alert heard, "Sleep."
> The one who was always asleep heard, "Wake."
> The one who wanted to stay heard, "Depart."
> The one who never spoke heard, "Preach."
> The one who always preached heard, "Pray."

I have to ask myself, "What word do I hear at this time in my life?" What word do you hear? If only we could sit at the feet of the world and listen.

Passages

"What is to give light must endure burning."

Viktor Frankl

"All of my work is meant to say, you may encounter defeats, but you must not be defeated."

Maya Angelou

Aesop

"An oak and a reed were arguing about their strength. When a strong wind came up, the reed avoided being uprooted by bending and learning with the gusts of wind. But the oak stood firm and was torn up by the roots."

"Your pain is the breaking of the shell that encloses your understanding."

Kahlil Gibran

"Gray skies are just clouds passing over."

Duke Ellington

Adrienne Rich

"If only we could learn from pain even as it grasps us."

"Although the world is full of suffering, it is also full of the overcoming of it."

Helen Keller

Confucius

"Our greatest glory is not in never falling, but in rising every time we fall."

Helen Keller

"We could never learn to be brave and patient if there were only joy in the world."

"By our stumbling, the world is perfected."

Sri Aurobindo

Albert Einstein

"You can't solve a problem on the same level that it was created. You have to rise above it to the next level."

"Life does not accommodate you, it shatters you. It's meant to, and it couldn't do it better. Every seed destroys its container or else there would be no fruition."

Florida Scott-Maxwell

"The snail has no hand.
The snail has no feet.
Gently the snail climbs the tree."

West African proverb

Corita Kent

"Flowers grow out of the dark moments."

Charlotte Bronte

"A depressing and difficult passage has prefaced every new page I have turned in life."

"Learn to drink life as it comes, without stirring it from the bottom."

Agnes Turnbill

"Experience may be hard, but we claim its gifts because they are real, even though our feet bleed on its stones."

M. P. Follett

"You may trod me in the very dirt,
but still, like dust, I will rise."

Maya Angelou

"Soul enters life from below, through the cracks, finding an opening into life at the points where smooth functioning breaks down."

Thomas Moore

"The secret of success is to fall down seven times and get up eight."

Chinese proverb

"The obstacle is the path."

Chinese proverb

"Water which is too pure has no fish."

Lao Tzu

"Everything has its wonders, even darkness and silence, and I learn, whatever state I may be in, therein to be content."

Helen Keller

"We never know how high we are
Till we are called to rise.
And then, if we are true to plan
Our statures touch the skies."

Emily Dickinson

Jeremy Taylor

"No man is more miserable than he that hath no adversity."

"Winning does not tempt that man.
This is how he grows:
By being defeated, decisively,
By constantly greater things."

Rainer Marie Rilke

"Life itself is the great sacrament through which we are wounded and healed. If we live everything, life will be faithful to us."

John O'Donohue

Mike Mathers

"When bad things happen, there is some good in it. When good things happen, you don't need a philosophy."

"We must not despise the rough, the dark, the empty, the cowardly, the flawed or the crooked. It is a package deal."

John R. Mabry

To Ponder and To Practice

- What are some of the most profound lessons you have learned through pain and adversity?
- What are some of the most profound lessons you have learned through joy and good fortune?
- Which lessons in your life seem to repeat themselves over and over?
- What people, situations or circumstances in your current life seem to be your greatest teachers?
- What is the last coconut to hit you in the head? How could you open it to eat its meat and drink its milk?
- Make a list of difficult situations you have handled well in your life. Make a list of those you wish you had handled better. What lessons do these two lists bring home to you?
- Think about your most persistent complaints, in or outside of work. Draft a list of the most persistent challenges or issues that keep returning to you, and consider the following questions in relation to your list:
  - Do you recognize common themes surfacing from this list of challenges (e. g, boredom, stress, personality conflicts, lack of purpose)?
  - If you were to consider each of the challenges you identified above as a door, how would your life change if you moved through each of those thresholds?
  - Some problems aren't meant to be solved—just outgrown. Is that true of any of the challenges you identified above?
  - What deep yearnings or desires do your challenges reflect?
- Draft a list of the many things that are going well for you right now and give thanks for all that is *not wrong.*
- Booker T. Washington once advised that we measure our success not so much by the position we have reached in life as by the obstacles which we have overcome while trying to succeed. Draft a résumé not of your accomplishments, but of the obstacles you overcame to reach them.
- Who could you enlist for one small act of support to ease your challenges or difficulties at home or at work? To whom could you offer some support right now?

Practice

- A deep river is not troubled if you throw a stone into it. What daily or weekly practices could help you foster the serenity and depth of a river so that you are not as affected by daily challenges?
- In what current situation in your life do you need to remember that "This, too, shall pass"?
- Select a quote from this chapter's *Passages* which speaks to you with regard to facing adversity and post it where you will see it until it is internalized.
- Given everything you have read in this chapter, what do you want to *keep* doing? What do you want to *stop* doing? What do you want to *start* doing?

Notes

A Heart Contained

Chapter

Choosing Joy and Practicing Gratitude

Cultivate joy by acting joyful

Cultivate joy by acting joyful

Be easily pleased

Be easily pleased

Make a practice of gratitude

Make a practice of gratitude

Redefine your wealth

Redefine your wealth

Increase joy by lessening desires

Increase joy by lessening desires

Discover joy rather than pursue happiness

Discover joy rather than pursue happiness

Learn to love many things

Learn to love many things

A Heart Contained

I know that the earth wants me to dance on her back,
to roll around, giddy, on her green belly.
I am confident that every star sparkles in anticipation
of being the one I will wish on tonight.
I am certain that every flower in my garden
is as nurtured by my profuse oohing and ahhing
as they are by the warmth of the noonday sun.
Every corner of the universe speaking to me through my intuition
offers me encouragement
for living life at full tilt—with no holding back.

It is only among people
that I have learned to withhold—
to water down my joy for public consumption.

We know the rules—
Laugh—but not too heartily! Jump—but not too high!
Show your pleasure—but don't overdo it with squeals or,
God forbid, tears of gladness.
Happiness is to be doled out a bit at a time.
Exuberance is fine on Christmas morning.
Enthusiasm we can take, in moderation.
And elation, well, let's reserve that for special occasions like graduations,
the birth of a baby, and most weddings.

When did the conspiracy against joy begin?
I, for one, refuse to participate.
You may think me a half-witted fool,
but I want you to know the truth of it!
You are only seeing the tip of an enormous iceberg.
If I had any real courage,
my joy would probably defy the laws of gravity
and lift me on wings of pure wonder.

I often wonder how it is that I am able
to contain the wild fire that burns within me.
How does anyone? How do you?
How do you stand at the edge of the pounding sea
and not thrill to the waves that rush through you?
How do you stand under a towering oak
and not get weak at the knees?
How do you hold the infant baby in your arms
without your heart blossoming like a lotus flower?

And yet, if you look around,
it appears as if so many are bored or unimpressed with this world.
They move through life in silent apathy,
lumbering as if through thick mud.
Are they, too, struggling under the weight of a contained heart?

I don't know how or why joy got a bad name,
but I believe that it is as basic to our nature as fear and hope—
and as essential to our lives as bread and water.

With the gift of age,
I care less how I appear and I care more about how I live.
I am going to keep on dancing on the belly of the earth.
I will wish on every star in sight.
I will ooh and ahh in celebration of each small bud in my garden.
In fact, I plan to go hang out with the lupine and the daisies
and learn from them how to blossom boldly,
as if my joy and beauty mattered.

Reflections

> "Most of us miss out on life's big prizes. The Pulitzer. The Nobel. An Oscar. But we're all eligible for life's small pleasures. A pat on the back. A kiss behind the ear. A four-pound bass. A full moon. An empty parking space. A crackling fire. A great meal. A glorious sunset. Hot soup. Cold beer. Don't fret about copping life's grand awards. Enjoy its tiny delights. Know joy."
>
> – Author Unknown

How I would love to have met the person who authored those words! I found them years ago in a splendid little book of quotations that is now worn and mildewed, but still precious to me, like a four pound bass is precious to someone else.

Ever since I was a child I have been blessed with the gift of joy, deep joy. The kind that drives other people crazy. Truly, of all aspects and quirks of my personality, it is my joy that has been the brunt of the greatest criticism I have taken in my life. The plain and simple truth is that to be joyful in this culture is to be suspect. People figure that you are either on drugs, totally fake or hiding behind a smiling mask. You can't be real or taken seriously if you are too happy. At the very least, the happy person is a little "off." Somehow there is the idea in our culture that it is mature to be cynical and immature to be innocent and joyful.

This story I know well, along with all of the other "happy fools" on this beloved earth who wish on stars and talk to the flowers and howl at the moon. But I meant what I said in "A Heart Contained." The older I become, the less I worry about what other people think and the more I care about how I live. I am more and more willing to come out of the closet with my unbridled enthusiasm. In fact, I want to ride her like a stallion.

How do we put joy back in our lives as an essential ingredient? How do we take seriously the advice of André Gide who wisely reminds us,

> "Know that joy is more rare, more difficult, and more beautiful than sadness. Once you make this all-important discovery, you must embrace joy as a moral obligation."

Here are a few insights and suggestions for allowing joy to bubble up from the fountain of our hearts, even when we've become so accustomed to doling it out a drop at a time.

Cultivate joy by acting joyful

Vietnamese poet and author Thich Nhat Hanh says, "Sometimes your joy is the source of your smile and sometimes your smile is the source of your joy." The physical acts of reverence and devotion, like kneeling, bowing or making the sign of the cross, can make us feel devout. When we extend a courteous gesture we increase our feelings of respect for others. To act lovingly is to begin to feel loving. In the same way it is true for these other qualities and emotions, to act joyfully brings joy to others, which in turn brings us joy. It follows the age-old advice "Act as if." Act as if you are happy and you may just feel the thump of your old heart beating to a livelier tune. Pretend to be grateful for all you have and just see if a little blade of joy doesn't come sprouting up from the hard ground of your life.

You know how it is when you don't want to go somewhere but you push yourself to go anyway, figuring that you will be glad you went once you get there? "Acting as if" works the same way. When you show up with your body, your spirit often follows. When you show up with the spirit of joy or gratitude, sometimes the real experience of it goes along for the ride. As Ralph Waldo Emerson says, "You must believe in the possibility of happiness in order to be happy." I think we need to match that belief with our actions.

I know that the earth wants me
to dance on her back,
to roll around, giddy,
on her green belly.
I am confident that every star
sparkles in anticipation
of being the one
I will wish on tonight.
I am certain that every flower
in my garden
is as nurtured by my profuse
oohing and ahhing
as they are by the warmth
of the noonday sun.

As I reread that first stanza of "A Heart Contained" I realize that I have been "acting as if" my whole life. My actions and beliefs have solidified into a hearty, unbreakable confidence that as I speak to the earth, it speaks back to me. As I nod to the moon, it nods back. Some would call this delusional. I call it open-hearted—when you open the door to your heart just far enough to let magic and mystery enter.

Be easily pleased

Marcus Aurelius, the 2nd century Roman philosopher, told us something that we have not quite understood, even until now. He said, "You should live your life as if you are ready to say good-bye to it at any moment, as if the time left you is some pleasant surprise." From that perspective, we would find delight in the very breath flowing in and out of our lungs, in the colors we see and the voices we hear. We would be so easy to please and joy would be our daily bread. Instead, we live like the fish searching for the ocean.

One day a very inquisitive and curious fish decided that he would head out for the great beyond known as the Deep Blue Sea. Problem was, he didn't know where to find it! So, he stopped and inquired of the first starfish he spotted, "Starfish, can you please point me in the direction of the Deep Blue Sea?"

The starfish beamed back brightly, "It is this, our home, dear fish." The fish rolled his eyes thinking, anything shaped like a star has got to be a bit soft in the head.

Then the fish spotted an octopus swimming along and popped the question, "Octopus, can you please point me in the direction of the Deep Blue Sea?" The octopus unfolded his elegant arms and pointed them in all directions, "It is there, dear fish!" Again, the fish rolled his eyes, wondering how he could ever expect something with eight arms to give him a straight answer.

Finally, the fish perked up at the sight of a huge ocean liner, sporting the name "The Deep Blue Sea." "There it is," he gasped, "There it is!" He decided he would follow it all the way to the great ocean! Of course, a fish has to eat along the way to keep up his energy, right? He was coming along nicely until a passenger on The Deep Blue Sea cast his line into the water…

We swim in the waters of joy and wonder every day, yet we live our lives in pursuit of it, as if it is outside our grasp. We get hooked, just like our friend the fish, by everything bearing Joy's name… be it the new car, a dashing outfit, a total makeover, or season's tickets to the football game. Not to begrudge our toys and pleasures, but if we are not happy before we get them, we probably won't be happy afterwards either. Sometimes we're like children at McDonald's ordering a Happy Meal, thinking that the happiness will somehow outlast the devouring of the burger and the fries. And all the while the potential for real joy laps around us like the ocean around the fish.

A great way to know joy is by simply finding delight in the people and things in front of you—to delight in the everyday experience, a gift that George Burns obviously cultivated and expressed in the following passage:

> "Everyday happiness means getting up in the morning,
> and you can't wait to finish your breakfast.
> You can't wait to do your exercises.
> You can't wait to put on your clothes.
> You can't wait to get out—
> and you can't wait to come home,
> because the soup is hot."

Let's loosen up and be easier to please, not holding to high standards in terms of what will blow our hair back. Let's not play hard to get where joy is concerned.

Make a practice of gratitude

Nothing can bring us joy faster, nor more assuredly, than being grateful for the many blessings we already enjoy. There is a myth in our culture that once you are happy, then you can be grateful. But it's a chicken and the egg thing. The sooner we are grateful, the sooner we find joy. Make gratitude for simple blessings a daily practice as Frederic and Mary Ann Brussant suggest in this passage from their delightful book, *Spiritual Rx: Prescriptions for Living a Meaningful Life:*

> "The spiritual practice of gratitude has been called a state of mind and a way of life. But we prefer to think of it as a grammar—an underlying structure that helps us construct and make sense of our lives. The rules of this grammar cover all our activities. Its syntax reveals a system of relationships linking us to the Divine and to every other part of the Creation. To learn the grammar of gratitude, practice saying "thank you" for happy and challenging experiences, for people, animals, things, art, memories, dreams. Utter blessings and express appreciation to everything and everyone you encounter. By blessing, we are blessed."

"The more you praise and celebrate in life, the more there is in life to celebrate." Those are the words of Oprah Winfrey. What an amazing woman. A lot can be said about her in terms of her achievements, her ability to overcome adversity, her vision and resolve to build an empire based on the ideas of service and spirit, not just entertainment. But what is so contagious about Oprah is her joy, her laughter, and her humility. I believe that as a child, regardless of her circumstances, she must have praised and celebrated life to the max. The evidence is in all that she has to celebrate today. Joy begets joy. Her words bear repeating, "The more you praise and celebrate in life, the more there is in life to celebrate."

I will never forget hearing the story of a man who was a survivor of the Nazi concentration camps. He said that he got down on his knees every night and thanked God profusely. When the person interviewing him asked what he could possibly have to be thankful for in such dire circumstances, he replied, "I was surrounded by men who killed and tortured daily without giving it a second thought. I thanked God daily that I was not such a man!"

This is an extraordinary example of a blessings perspective—not one that most of us feel capable of living up to, especially if we imagine ourselves in such a dreadful situation. But how about our ability to cultivate this perspective in relation to situations that are not so drastic, like our everyday experiences?

A friend of mine who spent time in a Buddhist monastery shared with me that the meal time prayer begins with this phrase:"First, seventy-two labors brought us this food; we should know how it comes to us." What if before each meal we were to give thanks not just for the feast, but for the efforts of all those who have participated in making the meal possible? What if we stopped to thank and bless the farmers, the laborers, the gardeners, the plumbers who brought water, those who made the boxes to carry the vegetables, the truckers who transported the food?

I live near the strawberry fields of Watsonville, California. Every year I am witness to the arduous work of migrant workers and their young families as they labor under a hot sun to pick and care for the harvesting of these berries. I am glad for those times, when before feasting on this sweet, red fruit, I remember that it is a gift not just from creation and the miracles of earth, but of the work and sweat of many people. I reflect on the words of poet Alison Luterman:

> "Strawberries are too delicate to be picked by machine. The perfect ripe ones bruise at even too heavy a human touch... Every strawberry you have ever eaten—every piece of fruit—has been picked by calloused human hands. Every piece of toast with jelly represents someone's knees, someone's aching back and hips, someone with a bandanna on her wrist to wipe away the sweat."

How do we make mindfulness of the gift as automatic as our delight in the fruit? This question is relevant to many other aspects of our lives. We take so much for granted—our families, our friends and neighbors, the privileges of living in a democracy, the natural resources availed to us through the fruitful earth, our many abilities and physical capabilities. But there is perhaps nothing we take more for granted than our health. A participant in one of my workshops shared this profound thought with me:"A person who has health has a thousand wishes, the person who doesn't has but one." How very true!

Let's allow the words of e. e. cummings to touch us somewhere deep:

> *i thank you God for this most amazing day:*
> *for the leaping greenly spirits of trees*
> *and a blue true dream of sky;*
> *and for everything which is natural,*
> *which is infinite, which is yes.*

Redefine your wealth

By fostering a blessings perspective in relation to all of life we would awaken to the myriad ways in which we are abundantly rich. In so doing, we would redefine our wealth. Think about what Christ, Buddha, Mohammed, and Gandhi had to say about wealth. None of them taught us how to acquire real estate, or how to make a mint in the mail order business, or how to better manage money market accounts. Prince Siddhartha gave up his fortune as a young man and Christ certainly never reached his true income potential. What they taught us was that the riches of the soul dwarf all others and endure like no other form of wealth. They taught us that true wealth is to be found in living with convictions and character, in loving and being loved, and in serving the world by making use of our gifts.

A great question that leads to a deeper awareness of the richness in our lives is "What do you have right now that you would not sell for all of the money in the world?" (For example, how much would you take for your eyesight? Your faith? Your friendships? Your sense of humor?) Another question that takes us down a similar path is "What would be left of you tomorrow if you should lose every dollar you own tonight?" The extent to which you would be grievous of your losses and grateful for what has not been lost is the extent to which you already live in abundance.

One of my favorite training exercises is to have everyone in a group write down aspects of their lives which make them feel rich. I then ask each person to share one item from their list, requesting that there be no repeats of a response in the group. People often fear that we will not be able to make it around the room without repetition of blessings. Once we go around the room, however, it is clear to everyone that we could go around the room all day without having to repeat ourselves once. We will hear numerous blessings we never thought to consider before which, of course, spur more and more ideas. Here is a list of the kinds of blessings mentioned which many people (myself included) had never considered before:

- My memories
- To be born to non-substance abusing parents
- To be able to think for myself
- The ability to read and write
- My ancestors and the heritage they left me
- The mistakes I've made and learned from
- Having free will
- Springtime
- My resilience and courage
- My ability to love and be loved
- All the people who have forgiven me something
- To have given birth to healthy children
- My love of music (or dogs, gardening, photography) and the immense pleasure it brings me
- Having a strong heart, both physically and emotionally
- The sound of laughter from those I love
- Having air to breath and the lungs to receive it

I have always appreciated this advice from medieval scholar and Christian mystic, Meister Eckhart: "If the only prayer you should ever pray is 'Thank you,' it would be enough." Merci. Muchas gracias. Danke. Arigato. Grazie. Thank you—it's beautiful in every language!

Increase joy by lessening desires

Many spiritual traditions support the idea that joy and peace are as much a part of our nature as the desire to breathe. From this perspective, joy is not something to be cultivated because it is already there within us. The challenge is to peel away the layers of discontent that we have allowed to cover our original joy. Typically, the source of discontent is our suffering from what we do not have.

There are two ways to not suffer from want of what we do not have. The first is to acquire more wealth so that we can obtain what we desire. The second is to limit our desires. The first is not always within our power—but the second is.

Here's a great story I heard a long time ago from a friend who had a gift for living simply, even in the face of criticism from those who would have had him clean up and "get a real job." I do not know the origin of the story, but the tale certainly rings a contemporary bell.

> Once upon a time a rich businessman from the city was horrified to find the rural fisherman lying lazily beside his boat, smoking a pipe.
>
> "Why aren't you out fishing?" said the businessman.
>
> "Because I have caught enough fish for the day," said the fisherman.
>
> "Why don't you want to catch some more?"

"What would I do with more?"
"You could earn more money" was the reply. "With that you could have a motor fixed to your boat to go into deeper waters and catch more fish. Then you would earn enough money to buy nylon nets. These would bring you more fish and more money. Soon you would have enough money to own two boats… maybe even a fleet of boats! Then you would be a rich man like me."

"What would I do then?"

"Then you could really enjoy life."

The fisherman leaned up on his elbow as he took the pipe from his mouth, and asked, "And what do you think I am doing right now?"

This story does not begrudge the businessman's entrepreneurial spirit—all the power to him. But this story does support the idea that the fisherman has his own definition of satisfaction and success. The only real joy we will ever know must spring forth from our own hearts and souls, not someone else's. The fisherman's contentment may have as much to do with the limits of his desires as the attainment of the desires he has.

The idea of lessening desires to attain joy has long been understood within the Buddhist tradition. Buddha summarized his discoveries in the Four Noble Truths which constitute the very heart of Buddhism:

1. Life is imbued with difficulties and suffering.
2. The cause of suffering is attachment.
3. Freedom from attachment brings freedom from suffering.
4. Freedom from attachment and suffering can come from practicing the Eight-Fold Path which centers on ethics, wisdom and meditation.

It is clear that the Buddha is suggesting not only that our perceptions of what we think we need (our attachments) is the cause of our greatest angst, but that the quickest way to our own contentment is by changing our minds about what we think we need. This lesson is beautifully portrayed in a story popular among the Islamic mystics known as Sufis. One of the Sufi's favorite characters is the trickster Nasrudin. Often Nasrudin appears to be a complete idiot, but he is actually a wise and cunning man whose tricks contain brilliant lessons about life.

One day Nasrudin was out walking and found a man sitting on the side of the road crying. "What is the matter, my friend?" asked Nasrudin. "Why are you crying?"

"I'm crying because I am so poor," wailed the man. "I have no money and everything I own is in the little bag."

"Ah-ha!," said Nasrudin, who immediately grabbed the bag and ran as fast as he could until he was out of sight.

"Now I have nothing at all," cried the poor man, weeping still harder as he trudged along the road in the direction Nasrudin had gone. A mile away he found his bag sitting in the middle of the road, and he immediately became ecstatic. "Thank God," he cried out. "I have all my possessions back. Thank you, thank you."

"How curious!" exclaimed Nasrudin, appearing out of the bushes by the side of the road. "How curious that the same bag that made you weep now makes you ecstatic."

How do we remind ourselves that unhappiness reflects the difference between what we crave and what we have? If we could relinquish our attachments by accepting what we have, the gap would dissolve and so too would much of our unhappiness. This is why Gandhi, when asked to describe his philosophy of life, needed only three words: "Renounce and rejoice."

Discover joy rather than pursue happiness

Contrary to the U. S. Constitution which upholds the right of every person to life, liberty and the pursuit of happiness, I do not think that joy is something to be pursued, like one would pursue a career goal or a hawk pursues its prey. It is something that one stumbles upon while involved in other things. I believe that joy prefers to travel on the wings of purpose, passion, and even persistence. She likes to surprise us and show up in unsuspecting places, like in the relief of speaking your mind in an awkward situation, in the letter received from a colleague with whom you had lost touch, or in the gratitude from a customer for whom you went the extra mile. Perhaps we should cease seeking happiness, but focus our attention instead on opportunities to give of ourselves. Perhaps we should take to heart the words of W. Beran Wolfe:

> "If you observe a really happy man you will find him building a boat, writing a symphony, educating his son, growing double dahlias in his garden, or looking for dinosaur eggs in the Gobi desert. He will not be striving for it as a goal itself. He will have become aware that he is happy in the course of living life twenty-four crowded hours of the day."

This wisdom was manifested beautifully in the life of one of the world's most celebrated artists. For thirty-five years Paul Cezanne lived in obscurity, producing masterpieces that he gave away to unsuspecting neighbors. So great was his love for his work that he never gave a thought to achieving recognition, nor did he suspect that someday he would be looked upon as the father of modern painting. He owes his fame to an art dealer in Paris who chanced upon some of his paintings, put some of them together, and presented the world of art with the first Cezanne exhibition. The world was astonished to discover the presence of a master. Evidently, the master was just as astonished. He arrived at the art gallery leaning on the arm of his son and could not contain his amazement when he saw his paintings on display. Turning to his son he said, "Look, they framed them!"

Cezanne's story encourages us to worry less about pursuing vocational goals and to focus more on listening to our instincts, following our spirits, and obeying our dreams. It reminds us to be content with life because we are allowed to love and work and play, to plant gardens and walk barefoot on the beach, to make a difference in someone's life and leave a mark on the world. Such is the journey of joy.

Learn to love many things

By attaching ourselves to the world through what we love, we experience the richness of life. When we love, we listen, we pay attention, we throw back the curtain of our cynicism so that our hearts become an open window. Those who love deeply simply cannot escape joy. (And of course, what we love, we cannot help but be grateful for. What we are grateful for brings us joy. It is a lovely, endless spiral.)

Here is my own rendition of an old teaching story about the power of love.

Once upon a time there lived a woman who was very discouraged because, try as she may, she could not find a way to love and worship God. She went to church, but she would leave uninspired. She earnestly read texts considered sacred by various religious traditions, but they did not move her. She wanted to know and love God, but she didn't know where to start.

One day she was visited by a friend who she considered very insightful, wise and deeply spiritual. She poured out her heart to her friend, admitting to her failure to know and love God. Her friend responded kindly, "Is there anything you do love?"

The woman's eyes lit up as she declared, "But of course! I love my cats! I have eighteen of them and I never know when a stray will join our family. I live to care for these cats. And of course, my garden. Did you notice my sweet peas growing on the fence? They didn't get that tall and beautiful without a fair bit of tender loving care!" The woman glowed as she spoke of the loves in her life.

Her friend just smiled saying, "You have failed at nothing. You know what it is to love your cats and your flowers… you have found your path to God."

The more we pour love into the things that we care for and about, the more joy we know and the closer to Spirit we feel. I remember a conversation I had with one of my nephews who is an avowed atheist. We spoke into the wee hours of the morning about the meaning of life and death and the mysteries of the beyond. There were many points upon which we disagreed, but we found our common ground once we started talking about love. I will never forget him saying, "The only thing I know of God is the fever of love… I would sacrifice everything and anything for my family. This isn't rational, but it is true." I remember thinking that we had argued and bantered through the night only to reach a common horizon we both call "Love," just about the same time the sun peeked over the horizon. And all was well with the world.

The writing of this chapter prompted me to identify in my personal journal the many loves of my life. My list began, of course, with all of the people I have loved—family, friends, teachers, colleagues, neighbors, etc. (That is a fun list to write!) The next time I opened my journal I attempted to identify other things I have loved through my life that have made it rich and made my heart glad. That list began with the most observable forms of things I love, like nature, music and books. As the list grew, the items became less and less tangible, like my love of celebration, festivity and communion with other people.

The writing of these lists brought home an essential insight—the deepest reservoir of power and vitality in my life is not in my intellect, my talents or my position in the world—my greatest source of power and vitality is in my love. That into which I invest and pour my love, that which ignites and stirs my heart and soul—these are the true testaments of the life I have lived and the life the world has lived through me.

Love has no limits—it increases rather than diminishes through its use. Love has no designs but to adore, delight and nurture its beloved. Love has fervor and strength and hope. It finds courage. Personally, I want to live with a deeper connection and alignment to that which stirs my heart and speaks to my soul—to that which I love.

With that intent, I chose one item from my List of Loves and decided to write more, to dive more deeply into the love of that one thing, and see where it would lead. I chose the topic of my hands. What resulted was the poem entitled, "Hands," included on the facing page. I look forward to attempting a similar exercise with my eyes, my feet, my imagination... Of one thing, I am certain—if we dive deeply enough into anything we love, there, at bottom, is joy!

For sure, great sadness and adversity make us understand the world. But it is great joy and gratitude that bring us to love this world. Both sides of the human experience are essential. There is a wonderful Apache myth about when the Creator gave human beings the ability to talk, to run, and to look. He found that He was not satisfied until He also gave them the ability to laugh and dance. Only then did the Creator say, "Now you are fit to live."

With the gift of age,
I care less how I appear
and I care more about how I live.
I am going to keep on dancing
on the belly of the earth
I will wish on every star in sight.
I will ooh and ahh in celebration
of each small bud in my garden.
In fact, I plan to hang out
with the lupine and the daisies
and learn from them
how to blossom boldly,
as if my joy
and beauty mattered.

I took it as a great compliment when one day, my friend and neighbor, Pearl Robinson, an accomplished poet from the 1930's, observed, "Denise, you get more excited about a budding lilac branch than most of us get in a lifetime of Easter Sundays. That's because you see resurrection in each branch, don't you?" Bless you, Pearl. Yes, I do.

Hands

I love having hands!
I love how, unlike the heart, they will open and close at will...
how, unlike the mind, they will shape themselves
to accommodate a foreign object.

I love having hands and the wondrous things they enable:
The braiding of my daughter's hair,
The paring of apples for pie,
The tilling of soil for seeds,
Tying ribbons, lighting candles,
Turning the pages of a great book,
Strumming the strings of an old guitar.

I love having hands!

I love how they fly like wild birds on the winds of my meaning as I speak...
How they provide the perfect mantle for my chin as I set myself to listen...
I love how they move with a fever across paper to midwife the infant poem.
I love how with the simple gesture of putting my hand in the hand of the
one I love, we cross an abyss of silence and find our way back home,
to one another.

I love having hands for waving hello, for blowing kisses,
for applauding beauty and raising a fist to injustice.
I even love them for signaling the occasional obnoxious driver.

But of all the miracles and movements of my hands,
I love them most when they are folded in prayer...
Palm to palm... fingertip to fingertip. . .
and they make that small, hollow, holy place between them—
As if inviting God to send a bird, the tiniest bird,
a bird of hope, a bird of faith
To make its nest.

I keep my hands busy all day with the activity of the world
but when they are folded in prayer I gather myself,
I return to the Source, to Spirit—
without whom I can do nothing.

If they were to serve no other purpose,
I would wish my hands to be a nest
for any small bird my God would send.

Passages

"God likes us when we work,
but he loves us when we sing!"

East Indian saying

"Row, row, row your boat,
gently down the sea,
merrily, merrily, merrily,
merrily, life is but a dream."

Children's nursery rhyme

George Satayana

"There is no cure for birth or death,
save to enjoy the interval."

Friedrich Nietzsche

"We should consider every day lost in which we have not danced at least once."

"Think of all the beauty still left around you and be happy."

Anne Frank

"Give thanks to God who made necessary things simple, and complicated things unnecessary."

Gregory Skovoroda

The Talmud

"Who is a wise man—
He who studies all the time.
Who is strong?—
He who can limit himself.
Who is rich?—
He who is happy
with what he has."

John Burroughs

"I am in love with this world. I have nestled lovingly in it. I have climbed its mountains, roamed its forests, sailed its waters, crossed its deserts, felt the sting of its frosts, the oppression of its heats, the drench of its rains, the fury of its winds and always have beauty and joy waited upon my comings and goings."

Emily Dickinson

"The mere sense of living is joy enough."

"This curious world which we inhabit is more wonderful than it is convenient; more beautiful than it is useful; is more to be admired and enjoyed than used."

Henry David Thoreau

"The best things are nearest: breath in your nostrils, light in your eyes, flowers at your feet, duties at your hand, the path of God just before you. Then do not grasp at the stars, but do life's plain, common work as it comes, certain that daily duties and daily bread are the sweetest things of life."

Robert Louis Stevenson

"I will not be a tourist in the world of images—just watching life pass by which I cannot live in, make love to, and possess as a permanent source of joy and ecstasy."

Anaïs Nin

Chinese proverb

"If I keep a green bough in my heart,
The singing bird will come."

"If you never want to see the face of hell, when you come home from work every night dance with your kitchen towel and, if you're worried about waking your family, take off your shoes."

Rabbi Nachman of Bratzlav

"The world seems to be divided into two groups of people: those who say you can never get something for nothing, and those muddled but happy creatures who maintain that the best things in life are free." Janet Gillespie

"A man comes into the world
with his hands pushed into fists,
as if he wants to say, "All this world is mine."
A man leaves this world with his palms open,
as if to say, "Look, I take nothing with me.""

The Talmud

"I love laughing." William Blake

Harvey Mackay

"Being rich isn't about money. Being rich is a state of mind. Some of us, no matter how much money we have, will never be free enough to take time to stop and eat the heart of the watermelon. And some of us will be rich without ever being more than a paycheck ahead of the game."

Colette "Be happy. It's one way of being wise."

Henri Matisse

"Ever since there have been men,
man has given himself over to too little joy.
That alone, my brothers, is our original sin.
I should believe only in a God
who understood how to dance."

"Scatter Joy!" Ralph Waldo Emerson

"Work is love made visible. And if you cannot work with love but only with distaste, it is better that you should leave your work and sit at the gate of the temple and take alms of those who work with joy. For if you bake bread with indifference, you bake a bitter bread that feeds but half a man's hunger."

Kahlil Gibran

"Be content with what you have;
Rejoice in the way things are.
When you realize there is nothing lacking,
The whole world belongs to you."

Lao Tzu

"A person will be called to account on Judgment Day for every permissible thing he might have enjoyed and did not."

The Talmud

"Joy to the World,
all the boys and girls,
Joy to the fishes in the deep blue sea.
Joy to you and me."

Three Dog Night

To Ponder and To Practice

- What have been some of the happiest periods of your life? What made them so?
- Who is the happiest, most joyful person you know? Consider what you believe to be the source of that person's joy.
- Who is one of the most miserable people you know? What do you think might be the source of that person's misery?
- George Sand once observed, "Happiness lies in the consciousness we have of it." Take a moment to consider the abundance of good things in your life. Does anyone love you? Celebrate it. Is there anything you do well? Take pleasure in it. Is your health good enough to survive the day? Revel in it. Begin to celebrate the ordinary.
- Identify three things in each of the following categories for which you are grateful:
  - Natural abilities or talents
  - Qualities or aspects of your personal nature
  - Conditions of your birth
  - Life experiences
  - What you have accomplished and enjoyed thus far in life
  - Memories you cherish
  - People who you are blessed to have in your life
  - Aspects of your home life
  - Aspects of your work life
  - Aspects of your spiritual life
  - Aspects of your physical being
- In addition to being thankful for what we are, what we have and what we receive, we should be mindful of what we have been fortunate enough to escape. What are some of the things in life that you have feared would happen, but that you have escaped thus far? What are some of the terrible things that happen to people around the world that you have never had reason to fear would happen to you?
- Wear a patina of joy and lightheartedness all day and observe how people respond.

Practice

- Remembering that unhappiness reflects the difference between what we crave and what we have, how can you live more like the content fisherman and increase your joy simply by lessening your desires? What three desires are you willing to let go of in terms of your home life? How about in your work life?
- Do something that brings you back to the delight you had as a child. Whistle as loud as you can for as long as you like. Blow bubbles. Spit watermelon seeds. Skip rocks. Jump rope. Inhale helium and talk like Donald Duck. Learn a new dance. Try juggling. Buy a coloring book and the deluxe box of 68 crayons! (Keep all the pointed ones for yourself.)
- Go outside tonight and look at the stars and claim one as your own. When you find yourself fretting about small cares, take a look at the stars and let them give you the gift of perspective.
- Select a quote on the topic of joy or gratitude from this chapter's *Passages* and post it where you will see it until it is internalized.
- Choose a daily habit, routine or symbol to help you remain conscious of the many blessings in your life. (e. g. Standing under a hot shower can be a great reminder of the many blessing showered upon us daily.)
- Given everything you have read in this chapter, what do you want to *keep* doing? What do you want to *stop* doing? What do you want to *start* doing?

Notes

I Want to Live in Color

Chapter 16

Living with Wholeheartedness

Consider your colors

Consider your colors

Accept the dandelions

Accept the dandelions

Feel with the whole heart

Feel with the whole heart

Fall into your inkpot

Fall into your inkpot

Be willing to be considered a crackpot

Be willing to be considered a crackpot

Believe in impossible things

Believe in impossible things

Increase your inquisitive quotient

Increase your inquisitive quotient

Be a heart-dweller

Be a heart-dweller

Refuse to be tamed by the world

Refuse to be tamed by the world

I Want to Live in Color

I don't want to live in the black and white of
conventional wisdom, of judgment and dogma,
in the security of my own fixed opinions,
though a certain comfort they bring.
I want to live in color!

With vitality, as green as summer grass and as enduring!
With purpose, as red as the blood coursing through my veins
and as deliberate!
With joy as yellow and shining as the face of the sun and as generous!
With passion, as purple as the clustered grapes hanging heavy
on the twiggy vine and as true to its source.
With courage, as brown as the redwood forest and as unrelenting.
With love, as blue as the sea and the sky and as infinite.
With wonder, as white as the virgin snow and as pure.

I want every color, every life-affirming quality
on the palette with which I paint my life!

And though the colors will mix and fade,
transmuting into the darker tones
of sorrow and doubt, even despair,
I want to live wholeheartedly.
I want a stained-glass life
through which Spirit may pour,
leaving not a pale shadow
but a rainbow of light!

Reflections

I want to belong to this world like the moon belongs to the sky or the fish belong to the sea… surrendered and wholehearted. I want to devote my work to life like the bird devotes its song to the morning or the candle devotes its light to the dark. Even as I work to free myself of social patterning and worn-out scripts, I want to bind myself to this world by attaching my heart to family, to friends and to those with whom I work and live in community. Even while I fluff the wings of my own independence, I want to fasten myself to the cradle of humanity with ribbons of compassion and tenderness and purpose. Even as I set sail on a sea of extravagant ideas and elegant notions, I want to find my moorings in the simpler yet more commanding loyalties of my own convictions. In large, bold letters I want written on the banner of my life, "She lived and loved and released all her petals to the wind."

I really do want to live in color. Whether or not my life is long, I wish for a life that is deep.

But daily life has a tendency to grow dull, monotonous and predictable, where our colors fade into black and white and shades of gray. We wake, we shower, we dress, we go to work. We do our time. We come home, we prepare dinner, we eat, we do the dishes and we tend to the needs of the kids. We watch the news and shake our heads at how royally we have screwed up the world. We go to bed, but we do not sleep. We toss and turn. We fluff and refluff the pillow as we start preparing for the morrow. (Then again, agonizing and worrying doesn't exactly qualify as preparation.) We eventually drift off. Just as we hit the deep level of REM sleep, the alarm goes off. We wake, we shower, we dress and we go to work again.

This is not how any of us wish to live. This is no moon of a life, betrothed to its sky. There is no birdsong in this existence nor are there sails set to any wind. This is a life deprived of sky, much less a rainbow.

The problem is not that there is a shortage of wonder in the world. Nor is there a scarcity of ideas, ideals, causes or crusades to enlist our allegiance or to spark our enthusiasm. But life lived in black and white produces two culprits that steal into the night of our existence. They do not let their presence be known, they just settle bit by bit into the proverbial woodwork of our being. One is apathy, a loss of interest in life and its adventures, a loss of appetite for joy and wonder. Apathy's sidekick, cynicism, is always nearby. Cynicism is blind to meaning and purpose; in fact, it chokes on the very words. It has a ravenous appetite for suspicion, doubt and pessimism. Once these culprits steal into our lives it takes something powerful to evict them.

Indeed, there is still one magic talisman that has the power to bring freshness, novelty and surprise back into the blackest and whitest existence we can muster: *our own and one another's wholeheartedness.* It is available to us in endless quantities if we but entrust our loyalties with the colorful side of our nature. When we light up with enthusiasm or passion for something outside our own needs and desires, when a fire has been lit within us—well, it's enough to send apathy and cynicism running for their pitiful little lives. Like throwing water on the Wicked Witch of the West.

Wholeheartedness means being present with the whole heart, not half of it. The word "enthusias," of Greek origins, literally means "a God within." How do we restore these qualities and our capacity for them again, to bring every color onto the palette of our lives so that our days fit more of this description?

We awaken. We slowly realize that we have been gifted with another day. We smile and rise to greet it. We bow to a rising sun. We carry that bit of rosy light with us as we greet the others with whom we share home. We feast on something marvelous like an orange or a banana and wonder how the banana tree could be so brilliant in the packaging of its fruit. We shower, inviting the warm water to rush over us as if we were under a waterfall in some tropical paradise. We dress, amazed at our own affluence and the choices of clothing in our closet. We smell the afternoon wind on the cotton shirt that hung on yesterday's clothesline. We go to work, grateful for the opportunity to use our God-given talents in some way that will affect someone or something outside ourselves…

You catch my drift.

I can hear you through the pages… "Denise is crazy! She's lost it! She's certifiable!" Well, I will let you draw your own conclusions as to what I am certifiable *for,* but before you do, let me plead "guilty," in the first degree, to living life in far less color than I wish to admit.

Consider your colors

In the midst of writing this chapter I had an idea. I thought I would draft a list of all the ways in which I already feel as if I *live in color,* examples of living wholeheartedly and true to the qualities I value. I cheerily wrote examples such as:

- I express my joy unabashedly.
- My home reflects my celebratory nature.
- I compliment people freely, even people I do not know.
- I am able to relate to children on their level—I can drop my adult posture in a second flat.
- I can apologize freely and humbly—I am not afraid to admit being wrong.
- I take a lot of risks as a trainer and as a writer; I do not hide from vulnerability.
- I can make any gathering of friends or family feel like a celebration.
- I am not afraid to show my affection or emotion.
- I am a generous person.
- I am conscientious about walking my talk.

That was all fine and good, and I was actually feeling pretty pleased with myself, until the next thought came to me and I drafted a different list. This time it was a list of examples of what my life would look like if I lived *more* in color, truer to those qualities I value. I was astounded not only by the quality of differences but the sheer quantity of them! The second list made the first list pale by comparison. It included examples such as:

- I would say "no" when I mean "no."
- I would only say "yes" when I mean "yes."
- I would stand up for people and principles, even when I know it might cause disharmony in the moment.
- I would not avoid important conversations.
- I would be less quick to judge and more inclined to see other points of view, especially on issues of politics and religion.
- I would speak up more often for my own needs and worry less about pleasing everyone else.
- I would participate more in local community projects and volunteer my time in causes I find important.
- I would engage in artistic and athletic endeavors, not worrying about whether or not I was good at them.
- I would never say anything about other people that I would not be willing to say in their presence.

- I wouldn't hesitate to look the homeless person in the eye and smile, even when I am not inclined to put money in the cup.
- I wouldn't worry about having to run into the store in my pajamas.
- I would be willing to sing as loudly and enthusiastically in front of other people as I am in my car with the windows rolled up.
- I would be more willing to be the first to stand in a standing ovation.
- I wouldn't have to wait until the dance floor is half filled before I was willing to shake my bootie.

For weeks after writing these lists, new examples continued to surface right and left. Not always conveniently. A few days after writing this list I shared these insights with my daughter, who was accompanying me on a work trip. The next morning as I was readying myself to deliver a day of training, I realized that I had left my makeup bag at home. I was horrified. In the midst of my frenzy, Jessica looked at me calmly and said, "That really shouldn't be a problem for someone who lives in color. I think you can survive a day without makeup, Mom."

From the mouths of babes. Somehow hearing the word "survive" in the same sentence with "makeup" brought it home to me. I knew in my heart of hearts that if I really lived in color, I would care less about my physical appearance. So it would be an experiment! Could I stand up and deliver, looking pale, peaked and washed out? (Which is how we women always look to ourselves sans Clinique.) Well, I survived the morning just fine. No one even asked me if I was feeling okay. It was weird. They just thought that's how I look. It was a wonderful, freeing feeling in the end, and it lasted all the way to the makeup counter at the local WalMart during lunch.

Another time, I was standing in line at a bank and watched a young man subtly make his way in front of an elderly woman in line. She was oblivious to it, but I wasn't. I started thinking about how rude we are in this culture towards elders and how in other cultures no one would ever think of doing such a thing. And then it hit me, "Well, if you lived more in color, you would say something… now." My heart was pumping nearly out of my chest as I tapped the young man on the shoulder and said, "Excuse me, but I think this woman was here before you." At which point, he looked me as if I was crazy and said, "Yeah, I know. That's my grandmother. I'm here to help her make a deposit."

Talk about living in color—my face turned a nice, bright shade of red! Still, once over my embarrassment, I felt happy and proud that I had followed an inkling to speak up on behalf of fairness. The gesture may have been wasted on the situation, but it wasn't wasted on me and my own growing sense of personal power to live in a conscious manner.

I am so grateful for having written the poem, "I Want to Live in Color," because it has served as a kind of wake-up call for me to put more color back into my life—not the kind that comes from a bottle but the deep and vibrant hues that come from wholehearted living.

With vitality,
as green as summer grass
and as enduring!
With purpose,
as red as the blood
coursing through my veins
and as deliberate!
With joy as yellow and shining
as the face of the sun
and as generous!

With passion,
as purple as the clustered grapes
hanging heavy on the twiggy vine
and as true to it source.
With courage,
as brown as the redwood forest
and as unrelenting.
With love,
as blue as the sea and the sky
and as infinite.
With wonder,
as white as the virgin snow
and as pure.

Here are some ideas and reminders of how we can put wholeheartedness into practice not only in our doing, but also in our *thinking* and our *being.*

Accept the dandelions

This spring I was visiting dear friends who live on beautiful Prince Edward Island in Atlantic Canada. Having arrived in the dark, I awoke in the morning to a splendid surprise. Their entire two and a half acres of yard was a meadow of delicate yellow and white flowers. I was enchanted. In the midst of my profuse emoting over this wild abandonment of beauty, one of my friends laughed and said, "Denise, you can make even a field of dreaded dandelions look beautiful." To my surprise, I learned that these "flowers" were the bane of their spring existence.

This reminded me of one of my favorite Sufi stories shared in the book, *Stories of the Spirit, Stories of the Heart,* by Christina Feldman and Jack Kornfield, which speaks to an essential aspect of true wholeheartedness.

There was once a woman who decided to start a flower garden. She prepared her soil and planted seeds of many beautiful flowers. But when they came up, her garden was filled not just with chosen flowers but also overrun by dandelions. She sought advice from gardeners all over and tried every method known to get rid of them but to no avail. Finally she walked all the way to the capital to speak to the royal gardener at the sheik's palace. The wise man had counseled many gardeners before and suggested a variety of remedies to expel the dandelions but the woman had tried them all before. They sat together in silence for some time and finally the gardener looked at her and said, "Well, then I suggest that if you want to continue with your flower garden, you learn to love the dandelions too."

If we only bring an open heart to those aspects of our lives in which the flowers we've planted remain within their neat little borders without any interference from the rest of nature, we are bound to live half-heartedly. No life, no job, no household is without its dandelions. No relationship is either. But it is the dandelions in our lives that keep us awake as gardeners. We must be careful to not grow impatient with other people, with circumstances or with ourselves when we meet dandelions in our own experiences. I don't know about you, but I have yet to know of, much less experience, a part of life that was dandelion-free. But take heart, because from another point of view, they may be mistaken as flowers.

Feel with the whole heart

In *The Book of Awakening,* Mark Nepo writes,

> "Amazingly, as the infinite forms of flowers arise from the same earth, the earthly garden of emotions—in all their delicate shapes and colors—all rise from the same earth of heart. What this opens for us is the often hard to accept fact that underneath, there is only one unnamable emotion, which all feelings know as

> home. . . . Despite our efforts to be happy and not sad, to be calm and not anxious, to be clear and not confused, to be understanding and not angry; it is feeling each of them all the way through that lands us in the vibrant place that is often healing."

I know people who shy away from anger, who never express it regardless of the cost to their inner world, where it hovers like a thundering storm. I know people who shy away from sorrow, who never express it regardless of the cost to their inner world, where their tears are held against a dam that is ready to burst. I know people who shy away from love, who rarely express it regardless of the cost to their inner world, where the need to love and be loved exists like the wilting flower that has no drink nor sun to grow by.

But our not wanting to feel or express various emotions does not stop them from existing within us. Avoidance of emotion in any of its colors exacts a price in our personal relationships. How can it not? The more wholehearted we are in a relationship, the more we bring to each other and the more the relationship can bring to us, to our mutual flowering. The more we withhold, the less life-giving power we bring to the relationship. To feel with every emotion, we create a life with every color on our palette.

It is true in work as well. Have you ever seen the person who brings half their heart to work? And while they may be very professional, rational, logical, and keenly accountable for their every action, you feel no personal or emotional connection to this person as a fellow human being. All their ducks may be in a row but their ducks have no quack, no waddle, no spark. You know that you have never heard his real laugh, the kind that erupts from the gut. You know that you have never seen her eyes come alive, with joy or frustration. You can't help but wonder how people can set aside the emotional side of their being in order to go to work. They may produce results of a certain kind, but it will be the kind that is bereft of imagination, vitality, creativity or passion because those qualities spring from the joining of the intellect with the heart and soul of the person. Leave the heart at home and we produce mechanical ducks, the kind that sit in a neat little row, unable to skim the water with a flourish before rising on wings.

Fall into your inkpot

The great Ralph Waldo Emerson proclaimed, "I dip my pen in the blackest ink, because I am not afraid of falling into my inkpot." How's that for living in color?

"Living in color" requires an acceptance that things get messy and out of order. As we paint the portrait of our own lives, we do not want paint-by-number lives. We were made for the kind of joy that results from experimenting with paint on canvas, of mixing colors and brandishing the paintbrush with the vigor and power of a samurai's sword. Actress and author Carrie Fisher suggests that "Our lives should not imitate art. They should be art."

Really, if you think about it, we are art. Fine art! The medium for our art lies in the choices we make at the intersection of our capacities and our circumstances. Have you ever seen someone who lives artfully, not just in terms of his or her dress and home décor, but in their decorum? Have you ever been invited to a meeting in which you were made to feel as if you were a valued guest, rather than just another name on the list? How about the housekeeper who folds the hand towels into an origami swan, the cosmetologist who finishes a haircut with her signature neck massage, the bagger at the grocery store who has learned the names of your children? What is this, if not living art?

It is possible for us to not only live artfully, but to die with equal elegance and grace. I know this because I was privileged to know such a person and I would like to share one of my most memorable vignettes of my dear friend and neighbor, Pearl Robinson, who was a celebrated poet in her day.

Pearl was in her 90s and living with brain cancer when she entreated me to record her poetry as she recited from her deathbed. One day a neighbor stopped by for a visit while Pearl was visited by the Muse. As he popped his head in the door, I suggested that he return later as Pearl was working. He came over to the bed, patted Pearl on the head and said, "Aren't you amazing? Ninety-something years old and still writing poetry!" Once he left, Pearl responded to his comment with her eyes dancing, "The poor fool—what he doesn't understand is that I am just at the top of my game!"

Pearl fell into her inkpot at about 22 years old and never recovered. May we be so blessed!

Be willing to be considered a crackpot

I grew up in a household where "using your brain" was important and you avoided being considered a crackpot at any cost. This is a culture that likes people who follow the party line and values conformity over controversy. Thomas Watson, the founder of IBM, didn't agree. He said,

> "Follow the path of the unsafe, independent thinker. Expose your ideas to the dangers of controversy. Speak your mind and fear less the label of 'crackpot' than the stigma of conformity. And on issues that seem important to you, stand up and be counted at any cost."

Living according to the party line gives us security and identity, but it also creates selective blindness, narrowness and rigidity because it is intrinsically conservative. Contrary to popular belief, there is nothing sacred about the status quo. It is radical thinking and revolutionary thought that bring change and progress, not groupthink. As contemporary writer Wes Scoop Nisker put it, "We live in a world of many illusions and much of human belief and behavior is ritualized nonsense." Isn't "reality" to a large degree whatever the masses at the time agree it is?

Not one of the founders of the great religions was orthodox—they were all independent thinkers. Jesus was not a Christian, Siddhartha was not a Buddhist, and Mohammed was not a Muslim. All were charismatic spiritual seekers, mystics, and prophets who were considered troublemakers and critics of the establishments of their day. Surely, by thinking for ourselves, we will be criticized and misunderstood. But is being misunderstood such a terrible thing? Pythagoras was misunderstood, and so were Socrates, Luther, Copernicus, Galileo, and Sir Isaac Newton. In fact, Ralph Waldo Emerson suggested that "To be great requires a willingness to be misunderstood."

It is said that whoever rocks the boat will be asked to sit down, but once in awhile we need the devious among us who just tip the whole thing right over. Let our old, dried up notions get all wet. It is the idealists, not the pragmatists who have advanced and enriched the world in astonishing ways. It is those who are foolish enough to throw caution to the winds who change the world with their discoveries or their revolutions. As Oscar Wilde observed, "An idea that is not risky is hardly worth calling an idea."

Believe in impossible things

Did you know that according to the theory of aerodynamics, it is impossible for the bumblebee to fly? Due to its size, weight and the shape of its body in relation to the total wingspan, bumblebees should not be able to be airborne. But the bumblebee, being ignorant of these profound scientific truths, goes ahead and flies anyway and manages to make a little honey every day.

I think we should live like the bumblebees. In fact, we should live like Lewis Carroll who says in *Alice in Wonderland,* "Sometimes I've believed as many as six impossible things before breakfast." Do you know who believed in impossible things? People like the Wright Brothers, Thomas Edison, Alexander Graham Bell, Mahatma Gandhi, Nelson Mandela and Jonas Salk.

The world sorely needs people who not only believe in the impossible but act out on those beliefs. I want to be in the company of people who have refused to deem as "impossible" a cure for Aids, cancer and other deadly diseases. I want to join the band of idealists who struggle to put an end to world hunger and the myriad factors leading to it. I wouldn't mind being counted among the crackpots who work to grow the consciousness about the health of the planet and are leading a movement to turn the tide of recklessness to caring for this blessed globe. I want to be a "fool for justice" in a world where the violation of civil rights is accepted as part of "the way things are."

One of my aunts to whom I have dedicated this book is a rebel to the bone. My Aunt Anna is a true renegade. Having been trained as a registered nurse, she began teaching in the Gerontology Department of Boston University. She recognized that many of the city's elderly did not have the ability nor the resources to be seen for medical care. She started one of the first programs in the U. S. where the students began knocking on doors of the tenements and apartment buildings that housed elders who may be in need of medical care. As time went on, a far more urgent need caught her attention, housing for elders living on the streets of Boston. My aunt spearheaded The Committee for Ending Elder Homelessness, which has provided hundreds of elders with housing, complete with furnishings, a well-stocked kitchen and round the clock nursing care. The fourth such house was named The Anna Bissonnette House.

My sisters and I were privileged to be present when my Aunt Anna received a prestigious award from the Massachusetts Health Council in 1999. I will never forget her words as she accepted the award "on behalf of all of the nurses present." With great humility, she said, "Shame on us that we would see fit to give an award to someone for the very basic act of putting a roof over an elder's head. It just shows how far we still have to go." If there was anyone present who was not yet aware of the work of Anna Bissonnette, by the end of that speech they were standing and applauding with as much fervor and enthusiasm as the rest of us.

God bless those who look deeply at the world and say, eye to eye with the status quo, "I don't think so."

Increase your inquisitive quotient

Martin Luther King, Jr. once said that you know a man more by his questions than by his answers. I agree. In today's fast paced and quickly changing environment, it is more important that we be teachable than that we be learned. As Alvin Toffler predicted, "The new literacy in the 21st century work world is not reading and writing, it will be learning, unlearning, re-learning, unlearning, learning…." We know that to stay healthy, the body needs exercise and movement, but we rarely recognize that it is equally important to keep our thinking in motion. We need aerobics for the mind—

jumping jacks for the imagination, stretches for the intellect—lest we settle for a fixed, unquestioned view of the world.

I love this passage from Sam Keen's wonderful book, *Hymns for an Unknown God,* in which he urges us to embrace our ignorance: He writes,

> "Each of us creates a picture of our world by connecting only a dozen or so of the trillions of dots that would have to be connected to make a "true" portrait of the universe (if indeed, the notions of knowing the universe and the truth make any sense at all.) Considering the inherent limits of the finite human mind and our nearly inexhaustible capacity for self-deception, we may actually be closest to the truth when we remain acutely aware of our ignorance."

When we embrace our ignorance, our inquisitiveness grows. Inquisitiveness, the desire to learn and grow, and curiosity are critical qualities not only for living in color, but for staying in the game of life. These qualities, in fact, may matter more in the long run than our ability to perform and conform within the confines of conventional wisdom.

The marvelous book, *Cradles of Eminence,* by Mildred and Victor Goertzel, describes how three-fifths of four hundred famous modern people performed less than brilliantly in school, but practiced independent thinking outside of school. Gandhi, Einstein, John Lennon, George Patton, Robert Browning, Pearl S. Buck, Isadora Duncan and Gertrude Stein—to name a few—all had problems conforming to a system into which they did not fit. It makes you wonder, did their original, non-conforming ways of thinking and being have anything to do with the kind of greatness they achieved?

One of my favorite examples is that of scientist, painter and inventor Leonardo da Vinci. Today he would probably have ended up in a class for the learning disabled. Historians claim that his writing was atrocious, he had trouble reading some of the basic texts of his time and he hated math. Yet he became a musician, anatomist, poet, engineer, geologist, astronomer, philosopher, inventor and creator of some of the world's most celebrated masterpieces. He is a role model for our age because he continually pushed his boundaries to know and learn while applying his unlimited curiosity in diverse directions. Oddly, it is reported that on his deathbed he expressed regrets that he had not lived up to his potential.

Be a heart-dweller

There is a wonderful Native American story about how the Creator decided where to put the secrets of the universe. He considered placing them in the trees, but realized that monkeys, squirrels and other tree-dwelling critters may disturb them. He considered putting them in caves, but was concerned about interference from bats, spiders and other cave-dwelling creatures. He considered the deep blue sea but worried about possible intrusion from the sharks, the squid and other sea-dwelling creatures. He finally got his answer. Why not put it in the hearts of the two-legged creatures, for few dwell there for more than a minute, and it is the last place anyone would look for the secrets of the universe.

I don't know about the secrets of the universe, but surely the secrets to each of our heart's desire has been planted there. Rumi, the Sufi mystic poet of the 13th century, professed that everyone was made for some particular work and the desire for that work has been put in every heart.

I think that sometimes the desire for our true work shows up as passion or purpose as forthright as an arrow aiming for its target.

But that is rare. Far more typical is the desire for our true work showing up as boredom, angst or discontent. Sometimes this is referred to as "divine discontent"—the knock at our heart's door from a messenger of the soul that it is time for us to move on.

It will only be through a willingness to *dwell in the whole heart* that we will respond with equal fervor to the pangs of woe and to the pitter-patter of happy feet of the heart. Both are messengers and both point in the direction of hidden secrets. In the words of Norman Vincent Peale, "Throw your heart over the fence and the rest will follow."

There will be some who tell you that dwelling in the heart is illogical and foolish. That our lives are better lived in the realm of logic and rationality. That we should lean on *what we know* as the basic pillar of our lives, not what we feel. But I, for one, do not buy that. I think back to the words of Socrates, who said,

> "The Delphi Oracle said that I was the wisest of all the Greeks. It is because I alone, of all the Greeks, know that I know nothing."

We are not really all that wise. Learning to be comfortable with that fact is not only an important discovery, but also the first step in our recovery from "know-it-all-ism." Even Thomas Edison, who was considered a pretty intelligent chap, proclaimed, "We do not know one-millionth of one percent of anything!" So if all of our analytic reasoning tells us that what the heart has to say is faulty or stupid or amiss, let's not give up on the heart, let's give up our reasoning.

Refuse to be tamed by the world

With the desire to appear practical, reasonable and well adjusted, we are tamed by the world. Thomas Moore describes our need to be "normal" as the predominant anxiety disorder in modern life. He poses the question, "Who really is insane? The person who sacrifices deep desire for the sake of propriety and respectability or the one who risks disapproval in the name of vitality?" Is our preoccupation with "being normal" helpful in our desire to be well adjusted or is it a disorder?

It is important that, if we want to appear well adjusted, we ask what it is we are "adjusting to." To a great degree, we come to see and act as society suggests. We tend to assume that our culture's beliefs are valid, its morals appropriate and its values fulfilling. We also accept its worldview—its pictures of the universe and of ourselves. In the literature on cross-cultural awareness, this notion shows up in terms like a "consensus trance" or a "shared hypnosis." It is not unlike being in a trance in that we have been hypnotized since infancy, we all share in it and it goes unquestioned. We are members of the biggest cult of all, namely, *culture.*

Living truer to a culture than to one's own heart poses a problem for wholehearted living because by definition, a culture comes with a particular set of colors that can only be used and mixed in certain ways and under certain conditions. Acting outside the prescribed "normalcy" will definitely raise a few eyebrows. I say, "Wink back."

Trust me: the more wholeheartedly you live your life, the more people will suggest that you calm down. Or as my father would say when I was a child, albeit with affection, "Denise, harness yourself." But telling the human spirit to calm down is like asking water to run upstream. The nature of the spirit is not to withhold but to lavish its exuberance. It's like other forces of nature that will not be contained, like fire or ocean, like wind or rain. It is taught in the Native tradition, "We were once wild here, don't let the world tame you."

So go ahead, wear pink with red, don your white shoes in winter. Start your sentences with "and." Pronounce "data" any which way you want! Howl at the moon, even if the neighbors are having a yard party. Embrace your boss… mess her hair. Take the advice of Mourning Dove who says,

> "Life is a gamble, a chance, a mere guess. Cast a line and reel in a splendid rainbow trout or a slippery eel."

Living wholeheartedly is a bold and adventurous gesture—a sign of our willingness to create, not from our thinking but from our being. Without wholeheartedness, we cannot give our truest gifts to the world. Like the "cante jundo" that comes from Spain, meaning "songs from the deep." Or the dance that takes our breath away as we watch a human body take on a swan-like quality.

Our lives ask that we seek the clay at the core of them and sculpt something beautiful, that we find the words that breathe just beneath our careful thinking and give them voice, be it in a poem, a prayer or a shout of protest. Our lives ask to be lived in a way that brings light to the dark or meaning to the night and fullness to our hearts. As celebrated poet e. e. cummings expressed so succinctly,

> "I would rather learn from one bird how to sing than teach ten thousand stars how to dance."

I want every color,
every life-affirming quality
on the palette
with which I paint my life!

And though the colors
will mix and fade,
Transmuting into the darker tones
of sorrow and doubt, even despair,
I want to live wholeheartedly.

I want a stained-glass life
through which Spirit may pour,
leaving not a pale shadow
but a rainbow of light!

The only gift we have to give this world and to our loved ones is the gift of ourselves. A watered down version really doesn't cut it. We mustn't tame our passions or suppress our beauty. We need to live our joy, to wear it like the favorite cap the twelve-year-old wouldn't be seen without. We need to be willing to be rebels, outlaws in the face of what the world has told us to be. We need to paint our canvases, dance our dances and sing our songs.

We must trust that everything we do with wholeheartedness will receive the Light through a puddle of its color… leaving it's blush like the rosy light that fills a temple of prayer.

Passages

"Don't be an ox pulling the wheel of the plow.
Turn with the stars that wheel above you."

Rumi

"You don't get to choose how
you're going to die. Or when.
You can only decide how
you're going to live. Now."

Joan Baez

Mary Cholmondeley

"Every year I live more convinced that the waste of life lies in the love we have not given, the powers we have not used, the selfish prudence that will risk nothing."

Eleanor Roosevelt

"Life was meant to be lived and curiosity must be kept alive. One must never for whatever reason, turn one's back on life."

"Do not be conformed to the world but be transformed by the renewal of your mind."

Saint Paul

"With life I am on the attack,
restlessly ferreting out each pleasure,
foraging for answers,
wringing from it even the pain.
I ransack life; I hunt it down."

Marita Golden

"Years may wrinkle the skin but to give up enthusiasm wrinkles the soul."

Anonymous

Elizabeth Kübler-Ross

"It is only when we truly know and understand that we have a limited time on earth, and that we have no way of knowing when our time is up, that we will begin to live each day to the fullest as if it is was the only one we had."

Julia Child

"Life itself is the proper binge."

"I will sail my vessel, 'til the river runs dry.
Like a bird upon the wind, these waters are my sky. I'll never reach my destination, if I never try,
So I will sail my vessel, 'til the river runs dry."

Garth Brooks

"Life is a gift… accept it.
Life is a mystery… unfold it.
Life is beauty… praise it.
Life is an adventure… dare it."

Anonymous

Never lose a holy curiosity."

Albert Einstein

Princess Marthe Bibesco

"One should make one's life like a mosaic. Let the general design be good, the colors lively, and the materials diversified."

Cherokee saying

"When you were born, you cried and the world rejoiced. Live your life so that when you die the world cries and you rejoice."

Cheyenne saying

"The human being, a partridge and a spruce tree cannot be tamed."

Brenda Ueland

"The true self is always in motion,
like music, like a river,
changing, moving, failing,
suffering, learning and shining!"

"Our aim should not be to detach, but to be more attached—to be attached to working; to be attached to making something that matters to other people; to be attached to beauty; to be attached to music."

Robert Bly

"Wonder, not doubt, is the root of knowledge."

Abraham Joshua Heschel

"All truth goes through three steps:
first, it's ridiculed;
second, it is violently opposed;
finally, it is accepted as self-evident."

Arthur Schopenhauer

William James

"Genius is the art of non-habitual thought."

"Art is a collaboration between God and artist—the less the artist does the better."

André Gide

Auguste Comte

"Live in the open."

Adam Clayton Powell

"I believe in hearing the inaudible,
touching the intangible,
and seeing the invisible."

"We are here to live out loud."

Balzac

"If I had my life to live over...
I would perhaps have more actual troubles,
but I would sure as heck have less
imaginary ones!"

Nadine Stair

"I would rather be the person who bought the Brooklyn Bridge than the one who sold it."

Will Rogers

"Every great and commanding moment in the annals of the world is the triumph of some enthusiasm."

Ralph Waldo Emerson

Bertrand Russell

"Even when the experts all agree, they may well be mistaken."

"I don't want to get to the
end of my life and find that
I lived just the length of it.
I want to have lived the
width of it as well."

Diane Ackerman

To Ponder and To Practice

- Who are a few of the people you have known who truly live in color and embrace wholeheartedness? In what ways would you like your life to more closely reflect theirs?
- Think of those times when you feel most alive and fully engaged in your life or work. What elements are present at those times which you would like to bring into other areas of your life or work?
- In the poem, "I Want to Live in Color," I identified the qualities that I most want to bring to the fore in my life. What qualities would you identify for yourself as being essential in living a wholehearted life?
- Do your own self-assessment by listing examples of how you already live true to the qualities you identified as being essential to wholehearted living.
- Draft another list of ways in which your life would be different if you were to live *more* in concert with those qualities.
- Make a list of some of the "dandelions" in your personal life and/or professional life.
  - Could any of the items on your dandelions list be pulled from the roots with an action or a decision you could take?
  - Are any of the items you listed part and parcel of the circumstance, which you may need to accept?
  - Could any of them be mistaken as flowers if looked at from a different perspective?
- Which emotions are you really good at expressing in your life? Which emotions are you pretty good at avoiding or managing? What is one emotion to which you would like to become more hospitable in your life?
- When was the last time you "fell into your inkpot"? What is one aspect of your life or work that you could do with a touch more abandon?
- When was the last time you were willing to be a crackpot, a renegade or a believer in impossible things? What is one cause, issue, question or problem that you are willing to stand up for and act upon in your community or workplace?
- We are all artists. We can't help it. In which areas of your life are you an artist—your work, home, clothing, cooking, gardening, writing, delivery of training, customer service, homemaking? In which area of your life would you like to bring more of your artisanship?
- What kinds of stimuli do you gravitate toward that foster your creativity, confidence and self-expression? How can you increase the presence of these stimuli in your life and work?

Practice

- What current shadow of angst, ennui or boredom is cast upon your heart which could be an arrow of "divine discontent," pointing to a secret in some hidden chamber?
- In what areas of your life do you feel tamed by the world? In what small ways could you free yourself of unspoken claims, demands or expectations on your spontaneity? Where would your wildness really like to express itself? What are you waiting for?
- Choose a quote from this chapter's *Passages* that hits you on a deep level and will remind you of your intention to *live in color*. Post it where you will be able to read it frequently.
- Choose a daily habit, routine or symbol that will remind you of your desire to live in color, with wholeheartedness and spirit—with no holding back (e. g., a rainbow in resplendent color across the sky, the sound of unbridled laughter, or opening the garage door as a signal to open the door to your heart to the day's possibilities)!
- Choose a color that represents the quality you most want to foster or cultivate in your life or work and wear that color as a reminder to practice that quality. Use that color as a cue in the world to remind you of an essential quality (e. g., green for vitality, red for purpose, white for wonder, etc.).
- Given everything you have read in this chapter, what do you want to *keep* doing? What do you want to *stop* doing? What do you want to *start* doing?

Notes

Chapter 17

Not One Alike

Valuing Your Part in the Whole

Recognize your brethren

Recognize your brethren

Judge not

Judge not

Beware the danger of empathy

Beware the danger of empathy

Practice compassion

Practice compassion

Make haste to be kind

Make haste to be kind

Acknowledge our interconnectedness

Acknowledge our interconnectedness

Not One Alike

Each of us is born into this world distinctive—
Like flowers or stars, each one like no other.
And yet, at the core of what makes us different,
lies the universal...
as ancient as mankind,
as common as mud.
Not one alike, yet none so very different.

While each of us comes in our own body
bringing an unrepeatable mix of facial features,
skin color, hair texture and muscle tone,
bringing laughter,
contributing new notes to the music of the universe,
we each inhabit a physical body
made of blood and bone, heart and lungs,
all of us bald just underneath our hair.
Each of us tracing new lines along our hands and around our eyes
as we watch our bodies grow, develop and age.
Not one alike, yet none so very different.

While each of us possesses a personal culture,
our own cherished ways of viewing and celebrating life,
to some degree we are all products of our environment,
our heredity and the historical realities of our times.
While each of us clings to our individual versions
of truth, belief and doctrine—
holding to our own perceptions, precepts and prejudice—
we all share both the magnificence and the smallness of mind
from which these choices spring.
Not one alike, yet none so very different.

While we each come with our own songs to sing,
our own lessons to learn and our own paths to tread—
each of us experiencing a unique blend of
appetites, ambitions and anxieties,
loves, losses and loyalties,
dreams, doubts and disappointments,
in all of our lives we will experience
enough sorrow to cry a river
and enough joy to give our hearts wings.
We are each troubled and challenged in multiple ways,
full of beauty and brilliance in others—
lifting someone's burden in one moment,
needing a burden lifted in the next.
Not one alike, yet none so very different.

But because our lives are taking place
in the greater backdrop of triumph and tragedy,
merry-making and melodrama,
we share something even more basic—even more fundamental—
and that is the need for each other.
We're in this together, in the same boat, pilgrims side by side.
Our connectedness is not a luxury;
it is the longing of our hearts to give ourselves away,
and in so doing, to share the incredible journey of living.

While we may forget from time to time to be kind,
to listen, to choose words and deeds carefully,
to give one another the benefit of the doubt—
we share the capacity, at any moment,
to re-open our eyes, our hearts and our minds,
and extend the ultimate gift in human community—compassion.

For just as the flowers in the field belong to one another
and the stars are connected by the forces of the night sky—
our lives are intertwined.
This connectedness, like everything else we share, is universal.
And while it may be as ancient as mankind and as common as mud,
when recognized and realized, it is as stunning as love.

Reflections

We love that we are born into this world as distinctive as an individual flower or star. It is almost as if Creation stood aside saying, "Now for something really special!" There has never been and never will be again the combination of molecules and atoms that each of us has presented to the world. We take pride in our originality and cherish our individuality. Especially when we are on top of the world and things are going our way. When we are winning the prize or taking the bow—how we love our distinctiveness! We love how no one has made the same mark as us, how we add a new color to the human palette.

Ah, but whoever said that "misery loves company" was right as rain! What comfort we take, when in our tough moments, when we stumble and fall, we are reminded that we really aren't so different from anyone else, that everyone fails equally shamefacedly. What comfort we take in knowing our mistakes simply belong to a greater treasure trove of human failings—that somehow our flaws and frailties are just part of the universal story of humankind.

How do we learn to recognize and embrace our connectedness as wholeheartedly in our moments of celebrity and celebration as we do in our angst?

Recognize your brethren

I am happy to share this powerful Hasidic tale I found in the book, *Peacemaking Day by Day.*

> One day an old rabbi asked his pupils how they could tell when the night had ended and the day had begun.
>
> "Could it be," asked one of the students, "when you can see an animal in the distance and tell whether it's a sheep or a dog?"
>
> "No," answered the rabbi.
>
> Another asked, "Is it when you look at a tree in the distance and can tell whether it's a fig tree or a peach tree?"
>
> "No," answered the rabbi.
>
> "Then when is it?" the pupils demanded.
>
> "It is when you can look in the face of any man or woman and see that it is your sister or brother. Because if you cannot see this, it is still night."

While we have all experienced moments of daylight with those with whom we work and share community, I think we would have to agree, at least by the rabbi's definition, we are all working the night shift.

Mark Twain once said, "I am the entire human race compacted together. I have found that there is no ingredient of the race which I do not possess in either a small way or a large way." Wise beyond her years, Anne Frank put it this way, "We all live with the objective of being happy; our lives are different… and yet the same."

How do we begin to recognize and appreciate the interconnection between us? How do we extend the gift of courtesy to one another in the midst of daily pressures? How do we extend respect and support to one another in work environments that promote competition over cooperation? How, as we are swept up in the steady flow of minutia, do we not trip over each other, inconvenienced by our differences, whether they are differences of opinion, cologne or communication styles? How do we keep the presence of mind to notice each other as we pass in the halls, even daring eye contact with the person in the next car as we crawl side by side through rush-hour traffic?

Of all the effects that changes in the 21st century work world have brought to us as workers, perhaps the most profound has been the replacement of our old sense of security with that of insecurity and vulnerability. In many ways, just to be alive is to be vulnerable, but what happens in an environment of massive lay-offs, of mergers and acquisitions, of what business writer Peter Vaill so aptly referred to as "the permanent white water of the business world"? I think the vulnerability that we all feel in today's work world prompts us to put up a protective armor. The spirit of "Kumbaya" slips right out the door as a new spirit enters… the one that warns us to look out for "Number One."

The survival of the fittest mentality does not bring us together, it tears at the seams of the blessed fabric we call human community. We must work to mend that garment, perhaps with the silken threads of our new vulnerability. This vulnerability is a gift, because in the attempt to bear the weight of it, we find ourselves reaching out and taking hands with anyone and everyone who will make a larger circle that will help sustain us in our own uncertainty. What prompts us to join hands may be fear, but once in the circle, we find ourselves drawn by something even stronger: the gravity of hope, connection and mutual support. We are like the antelope in West Africa; it is because one antelope will blow the dust from the other's eye that two antelopes walk together.

You will recognize the antelope spirit in these words spoken by the incredible Buckminster Fuller, following a crisis in which he came extremely close to taking his own life.

> "So I vowed to keep myself alive, but only if I would never use me again for just me—each one of us is born of two, and we really belong to each other. I vowed to do my own thinking, instead of trying to accommodate everyone else's opinion, credos and theories. I vowed to apply my inventory of experiences to the solving of problems that affect everyone aboard planet Earth."

Judge not

We assume that each of us comes into the world with both a unique set of gifts as well as a unique set of limitations. We hope that our gifts will be seen and appreciated and that our limitations will be overlooked. In the meantime, however, we cannot help but take notice of other people's shortcomings. We would be wise at those times to recall Aesop's fable, "The Crab and His Mother."

> An Old Crab said to her son, "Why do you walk sideways like that, my son? You ought to walk straight." The Young Crab replied, "Show me how, dear Mother, and I'll follow your example." The Old Crab tried, but tried in vain, and then saw how foolish she had been to find fault with her child.

Someone once told me that at the heart of what drives us most crazy about other people is a fault of our own. On the flip side, at the heart of what we most admire in other people is one of our own gifts. To the extent that both are true, the world is a kind of looking glass.

Inspired teachers admonish us to remove the beam from our own eye before we attempt to take the splinter from our brother's eye, to become acquainted with our own demons before we try to become angels. Our ability and propensity to "judge not" is probably in direct proportion to our willingness to view the world through the lens of our own brokenness—our own tendencies toward selfishness, greed, arrogance, disregard for other people and our cowardice. Each of us must deal with our particular blend of gifts, problems and woundedness in life. By claiming our own faults and frailties, we are less prone and anxious to point out those of others.

We must each of us cherish the grain of our own wood before we can fully appreciate the grain of one another. This means accepting that we are both good and bad, wise and foolish. It requires courage to face our personal shadows, but this is required if we want to cultivate relationships based on generosity, understanding and compassion—the qualities upon which a healthy community thrives.

William Butler Yeats goes beyond the idea of "judging not" by encouraging us to look at one another through eyes of confidence and belief, the other side of judgment.

> *I have believed the best of every man.*
> *And find that to believe is enough*
> *To make a bad man show himself at his best*
> *Or even a good man*
> *to swing his lantern that much higher.*

I know that I need other people's faith in me to do the work I am meant to do as much as I need air to breathe. It is a worthwhile habit to cultivate the eyes to see potential—even the crumbs of the slightest potential in one another's actions and deeds—if we are to live in a world in which we give our best and hold our lanterns high.

... because our lives are taking place
in the greater backdrop
of triumph and tragedy,
merry-making and melodrama,
we share something
even more basic—
even more fundamental—
And that is the need for each other.

Life seems somehow less painful and lonely—more hopeful and beautiful—when we share our experiences. Although each of us is unique, there are familiar responses and doubts and joys that let us know we are kindred. We all know joy and we all know sorrow, though we laugh and cry in different voices. Our hopes and dreams vary, but what sets us to dream is the same. We differ from one another in what we do and don't do—but not in what we are.

That we need each other is painfully obvious. One of the more beautiful truths of human life is that whatever we are experiencing, we can be sure to meet someone on the road experiencing the flip side. When I am down, you may be the one to cheer me up; when you are sick, I'll bring the chicken soup. While one of us grieves in darkness, the other will hold up the lamp. While all of us experience life "in the backdrop of triumph and tragedy, merrymaking and melodrama," we do take turns.

Beware the dangers of empathy

One of the most popular pieces of advice in working and living in community with other people is to "practice empathy." The idea is to put yourself into another's place, to walk a mile in another's moccasins before passing judgment or making false assumptions. The intent is to foster greater understanding by looking at the world from another person's perspective.

I would venture to say that while this advice comes with the purest of intentions, it is dangerous—for we can no more see the world through another person's eyes than we can breathe their next breath or swallow their food.

I learned this lesson the hard way—by attempting to empathize with a former client who I was supposed to assist in finding employment. He was a Vietnamese refugee in his fifties who spoke very little English. I was employed as a job developer in a program for welfare recipients. When I met this gentleman I was very anxious to assist him in any way I could... until we started the interview.

To make a long story short, he refused to give me eye contact, he never stopped shifting in his chair and he answered every question I asked in grunts and groans. Being of the "empathic type" I attempted to walk a block, if not a mile, in his shoes. I remember thinking to myself, "Denise, what do you expect? He was a wealthy landowner who lost everything. He lost many members of his family in the war and does not know of the whereabouts of many who survived. Naturally he is traumatized. Of course he has lost his sense of self-esteem. He has little confidence—thus the lack of eye contact. I am not going to open any doors with this guy—but I bet I can find an employer who has a place for him where he does not need to interact much with other people."

A couple of weeks later I was invited to a martial arts symposium in which teachers of various martial arts would show their stuff and demonstrate the difference and similarities among their disciplines. Practicing Aikido at the time, I attended the symposium. As I had never been to that particular dojo, I was surprised that the karate instructor looked so familiar to me. It struck me who he was when he recognized me, folded his hands and bowed. There was my insecure client kicking butt among the top martial artists in the county! There was my client, who I deemed as an unfortunate fellow who had lost his self-esteem, strutting his stuff in front of hundreds of people, moving with incredible power and grace! It occurred to me as I watched him move with the fervor of a tiger, that if I had a chance, I would put him in the position of a supervisor!

In my sincere attempts to "empathize," I had totally misjudged this man. The truth came out at our next meeting—he had no interest in receiving assistance from a young American woman—three counts against me according to his cultural mores. What I perceived as a lack of confidence and the results of trauma was this person's polite way of saying, "No, thank you. I really do not need or want your help."

Empathy is a great ideal but a difficult end because we rarely see "the whole picture." We see through our own eyes, whether we like it or not. To bring this lesson home to other employment counselors, I designed a training activity I call the "Empathy Exercise." Towards the end of a two-day workshop I ask everyone to write down something that has been going on for them during the training to which no one else in the room would necessarily be privy. I have them write it down anonymously and hand their papers to me to be read. Here are the kinds of things that people have written:

- Today is the anniversary of my father's death.
- My friends are having a surprise party for me tonight and I don't know how I am going to act surprised.
- I fear my wife is having an affair.
- I am wondering if I turned the iron off this morning.
- I hate my job and want to look for a new one.
- I am having doubts about my wedding engagement.

- I am awaiting the results of a blood test, the result of which could be quite serious.
- My daughter ran away four days ago—I am beside myself with worry and regret.

It is always an astounding and powerful experience to learn what is happening to people in the room of which no one else is aware. The lesson becomes self-evident—we never know what is happening to anyone at any given time. Is your co-worker awaiting the blood test? Is the waitress who messed up your order the one who is sick with worry about her runaway daughter? Your boss who was so rude in this morning's meeting—is it the anniversary of her father's death? We never know. Beware the dangers of empathy.

Practice compassion

While we may forget
from time to time to be kind,
to listen, to choose words
and deeds carefully,
to give one another
the benefit of the doubt—
We share the capacity,
at any moment,
to re-open our eyes,
our hearts and our minds,
and extend the ultimate gift
in human community—
compassion.

Thich Nhat Hanh, the gentle Buddhist poet and teacher from Vietnam, says of compassion,

> "It is through our compassion that we care for the dignity, well-being and integrity of every person around us. Our capacity to embody this quality, simple as it may seem, is the strength that can change the world around us."

What if we made a habit of looking at the people around us each day and choosing someone who we think could use a little compassion and finding some small way of offering that gift? If such a habit were woven into the fabric of our families and our workplaces, I believe it would change the world, or at least our experience of it.

We all live in the constant fear of being judged by others, while the empty space between us is waiting to be filled by a simple gesture of honest caring. Rudeness, the absence of this caring, is a symptom of living our lives as if our time was money. We need to start a campaign to eliminate rudeness from the workplace and replace it with the sacrament of small considerations. Our hearts and lives are fed by kind words, small decencies and gracious behavior. We are fed by words like "excuse me", "I'm sorry", "please, go ahead", and other simple courtesies.

Our spirits are also richly fed on compliments and praise, even for seemingly insignificant acts like holding the door for someone, asking to refill someone's coffee when you are going for your second cup or noticing the updated photo of someone's grandchild on their desk. It is the gravity of these small kindnesses that pulls us into communion with one another.

I have dreamed of a world in which every person is perfectly loved from birth right into adulthood—and in this world, everyone is spontaneously and effortlessly open-hearted and loving. But in the world outside my daydreams, we have all been wounded or hurt by being loved too little, too much, too late or in unhealthy ways. As a result, as we attempt heartfelt communion with others, we limp along the path. Living with an openness to love requires resolve, courage and will. We each know this to be true in our own lives. How can we extend anything less than kindness to those we meet along the way?

Here is one of my favorite stories of human kindness which I first heard at a conference many years ago. I have liberally adapted it, hopefully with the originator's approval.

Once upon a time God was asked for the millionth time from one of his most curious children, "What is the difference between heaven and hell?" God decided that this inquisitive child deserved a personal tutorial on the matter so arranged for back-to-back field trips into hell and heaven so that child could experience for herself the difference between them.

The child was shocked to find that hell was nothing more than a long banquet table of beautifully prepared foods. Everyone was called to the table and told to enjoy themselves. The only problem was that the utensils with which they were to eat were twice the length of a person's arm. So as they would try to put the food in their mouths they would find that they couldn't possibly do so because the utensils were too long. The feast looked good, it smelled good, but they couldn't access it—this was hell!

The child was then escorted through the pearly gates. How surprised she was to find that paradise had the same banquet table with the same beautifully prepared foods! Everyone was called around that table and told to enjoy themselves. The biggest shock was that in paradise people had been given the identical, ridiculously long utensils. The child was about to burst out in protest when she looked up and noticed something different—people in paradise fed each other!

The simple shift in focus from getting to giving could completely change our experience of the world!

Make haste to be kind

The great writer Henry James advised, "Three things in human life are important: the first is to be kind; the second is to be kind; the third is to be kind." A more current writer, Wayne Dyer, shared similar advice when he said, "If you must choose between being right or being kind, always choose kind." When discussing in my workshops the idea of making kindness a practice at work and in our larger lives, many wonder why we should consider responding with kindness to situations of ignorance, cruelty or injustice. Offhand, I can think of think of three very good reasons.

First, kindness might be your best option! We could fight fire with fire, but that only escalates the situation. For example, insulting someone who has been insulting or yelling back at someone who yells. But why play a game that we find distasteful in the first place? Instead, we can demonstrate the power of kindness. Water works better than fire when trying to put a fire out. As Gandhi once said, "Taking an eye for an eye is a great way to blind the world."

Secondly, sometimes kindness is exactly what other people need most when they have behaved in an inappropriate or offensive manner. Have you ever said or done something hurtful to someone not because they deserved it but because they just happened to be in the path of your arrows? Often we are not the target of people's anger, but we happen to be within range. What if we were to give people the benefit of the doubt that we were not the intended target? Who knows—their cat could have just died, their child might be in trouble at school, their mate might have just left town without so much as a note. As Plato put it, "Be kind, for everyone you meet is fighting a hard battle."

The third reason why we might take the advice of Henry James is that kindness works! Even when it's not what the person needs or deserves, kindness is a great option. By responding to conflict with an even-handedness we are practicing a strength and eliciting a power that is almost impossible to overcome. In the martial arts they talk about "keeping your center"—not letting people knock you off guard. Well, it is impossible to be "off center" and to be kind... one begets the other. Besides, as Martin Luther King, Jr. professed, "Forgive your enemies. It will drive them crazy."

Best-selling author and modern day philosopher Og Mandino makes an outrageous and compelling suggestion. He says:

> "Beginning today, treat everyone you meet as if they were going to be dead by midnight. Extend to them all the care, kindness and understanding you can muster, and do so with no thought of any reward. Your life will never be the same again."

Many people think of kindness as a quality that we are born with in varying amounts, like intelligence or athleticism. I do not see it that way. I believe that kindness, like compassion or patience, is something that we practice. The more we practice it, the more of a habit it becomes and the greater our ability to extend these gifts to ourselves and to each other. In the words of Henri Amiel, "Life is short. Be swift to love! Make haste to be kind!"

Acknowledge our interconnectedness

> Once upon a time a hunter sent his dog after something that moved behind the trees. It chased out a fox and corralled it into a position where the hunter could shoot it.
>
> The dying fox said to the hound, "Were you never told that the fox is brother to the dog?"
>
> "I was indeed," said the dog. "But that's for idealists and fools. For the practical minded, brotherhood is created by identity of interests."

When coming by this story I couldn't help but wonder if Democrats and Republicans have had a similar conversation. Or Jews and Muslims, Christians and Buddhists. I even recall a similar dialogue taking place between the marketing and production departments of the same company. A funny breed, we human beings, preferring the dim light of our individual interests to the brighter light of our shared values and commonality.

I love how these simple words from Jane Howard express an important truth:

> *Call it a clan, call it a network,*
> *Call it a tribe, call it a family.*
> *Whatever you call it, whoever you are,*
> *You need one.*

Did you know that it is a biological fact that if you place two living heart cells from different people in a petri dish, they will in time find and maintain a third and common beat? This fact, writes author and poet Mark Nepo, holds the secret of all relationships. He says,

> "It is cellular proof that beneath any resistance we might pose and beyond all our attempts that fall short, there is in the very nature of life itself some essential joining force. For if two cells can find the common pulse beneath everything, how much more can full human hearts feel when all our excuses and fears fall away. This drive toward a common beat is the force beneath curiosity and passion. It is what makes strangers talk to strangers, despite the discomfort."

How cool is that? If only this drive toward a common beat could be the force we need as a planet to take care of one another, despite political and economic boundaries. On a large scale, I wax philosophic and idealistic, but in the corners of the world that each of us occupy is a great place to start! Could we take to heart this advice from the great Albert Einstein?

> "We are part of the whole which we call the universe, but it is an optical delusion of the mind that we think we are separate. This separateness is like a prison for us. Our job is to widen the circle of our compassion so we feel connected with all people and situations."

Systems theory supports Einstein's philosophy. It has emerged as the dominant trend in most disciplines, from psychology to computer science, replacing the old myth of piecemeal analysis, in which everything is broken down into its component parts. The tendency in recent thought is to stress synthesis, networks, interaction and process. The old notion that the whole is greater than the sum of the parts has been replaced by the idea that the parts can only be understood in relation to the dynamics of the whole. The 19th century vision of lonely billiard-ball atoms accidentally colliding with each other to form the varieties of life has been replaced by a vision of a universe made up of an intricate web of relationships, a net of jewels.

We are being told by physicists the world over that no matter how deeply we look into the fabric of material being—the biological level, the chemical level, the subatomic level—we see that life forms are interdependent, co-conditioning and co-evolving. Every human effort, civilization, thought and spiritual insight requires and is supported by the whole of organic life. As Margaret Wheatley explains in her book, *The New Leadership Science:*

> "We live in a universe where relationships are primary. Nothing exists independent of its relationships. We are constantly creating the world—evoking it from many potentials—as we participate in all its many interactions."

Reverend Martin Luther King, Jr. said the same thing in a different way decades before in *The Trumpet of Conscience:*

> " It really boils down to this: all life is interrelated. We are all caught in an inescapable network of mutuality, tied into a single garment of destiny. Whatever affects one directly affects all indirectly."

May we come to accept a little more, day by day, our particular place in the fabric of the world and our holy connection to each other. May our integration be less about standing shoulder to shoulder, and more about living heart to heart.

Passages

"We may have all come on different ships, but we are all in the same boat now."

Martin Luther King, Jr.

"What do we live for if not to make life less difficult for each other?"

George Eliot

Sam Keen

"What all persons have in common is their uniqueness."

"If we could read the secret history of our enemies, we would find in each man's life a sorrow and a suffering enough to disarm all hostility."

Henry Wadsworth Longfellow

"Just as the wave cannot exist for itself, but is ever a part of the surface of the ocean, so must I never live my life for itself, but always in the experience which is going on all around me."

Albert Schweitzer

"How far you go in life depends on being tender with the young, compassionate with the aged, sympathetic with the striving and tolerant of the weak and strong. Because someday in your life you will have been all of these."

George Washington Carver

"Let he that is without sin cast the first stone."

Jesus

"We all have the same color bones."

Langston Hughes

"There are only two or three human stories and they go on repeating themselves as fiercely as if they had never happened."

Willa Cather

Mahatma Gandhi

"I am part and parcel of the whole and I cannot find God apart from the rest of humanity."

"Our humanity would be a poor thing, were it not for the diversity stirring within us."

Francis Bacon

Ram Dass

"Compassion simply stated is leaving other people alone. Not laying trips. You exist as a statement of your own level of evolution. You are available to support other people but you do not lay trips on another person."

"Whatever you may be sure of, be sure of this—that you are dreadfully like other people."

James Russell Lowell

"Kindness is the language which the deaf can hear and the blind can see."

Mark Twain

"Human beings are actually created for the transcendent, for the sublime, for the beautiful, for the truthful… and all of us are given the task of making this world a little more hospitable to these beautiful things and to each other."

Desmond Tutu

John Donne

"No man is an island, entire of itself. Every man is a piece of the continent."

Harry Overstreet

"A person remains immature, whatever his age, as long as he thinks of himself as an exception to the human race."

Krishnamurti

"In oneself lies the whole world."

"At bottom every man knows well enough that he is a unique being, only one on this earth; and by no extraordinary chance will such a marvelously picturesque piece of diversity in unity as he is, ever be put together a second time."

Friederich Nietzsche

"The question of bread for myself is a material question, but the question of bread for my neighbor is a spiritual question."

Nikolai Berdyaev

Joanna Macy

"Our lives extend beyond our skins, in radical interdependence with the rest of the world."

"Listen. In every office
You hear the threads
Of love and joy and fear and guilt,
The cries for celebration and reassurance,
and somehow you know
that connecting those threads
is what you are supposed to do
and business takes care of itself."

James Autry

Chinese proverb

"When you see a good man, think of emulating him; when you see a bad man, examine your heart."

Martin Luther King, Jr.

"We have flown the air like birds and swam the sea like fishes, but have yet to learn the simple act of walking the earth like brothers."

"There is no need for temples; no need for complicated philosophy. Our own brain, our own heart is our temple; my philosophy is kindness."

The Dalai Lama

"If you knew all, you would pardon all."

Leo Tolstoy

To Ponder and To Practice

- Think about some of your defining traits that distinguish you from others. Consider, in turn, some of your defining traits that you have in common with others.
- In what area of your life do you need to extend more compassion to yourself?
- How can you extend more compassion to the people around you?
- Reflect on how dangerous the concept of "empathy" can be—given how little we really know about each other. Try approaching people, instead, with the humble knowledge that you are not working with all the facts. Be willing to give them the benefit of the doubt and trust that "if you knew all, you would pardon all." Wash the conclusions from your eyes before you relate to people today, and view them with the eye of your heart.
- Ask someone a question that you know they would love to answer and listen with the intention to understand.
- In Hindu and Buddhist cultures it is the custom, when meeting another, to fold the hands together in the gesture of a prayer and bow to the divinity within that person. The same basic attitude is contained in Jesus' maxim: "In as much as you have done it unto one of the least of these, my brethren, you have done it unto me." Approach the strangers you meet as if everyone were a sacred being. Begin by offering a half-smile to the corner grocer or the crossing guard at your child's school.
- When was your last experience of feeling deep affiliation and true belonging in a group or team? In what context can you re-create an experience which could feed your soul in a similar way?
- Who is one of the kindest people you know? How would you like your life to more closely reflect that person's life?
- Consider who has been supportive of you lately and thank them.
- Buckminster Fuller once said that everyone is ignorant, only on different subjects and that everyone is a genius, only in different contexts. Resolve to practice diversity from the bottom up by noticing and celebrating the genius of each person around you. Pass on genuine praise to individuals in the company of others who may be overlooking the person's gifts.

Practice

- It is said that it far easier to love humanity as a whole than to love one's neighbor. Think about someone you have had some distaste for and meet that person fresh, seeing them this time with the eyes of your heart.
- Start a "Respect Campaign" or a "Compassion Crusade" around your home, neighborhood or workplace. Make a concerted effort to treat everyone with extraordinary respect.
- Select a quote on the topic of kindness, diversity or interdependence from this chapter's *Passages* and post it somewhere you will see it until it is internalized.
- Choose a daily habit, routine or symbol to help you remain conscious of your interdependence with those around you (e. g., while watering or tending the flowers in your garden, notice how much more beautiful your garden is as a result of its diversity).
- Given everything you have read in this chapter, what do you want to *keep* doing? What do you want to *stop* doing? What do you want to *start* doing?

Notes

Rhythm

Chapter 18

Cultivating Balance in Life and Work

Make balance a priority

Make balance a priority

Live in clusters and learn to juggle

Live in clusters and learn to juggle

Be the grasshopper *and* the ant

Be the grasshopper and the ant

Unpack the Swiss cheese

Unpack the Swiss cheese

Don't mistake busyness for engagement

Don't mistake busyness for engagement

Practice "voluntary simplicity"

Practice "voluntary simplicity"

Honor the need for solitude

Honor the need for solitude

Learn to say "no"

Learn to say "no"

Rhythm

My spirit bobs between two shores of my being.
I want to rise like the sun, each day, on a steady horizon.
I want to employ every tool of my being
to participate in the ongoing creation of the world.
I want to stand up and be counted among those who dare to dream
and believe in those dreams enough to act on them.
I want to dance to the drumbeat of passion
and swoon to the high notes of joining my purposes
with the demands of the world.

And… I want rest.
I want to put all my tools away and
put a closed sign on the door.
I want to remove my dancing slippers and
cradle myself in a warm cocoon…
high up in a tree where no one can reach.
I long to sleep the deep, dreamless sleep
of a thousands days.

I want both.

I am split between two branches of my nature.
I want all sorrow and glee to bubble up from the fountain of my heart,
to move like a river through my throat
and out my mouth in joyful and desperate sounds—
in tears and laughter unbridled.
I want to scream and chant and howl,
to sing carols and ballads and lullabies, too.

And yet, I crave solitude.
I long for silence as deafening as the winter snow.
I want to wrap a thick blanket around all my senses and emotions,
to still them so that I may dip down into the well of my being
where serenity resides.
Where there are no words, no sounds,
outside the holy hum of my own existence.

I want both.

I possess a dual citizenship within my own life.
For there is a gypsy in my bones!
She loves the wind in her hair as she faces an open road.
She harbors the hunger of a hunter, the spirit of an explorer,
and the heart of a pilgrim.
She thrills to the sound of a train or
the haunting call of a fog horn at sea.
She keeps a quest flickering inside her like a torch that lights her way.

And yet, I am also the mother bear who is happiest in her cave,
a nester of the highest order.
The comforts of home—be they flowers on the mantel,
a lit candle by the bed, friends around the table—
these are the medium of my deepest joy.
No worldly wonder could possibly move me as profoundly
as the blossoms at my own front gate.

I want both.

And as I consider these differing yearnings within my heart,
I realize that they are not enemies or opposing forces.
In fact they are twins, loyal to the same mother.
Life does not ask me to choose between them,
but beseeches me to accept them both…
for it is in their mutual embrace that I will find my rhythm,
the rhythm found in all nature.

Sleep will replenish my work.
Silence would only enhance my song.
And with the small stones gathered from the travels of the gypsy
I will fashion a trail leading back to my own front door.

My life is not two-sided, it is simply devoted to its own rhythm.

Reflections

We love fast things like deer and lightning and rushing rivers. We love slow things too, like the dying ember of a fire or the greening of a forest. Loud things are great, like fireworks and thunder and the choir's song. Quiet things are lovely too, like falling snow, the first light of morning, or dandelion puffs on the wind. Big things are fine, like elephants and planets and epiphanies. Small things are fine too, like ladybugs and seashells and moments. Flying things are wonderful, like dragonflies and kites and ideas, but the world needs grounded things too, like trees and mountains and convictions.

Much of the wonder in this world is in its diversity and the spaces between opposites. We would not want to choose between hot and cold, up and down, or in and out. We embrace soft and hard, narrow and wide, more and less because one cannot exist without the other. There is no division in nature, it exists in splendid balance, until that is, we observe how we humans live.

Deborahann Smith, author of *Work With What You Have,* describes the rhythm she perceived in the animal world by watching them in their natural habitat. She writes,

> "As I watched deer, ground squirrels, soaring eagles and a mountain lion, I realized that the difference between human beings and animals is that animals don't hunker down, put their noses to the grindstone for eight hours, and then go home and attend to their personal lives. Instead, their days are integrated with everything their existence is about. Their office is an entire mountainside, a meadow, a creek, acres of sky, and the entire territory where they live and breathe. Their hours are interspersed with hunting, building nests, socializing, grooming, mating, playing and resting. Their existence is a rhythm of survival and spirit, rest and work—the work of living their lives."

As natural creatures, we seek that birthright, to live in natural rhythm with the world. But stop to observe us in the human realm and you will see that we live out of balance. We have created an abyss between ideas and feelings, logic and art, science and religion, work and play, heart and mind, the practical and the inspirational. We do not live in rhythm with our nature; we have sped up and ordered our lives around the frenzied beat of the 21st century workplace.

I can just hear it now, "Yeah, but what about heavy workloads, tight deadlines, difficult coworkers, and even more difficult bosses? How about impending layoffs, budget cuts, and re-org plans all wrapped up with a tangled bow of office politics and personal agendas? Where, for heaven's sake, are we supposed to find balance amidst all of this REALITY?"

Let's face it, it's not easy to preserve our sanity much less serenity when reality refuses to cooperate. We are told by time management specialists to take one problem at a time; that would be great, if it were in the nature of our problems to get in line.

But the truth remains that unless we operate from a healthy sense of balance and rhythm, we will not have the inner resources to respond to a hectic work environment, much less juggle the needs of home and family, friends and community, as well as our own physical, creative and spiritual needs. The qualities needed to live busy, bustling lives and still maintain a sense of sanity include patience, calm, fortitude, poise, and an inner sense of serenity. These qualities come only on the wings of rhythm and balance.

Anne Morrow Lindbergh, in her classic and beautiful book, *Gift from the Sea,* writes:

> "The problem is not entirely in finding a room of one's own, or time alone, difficult and necessary as that is. The problem is how to still the soul in the *midst* of its activities. Without a sense of balance in one's life, that is impossible." (my emphasis)

Here are some suggestions and insights for restoring a sense of balance in our busy lives and living in tune with our natural rhythm so that even in the midst of activity we may "still the soul" and maintain not just a sense of sanity, but a sense of serenity as well.

Make balance a priority

In writing this chapter, I thought a lot about the issue of balance and its place in my life. The truth is that being "out of balance" is what feels normal to me. Too much work, not enough play. Living too much from the heart, not enough from the rational, planning side of my brain. Not able to match my feelings for people with the investment of real time and attention. I live out of whack. But it's like bowling. It's not uncommon for us to throw the ball with a bent that leans to one side of the alley. My natural throw of the ball goes to the left—so I stand to the left of the alley in order to bring my swing more to the right. We have to know where and how we are out of balance before we can compensate and bring ourselves back into equilibrium. But once we have found that balance, we can find the power to maintain it.

Striking a healthy balance between our personal lives and our work lives is a hot topic in our culture today, but are we prepared to take the steps and make the choices which would make that possible? We are swallowed up only when we are willing for it to happen. If we were convinced that a day off or an hour of solitude was a reasonable ambition, we would find a way of attaining it. As it is, we feel so unjustified in this demand that we rarely make the attempt. The fact that we need more balance seems insufficient reason for us to attain it. What would it take for us to make the kind of choices that put our sanity, serenity, and need for balance before the demands of the world?

One of my dearest friends developed breast cancer a few years back. I watched her struggle through the day-by-day fight for her life, complete with chemotherapy, radiation, a mastectomy, and a dining room table turned into a veritable buffet of homeopathic supplements and vitamins. She suffered every pain and indignity that cancer can bring: fatigue, nausea, depression, the loss of her hair, not to mention desperation at the thought of losing her life.

And then I saw something glorious happen to Christina. In the midst of the fight for her life, I watched her take her life in her very hands. I witnessed the change of choices that she made day to day—more time in the garden, less time in the kitchen—more time reading to her girls, less time watching television—more time with friends, less time at work. I saw her view time and money differently—she could learn to do with less of the things that money could buy, but as time could not be bought, she valued her moments more.

Believe it or not, I came to envy my friend. I certainly did not envy her illness or the torturous means by which she had to fight it. But I envied the new lease that she had on life and the tremendous freedom (and even urgency) she felt in making choices that put her well being and her happiness first. Without guilt or shame or feeling self-absorbed, my friend was making choices for herself—unabashedly, absolutely and wholeheartedly! Amazing the gifts that a life-threatening illness can bring.

Then it occurred to me—we've already been given the same diagnosis; we are all going to die, and none of us know when. Thankfully, Christina survived her cancer and, God willing, she may live another half-century. But I pray that with the growth of her long pretty hair, she never regains the perverse but all too prevalent attitude that would have her put the demands of the world before her own joy and well-being. I hope that one of the lasting treasures that comes from having experienced the trial and tribulation of cancer, is her life-long devotion to the gift of balance in her life. And the reminder to her friends to find balance in their own lives.

Live in clusters and learn to juggle

I am not suggesting that we devote equal time to our personal lives and work lives. While that would be nice, I think that the goal of achieving personal and professional balance is not necessarily to have the scale sitting still with both sides equally full. Surely the demands of the world may outweigh our needs and wants for personal care and solitude, at least at times. Our lives need to work as a scale that can tip one way or the other as the situation demands, so we don't become stuck with one side of our life consistently dominating the other. There is a time to act and a time to remain still. There is a time to push and a time to wait. There is a time to engage and a time to retreat. If we could feel the truth of this fundamental law of expansion and contraction in all things, we would cultivate a greater sense of peace in our lives.

Life comes in clusters: clusters of solitude, then a cluster when there is hardly time to breathe. But the solitude is what prepares us for the busyness. Our challenge isn't to simply cut out whatever it is that throws things out of whack. That isn't really dealing with the issue. Our challenge is to reestablish a dynamic equilibrium that is energizing, allowing us to jump into work when that is necessary and to be fully involved in our personal lives at other times. What we need is rhythm.

We establish this rhythm through our choices, creating a dynamic interplay between the various aspects of our lives. We need to give full attention to work if it demands that—temporarily. In addition to professional success, we need to relax, to take care of ourselves, and tend to our relationships. We need to have the fortitude to make new choices that will get us back into balance when we find ourselves tipping off one end of the scale. We need a dynamic synergy between the personal and professional aspects of life, such that each aspect seems enriched by the other.

Joan Borysenko, in *Inner Peace for Busy People,* distinguishes between balancing and juggling. She reminds us that there will always be balls in the air—maintaining a sense of balance and peace within ourselves while we juggle is more the issue. With this idea she suggests that we give up the idea of being tightrope walkers with our lives—and learn to juggle instead.

To take the juggling metaphor further, it is worth considering what balls we have in the air—family, friends, work, home, school, community, health and faith may be among them. As we consider each of these balls, it is also worth noting that they are not all made of the same stuff—some are more fragile and delicate than others, some require more attention than others. Some, if dropped, may not bounce back. Surely we have seen people who have ignored a relationship long enough, then when it finally dropped out of the air, it did not bounce back. Friendships do not always bounce back, nor does health. The key question is "Which ball am I attending to most—which of them receives most of my attention?" Typically, the answer is "Work." Ironically, of all the balls in the air, work is the one that if dropped will bounce back in one form or another. The point being—we need to juggle priorities with care.

Be the grasshopper *and* the ant

In Chinese philosophy the idea of interrelationship and mutual synergy is known as Tao, or "the way." The way to have a satisfying life is to live in such a manner that the various parts of one's life flow naturally from each other, and are not compartmentalized or at odds with each other as they vie for our attention. This is represented by the symbol of two complementary opposites interrelated in such a way that both together are necessary to form a whole. You are probably familiar with the symbol of the union of the Yin and Yang. The black (Yin) represents the mystery, the realm of receptivity and depth, the symbolic realm of the female. The white (Yang) represents the realm of bright light where things are known and clear, the realm of activity and achievement, the symbolic realm of the male. Together they form a circle, the symbol of fullness and infinity. They are not two alien entities—within each one is a perfect circle of the opposite.

What a powerful symbol for the balance of our professional and personal lives. This is definitely not the balance of static, separate, clearly defined, unrelated aspects of life; this is a dynamic and fluid balance where the two are inextricably related, and therein lies their power. In fact, each side of the circle enhances the other—like play enhances work, like silence enhances song.

And as I consider these differing
yearnings within my heart,
I realize that they are not
enemies or opposing forces.
In fact they are twins,
loyal to the same mother.
Life does not ask me
to choose between them,
but beseeches me
to accept them both...
for it is in their mutual embrace
that I will find my rhythm,
the rhythm found in all nature.

Reading Aesop's fable of the grasshopper and the ants raises the question, "Need we be all ant or all grasshopper?"

> One fine winter's day some Ants were busy drying their store of corn, which had gotten rather damp during a long spell of rain. Presently, up came a Grasshopper and begged them to spare her a few grains. "For," she said, "I'm simply starving."
>
> The Ants stopped work for a moment, though this was against their principles. "May we ask," said they, "what you were doing with yourself all last summer? Why didn't you collect a store of food for the winter?"
>
> "The fact is," replied the Grasshopper, "I was so busy singing that I hadn't the time."
>
> "If you spent the summer singing," replied the Ants, "you can't do better than spend the winter dancing." And they chuckled and went on with their work.

I admire the ant, carrying twice it's weight up and down the slants of the broken sidewalk, deliberate in its actions and deeds, dedicated to the colony. But the grasshopper has such a good life, being lean and green like grass, yet double-jointed and springy. Singing through the summer and hanging out at other people's picnics. What a life!

Personally, I want both. As it is said in the Indian proverb, "God likes us when we work, but he loves us when we sing!" If that is true, can you imagine the delight in the heavens when we are found singing while we work? When was the last time you worked with the cadence of a song? When did you find yourself singing to the rhythm of your work?

I want to dance
to the drumbeat of passion
and swoon to the high notes
of joining my purposes
with the demands of the world.

I want to remove
my dancing slippers
and cradle myself
in a warm cocoon...
high up in a tree
where no one can reach.
I long to sleep.
The deep, dreamless sleep
of a thousands days.

I want both.

Unpack the Swiss cheese

Someone once asked composer Anton Bruckner—"Master, how, when and where did you think of the divine motif of your Ninth Symphony?"

"Well, it was like this," Bruckner replied. "I walked up the Kahlengerg and when it got hot and I got hungry, I sat down by a little brook and unpacked my Swiss cheese. Just as I opened the greasy paper, that darn tune popped into my head."

We've heard it many times, by many great artists—their best ideas come while taking a shower. Inspiration for the most glorious of paintings and symphonies, the most brilliant of marketing ideas, are known to come to those who are engaged in anything but work.

When I am in the midst of developing a new product or program, there are two things that I can do to open the floodgates on my creativity; some kind of physical exercise (preferably a walk along the ocean) or engagement in some creative activity, be it an art project, gardening or cooking. It is amazing what the scent of ocean in my hair, the repetitive act of digging and weeding, or the colorful array of felt, ribbons and beads spread out before me will do for my thinking! A friend of mine finds a special kind of peace and renewal riding on the back of his lawn mower as he peruses the open green spaces of his Alberta property. Another friend finds the cast and reel motion of fishing the perfect mantra for entering the muse.

My eldest brother, Andy, is amazing in many ways, but there is one characteristic I see in him that I have not seen equaled by any other person, and that is his penchant for being the Jack-of-all-trades. He lives a rich and busy life investing his time, talents and interests in myriad and diverse ways.

On any given weekend day, you might find Andy tending the tomatoes in his garden, conjuring up his newest muffin recipe or working a piece of wood into an exquisite elfin creature who will join the merry band of his Santa Claus collection. Then again, he could be engaged in painting a watercolor, writing goofy lyrics for a song or spinning a colorful poem for someone's birthday. If he's with one of his three sons, you'd best look for him in a canoe, on a hiking trail, in a fishing boat, or amidst a cheering crowd for the Wisconsin Badgers. Unless it's on a Sunday, when he is singing in the church choir or on a men's spiritual retreat.

On any given weeknight, you might find Andy on a walk with his wife, at the gym, or on a tennis court. That's if he's not already committed to a board or committee meeting of some community group, except this year, of course, when he's busy starting up the local chapter of Habitat for Humanity. I wouldn't be surprised, however, if you spotted him at a play, a local art fair or attending a class 30 miles away on the Structures of Medieval France. What about weekdays, you ask? Oh, just look for the guy in the long black robe with a gavel in his hand in the Circuit Court of Dodge County, Wisconsin. I think they call him "Your Honor." (Did I mention he's also a great brother and a proud new grandfather?)

As one of my sisters said of Andy, "He is a butcher, a baker and a candle-stick maker, all rolled into one." The only person I know who has just about as many irons in the fire at one time is his wife, Debbie, who is an inspiration to me in many ways. Debbie models the tenets of "true livelihood" outside the economics of the workforce, finding numerous ways to give of her time and talents to her family, her community and her church. I have watched her grow in wisdom, fortitude and in the proficiency of her gifts throughout the years. I doubt very much that without the necessity of earning a living, I would have had the same kind of discipline and devotion to develop my true livelihood in equal measure. How perfect that these two are mated to one another, being such birds of a feather.

I give you the example of my brother and his wife because from watching and listening to them over the years, I am convinced that their engagement in so many activities does not diminish their involvement in each one, but enhances it. I can only imagine how my brother's thoughts regarding a difficult court case might uncurl and unfold with each chip of wood as he carves and chisels. How, as he sows seeds for the next summer's vegetable patch, he is sowing seeds in his mind for the way Habitat will secure its next piece of property for a hopeful family. Surely his signature coffeecake is made that much more delicious as he works the dough to the songs of next Sunday's choir recital. To be sure, my brother complains like the rest of us that he is exhausted and over-committed. The beauty about my brother's life, however, is that he has many gifts, loves and hobbies to which he can bring his exhaustion and renew his spirit.

So here is further justification for balancing leisure with work, our lives in the world with our lives at home—each will be enhanced by the other. If going on a leisurely picnic produced Bruckner's Ninth Symphony, imagine how our work might be enhanced by deliberately adding a tad more pleasantness to our lives. We might consider fishing, sewing, taking a walk under the moon, and maybe even unpacking the Swiss cheese and uncorking a bottle of something nice. In the words of the Chinese poet, Li Po:

Since water still flows,
though we cut it with swords,
And sorrow returns,
though we drown it with wine,
Since the world can in no way
answer to our craving,
I will loosen my hair tomorrow
and take to a fishing boat.

Don't mistake busyness for engagement

As much as I adore all of the growing things in my yard and the many lessons the earth has to teach through my garden, I hate the whole pruning thing. I hate having to cut back the beautiful rose bush or the apple tree. But much of our ability to live a spirited and soulful life has to do with a similar kind of cutting away and letting remain what must remain. Knowing what to cut—that is wisdom. Being clear and strong enough to make the cut when it is time for things to go—that is courage. Together, the practices of wisdom and courage enable us, day by day and task by task, to gradually simplify our lives. In order to cultivate a richer *inner* life, we might begin by pruning our *outer* lives.

Living a complex and intricate existence keeps us busy, but busyness doesn't mean we are fully engaged in what we are doing. Usually, it's just the opposite. Complicated lives often show the extent to which the person is lost in the busyness of the world. To the extent that we are busy, we often feel neurotically active in trying to get things done which do not matter much in the long run. We might run a successful business that requires sixty hours of work a week while the simple pleasures of home are neglected. So success in one part of life usurps peace in another. With all of the complexities and complications of our lives, by simplifying them we will find a sharp articulation of our true values and interests.

The metaphor of the bee is a good one for human engagement. The bee is stuck in the kitchen, busily buzzing from corner to corner of every window, while just a few feet away there is an open door from which to escape the house and gain the sky. It is so busy trying to get through the window, it remains unaware of the open door. The bee is busy, yes, but not very bright. Wouldn't it be interesting if we could truly see how much of our daily activity is as fruitless as the bee at the window? What would be more enlightening, of course, is if we could see how many opened doors there are just within reach, if only we had the eyes to see them.

There are three important practices that can help us retire the role of the busy, if not too bright, buzzing bee clamoring for freedom at the window panes of our complex lives: simplicity, solitude, and naming our boundaries.

We must remember that we are designed for balance. We've been given two hands and two arms, and two eyes and two halves of our brains to work together. We walk, one foot in front of the other; we hear both sides of a story. Every aspect of life is in a dance with its opposite. Talking is great, and so is listening. Teaching is great, and so is learning. Pride is beautiful, and so is humility. Certainty feels good, and so does surprise. Saying "yes" feels good, but saying "no" has its place, too. Life is a dance of giving and receiving, action and reflection, movement and stillness.

Practice "voluntary simplicity"

Contemporary American author and minister, Robert Fulghum, says in his book, *Words I Wish I Wrote:*

> "As with language, so with life: Less is often more. The quality of life is marked by what you can do without and still do well. The best things in life aren't. Simplify. Thoreau subscribed to this line of thinking. So did Buddha, Lao-Tzu, and Jesus. Possession is nine tenths of our flaw."

"Possession is nine-tenths of our flaw." I love that. What is it with us humans and our need to collect, hoard and hang on to things as if they were the true source of our joy? Sure, I treasure every photo I have ever taken of my daughter, but I have also saved all of her favorite clothing, stuffed animals, toys, books and artwork from each age. My storage unit looks like a kindergarten classroom. She's now a teenager. You don't think I am having a hard time letting go of my little girl, do you?

We won't even discuss how many boxes of "stuff" I have in storage for each holiday. In thinking more about scaling down and practicing what Duane Elgin calls "voluntary simplicity" (introduced in his book by the same title), I was thinking that just for fun, I should go through a whole year without taking out any of my holiday or seasonal boxes. I am so curious—would the seasons still change? Would autumn arrive without dried corn, oak leaves and pumpkins in every nook and cranny of my house? Would Christmas have the gall to come without my halls thoroughly decked? How could spring even consider lifting her sleepy head if I haven't changed my tablecloths, and draped the tiny lights around my windows with birds on their flowered nests?

The idea of voluntary simplicity is living "outwardly simple and inwardly rich." It means living life more fully, placing less value on money and objects and putting more focus on a higher quality of life. Doesn't just the sound of it feel good? Meister Eckhart suggests that "God is not attained by a process of addition of anything to the soul, but by a process of subtraction." Like peeling an artichoke to get to its heart, we need to peel back the layers of our possessions, our attachments, and our obsessions in order to get back to the heart of us. It's not just things that we acquire, but we also add layer upon layer of habits, obligations and expectations that are not necessary. My daughter recently pointed out that I may not be so exhausted after hosting a dinner party if I didn't think that I had to redecorate the house for the occasion, with matching candles, napkins and food in the same color scheme. (She was exaggerating, of course.)

I remember the year that a friend of mine died the week before Christmas. Typically I would have spent those last seven days leading up to the 25th frantically baking, shopping, wrapping, visiting, caroling, over-extending both my credit line and my energy—only to remember on the night of the 24th, with a little help from Andy Williams, that it's all meant to be about a Silent, Holy Night. But the year my friend, Dhyan, died, I was so overwhelmed with the grief of his sudden passing, that I let go of the Christmas reins. I flew to Oregon for his funeral and returned a few days before Christmas. I did not buy or wrap another gift that year. I did no baking. Our stockings were not overflowing with carefully wrapped goodies. Oddly, it was a most beautiful and peaceful Christmas. Surrounded by the ones I love, present with my whole heart and a renewed urgency to live life to the fullest, my friend's parting gift to our household was serenity—like one would feel if wrapped in swaddling clothes.

In the midst of holiday frenzy all I have to do is think back to that Christmas of 1987, and slowly but surely, I release the reins. We need such prompting and reminders for living more simply in our consumer-oriented world. "Possession is nine-tenths of our flaw."

Honor the need for solitude

The great philosopher, Pascal, once said that many of our major problems derive from our inability to simply sit in a room and be still. Stillness is vital to the soul. Many people miss out on themselves completely as they journey through life. They know others, they know places, they know the industry, they know their business, they know their essential functions, they know skills, they know their customers and their competitors, but tragically, they know little about themselves. How much of our ability to know ourselves, I wonder, is connected to our ability to be alone and to be still?

The benefits of solitude have long been praised. Consider the examples of the great religious founders: Buddha's long years of meditation in the forest, Mohammad's prayer in a cave, or the forty days Jesus spent in the wilderness. All would have agreed with contemporary Native American wisdom that: "The power of solitude is great and beyond understanding."

The great poet, Pablo Neruda, put it beautifully in this remarkable verse entitled, "Keeping Still:"

> *If we were not so single-minded*
> *about keeping our lives moving,*
> *and for once could do nothing,*
> *perhaps a huge silence*
> *might interrupt this sadness*
> *of never understanding ourselves*
> *and of threatening ourselves with death.*

Perhaps one of the reasons we are so stressed is not that we are doing stressful things, but that we allow so little time for rest and silence. We cannot know a fruitful solitude without silence and space. It is the space between notes that allows music to come forth. It is the holes in lace that render it beautiful. Our experience has this musical and lacy structure. We need to attend to the spaces in our daily life experience that render it more beautiful. We need to ask where we can add more of these empty spaces between notes, allowing more lovely holes in the pattern of our lives.

Learn to say "no"

Before we can enjoy and reap the benefits of solitude and simplicity, we have to make room for them. I will speak for myself in saying that it can only happen in my life if I say "no" to other things, to other people, to other obligations and responsibilities. Before I can say a wholehearted "yes" to those aspects of my life that would in fact bring me into greater balance within myself, I have to say "no" to those things that keep me juggling like a mad woman. This is one of those principles that is far easier said than done.

Turning forty was wonderful for me! The lead up to it was awful—I felt the proverbial shock and angst that went with "going over the hill." Little did I know how beautiful and expansive the view would be on the other side. There was something about turning forty that awakened in me a sense of this life that I am living being *my* life. I found a new quality in my voice and the courage to use it. I found myself willing to speak up more for my values, my convictions and, to my great surprise, my boundaries! That is what being able to say "no" can mean—the power and willingness to name our boundaries so that we can choose with discernment the territory in which we want to live our lives.

Still, as I approach ever so quickly the next decade of my life, I find that my natural reflex when being asked a favor or being made a request is "Sure", "Absolutely" or "Why not?" I am working hard to listen more closely to my own question—"Why *not?*" For if I were to genuinely pose the question to myself, in most situations, I could probably draft a list of 10–20 very good reasons why not! Among them might be—my time, my priorities, my inner peace, and my desire to say "yes" to something else! The strangest thing I have found in my slowly but surely evolving ability to say "no" is that the uttering of this single syllable does not cause the world to end; my family and friends do not desert me; I do not lose the customer for life, the telemarketer does not burst into tears; and somehow, my daughter's school stays standing. Amazing.

Larry Boldt, author of the wonderful book, *Zen and the Art of Making a Living,* speaks to this aspect of human life:

> "You have heard that life is a dance. And if you have seen cells dividing or the sun on the water, or birds before they mate, you can see that it is a dance. If you think too much when you are dancing, you trip over your feet. In the same way, if you miss the rhythm of your life, you'll stumble through it a bit awkward and out of place. The graceful dancer listens for the music and trusts her feet to respond."

Learning the poise and balance in the dance of life is one of the greatest skills we can hone. For example, knowing when energy and resolution is needed and when it is time to soften and surrender. Knowing when we need greater faith or greater inquiry into a situation. Listening to the rhythms of our own hearts telling us it is time to seek greater solitude and simplicity or telling us to make our care and love more visible. There is no formula for this kind of responsiveness, no known steps for this dance. We must simply learn to listen with an open heart to whatever is in this moment, this day, this life. We have to learn to trust our feet.

Cultivating balance and a deeper sense of rhythm in life and work necessitates making choices. Practicing simplicity and honoring the need for solitude means giving up complexity and not surrendering to every pull that the world makes on us. We will live truer to our dual nature when we value inner peace enough to make it a priority and allow our lives to reflect that priority. Indeed, there are times when we will feel our spirits bobbing between the two shores of our being, when we feel split by two branches of our nature, as if we hold a dual citizenship within our own lives. And we should be grateful for both sides of the circle, because that is what makes the dance of life so rich, so entrancing and so merry. By embracing with gratitude these varying aspects of our nature, we may enable ourselves to live as Rumi, the 13th century Sufi poet, suggests in this small, powerful poem:

Why do you stay in prison
when the door is so wide open?
You must have shadow and light source both.
Listen, and lay your head
under the tree of awe.
Your way begins on the other side.

Become the sky.
Take an axe to the prison wall.
Escape.
Walk out like someone
suddenly born into color.
Do it now.
Unfold your own myth.

Passages

"There are two worlds:
the world that we can measure
with line and rule,
and the world that we feel
with our hearts and imagination.
One does not dismiss the other."

Leigh Hunt

"Just as your car runs more smoothly and requires less energy to go faster and farther when the wheels are in perfect alignment, you perform better when your thoughts, feelings, goals and values are in balance."

Brian Tracy

"There are some things you learn best in calm, and some in storm."

Willa Cather

"Take rest; a field that has rested gives a bountiful crop."

Ovid

"As there is design and symmetry in nature, I believe that there is also design and symmetry in human experiences if we learn to yield ourselves to our destinies."

Katherine Butler Hathaway

"We stand somewhere between the mountain and the ant."

Hopi saying

Nisargadatta Mahara

"Wisdom tells me that I am nothing.
Love tells me that I am everything.
And between the two my life flows."

Patricia Digh

"I need to recover a rhythm in my heart that moves my body first and then my mind second, that allows my soul to catch up with me. I need to take a sacred pause, as if I were a sun-warmed rock in the center of a rushing river. In essence, I need to come home to myself."

"A strong woman is a woman who loves strongly and weeps strongly and is strongly terrified and has strong needs."

Marge Piercy

"The path of heart is not a road of incessant introspection or mystical flight, but a way of engaging the joys and sorrows of the world. It is a path into the depths, not out of them—a path that leads us to the truth behind our illusions, to the oneness that dwells behind our dualities."

Jan Phillips

"Activity and reflection should ideally
complement and support each other.
Action by itself is blind;
reflection by itself is impotent."

Mihaly Csikszentmihalyi

Susan McHenry

"Work when there is work to do.
Rest when you are tired.
One thing in peace will most likely be better than ten things done in panic…
I am not a hero if I deny rest;
I am only tired."

Zen saying

"After ecstasy, the laundry."

"To attain knowledge, add things every day.
To attain wisdom, remove things every day."

Lao-Tzu

"The notes I handle no better than many pianists. But the pauses between the notes—ah, that is where the art resides!"

Artur Schnabel

"Sunshine is delicious, rain is refreshing, wind braces us up, snow is exhilarating; there is really no such thing as bad weather, only different kinds of good weather."

John Ruskin

"To everything there is a season…
a time to weep, and a time to laugh;
a time to mourn, and a time to dance…"

Ecclesiastes, Chapter 3

Walt Whitman

"Do I contradict myself?
Very well then…
I contradict myself;
I am large…
I contain multitudes."

"I learned inspiration does not come like a bolt, nor is it kinetic, energetic, striving, but it comes to us slowly and quietly and all the time, though we must regularly and every day give it a little chance to start flowing, prime it with a little solitude and idleness."

Brenda Ueland

Thomas Merton

"We cannot be happy if we expect to live all the time at the highest peak of intensity. Happiness is not a matter of intensity, but of balance and order and rhythm and harmony."

Lin Yu-Tang

"Besides the noble art of getting things done, there is the noble art of leaving things undone. The wisdom of life consists of the elimination of nonessentials."

To Ponder and To Practice

- Who do you know who lives with a great sense of balance and rhythm? How would you like your life to reflect the life of that person?
- If your mind, body and spirit could carry out a conversation with one another, what do you imagine each one would have to say to the other? What requests or suggestions would each offer the other?
- The day is set to the rhythm of the sun, the month to the rhythm of the moon and the year to the rhythm of the seasons. What is the rhythm to which you have set your yearly cycle? Make a list of daily, weekly, and yearly rituals that help you organize the rhythm of your life and give you a feeling of continuity and predictability.
- Identify a few ways that you can bring "voluntary simplicity" into your life.
- In order to attain a more peaceful state of being, what five distractions could you eliminate from your life? What new boundaries could you set or let go of that could allow more peace or serenity into your life?
- What physical clutter are you completely ready to be rid of? Look at your work area—throw five things away. Look at your living space—give five things away. Open your closets and drawers—fill a few boxes to donate to the nearest homeless shelter.
- What is the one thing you need more of in your life right now? Choose a word from the list below and come up with a practical idea of how you can bring more of that quality into your life.

Solitude	Peace	Love	Friendship	Celebration
Grace	Touch	Creativity	Movement	Communication
Fun	Silliness	Nature	Spontaneity	Order

- Step out of your normal routine in a way that would feel good to you and would help bring a sense of balance to some area of your life. Here are some examples:
  - Turn off the answering machine and unplug the phone to create a silent space free from the intrusion of others.
  - Stay in bed for an extra hour or get up an hour earlier than usual.
  - Finish the project that's been hanging over your head and feel the relief that accompanies completion.
  - Put something off until tomorrow with the knowledge that it will still be waiting for you and the world will not come to an end as a result.
  - Write a letter to someone you really care about but never seem to find the time to correspond with.

Practice

- Step out of character to bring more balance to your relationships. For example,
  - If you are always the helper, ask for help from someone today. If you are the often the recipient of someone else's care, turn the tables and offer your services today.
  - If you tend to be the follower, be the leader today… whether it's to lead a discussion, a group of hikers or a team of people to a new idea. If you are usually the leader, try following today… surprise those around you with your interest in listening and learning.
- Write your own poem that expresses different sides of your own life, putting a voice to your own sense of rhythm.
- To what and whom would you like to practice your ability to say "no"? Draft a two-sided list: on one side write down some of the things to which you could say "no"; on the other side write down some of the things you would be saying "yes" to by having named your boundary.
- Select a quote from this chapter's *Passages* which you can use to remind yourself of the importance of cultivating rhythm and balance in your life.
- Choose a daily habit, routine or symbol to help you remain conscious of your intention to bring a greater sense of rhythm and balance into your life (e. g., as you open the curtains in the morning and draw them in the evening, become aware of the windows you open and close within yourself which will allow you to honor your natural rhythm).
- Given everything you have read in this chapter, what do you want to *keep* doing? What do you want to *stop* doing? What do you want to *start* doing?

Notes

Veil of Wonder

Chapter

Seeing through New Eyes

Remember the three secrets of the universe

Remember the three secrets of the universe

Consider the lilies of the field

Consider the lilies of the field

Let mystery have its place in you

Let mystery have its place in you

Listen for the squirrel's heartbeat

Listen for the squirrel's heartbeat

See the pearl

See the pearl

Make every day a "holy day"

Make every day a "holy day"

Trust the sermon of a bird

Trust the sermon of a bird

Veil of Wonder

We feel a duty to be timely, we feel a duty to be right,
but do we feel a duty to wonder and delight?
We speak of essential functions that constitute the job,
but what is essential to the soul, we cannot ignore or rob.
We are pressured, we are challenged, God knows that we are stressed,
but seldom do we contemplate how immensely we are blessed.
The glorious, green and fruitful earth, lives laced with love and grace,
a heart, a mind, two legs and hands, two eyes and ears, a face!

The world's frantic with activity, the telephone is ringing,
but just outside these busy walls there is a small bird singing.
We hear the clock a tickin', eyes glued to a computer screen,
while daily beauty glides right by, unheard, untouched, unseen.
The sun rising from its slumber, a crocus poking through the snow,
the child skipping merrily, across the street she goes.
Immeasurable beauty on the loose disguised as daily bread,
deep of sea, expanse of sky, fields of wheat on which we're fed.

We keep ourselves accountable, our hours neatly planned,
the schedule is tight, no time to breathe, this we understand.
But we're also made to celebrate, to thrill from head to toe,
to be speechless and bewildered by what we cannot know.
To be transfixed, befuddled and wrapped in mystery,
to ponder with our wild hearts, life's possibility.
We gather data, we love our facts, we've stored our information,
but where's the room for epiphany, for the voice of revelation?

We're committed to the things we do, and so, we earn our wages,
but this world is a treasure trove, passed down throughout the ages.
Let's set our souls on tiptoe lest we miss what passes by,
a steady stream of miracles if seen through wonder's eye.
The stunning gift of the everyday in all its simple glory
comes streaming from the moments that shape each person's story.
We live and work as humans will, but as we tell the tale,
let's lift the blinders from our eyes, let wonder be our veil.

Reflections

> "Today, like every other day,
> we wake up empty and frightened.
> Don't open the door to the study
> and begin reading.
> Put away the books.
> Take down the dulcimer.
> Let the beauty of what we love
> be what we do.
> There are a thousand ways
> to kneel and kiss the ground."

These words from Sufi mystic Rumi are so simple, beautiful and true. Life is difficult and trying—there is hardly a morning we do not awaken to that reality. And yet life is so stunning, so astonishing and so full of beauty, we can hardly take in its wonders. And so we awaken each day with a choice. We can delve into our books or we can take down the dulcimer. How many ways, I ask myself, do I know to kneel and kiss the ground? What astounds me to the point where I can do nothing but sigh and bow? I want to live with an ever-increasing sense of wonder at the miracle of earth, of life and of love. I want to open my eyes and *really* see. I want to open my heart and *really* feel. I want to awaken and be *really* alive. I want wonder to be my veil.

Wonder encourages us to stand before the unfathomable mysteries of human life, and if only for a split second, to encounter the divine. Some of the greatest writers, poets and thinkers of the ages have used *wonder* as their axis, the point around which the volume of their work revolved. Here are a few recommendations gleaned from the words and images of some of my favorite writers on bringing true attention to this moment of our lives, on truly listening, fully seeing, really touching the world around us.

Remember the three secrets of the universe

A spiritual seeker once heard that there lived a true spiritual master who knew the three secrets to the universe. The seeker traveled long and far to reach the mountaintop where the sage lived. He was granted a meeting with the master with whom he pleaded to be told the three secrets to the universe. The master looked into the other man's eyes and saw that he was ready to receive this great wisdom. The master smiled kindly and said, "The first secret is very important. Listen closely. The first secret is *pay attention."*

He paused before revealing the second secret, which was even more critical. With a serious face, he warned, "Listen closely. The second secret is *pay attention."*

Finally, the master held the seeker's hands in his and told him that the third secret would have the most profound affect on his life, if he could but follow it. "Listen closely. The third secret is to *pay attention."*

The secret to living a life with the *veil of wonder* lies in our willingness to pay attention. Our growth as conscious, awake human beings is marked not as much by grand gestures as it is by extending loving attention to the minutest particulars of our lives. Every relationship, every thought, every gesture is blessed with meaning through the wholehearted attention we are able to bring it. It is interesting that the word "revelation" comes from *re-valere,* literally "to veil again." Through the veil of wonder and the gift of our attention, the world itself is revelation.

Learning to pay attention to something as mundane as the inhaling and exhaling of breath can make a huge difference in our day. This is perhaps the world's most common contemplative exercise and a central element of yoga. Paying attention to breath is a delightfully simple and easy meditation that can be practiced at almost any time and quickly lift the veil of complacency. All we have to do is turn our attention to our breath and take three long, slow breaths, breathing in slowly and deeply, and then relaxing and letting go as the air falls out. A few mindful breaths before a meeting or a little while before the kids come home can help salvage a little sanity. A few mindful breaths before a business call can restore a sense of peace. Likewise, some calming breaths can be a wonderful way to start each hour. In just a minute or two you can release tensions accumulated in the last hour and bring a clear, fresh mind to the hour ahead.

I loved this idea offered by Roger Walsh in his book, *Essential Spirituality*. He suggests that rather than simply do "breath meditations," we up the ante with a "First Breath, Last Breath" meditation. First, to breathe as if it is the first breath, and then to imagine that you are at the end of your life and breathing your last breath. I find this a nice practice upon awaking in the morning and before going to sleep at night. By doing it the morning, I am more inclined to grant a purpose to my day. By doing it at night, I am more inclined to let go of the trivial concerns that would otherwise keep me tossing and turning.

Consider the lilies of the field

"Consider the lilies of the field," Jesus says in the Bible, and it is reported that 19th century poet Emily Dickinson claimed that this was the only commandment she never broke. Anyone familiar with her poetry would just nod, knowing that, among others, that was her gift—paying attention.

It is said that God is in the details. But we cannot recognize the divine without first paying attention. This requires discipline and practice. "For lack of attention," writes English mystic Evelyn Underhill, "a thousand forms of loveliness elude us every day." Moments of grace, epiphanies and great insights are lost to us because we are in too much of a hurry to notice them.

Writer and poet Wendell Berry reminds us that wonder surrounds us in this passage from his essay, "Sex, Economy, Freedom and Community":

> "We are confronted everywhere with wonders. We see that the miraculous is not extraordinary but the common mode of existence. Whoever has considered the lilies of the field or the birds of the air and pondered the improbability of their existence in this warm world within the cold and empty stellar distances will hardly balk at the turning of water into wine—which was, after all, a very small miracle. We forget the greater and still continuing miracle by which water (with soil and sunlight) is turned into grapes."

And yet, in our hurriedness, amongst all of the miraculous, we often find ourselves bored. From what could our boredom stem, if not lack of attention? It is as if our perceptual senses are on automatic pilot. We are a culture that feeds itself on entertainment—we like to sit and watch—be it a sports event, a video game or a movie rental. Our children learn from us that they must be entertained instead of creatively filling their time by themselves. Heaven forbid they might ever find time alone—what would they do? With our need for constant entertainment, I think we dull both our senses and our sensibilities.

I plead guilty in the first degree to being very good at distracting myself—I use books when traveling, and I always make sure to have a few new books for the trip. I can hardly imagine being a passenger on an airplane without devouring a book or two in flight. On a trip I made with my daughter when she was twelve years old, I remember settling into my seat with a new book, a journal and a pen as I watched her slip her backpack under the seat without having opened it. She just sat with her hands in her lap, her eyes open, in silence. After about half an hour, it was driving me crazy! I asked her why she wasn't engaging herself in something. "Didn't you bring something to read?" I asked. "Where's your sketchbook?" (There was definitely an edge to my voice.) Her reply astounded me. She just looked at me perplexed and responded, "I am doing something, Mom. I am thinking."

It had never occurred to me to just sit and think on an airplane. I have since tried it many times—at least once per flight. I can't help smiling as I admit that it takes conscious effort for me to put the book or pen down and just be present with my thoughts on an airplane. What has resulted from this little "practice" is an awareness of the amazing experience of being in a mechanical bird flying over fields, mountains and plains. Unlike the awareness that unexpected turbulence can bring, I find myself in awe of the breathtaking beauty of the ever-changing skies as we weave (or bounce) through the clouds. I take in the people around me and notice who is in my presence. Is there anyone who might need assistance in some way? Is there a child near me who could use a little attention? And always, the thought will occur to me, if something happens to this plane or on this flight, are these the people with whom I may die today?

As I discussed in the first chapter of this book, it is a plain and simple truth that we cannot live a rich and spirited life while on automatic pilot. We can neither see anything nor truly love anything while on automatic pilot. George Washington Carver wisely posed, "If you love it enough, anything will talk with you." What does it mean to love something, if not to give it our full, undivided attention? Have you ever noticed that what is loved, spills over with its loveliness? It is true of flowers and of trees and of lakes. It is especially true of children, of elderly people and of people of every age in between. Consider the lilies of the field. Consider the people in your midst.

Let mystery have its place in you

With characteristic flair, poet Mary Oliver articulates the urgency to make room for mystery, indeed, amazement with the world, in this verse from her poem "When Death Comes," included in her book, *New and Selected Poems:*

All of my life I was a bride
married to amazement.
I was the bridegroom,
taking the world into my arms.
When it is over I don't want to wonder
if I have made of my life something particular,
and real.
I don't want to find myself
sighing and frightened, or full of argument.
I don't want to end up
simply having visited this world.

We love knowing everything we can know. We love our data and our information. We love having the facts. But where is our appetite for mystery and the unknown? There is a beautiful poem by the wonderful Czeslaw Milosz called "A New Province," which speaks with equal power to the idea of allowing mystery to have its place in our lives. This is the last verse:

I would prefer to be able to say: "I am satiated,
what is given to taste in this life, I have tasted."
But I am like someone in a window
who draws aside a curtain
to look at a feast he does not comprehend.

Mechthild of Magdeburg, 13th century mystic, mirrors this sentiment in her own lovely verse:

Of all that God has shown me
I can speak just the smallest word,
No more than a honey bee
Takes on his foot
From an overspilling jar.

The truth is that the world is a miracle and it is not meant to be comprehended. Wonder accompanies us every step of the journey. But we must be alert and awaken to the moments when it shines its face even as it peers from places we wouldn't expect. The shy smile from a child in the grocery store line, someone letting you into the next lane during rush hour, that brief moment of sun leaving a water-colored shadow from the glass vase on your window sill. I believe that beauty wants to be seen and wonder watches for us too. I believe even our dreams are waiting for us to come true. The universe is just full of magical things patiently waiting for our senses to grow sharper. Like new parents mesmerized with the face of their sleeping infant, creation is watching us, waiting for our eyes to open.

It is said that Claude Monet lived in Germany for thirty-five years, painting the same water lilies year after year in each new day's light. To look with the freshness of eyes that see today's light anew—this is the everyday magic we are capable of experiencing. Unfortunately, we lose the wonder and magic of our everyday surroundings by wrapping them in an attitude and seeing through the lens of "familiarity."

When we are familiar with something it loses its energy, its edge and its excitement. This is probably true of how we see our homes, our towns, our yards, our friends and co-workers, even our workplaces. We need to remove the cloak of familiarity from our surroundings and see them fresh.

We can still our yearning hearts not by finally finding the perfect mate, the dream house or success in the workplace, but by perceiving the pulse of eternity in the moment at hand and in the beauty of the world we have come to see as "ordinary." I love these words of Boris Pasternak: "When a great moment knocks on the door of your life, it is often no louder than the beating of your heart, and it is very easy to miss it." We must remain attentive in order to hear and receive... to be open to the paths our feet may take.

Listen for the squirrel's heartbeat

In her beautiful poem, "The Swan," Mary Oliver says,

> "Paradise, of course, does not lay out in flat miles.
> It is in the imagination with which we perceive the
> world and the gestures with which we honor it."

Our first gesture may be to look with more than our eyes and to listen with more than our ears—to be here not only with our senses, but with the imagination of the heart as well. It is a startling truth that *how* we see and *what* we see largely determines *who* we will be. When we look through eyes of fear and suspicion, we see evidence of it and we become distrustful, living like turtles in our shells. When we look through soft and loving eyes, we see a world that we want to take into our arms and in whose arms we want to be held. It is not uncommon in a competitive workplace to see people looking through eyes of judgment, blame or inferiority. Unfortunately, through such a lens, they will find plenty of reason to harbor such feelings.

We can choose the lens through which we view the world, and in doing so, alter our experience and perceptions.

How do we look out at that the world with fresh eyes, free of the filters or our judgment and labels? To what extent are our perceptions really just old tapes of what we expect to see and hear? What would we think about, wonder about and explore if we were not conditioned to seeing and thinking in a rational way? I love the way George Eliot, English novelist of the 1800s, put it:

> "If we had a keen vision and feeling
> of all ordinary human life,
> it would be like hearing the grass grow
> and the squirrel's heart beat,
> and we should die of the roar
> which lies on the side of silence."

I remember walking hand in hand with my daughter in the redwood forest when she was five years old and her saying in a very matter of fact way, "Mommy, life is very big." It was a strangely revelatory moment for me, because I realized that life was indeed big—big enough to contain my joy and my sorrow, my wonder and my tiredness, my hopes and my fears. It made me feel wonderfully small and insignificant, yet held by something large enough to contain everything the Great Spirit intended for my life. Now, among its other glories, the redwood forest is a place where I can go to lose my preoccupations and self-absorption. It is a place to re-enter my life again, fresh and willing to awaken to the largeness of the world. From the mouth of babes: "Life is very big."

In the very same forest a decade later, I walked with my nephews, Conor and Luke, who were then six and eight years old. We hadn't walked two-hundred yards, before they had become Ewoks in an enchanted forest. Every nook and cranny of the Henry Cowell Redwood State Park became a magical world of gnomes and fairies and tree elves as well as the hiding place for every character from Star Wars who was on the "good side." They even found the roots of an old tree which they quickly made into their home. Children have a natural gift for seeing through eyes of wonder. We need children in our lives to restore that sense of awe, even momentarily. Listen, watch, beware… who knows what we may spot in the corner of the forest….

See the pearl

We often fail to realize that we are in the presence of the everyday miraculous because we are so preoccupied with practical matters. See if you can relate to St. Peter in this story:

> One Sunday morning after church, God and St. Peter went to play golf. God teed off. He gave a mighty swipe and sliced the ball off into the rough beside the fairway.
>
> Just as the ball was about to hit the ground, a rabbit darted out of a bush, grabbed it with his mouth, and ran with it down the fairway. Suddenly an eagle swooped down, picked the rabbit up in its claws, and flew with it over the green. A man with a rifle took aim and shot at the eagle in mid-flight. Dodging the bullet, the eagle let go of the rabbit. The rabbit fell onto the green and the ball rolled out of its mouth and into the hole.
>
> St. Peter turned to God in annoyance and said, "Ah, come on now! Do you want to play golf or are you here to fool around?"

Isn't it true that we are too preoccupied with the seriousness of life, with playing the game of life as we know it and understand it to be bothered with wonder? We don't have time to fool around with miracles!

We feel a duty to be timely,
we're committed to being right,
But do we feel a duty
to wonder and delight?
We speak of essential functions
that constitute the job,
But what is essential to the soul,
we cannot ignore or rob.

And even if we did make time for wonder and delight, we may still miss it because we have trained our eyes to look in the wrong places, much like the pearl diver in this story:

> An oyster saw a loose pearl that had fallen into the crevice of a rock on the ocean bed. After great effort she managed to retrieve the pearl and place it just beside her on a leaf.
>
> She knew that humans searched for pearls and thought, "This pearl will tempt them, so they will take it and let me be."
>
> When a pearl diver showed up, however, his eyes were conditioned to look for oysters and not for pearls resting on leaves.
>
> So he grabbed the oyster, which did not happen to have a pearl, and allowed the real pearl to roll back into the crevice in the rock.

We are trained to look for oysters, not the pearls of everyday existence. True wonder often escapes the net of our logic, our language and our expectations.

I know that as a child I missed much of the miraculous in the everyday wonder around me because I was waiting for "The Holy" to reveal itself through a supernatural event—like a choir of angels, a burning bush, or the voice of God cutting through the skies like thunder. I remember praying fervently to be chosen, like the children at Fatima, and see the Virgin Mary appear before me, levitating above the Kankakee River. I remember kneeling before the statue of Mother Mary in St. Patrick's Church, closing my eyes tightly, and praying a most deep and sincere prayer. I would then open my eyes, oh, so slowly, half-expecting to see Her moving before me. Disappointed, I would steal out of the church believing that the day I was holy enough, it really would happen. In the meantime, I knew I had a lot of work to do cleaning up that selfish soul of mine with all the dust and dirt in its corners, the hairballs under its bed.

I wish that someone would have met that child coming out of the church, taken her hand and led her on a little escapade through *the holiness* in her own town, in the park at the end of her block or at the river's edge. The butterfly alighting upon the flower, a field of new green grass, leaves of orange and gold falling from the trees, the silent, falling snow. The child I was would have seen the miracles of each of these, had she been prompted to look through those eyes. That's all that it takes—a change in perception—and an ordinary object can carry the fire and power of epiphany. The bush of red and golden leaves is a burning bush if seen through the eyes of soul—the sound of rain on the rooftop is the perfect homily if listened to with the ears of soul.

I have come to believe that what we think of as spirit and soul is not something to see or experience in ourselves or in the world, but in the way we perceive the world. Children have the eyes and sensibilities to perceive in a soulful way. We are children who have just lived a little longer—if we can but look again, see again, listen, sense, touch and taste from a soulful place.

Sam Keen speaks to this kind of soulful seeing in this passage from his book, *Hymns to an Unknown God:*

"Everything solid melts the moment our perspective changes from common sense understanding to wonder. We become like the physics professor who was so awed by the vision of the insubstantiality of atoms that he walked around wearing snowshoes so he wouldn't fall into the void between the whirling electrons. Once we see the universe as a never-ending process and ourselves as ever-changing moments with that process, it is difficult to get too excited by the daily fluctuation of the Dow Jones average. When we touch the wonder of all things, we become weak at the knees. We tremble and are struck dumb by the intense awareness of the fragileness of the universe."

Make every day a "holy day"

I used to be obsessed with holidays and all of the hoopla that went with them. I understand now that I loved holidays because they felt like "holy days." Days when we would stop long enough from the routine of our lives to love one another, to celebrate one another, to honor our fathers or mothers, to honor the people who have passed before us, to consider the journey of pilgrims and give thanks for our abundance, to celebrate rebirth and resurrection… to write love notes on paper hearts.

For years I lived from holiday to holiday and my home reflected it. One day my Aunt Anna, who pretty much detests holidays and all that goes with them, asked me, "Denise, what's with all this holiday stuff? Why can't you just celebrate regular days?" I realized that I was investing my thoughts and energy into holidays in order to reap what holiness I could from the rituals and symbols of those days. I have since learned to enjoy the holiness of each day and season without the trappings of a holiday. By welcoming the morning with a moment of solitude before entering the day, by stopping long enough to feel the noon day sun on our faces or its sparkling affect on the winter snow, by allowing the darkness of night to cause us to reflect on the light within—lighting a small candle as a symbol of our love and faith for that which sustains us but which we cannot see. Without boughs and wreaths and blinking lights, without banners and parades and fireworks—we make each day a holy day with these small, humble gestures.

It's strange for me to admit that January has become one of my favorite months of the year. I adore the silence and stillness, the dark and cold that January brings—the time to go inside and be home without the pressures of a holiday. I think back to the young woman I was who lived from holiday to holiday—I sigh and give thanks that my journey has brought me to a place of living each day as its own holy day. I am less exhausted and no longer need to spend half my income on the accoutrements of a commercial holiday.

Trust the sermon of a bird

I have always had a sense that when I am most awestruck by the world (or something in it), I am nearer to understanding the world than at any other time. Anthony de Mello, a great spiritual teacher and writer, shares this story which speaks to the wisdom that can come from wonder.

Once upon a time there was a minister who, new to the church, really wanted to make a great impression on the congregation with his first sermon on Sunday morning. He wrote it and he rewrote it, then he deliberated more until he had just the right mixture of Biblical verse, practical application and inspiration. He was ready!

The crowd gathered in great numbers, curious to check out the new minister. After a few opening hymns, he gathered the notes for his sermon and walked up to the pulpit. His heart beat fast and there was sweat on his brow. He prayed to be used as an instrument of divine inspiration. Just as he finished his prayer and was about to deliver his sermon, he noticed a small bird land on the open sill towards the front of the church. The bird began to tweet and chirp and then to sing, filling the church with the pure, clear sounds of its merry tune. Then the fledgling flew off into an expanse of blue.

The minister gathered the notes, cleared his throat, and announced to the congregation that they had just received a sermon, the likes of which he could not possibly match. Then he closed with a prayer.

With the complexities of the mind and the busyness of our lives, we easily forget the powers of our attention and the presence of wonder in our everyday lives. Yet without an awareness of the beauty and wonder of the world, we find ourselves living on the surface of existence rather than in its depths. It is just simple attention that allows us to hear green in the frog's voice, to see and smell glory in the autumn leaf, to touch the heart of another person and to be touched. Mary Roberts Rinehart tells us, "Life is not so very long… a little work, a little sleep, a little love and it's all over." What other place can we begin to live with the wisdom of wonder, but here? When will there be a better time to take the blinders off than now?

The sun rising from its slumber,
a crocus poking through the snow
The child skipping merrily,
across the street she goes.
Immeasurable beauty on the loose
disguised as daily bread,
Deep of sea, expanse of sky,
fields of wheat on which we're fed.

Let's not miss the sermon.

Passages

Albert Einstein

"The man or woman who possesses no awe or sense of mystery is a candle without a wick."

"You cannot avoid paradise— you can only avoid seeing it."

Charlotte Joko Beck

"Wonder, not doubt, is the root of knowledge."

Abraham Joshua Heschel

"It is good to remember that all ground is sacred where life is honored and that you can build a temple in the space between your eyes."

Jan Phillips

"Earth's crammed with heaven,
And every common bush afire with God;
But only he who sees takes off his shoes;
The rest sit round it and pluck blackberries."

Elizabeth Barrett Browning

Pearl Buck

"I am so absorbed in the wonder of the earth and life upon it that I cannot think of heaven and angels. I have enough of this life."

Native American saying

"If we wonder often enough, the gift of knowledge will come."

Crowfoot

"What is life?
It is the flash of a firefly in the night.
It is the breath of a buffalo in the winter time.
It is the little shadow which runs across the grass and loses itself in the sunset."

Ojibway saying

"Sometimes I go about pitying myself
and all the time I am being carried
on great winds across the sky."

"We milk the cow of the world,
and as we do we whisper in her ear,
'You are not true.'"

Richard Wilbur

"I believe a leaf of grass is no less than the journey work of the stars. And a mouse a miracle enough to stagger sextillions of infidels."

Walt Whitman

Albert Schweitzer

"Let a man once begin to think about the mystery of his life and the links which connect him with the life that fills the world, and he cannot but bring to bear upon his own life, and all other life that comes within his reach, the principle of reverence for life. . . ."

Emily Dickinson

"The soul should always stand ajar, ready to welcome the ecstatic experience."

"We all grow up fast and lose that first sharp vision of the world. We miss dew sparkle, leaf shadow, spider scuttle, puddle shine. We waste time on worry. And we find the days sweep by, each blurred, each like the other."

Pam Brown

"The man who cannot wonder, who does not habitually wonder and worship, is but a pair of spectacles behind which there is no eye."

Thomas Carlyle

Braden McInnes, 4 yrs. old

"Our airplane went higher than the sky, it went higher than the ABC's!"

"The same stream of life that runs through the world runs through my veins."

Rabindranath Tagore

Rumi

"Each thing in the universe is a vessel full to the brim with wisdom and beauty."

"Life is too wonderful, too full, too short, and strength too limited to contain its wonder."

Ruth Draper

André Gide

"I should like to enjoy this summer flower by flower, as if it were to be the last one for me."

Ralph Waldo Emerson

"If the stars would appear but one night every thousand years, how man would marvel and adore."

Henri Frederic Amiel

"Let mystery have its place in you; do not be always turning up your whole ploughshare of self-examination, but leave a little fallow corner in your heart ready for any seed the wind may bring, and reserve a nook of shadow for the passing bird; keep a place in your heart for the unexpected guest, an altar for the unknown God."

"Celebrate your existence!"

William Blake

"Life is this simple: We are living in a world that is absolutely transparent and the Divine is shining through it all the time. This is not just a nice story or fable. It is true."

Thomas Merton

To Ponder and To Practice

- What experience, event or person in your life aroused or renewed your sense of wonder?
- When was the last time you had a song in your step at work? What do you know in your heart of hearts would make you whistle while you work? Is there anything stopping you from taking that step?
- Albert Einstein, the greatest physicist of our time, observed, "There are two ways to live your life. One is as though nothing is a miracle. The other is as though everything is." What was the last miracle in your life? Resolve to notice the miraculous around you.
- Each day take the time to look at life with a sense of awe, for your liver, your hands, your invisible, incomprehensible, complex mind. Treat life with reverence a few minutes each day and you will contribute to your spiritual awakening faster than through any metaphysical course. Keep a "Wonders Journal" just to keep your perception on tiptoe.
- Take a few mindful breaths a couple of times each day. As time goes on, extend this practice to as long as a minute of mindful breathing. Try the "First Breath/Last Breath" exercise at the end of a long day and see if it doesn't help alleviate stress.
- Henry Miller wisely reminds us that "The moment one gives close attention to anything, even a blade of grass, it becomes a mysterious, awesome, indescribably magnificent world in itself." Choose someone or something that you will invest some undivided attention to today that you have perhaps ignored up until now, whether it be a person, a project or a peony bush. Carry a notepad and keep a running list of aspects of your work and home environments that you never really noticed before.
- Hold a baby and rejoice in the knowledge that miracles are real.
- Spend time anywhere in nature. Listen. Be still and watch. Touch the earth. Breathe deep, smell and taste the air.
- Spend time with a person much younger than you. Give that person your undivided attention. Open your eyes to see through this young person's eyes. Notice what is different. Do the same with an elderly person.
- Attempt to fine-tune your senses. When listening to music, become fully aware of its subtleties—the delicate notes, the background rhythms and the emotions they evoke in you. When eating, taste the earth in the apple; when getting under your covers, appreciate the miracles of cotton or silk.

Practice

- Choose a daily habit, routine or symbol to remind yourself, as Emily Dickinson suggests, to keep your soul ajar (e.g., use the sound of crickets, wind or birdsong as a cue, or follow the advice of poet and author Thich Nhat Hanh and use something as mundane as the telephone ringing as your prompt).
- Select a quote from this chapter's *Passages* that you can post in your work or home environment to remind you of the importance of fostering an acute sense of wonder.
- Given everything you have read in this chapter, what do you want to *keep* doing? What do you want to *stop* doing? What do you want to *start* doing?

Notes

Chapter 20

A Pilgrim's Plea

Remaining True to the Soul

Recognize your path as a pilgrim

Recognize your path as a pilgrim

Seek to know your soul so it can speak to you

Seek to know your soul so it can speak to you

Trust the compass of soul

Trust the compass of soul

Stand resolute that your soul is not for sale

Stand resolute that your soul is not for sale

Accept that the vocational journey is a spiritual journey

Accept that the vocational journey is a spiritual journey

Take the high road in life and work

Take the high road in life and work

Follow the beat of your soul's drum

Follow the beat of your soul's drum

Find and go to your forest

Find and go to your forest

A Pilgrim's Plea

Please don't ask us to "reinvent" ourselves
for yet another change in the work world
for we only wish to unfold,
to continue the miracle of having been born.
We long to greet each day as the world does,
fresh, new and ripe for living.
We long to lean towards the sun like flowers—eager to blossom
to move wild like waves under a silver moon—
drawn on the tide of our native longing.

Oh, we wish to belong to the world, yes.
But first and foremost, we wish to belong to ourselves.
For you cannot downsize, right size or minimize the human soul.
That place in each of us that is our true home
is totally immune to the corporate takeover,
to mergers and acquisitions,
because it's not for sale.

Please don't ask us to be so smitten with technology
that as we enter more deeply into the world of the virtual
we surrender what has always come natural.

Let us not be hypnotized by the 21st century mantra
"To embrace change as the only constant in our lives."
Can we not instead restore our faith in those things that never change?
Like the genius in the seed
to become a flower, a tree or a human being?
The faithful turning of the earth,
or the lovely way that gravity continues to hold us to her?
Can we not restore our faith
in the persistent beckoning of the human heart
to simply give and receive,
to love and be loved,
to fail with as much grace as we succeed?

As we become more firmly rooted in ourselves
we will cease to demand that the world navigate our work lives
with promises of more programs, more positions, more promotions.
We will have the maturity to see that
those in the oval office,
those in the board rooms, those on the trading floor
are not prophets. They, too, are pilgrims—
their every step remaining as much a mystery as our own.

For each of us must travel the uncharted seas of our own lives, alone.
Yet, blessedly, together, side by side.
Trusting that inner compass of hope and courage and imagination.
Never forgetting that when we bring heart to the journey,
we make it holy.
When we bring heart to the journey,
we will not lose sight of the brilliant stars in the immense night sky.

This is the pilgrim's plea at the onset of the 21st century.
To hear the echo of all who have gone before us
and the hopeful cry of all of those yet to come.
To bring all that we are and all that we have
to the joy and the sorrow,
the wonder and the terror,
the known and the unknown,
of daily living.

But please, don't ask us to "reinvent" ourselves
for yet another change in the work world.
For we only wish to unfold,
to continue the miracle of having been born.

Reflections

From ancient times the human being has been understood as a wanderer, a nomad, traversing foreign territories and exploring unknown places. Yet it is agreed among some of the most prolific and celebrated thinkers of every age (from Socrates and Plato to Einstein and Buckminster Fuller) that the longest, most exciting and most arduous journey is the journey inward… the journey to belong and to be at home in the world. That we move from unknown to unknown is not a choice in life… it is the sum and substance of the human condition. How we journey, however, is a choice.

Recognize your path as a pilgrim

We are born empty-handed and we die empty-handed. Contrary to popular bumper-sticker wisdom, the one with the most toys does not necessarily win, but simply leaves behind more toys. The only wealth we can take from this world is wealth of the soul. The gifts that we give and the gifts that we receive along the way are riches of the spirit. That we travel from infancy towards adulthood is inevitable. However, whether we are transformed, enriched and ennobled by this journey is up to us.

Author and poet, Mark Nepo, makes this important distinction:

> "To journey without being changed is to be a nomad.
> To change without journeying is to be a chameleon.
> To journey and to be transformed by the journey
> Is to be a pilgrim."

We all know what it is to be nomads—traveling mindlessly from one job to another, from one relationship to another or from one year of our lives to the next… the only significant changes marked by increases in pay, notches on the proverbial "dating belt," or dates on a calendar. In the back of our minds, we hear the low, incessant rumbling, "Are we having fun yet?"

We all know what it is to be chameleons—turning corporate when in the corporation, becoming yuppified when in the yuppie forest, playing spades when spades are trump… God knows we don't want to renege. Life—one big game of camouflage. And in the meantime, never discovering, much less showing, our true colors.

We all know what it is to be pilgrims—traversing dangerous territories, lush jungles and the quiet garden spaces, be they vocational, physical, emotional or spiritual. We are changed forever, in big and little ways, by each part of the journey. Experiencing along the way, breathtaking views of friendship, being windblown by an illness, or being stopped in our tracks by a penetrating insight, shipwrecked on the shores of a career move that had no sails, torn asunder by a tornado of a relationship, or having our feet blistered from walking the peaks and valleys of faith and understanding. Clearly, we are never the same again from these experiences.

Undoubtedly, for better or for worse (probably both), we are transformed when we undertake life's journey as pilgrims. Nomads have to be lonely, but they probably don't grieve as deeply. (Then again, they don't fly on wings of joy either.) Chameleons have a fine life, their colors decided for them. (Then again, I would personally prefer that I make of my life an original portrait rather than a paint-by-number replication.) Pilgrims have it tough. But in the end, the pilgrim has something that no one can ever take from them… they have soul. 11th Century Swiss philosopher, Henri Amiel, proposed:

> "The process of life should be the birth of the soul. This is the highest alchemy, and this justifies our presence on earth. This is our calling and our virtue."

Contemporary author, Annie Dillard, with characteristic flair, takes the metaphor of pilgrimage to sea:

> "The secret of sailing is to sail on solar wind. Hone and spread your spirit till you yourself are a sail; whetted, translucent, broadside to the merest puff."

It has been said a thousand and one ways, but I think one of the most basic and significant truths of our journey can be summed up in this metaphysical principle professed by 20th century Catholic priest and mystic, Teilhard de Chardin.

> *We are not human beings on a spiritual path; we are spiritual beings on a human path.*

From this perspective, life is not only a journey, but a pilgrimage and a quest. It is a quest for meaning, fulfillment and wholeness. It is a quest for purpose, wisdom and belonging. As individuals who are not satisfied to live the life of nomads or chameleons, or even great toy collectors, I believe that we want to return and restore our focus from the gravity of the world to the gravity of the soul.

For we only wish to unfold,
to continue the miracle
of having been born.
We long to greet each day
as the world does,
Fresh, new and ripe for living.
To lean towards the sun
like flowers—eager to blossom
To move wild
like waves under a silver moon—
drawn on the tide
of our native longing.
We wish to belong to the world, yes.
But first and foremost,
we wish to belong to ourselves.

How do we live more like flowers eager to blossom or waves drawn on the tide of our native longing? How do we belong to ourselves? How do we respond to Annie Dillard's challenge to live as a sail, honed by spirit, broadside to the merest puff of our experience? How do we restore our faith in ourselves and stand surefooted in a sense of soul? How do we undertake this pilgrimage as spiritual beings who, as Henri Amiel suggested, "...are here to give birth to our souls"?

I have been living in the flame of these burning questions since the writing of the poem "The Pilgrim's Plea." The book you are holding is a result of living these questions. Like all beautiful questions, they remain unanswered. But they continue to serve as arrows pointing the pilgrim in me in wonderful directions. Not the kind of directions you download from the Internet, telling you what turns to take in the increments of a mile. These directions are more like principles or precepts... whispers from the soul... promptings from the heart... musings from the mind. These directions suggest to me not where to go and what to do, but how to live as I journey into the unknown—the unknown of a day, of a vocation, of big and little choices, the unknown of a life.

Seek to know your soul so it can speak to you

I cannot count the number of times I attempted to find the stream of this chapter. I set out many times on my small, humble raft of hope and humility, only to see ahead the white waters of a subject I felt unqualified to ride, much less traverse: Soul. I would hear the wild waters just around the next bend of a paragraph and, swoosh I would bail... swimming to the shores of my *close file* button faster than you can say "Scaredy Cat." (The Scarlett O'Hara approach was a nice escape route: "I'll just think about that tomorrow.")

The theme of this chapter has been ruminating in me for months; for we are not pilgrims so much in our countries, our vocations, nor in our new understanding and use of technology, the global community or quantum physics—we are pilgrims, first and foremost, in the realm of soul. Our greatest pilgrimage is into those territories where soul guards the gate: realms we have tiptoed in throughout this book, like balancing the tension between longing and belonging, discovering and entering our natural rhythm, cultivating our native talents, igniting our imaginations, living with hearts wide open in order to not simply be a witness to the world, but to participate in its creation.

And while I have broached the subject of soul in myriad ways throughout this book, it has remained as an indirect object, not the subject. This is partly because I find it to be both an intimidating and a rather imposing subject. After all, who am I to write about such a grand and mysterious topic? I heard myself saying, "I am no priest. I am no rabbi. I am no monk." I am just a common seeker on a spiritual path, walking and stumbling at about equal intervals. All that I know of the soul is what I sense and believe about my own—that it is the custodian of my essence, my deepest truth, and my connection to the eternal.

Then the opposite question struck me right between the eyes, "Who are you *not* to write about soul, if that is, in fact, what you consider to be your essence?" I would not say, "Bread, what do you know of wheat?" or "Water, how arrogant of you to think that you know something of hydrogen and oxygen." "Sky, what could you possibly know of sun and moon and stars, you are not a scholar of astrology." On the same ground that these comments are absurd, so is this one: "Who are you, just a plain old human being, to speak of soul?"

As I contemplated this question I began to wonder why I take the time to write of anything else. After all, what subject, what arena, what realm is more deserving of my consciousness than that of my soul? I do not have to be privy to divine secrets to speak of soul; I just need to tune into my own and listen. In fact, I am the only one who can listen to my particular soul—the one and only receptacle of its wisdom.

I slowly realized that the real arrogance is not in attempting to speak for soul, but pretending that it does not have a voice. Or that we are too insignificant to hear it. In fact, I wonder if the experience of discerning the sacred is even available on the second hand market. It seems improbable to me that God would have whispered the meaning of my life into the ear of someone else (even if that someone is a priest, a rabbi or a monk.) Likely, my best chance to hear the still, small voice is to listen carefully for a sacred echo in the voices and silences that resound within my own mind, body and heart.

I have since entered the white water and have found myself in conversation with my own soul, stirred by wondrous, swirling questions like:

- What is the soul?
- Is the soul in my body or is my body in the soul?
- Does it belong to me or do I belong to it?
- Does the soul care for me or do I care for it?
- Is the soul something to be nurtured and cultivated like a garden, or is it an ever-blossoming arena, in which it is my own sensibilities towards it that need cultivating?
- What powers does the soul possess?
- What power do I give my soul and what power do I withhold from it?

- In what situations and circumstances do I have a sense of my own soul?
- What does my soul have to say to me at this particular time of my life?

I am so grateful that I have made room within my heart and mind to entertain these questions, to be hospitable and welcoming to the qualities of mystery and the elusiveness these questions carry. I understand more deeply what Leo Tolstoy meant in the following passage from his book, *A Calendar of Wisdom.*

> "We live in this world like a child who enters a room where a clever person is speaking. The child did not hear the beginning of the speech, and he leaves before the end; and there are certain things which he hears but does not understand. In the same way, the great speech of God started many, many centuries before we started learning, and it will continue for many centuries after we turn to dust. We hear only part of it, and we do not understand the biggest part of it, but nevertheless, a bit vaguely, we understand something great, something important, something of our own souls."

I sat myself down with a pen in hand and inquired of my soul, "What would you have me know of you?" I would like to share the response I received to this question, and so, have included it in the following pages. I entitled it, "Song of the Soul." If the writing of this book were to bring no other gifts, this piece of writing was gift enough. Not because it is particularly poignant or poetic, but because it is altogether important for me to delve deeper into the current which connects me more fully to this beautiful world and, ultimately, to the divine. With this piece of writing, I have dipped my big toes into those waters. Perhaps reading my response to the question of soul will help to stir your own. See if you (and your soul) can relate to any of the images or roles evoked in this poem.

Song of the Soul

I am the Soul. I am here.
A divine spark placed in the heart of you by the Hand of God.
I am the sacred territory where you can remove your shoes
and know for yourself, within yourself, the blessedness of holy ground.
I will be true to you… if you but seek the truth of me.

I am the Soul. I am here.
Custodian of your original nature.
All that is native to you, everything that is essential,
I have stored with the utmost care.
I am the keeper of your deepest secrets,
not the secrets that keep you tossing in your bed,
but those shaped liked keys to the Door of Truth.
I have held close the memories that would elude even the heart.
Fear not, I have not missed a thing—not a single Kodak moment is lost on me,
nor the millions of minor ones in between.
I will be the treasure chest where nothing that matters
has been forgotten nor ignored, if you but lift the lid.

I am the Soul. I am here.
Like a still surface of a lake that reflects the stars,
and your face among them.
I do not struggle for identity—I have no interest in position, roles or titles.
If ever you should forget who you are or to what and whom you belong,
I will hold up the mirror… if you will but gaze my way.

I am the Soul.
Come to me when you are worn and weary of the ways of the world
and I will restore magic and mystery…
not because I am the purveyor of potions, nor a fairy godmother,
but because I never forgot the songs you sang as a child
and the way you wished on stars,
the way you picked flowers at their blossoms instead of their stems
as they surrendered their petals in your innocent hands.
I am the tabernacle holding your deepest dreams and longings.

I am the Soul.
Come to me when you feel jaded and tired,
betrayed by the seductive powers of the outside world,
when the mask you wear grows thin,
and I will help you to renew faith in yourself.
I will restore your faith in this beautiful universe.
Not because you have laid me on an altar that promises a paradise…
but because I have witnessed your comings and goings,
…your winters and springs,… your sorrows and your celebrations.

And through the liturgy of these seasons
I have recorded in your depths, etched in the very stone of your being,
a testament to the powers of courage and hope,
...the way you buried your friend and carried her memory like a torch,
...the way you held the newborn infant as if all of Creation was bundled
in the soft folds of that blanket,
...the way you've stumbled and fallen... then gotten back on your feet,
time and again, willing to take another step.

I am the Soul. I am here.
A threshold to the Eternal...
I do not age, I only deepen and grow stronger.
I have no skin to wrinkle, no hair to lose, no bones to grow brittle.
I am a gateway that swings wide with the slightest prompting...
I will carry you like a warm wind to the Heart of God
if you but draw the curtain...
Then again, I am the only part of you to be carried home...
The rest shall remain as dust.

I am the Soul. I am here.
As an invitation to live more deeply,
as a promise to prompt you towards your possibility,
as a light in your inner window,
as an invisible arrow pointing your feet on this earthly journey,
as wings to return you to the One who made you.
All of this and more, Beloved One,
I aim to be... if you but pause to be with me.

Journal Entry, June 2001

Trust the compass of soul

We must seek to know our souls so that they can speak to us. What surprised me about this passage was not just the beautiful roles my soul has undertaken, but its relentless faith and immense patience in me to respond and receive its gifts—to pause long enough to be in its company. We must not concern ourselves that it is arrogant or presumptuous to do so, in fact, we should consider such an undertaking as necessary as eating and as urgent as loving. If we are not in communion with our own souls, how do we expect to be in communion with our lives, with the world, or with other human beings? Living a life that is cut off from the presence of soul is like a sailor who is lost upon wild seas with disregard for a compass or stars—it is to be drifting rather than directing one's journey.

I remember writing the following lines in "A Pilgrim's Plea" and feeling the truth of them in the marrow of my bones:

For each of us must travel
the uncharted seas of our lives, alone.
Yet, blessedly, together, side by side.
Trusting that inner compass of hope
and courage and imagination.
Never forgetting that
when we bring heart to the journey,
we make it holy.
When we bring heart to the journey,
we will not lose sight of the brilliant
stars in the immense night sky.

Perhaps what we call "heart" and what we call "soul" go together; the heart being the emotional side of soul, soul being the spiritual side of heart. When we bring these magnificent twins as companions on the pilgrim's journey, we will not lose sight of the brilliant stars, even if they are hidden behind dark clouds, or tucked under the blanket of day. It is in the nature of the heart to be loyal to the stars it loves, and it is in the nature of the soul to not be mistaken by appearances. Together they provide a steady compass.

Is it possible that our hearts and souls, when working in unison, know the secret geography of our destinies? Can we trust this invisible, mysterious part of ourselves to hold the map to our futures? What if we bequeathed our loyalty to the soul, trusting that it will take us where we need to go? What if we followed the soul in a way that it carried our feet and provided a kind of rhythm to the journey? I pose these thoughts as questions, yet as I write I feel a resounding "Yes" pounding in the middle of my chest. This beating of my heart tells me that I would love to delve into the meaning and mystery of being loyal to my soul. Something tells me it leads to magic.

Stand resolute that your soul is not for sale

Ralph Waldo Emerson claimed that the only thing in the world of value is the *active* soul. I put emphasis on the word active, because the inactive soul is not valuable. In fact, the soul exacts an enormous price on the person who would deny, ignore or repress it. This price is not measured in dollars and cents, but in the loss of energy, vitality and the quality of life itself.

We all know what that looks and feels like, trudging through the day under the weight of apathy rather than gliding on wings of purposefulness. Feeling the need to numb ourselves at the end of the day with mindless sitcoms because we have no mind left at the end of the day to engage in meaningful dialogue, a compelling read, or thoughtful silence. The soul is telling us that we sold out to the highest bidder and its vitality is the price we pay.

Social status and security can be such subtle traps on the vocational journey. They are traps because once drawn by the lure of these rewards, it is easy to let these run our lives detached from the energies and gifts of soul. We begin to operate only with one side of ourselves, mainly the strategic, tactical, mechanical side. Day in and day out, this "go to work and come home to get ready for the next day" becomes a mental habit that we come to apply to everything, including our homes, our families and our friends. (For example, we invite our friends to "do" lunch, we "pencil in" the kid's play performance, we schedule a "once a month dinner" with our loved one.)

Operating in strictly a "work mode" is great for work, but if we cannot put it down outside of the workplace, we begin to feel forlorn and lost. That is because we cannot repress the presence of soul and not pay the price. Work can be such an attractive way of betraying and denying the soul. We need to make a living, of course. But not at the expense of making a life. They need not be mutually exclusive.

Saint John Chrysostom warned us that, "The love of great wealth commends you, 'Bring me your soul as a sacrifice', and people will do so." We may roll our eyes and call such betrayal the reality of employment, but we are pointing to a symptom rather than a cause. Needing to earn our daily bread and put food on the table does not have to be done with total disregard to the need to feed our spirits as well. It is when we have invested ego and identity in the making of a living that we can block or poison the true making of a life. It is when the question "What do I do?" carries more weight than "Who am I being and becoming?" that we know we are in trouble.

I remember taking a lucrative contract for a company that, in the end, required me to compromise the integrity of my work for its purposes. The words of John Ruskin came to haunt me, "You cannot sell your talent or your genius; as soon as you do, you are a prostitute. You can sell your work, but not your soul." I will never forget looking in the mirror as I drove to work one morning and saying aloud "Denise, you are prostituting yourself." I suggested to the customer by the end of that day that they find another consultant for the project. It would mean meager earnings for the quarter, for sure, but I remember the richness of rolling down my window and joining voices with Tom Petty in a chorus of "... I will stand my ground... and I won't back down."

The great Mahatma Gandhi, a small man who spent his days crossed-legged at a loom, found the force (he called it *satayana,* meaning "passive resistance") which would bring an end to the British rule of India. He did not hire management consultants, he attended no conferences. He was a strategic genius, no doubt. But his genius was soul-based. In his words, "One needs to be slow to form convictions, but once formed they must be defended against the heaviest odds."

At another time and place Gandhi said, "We must be the change we wish to see in the world." I am sure that Nelson Mandela would nod in agreement. So would Martin Luther King, Jr. and the legions of individuals throughout time who have held their deeper convictions and purposes high in the face of powers that would bring them down, if not with physical force, with the promise of riches, prime stock options and great financial portfolios.

I do not expect you or myself to bring independence to an entire nation, nor to necessarily lead a great movement for justice. (Although, if that's where you're headed, "May the force be with you!") I employ these examples because they bespeak the lives of individuals whose own convictions and values were a grounding wire to themselves. Our convictions and values can be equally grounding in a way that we can belong to ourselves.

We wish to belong to the world, yes.
But first and foremost,
we'd like to belong to ourselves.
For you cannot downsize, right size
or minimize the human soul.
That place in each of us
that is our true home
is totally immune
to the corporate takeover,
to mergers and acquisitions,
because it's not for sale.

Sometimes our "selling out" is so subtle that we don't even know that it has taken place. Never having made an overt decision, it feels as if it just kind of happened to us. Selling out can be the result of not acting on principle, not responding to the call of soul, but sleep-walking through our days. We are just as culpable, of course, in our apathy. This kind of betrayal to the soul happens when we keep the same job for years, after it has failed to nourish us in any significant way. Or when we allow the job to drain the vital forces within us that would keep the soul afloat. That we are doing it for a paycheck does little to console the soul within us. That we should find ourselves dispirited should come as no surprise.

Maybe the problem is not with the job, but with who we have become in order to fit what we think we should be in that role or in that particular environment. For example, when we are in a situation that we know in our bones is wrong or unfair or unethical, but we acquiesce for the sole purpose of conformity or not wanting to rock the proverbial boat. Or, how about when we get into that classic workaholic mode and ignore for months at a time our personal and spiritual needs—like quality time with family, time in community or in nature, doing whatever it is that puts us in the stream of soul? Trust me—if there are a thousand and one ways to leave our lovers, there at least that many ways of ignoring or betraying our souls.

So how do we become vigilant in our aim to listen to and attune to the needs and desires of our souls? How do we stay awake and not sleep-walk through life? How do we belong to ourselves, through our values and convictions, without selling out to the highest bidder? How do we establish a kind of dominion, a place of calm within our interior worlds, where we can stand with a solemn dignity and self-assuredness even in the midst of a changing work world?

Accept that the vocational journey is a spiritual journey

To begin with, it is imperative that we set our compasses to our true purposes in life. Underneath all our worries about careers, jobs, and retirements our purpose really comes down to living fully, to bringing our gifts to the light of day, regardless of position, promotion, or pension. This is easy to forget given the incredible pressures and paradoxes that we face on the vocational journey in today's work world. We know the new rules:

- Get up, compete in the open market, show your stuff!
- Keep your skills marketable, add value to your workplace.
- Be responsible for your own continuous learning.
- Demonstrate that you are an independent thinker, a true maverick, but don't forget to be the ultimate team player.

- Cultivate a specialized skill set, but prepare to multi-task!
- Balance your life and work, but prepare to give 200%!

What is so spiritual about that, you ask? Precisely! Because the challenges that come with the need to earn a living in the world are so great, it can be nothing less than a spiritual practice to walk that road with a sense of integrity and dignity at our centers. To traverse the highways and byways of a career and maintain a strong sense of self at one's center takes discipline, courage and perseverance.

Indian philosopher and poet Sri Aurobindo reminds us, "The spiritual journey is one of continuously falling on your face, getting up, brushing yourself off, looking sheepishly at God and taking another step." In what area of our lives do we understand Aurobindo's dilemma more clearly than in our work lives? Every taking and leaving of employment, no matter how smooth the going, lands us on our behinds in one way or another. In a way, all work is temporary work. Especially in the western world, where moving from one opportunity to the next is almost a required rule of the road.

Consider too, how at their core, vocational issues are deeply spiritual issues. The questions that are at the heart of livelihood are questions of the soul:

- What do I want?
- What is my purpose?
- Where do I belong?
- What stage am I at in my journey?
- What am I looking for in the short term and the long term?
- What am I working towards?
- What am I working for?
- How do I know which way to go?
- What if I can't make a living doing what I consider to be my "real work"?

This last question is particularly deserving of our attention.

Take the high road in life and work

It is difficult at first to bring the world of work and the world of the soul together. We work in order to survive. Instead of approaching work as an arena of possibility and real expression, we often leave our true selves at the company door, feeling as if our contributions are merely functional, required and demanded. When we work like this, we do little to stir the soul. I think it just rolls over and goes back to sleep, saying, "Wake me when we're out of here!"

But as human beings, we desire expression. When we perform an action, the invisible within us finds a form and comes to expression. Therefore, our work should be the place where the soul can enjoy becoming visible and present. The rich, unknown, reserved and precious within us, can emerge into visible form. I believe our nature longs deeply for the possibility of expression in what we call work.

Lorna Catford and Michael Ray, in their delightful book, *The Path of the Everyday Hero,* make a distinction between work with a small "w" and work with a capital "W," one's essential "Work." Work with a small "w" is what we do every day, our job or profession. It is what we put on our tax forms and what we tell people when we are asked about our occupation. It's who we are on the everyday level of existence. Work with a capital "W" refers to our reason for being in the world. It embodies our highest purpose and transcends our everyday work. Our true work is what we would describe to friends around a roaring fire when sharing intimacies about what is meaningful in our lives. For example, you may be employed as a bartender, but your real "Work" may be coaching the kid's little league games, providing the alto voice in the church choir, and or being the best parent you know how to be.

In her book, *Take Your Soul to Work,* writer Tanis Helliwel refers to the high road of work and the low road. Most of our jobs contain aspects of both high road and low road work, aspects that satisfy the soul and others that satisfy the personality. We may take a job for monetary reasons, but the way in which we do it brings aspects of high road work to the position. The way we treat our customers and co-workers, as well as our competitors, brings us ongoing opportunities to walk the high road at work.

Only we know what our true calling is, but the necessity to make a living cannot snuff out that vital flame. Even if we are employed in what feels like low road work, we cannot afford to ignore our high road work. It is essential not just to the soul, but to our workplaces. Catholic scholar John O'Donohue in his beautiful book, *Anam Cara,* makes a great case to the corporate world for inviting the soul of the employee. He says,

> "We had better make room for the soul at work if we want to reap the benefits of its gifts which include creativity, imagination, innovation and resourcefulness, vitality, joy and energy. Imagination is the creative force of the individual. It will release possibilities of recognition and creativity that the linear, controlling, external mind will never even glimpse. When the imagination is allowed to stir it opens up the workplace in a brand new way. Our work should be expressive of our identity, dignity and giftedness. Sell your soul and you buy a life of misery."

O'Donohue makes the case that the contemporary workplace worships at the altar of functionality. Concepts such as "process", "method", "model", "system", "strategy" and "procedure" pretty much sum up our approaches and relationships within the work world. This functional perspective is critical. But the other side of our nature does not have to be sacrificed at this altar. The soul thrives on concepts like discovery, inquiry, mystery, passion, surprise, and wholeheartedness. Bridging these worlds within us would not diminish our results in the workplace, it would enhance and increase them!

In an earlier publication entitled *Cultivating True Livelihood,* I included a list of differences between the traditional view of employment and working with a capital "W" which I called True Livelihood. Some of the major differences included:

Employment	True Livelihood
Work that saps the spirit	Work that taps the spirit
Focuses on getting	Focuses on giving
Separates life and work	Sees life and work as two sides of the same coin
Success is tied to money and benefits	Success is tied to personal, spiritual and financial growth
Decisions based on scarcity thinking	Decisions based on abundance mentality
Views the demands of the job as a limitation of artful living	Views working as a springboard for artful living
Sees work as an obligation	Sees work as a privilege

So the question arises, how do we cultivate livelihoods which are in alignment with our spirits and do not disregard the soul? I wonder, could it possibly be as simple as Henry David Thoreau implies in this classic quote?

> "If a man does not keep pace with his companions perhaps it is because he hears a different drummer. Let him step to the music he hears, however measured or far away."

Follow the beat of your soul's drum

One of our most sacred duties in life is the duty to be ourselves. Wisdom, joy and peace can only come when we stop looking for them and start living the life intended for us. Each of us must live our own life, from beginning to end, no one else can do it for us. Our soul wants us to occupy our life right to the corners… living not just the length of our life but the breadth as well. Our soul beseeches us to live face to face with ourselves and skin to skin with the world. To see the false as false and the true as true. To look into our hearts and follow our true nature. To have faith in our longing and in the fierceness of its ache. Renowned mythologist, Joseph Campbell, echoed this wisdom when he said,

> "What each must seek in his life never was on land or sea. It is something out of his own unique potentiality for experience, something that has never been and never could have been experienced by anyone else."

John O'Donohue put it more emphatically,

> "Each destiny has a unique curvature and must find its own spiritual belonging and direction. Individuality is the only gateway to spiritual potential and blessing."

Clearly, it is the soul's duty to be loyal to its own desires. But it can only do that when we allow its voice to be heard and its dance to be danced. I believe that the soul speaks to us through our purposes and our passions, our longings and our need to belong. The soul dances when we speak our truth, when we make choices based on our deeply held convictions and when we work and live in the spirit of generosity and love. The soul carries its own small drum and that is what Thoreau was talking about when he urges us to follow the music we hear, however measured or far away.

Leo Tolstoy wrote about the voice of the soul in this passage from his book, *Calendar of Wisdom*.

> "The voice of your conscience, the voice of your soul, can always be singled out above the noise of your other wishes, because it always wants something seemingly useless, seemingly senseless, seemingly incomprehensible, but at the same time something actually beautiful and good, which can be achieved only through effort."

How do we hear the music of our souls above the cacophony of noise and sound that surround us in our inner and outer worlds? How do we make a place, even a small place, where the notes of the holy drum can beat and be heard?

Find and go to your forest

Regardless of where we are employed, what if we were to commit to the practice of starting each day with one endearing moment, before the bumps and nicks and noise rush in, before the confusions and conflicts tighten our sense of things? What if we followed the wild and wonderful advice of Joseph Campbell who suggested that we "make a small corner of our day, each day, where we do not know what or who we are responsible to." Where we can just breathe and let our spirits fly in the winds of our *being*… not our *doing*. A place for our spirits to soar on their own unencumbered wings. A place, perhaps, where we can feel the presence of God like the child in this wonderful Chasidic story.

There was once the child of a rabbi who used to wander in the woods. At first his father let him wander, but over time he became concerned. The woods were dangerous. The father did not know what lurked there.

He decided to discuss the matter with his child. One day he took him aside and said, "I have noticed that each day you walk into the woods. I wonder, why do you go there?"

The boy said to his father, "I go there to find God."

"That is a very good thing," the father replied gently. "I am glad that you are searching for God. But, my child, don't you know that God is the same everywhere?"

"Yes," said the boy, "but I am not."

We need the kind of time and space in our lives in which we can conceive, renew, embrace and enchant the life we want. Christian mystic Meister Eckhart suggests that we do not need the whole armory and vocabulary of therapies, psychologies or spiritual programs. He suggested that if we have trust in and expectation of our own solitude, everything we need to know will be revealed to us. Even if that solitude is found for a few moments in our kitchen before starting the commute, or in the car before we enter the work day, or at the end of the day—on the bridge between work and being with the family. But it must be found somewhere if we are to cultivate the capacity and readiness to receive the gifts of soul.

Irish writer, James Stephens, says, "The only barrier is our readiness." We often remain exiles, left outside the rich world of the soul, simply because we are not ready. Our task is to refine our hearts and minds. There is such beauty and blessing near us at all times that cannot enter our lives because we are not capable of receiving it. The handle is on the inside of the door; only we can open it. Our lack of readiness is often caused by our blindness, our fear, and our preoccupation with the million and one things that call for our attention in the outside world. When we are ready, our souls will be singing and our lives will dance to the deep melody. When we are ready, we will be blessed.

We need not cultivate our souls like we do the garden for our pansies or the earth for our summer tomatoes. We need to be more like the child who ventures into the forest, trusting that we do not have to create the divine, nor beg for a sense of the sacred to come to our side. What we need is to make the place within us where we can be ready and open to receive the grace that is ever present.

For we only wish to unfold,
to continue the miracle
of having been born...

Passages

"The soul would rather fail at its own life than
succeed at living someone else's."

David Whyte

"Each of us inevitable,
Each of us limitless—
Each of us with his or her right upon the earth,
Each of us allowed the eternal purports
Of the earth
Each of us here
As divinely as any here."

Walt Whitman

"You need chaos in your soul
to give birth to a dancing star."

Friedriche Nietzsche

"Creativity is foremost,
being in the world soulfully,
for the only thing we truly make,
whether in the arts,
in culture, or at home, is soul."

Leo Tolstoy

The Talmud

"You cannot see your soul, but only the soul can truly see the essence of things."

"A person will understand his place in the world only when he understands his soul."

Chinese wisdom

The Talmud

"The soul of a person is the lamp of God."

Henry David Thoreau

"Nothing is more terrible than activity without insight. Only work which is the product of inner compulsion can have spiritual meaning. The mass of men lead lives of quiet desperation."

"When you work you fulfill a part
of Earth's furthest dream assigned to you
when that dream was born.
And in keeping yourself with labor
you are in truth loving life,
and to love life through labor
is to be intimate with life's inmost secret."

Kahlil Gibran

"Some nights, stay up till dawn…
Be a full bucket pulled up the dark way of a well,
then lifted out into light.
Something opens our wings.
Something makes boredom and hurt disappear.
Something fills the cup in front of us.
We taste only sacredness."

Rumi

Edna St. Vincent Millay

"The world stands out on either side—
No wider than the heart is wide;
Above the world is stretched the sky,
No higher than the soul is high."

"Why do you hasten to remove a thing which hurts your eye, while if something affects your soul you postpone the cure until next year?"

Horace

"To a large extent, the future lies before us like a vast wilderness of unexplored reality. The God who created and sustained the evolving universe through eons of progress and development has not placed our generation at the tag end of the creation process. God has placed us at the beginning."

Sir John Templeton

"I am the master of my fate;
I am the captain of my soul."

William Henley

"Ordinary riches can be stolen.
Real riches cannot.
In your soul are infinitely precious things that cannot be taken from you."

Oscar Wilde

Diane Ackerman

"It began in mystery, and it will end in mystery, but what a savage and beautiful country lies in between."

"The seed of God is in us.
Now the seed of a pear tree
grows into a pear tree
and a hazel seed
grows into a hazel tree.
A seed of God
grows into God."

Meister Eckhart

Thomas Aquinas

"All that is true,
by whomsoever it has been said,
has its origin in the Spirit."

"Every time we walk down the street, we are preceded by hosts of angels singing, 'Make way, make way, make way for the image of God.'"

Rabbinic Phrase

"I live my life in growing orbits which move out over this wondrous world. I am circling around God, around the ancient towers and I have been circling for a thousand years. And I still do not know if I am an eagle or a storm or a great song."

Rainer Maria Rilke

"No job is large enough to contain even one human soul." John O'Donohue

Carlos Castaneda

"Eventually I saw that the path of soul requires a full gesture, a degree of abandon that can be terrifying. Only then is it possible to achieve a sparkling metamorphosis."

"Your role, however small, is just as important as the biggest in contributing to the success of the entire drama of souls on the stage of creation."

Parmahansa Yoganada

To Ponder and To Practice

- Using Mark Nepo's definition, when do you remember feeling like a "nomad"—journeying without being changed? When have you been the "chameleon"—changing without having journeyed? In what areas of your life have you been the "pilgrim"—journeying, and being transformed by the journey?
- Draft a list of your strongest convictions and values that could serve as a grounding wire for you as you traverse the rocky roads of life. Where are you walking your talk these days?
- Who is a person you have known who seems to live most soulfully? How does this person express or exemplify that quality? How would you like your life to greater reflect the life of that person?
- Think about three different times in your life when you felt connected to your soul in a meaningful way. What was happening during those times that made them such? How were those times similar or different to your current phase of life?
- 13th century mystic and poet Rumi wrote, "When you do things from your soul, you feel a river moving in you, a joy." Draft a list of 5-10 things that make you feel your river.
- Gifted writer Barbara Kingsolver told us something very important when she said, "People's dreams are made out of what they do all day. The same way a dog that runs after rabbits will dream of rabbits. It's what you do that makes your soul, not the other way around." What are you doing that is making your soul? When you think about how you spend your time, what qualities are you adding to your soul?
- Which aspects of your present life and work feel like the "low road" and which aspects feel like the "high road"? How could you bring more "high road" behavior into the "low road" contexts of your life?
- Instead of speaking to your soul, let your soul speak to you. Write a letter or a poem of what you hear your soul saying to you.
- Beatrice Lillie suggests that "The vows one makes privately are more binding that any ceremony." What private vows or silent promises could you make that could help you remain true to your own soul?
- Create a sacred place where you can go and be with your soul. This place can be in your home or yard, perhaps in your interior space shaped by your imagination or a spiritual realm you visit. Nothing is too mundane or exotic to name as your sacred place. Consider what kinds of objects you would like to have in that space, perhaps things from your childhood or from nature. What colors, sounds, smells and textures would you like in that space? Which most invite the qualities of spirit and essence of soul?

Practice

- Every so often, remember that this is your life and that you are the only one who can live it. What could serve as a faithful reminder of this important fact?
- If you were to put together a "Soul Chest," what would you put into it to help you remember and return to the sacred part of yourself?
- Select a quote from this chapter's *Passages* which you can use to remind you of the importance of being loyal to and attending to the needs and longings of your soul.
- Choose a daily habit, routine or symbol to help you remain conscious of your intention to "take the high road" in your life and work.
- Given everything you have read in this chapter, what do you want to *keep* doing? What do you want to *stop* doing? What do you want to *start* doing?

Notes

Appendix: Everyday Habits as Entrance to Soulful Living

Routines at Home

Putting on or removing your shoes
Putting on or removing your makeup
Brushing and flossing your teeth
Pouring the first cup of coffee
Taking a bath
Folding laundry
Setting the table
Washing the floor
Washing the mirror
Hanging up your clothes
Walking in and out of the door
Stirring something in a pot
Getting dressed or undressed
Brushing your hair
Taking a shower
Washing dishes
Throwing out the garbage
Bringing food to the table
Polishing the furniture
Vacuuming
Making the bed
Washing the car
Smelling something in the oven
Cutting vegetables

Examples

- Turn the mundane task of putting on your shoes into the ritual that reminds you to walk on the earth today with humility and gratitude. When taking off your shoes, put the world aside and attend, for even a few brief seconds, the ground of your own inner being.
- Stop for just a second to consider what thoughts, worries or concerns you are ready to throw out with the garbage. Don't forget to line your mind with clean thoughts before re-entering the house.
- When bringing food to the table, think of offering the gifts of love, care and communion as Christ brought to the Last Supper.

Events

Walking in and out of the door to work
Ringing telephone or cell phone
Shaking hands
When someone asks, "How are you?"
Opening and closing the garage door
Putting on and taking off your glasses
Waiting to cross the street
Getting lost
Sitting in a traffic jam
Waiting for a movie to begin at a theater
Defrosting the windshield
Greeting people at work
Connecting to the Internet
Signing your name
Standing in an elevator
Getting lost
Misplacing your keys
Waiting in line
Entering a dead-end street
Seeing graffiti
Crossing a bridge
Waiting for the bus

Examples

- Use the time you are waiting in line to observe the people around you and note how you are similar and different to those with whom you share the planet. Make eye contact with people and smile.
- Let the task of signing your name on a check or a receipt, serve as a reminder to ask yourself, "Who am I behind this name?"
- When defrosting the windshield on your car, pause to ask yourself, where am I frozen inside my heart? What needs thawing within me in order to receive and enter my day wholeheartedly?

In the Company of Others

Hearing someone cry
Hearing someone laugh
Watching a musician
Watching people dance
Being part of an audience clapping
Making eye contact with strangers
Taking orders from someone
Hearing gossip about others
Paying someone a compliment
Receiving a compliment
Going to someone for advice
Giving criticism
Hearing someone yell
Hearing someone brag
Seeing children at play
Seeing an elderly person
Being part of a cheering crowd
Being approached for money
Dealing with an irate customer
Feeling jealous of someone else
Apologizing to someone
Needing to confront someone
Receiving criticism
Giving a compliment

Examples

- Watch children at play as a tutorial in free-spiritedness.
- Use the event of cheering at a performance to cheer for life in general.
- When approached by someone on the street for money, take a second to give thanks for your own good fortune.

In Nature

A birdsong	The wind whistling	A dog barking
Sunrise or sunset	A spider web	A squirrel leaping
Apples on a tree	A butterfly	A crackling fire
The time change	The phases of the moon	Watering the garden
Planting seeds	Weeding the garden	Raking leaves
Shoveling snow	Watching a storm	Seeing a rainbow
The ocean	Mountains	A forest
A meadow	Flowers	An ant hill
Stars	Seashells	Rocks

Examples

- As you witness a squirrel leap from tree to tree, remember that as you leap from choice to choice, you, too, will land on your feet.
- Apply the principles of the ecology of the forest to the ecology of the workplace.
- Life, death, earth and sky all come together in the intimacy of a garden's space. It is a metaphor too rich to exhaust, a constant reminder that we must accept the forces of nature if we are to survive.

Sports, Art and Leisure

Lifting weights	Working out	Walking on a treadmill
Swimming	Diving into water	Floating on water
Casting a fishing line	Hitting a ball	Walking barefoot
Stretching your muscles	Taking a hike	Surfing
Walking on a beach	Arranging flowers	Playing an instrument
Painting a picture	Dancing	Kayaking
Singing	Sculpting	Needlework

Examples

- Use the motion of diving into water as an exercise of diving into life.
- While fishing, consider what lines you are casting into the greater waters of work, family and community.
- Offer the songs you sing as you play the guitar as a form of prayer.

Physical Ailments

Sneezing, watery eyes
Toothache
A paper cut
Stubbing your toe
Allergies
Menstrual cramps
Heartburn
Insomnia
Headache
Hot flashes
Fatigue
Chronic pain

Examples

- Allow the experience of heartburn to remind you to consider what is burning in your heart.
- When experiencing physical fatigue, ask yourself, "In what other areas of my life am I tired and needing renewal and rejuvenation?"
- Use the painful experience of a toothache or a headache to practice what Viktor Frankl called "the last of human freedoms"—to choose your response to circumstances.

Symbols

An airplane passing overhead
Passing a police car
Seeing a flag
Seeing a kite flying
Watching fireworks
Hearing a fog horn
Hearing a door bell
Passing a cemetery
Seeing a lighthouse
Passing a carnival
Seeing a sandcastle
Hearing a train whistle
Hearing church bells
Seeing an ambulance or a fire engine

Examples

- When passing a hospital, give thanks for your health and the health of your loved ones.
- Use the sound of a train or a passing airplane to remind you that life is a journey. Stop and consider how you feel about your present manner of traveling.
- When seeing a kite in flight, remember that you too are supported and sustained by an invisible force.

Bibliograpy and Suggested Reading

Angelou, Maya. *Wouldn't Take Nothing for My Journey Now.* London: Random House, 1993.
Autry, James. *Love and Profit.* William Morrow & Company, 1991.
Barks, Coleman. *The Essential Rumi.* San Francisco: Harper San Francisco, 1984.
Bender, Sue. *Everyday Sacred.* San Francisco: HarperCollins, 1995.
Bennis, Warren and Burt Nanus. *Leaders.* New York: Harper & Row Perennial, 1985.
Berry, Wendell. *Rememberings.* North Point Press, 1988.
The Selected Poems of Wendell Berry. Washington, D. C.: Counterpoint, 1998.
Blake, William. *The Portable William Blake.* Edited by Alfred Kazin. New York: Penquin Books, 1946.
Blanchard, Ken and Michael O'Connor. *Managing by Values.* San Francisco: Berret-Koehler, 1997.
Block, Peter. *Stewardship: Choosing Service over Self-Interest.* San Francisco: Berret-Koehler, 1996.
Bly, Robert. *The Soul Is Here for It's Own Joy: Sacred Poems from Many Cultures.* The Ecco Press, 1995.
Bissonnette, Denise. *Beyond Traditional Job Development: The Art of Creating Opportunity.* Milt Wright & Associates, 1994.
Cultivating True Livelihood. 1996.
30 Ways to Shine as a New Employee. 1999.
Boldt, Laurence. *Zen Soup.* New York: Penquin Group, 1997.
Borysenko, Joan. *Fire in the Soul.* New York: Warner, 1993.
Breathnach, Sarah Ban. *Simple Abundance.* New York: Warner Books, 1995.
Bridges, William. *JobShift: How to Prosper in a Workplace without Jobs.* Addison-Wesley Publishing Company, 1994.
Transitions :Making Sense of Life's Changes. Perseus Publishing, 1980.
Managing Transitions: Making the Most of Change. Perseus Publishing, 1991.
Brussat, Frederic and Mary Ann. *Spiritual Literacy.* New York: Touchstone, Simon and Schuster, 1996.
Cameron, Julia. *The Artist's Way.* New York: Jeremy Tarcher/Perigree, 1992.
Campbell, Joseph. *Reflections on the Art of the Living.* New York: HarperCollins, 1991.
Hero with a Thousand Faces. Princeton, NJ: Princeton University Press, 1968.
Carlson, Richard and Shield, Benjamin. *Handbook for the Soul.* Little, Brown and Company. 1995.
Catford, Lorna and Michael Ray. *The Path of the Everyday Hero.* New York: Jeremy Tarcher, 1991.
Chodron, Pema. *When Things Fall Apart.* Boston: Shambhala, 1997.
Chopra, Deepak. *Ageless Body, Timeless Mind.* New York: Harmony Books, 1993.
Covey, Stephen. *The 7 Habits of Highly Effective People.* New York: Simon and Schuster, 1989.
Csiksentmihalys, Mihaly. *Flow.* New York: Harper and Row, 1990.
cummings, e. e. *100 Selected Poems.* New York: Grove Press, 1954.
Dalai Lama. *The Art of Happiness: A Handbook for the Living.* New York: Riverhead Books, 1998.
de Mello, Anthony. *The Song of the Bird.* San Francisco: Bantam/Doubleday, 1982.
Depree, Max. *Leadership is an Art.* New York: Doubleday, 1989.
Dobson, Terry and Miller, Victor. *Aikido in Everyday Life.* Oakland, CA: North Atlantic, 1992.
Dorson, Richard. *African Folklore.* Bantam Doubleday, 1972.
Dreamer, Oriah Mountain. *The Invitation.* Harper San Francisco, 1999.
Elgin, Duane. *Voluntary Simplicity.* New York: Quill/William Morrow, 1993.
Eliot, T.S. *"Four Quartets" from Collected Poems 1909-1962.* London: Faber and Faber, 1974.
Emerson, Ralph Waldo. *The Portable Emerson ("Self Reliance").* New York: Viking Penquin, 1981. Edited by Carl Bode.
Estes, Clarissa Pinkola. *Women Who Run with Wolves.* New York: Ballantine, 1992.

Feldman, Christina and Jack Kornfield. *Stories of the Spirit, Stories of the Heart.* San Francisco: Harper San Francisco, 1991.

Feldman, Reynold and Cynthia A. Voelke. *A World Treasury of Folk Wisdom.* San Francisco: Harper San Francisco, 1992.

Fenchuck, Gary. *Timeless Wisdom: A Treasury of Universal Truths.* Virginia. Cake Eaters, Inc., 1994.

Ferguson, Marilyn. *The Aquarian Conspiracy: Personal and Social Transformation in Our Time.* New York: Jeremy Tarcher, 1980.

Ferguson, Alfred. *The Collected Works of Ralph Waldo Emerson.Vol. 1, Nature, Addresses and Lectures.* Cambridge, MA: Harvard University Press, 1979.

Fox, John. *Poetic Medicine: The Healing Art of Poem-Making.* New York: Jeremy Tarcher/Putnam, 1997.

Fox, Matthew. *The Reinvention of Work: A New Vision of Livelihood for Our Time.* San Francisco: Harper San Francisco, 1994.

Frankl, Victor. *Man's Search for Meaning.* Boston: Beacon, 1959.

Friedlander, Ida. *Wisdom Stories for the Planet Earth.* HarperCollins Publisher, 1973.

Gardner, Howard. *Creating Minds—An Anatomy of Creativity Seen Through the Lives of Freud, Einstein, Picasso, Stravinsky, Eliot, Graham and Gandhi.* New York: Basic Press, 1993.

Gibran, Kahlil. *The Prophet.* Alfred Knopt, Inc., 1923.

Goldberg, Natalie. *Long Quiet Highway.* New York: Bantam, 1993.

Writing Down the Bones. East Lansing, MI: Shambahala Publications, 1986.

Greenleaf, Robert K. *The Power of Servant Leadership.* San Francisco: Berett-Koehler, 1998.

Halifax, Joan. *The Fruitful Darkness.* San Francisco: Harper San Francisco, 1993.

Hammarskjold, Dag. *Markings.* New York: Knopf, 1964.

Hammer, Michael. *The Reengineering Revolution.* New York: Harper Business, 1995.

Handy, Charles. *The Age of Unreason.* Cambridge, MA: Harvard Business School Press, 1992.

Harvey, Andrew. *Teachings of the Christian Mystics.* Boston: Shambala, 1998.

The Essential Mystics: Selections from the World's Great Wisdom Traditions. San Francisco: Harper San Francisco. 1996.

Helliwell, Tanis. *Take Your Soul to Work.* Random House of Canada, 1999.

Helminski, Kabir. *The Rumi Collection.* Boston and London: Shambhala, 1998.

Hillman, James. *The Soul's Code: In Search of Character and Calling.* New York: Random House, 1996.

Hoffer, Eric. *The Ordeal of Change.* New York: Harper and Row, 1963.

Houston, Jean. *The Possible Human.* Los Angeles: Jeremy Tarcher, 1982.

Passion for the Possible. Harper San Francisco. 1998.

Jeffers, Susan. *Feel the Fear and Do It Anyway.* New York: Fawcett-Columbine, 1987.

Jung, Carl. *Man and His Symbols.* New York: Doubleday, 1964.

Kabat-Zinn, Jon. *Wherever You Go, There You Are.* New York: Hyperion, 1995.

Keen, Sam. *Faces of the Enemy.* New York: Harper Collins, 1988.

Hymns to an Unknown God. New York: Bantam Books, 1994.

Keen, Sam and Anne Valley-Fox. *Your Mythic Journey.* New York: Jeremy Tarcher, 1973.

Keats, John. *The Selected Poetry and Letters of John Keats.* New York: New American Library, 1966.

King, Martin Luther, Jr. *The Trumpet of Conscience.* New York: Harper & Row, 1967.

Kornfield, Jack. *A Path with Heart.* New York: Bantam Books, 1993.

After the Ecstasy, the Laundry. New York: Bantam Books, 2000.

Kubler-Ross, Elizabeth. *On Death and Dying.* New York: Macmillan, 1969.

Lao-Tzu. *Tao Te Ching.* New York: Concord Grove Press, 1983.
Levine, David. *The Fables of Aesop.* Boston: Harvard Common Press, 1975.
Lamott, Anne. *Bird by Bird—Instructions on Writing and Life.* New York: Doubleday, 1995.
Traveling Mercies. New York: Pantheon, 1999.
Levine, Stephen. *A Year to Live.* New York: Three Rivers Press, 1998.
Lindbergh, Morrow Anne. *The Gifts of the Sea.* London: Pantheon Books, 1955.
Lorca, Garcia. *Poet in New York:* New York: The Noonday Press, 1988.
Mandelker, Amy and Elizabeth Powers. *Pilgrim Souls: A Collection of Spiritual Autobiographies.* New York: Simon and Schuster, 1999.
Markova, Dawna. *No Enemies Within.* Berkeley, CA: Conari Press, 1994.
I Will Not Live an Unlived Life. 2000.
May, Rollo. *The Courage to Create.* New York: Norton, 1975.
McKenna, Megan. *Parables: The Arrows of God.* New York: Orbis Books, 1994.
McNamara, William. *Christian Mysticism.* New York: Continuum Publishing Company, 1981.
Merton, Thomas. *No Man is an Island.* New York: Harcourt Brace, 1955.
Merwin, M.S. *Flower and Hand.* Washington, D. C.: Copper Canyon Press, 1977.
Moore, Thomas. *Care of the Soul.* New York: HarperCollins, 1992.
Original Self: Living with Paradox and Originality. New York: HarperCollins, 2000.
Muller, Wayne. *Legacy of the Heart.* New York: Fireside, 1992.
How Then Shall We Live? New York: Bantam Books, 1996.
Needleman, Jacob. *Money and the Meaning of Life.* New York: Currency/Doubleday, 1991.
Nepo, Mark. *The Book of Awakening.* Berkeley, CA: Conari Press, 2000.
Nin, Anaïs. *Diary of Anaïs Nin.* New York: Harcourt Brace Jovanovich, 1966.
Novak, Philip. (Ed.). *The World's Wisdom: Sacred Texts of the World's Religions.* San Francisco: Harper San Francisco, 1996.
Nouwen, Henri. *Here and Now: Living in the Spirit.* New York: The Crossroad Publishing Co., 1994.
O'Donohue, John. *Anam Cara.* New York: Harper Perennial/Cliff Street Books, 1996.
Oliver, Mary. *New and Selected Poems.* Boston: Beacon Press, 1992.
Osbon, Diane K., ed. Joseph Campbell. *Companion: Reflections on the Art of Living.* New York: HarperCollins, 1991.
Peck, M. Scott, M.D. *The Road Less Traveled: A New Psychology of Love, Traditional Values and Spiritual Growth.* New York: Touchstone/Simon & Schuster, 1978.
Perry, Whitall. *The Treasury of Traditional Wisdom.* Pates, Middlesex, UK: Perennial Books, 1981.
Peters, Tom. *Thriving on Chaos: Handbook for a Management Revolution.* San Francisco: Perennial Library/Harper & Row, 1987.
Phillips, Jan. *Marrying the Muse.* Illinois: Quest Books, 1997.
Remen, Rachel Naomi, M.D. *Kitchen Table Wisdom.* Riverhead, 1996.
Richmond, Lewis. *Work as a Spiritual Practice.* New York: Broadway, 1999.
Rico, Gabrielle. *Pain and Possibility.* Los Angeles: Jeremy Tarcher, 1991.
Rilke, Rainer Maria. *Letters to a Young Poet.* New York: Random House, 1986.
Book of Hours, Love Letters to God. Translated by Anita Barrows and Seanna Macy. New York: Riverhead/Penguin Putnam, Inc., 1996.
Rinpoche, Sogyal. *The Tibetan Book of the Living and Dying.* New York: HarperCollins, 1992.
Safransky, Sy. *Sunbeams: A Book of Quotations.* The Sun Publishing Company, 1990.

Schaef, Anne Wilson. *Living in Process: Basic Truths for Living the Path of the Soul.* New York: Ballantine Books, 1999.

Schumacher, E.F. *Good Work.* New York: Harper and Row, 1979.

Small is Beautiful. London: Abacus, 1973.

Secretan, Lance H.K. *Reclaiming Higher Ground: Creating Organizations that Inspire the Soul.* Toronto: Macmillian Canada, 1996.

Seligman, Martin. *Learned Optimism: What You Can Change and What You Can't.* New York: Pocket Books, 1990.

Senge, Peter M. *The Fifth Discipline: The Art and Practice of the Learning Organization.* New York: Currency/Doubleday, 1990.

Sewell, Marliyn. *Claiming the Spirit Within.* Beacon Press, 1996.

Sinetar, Marsha. *Do What You Love the Money Will Follow.* New York: Dell, 1989.

Living Happily Ever After. New York: Villard Books, 1990.

Ordinary People as Monks and Mystics. Mahwah, New Jersey: Paulist Press, 1986.

Steinem, Gloria. *Revolution from Within.* Boston: Little Brown and Co., 1992.

Steindel-Rast, David. *The Music of Silence.* New York: HarperCollins, 1995.

Suzuki, David. *Wisdom of the Elders.* San Francisco: Bantam/Doubleday, 1992.

Tagore, Rabindranath. *Towards Universal Man: A Poet's School.* N.Y: Asia Publishing House, 1961.

Teilhard de Chardin, Pierre. *The Phenomenon of Man.* New York: Harper, 1965.

Teresa, Mother. *In the Heart of the World.* Novoto, CA: New World Library, 1997.

Thich Nhat Hanh. *Being Peace.* Berkeley, CA: Parallex Press, 1987.

Peace is Every Step. New York: Bantam, 1991.

Living Buddha, Living Christ. New York: Putnam Publishing, 1995.

Tolstoy, Leo. *Calendar of Wisdom: Daily Thoughts to Nourish the Soul.* Translation copyright—Peter Sekirin, New York, Scribner, 1997.

Vaill, Peter. *Managing as a Performance Art: New Ideas for a World of Chaotic Change.* San Francisco: Jossey-Bass, 1991.

Walker, Alice. *The Temple of My Familiar.* New York: Harcourt, Brace, Janovich, 1989.

Walsh, Roger. *Essential Spirituality.* New York: John Wiley & Sons, 1999.

Welwood, John. *Journey of the Heart.* New York: Harper Collins, 1990.

Ordinary Magic: Everyday Life as Spiritual Path. Boston & London, Shambhala, 1992.

Wheatley, Margaret. *Leadership and the New Science.* San Francisco: Berret-Koehler Publishers Inc., 1992.

Whitman, Walt. *Complete Poetry and Prose of Walt Whitman.* New York: Pellegrini and Cudahy, 1948.

Whitmeyer, Claude. *Mindfulness and Meaningful Work: Explorations in Right Livelihood.* Berkeley, CA, Parallax Press, 1994.

Whyte, David. *The Heart Aroused: Poetry and the Preservation of the Soul in Corporate America.* New York: Currency and Doubleday, 1994.

Crossing the Unknown Sea: Work as a Pilgrimage of Identity. New York: Riverhead Books, 2001.

Zerah, Aaron. *The Soul's Almanac.* New York: Jeremy Tarcher, 1998.

Zuskav, Gary. *The Seat of the Soul.* New York: Simon and Schuster, 1989

Source Index

Created and contributed by Kendra L. Webster

The following is a listing of each person and source quoted in *The Wholehearted Journey* with a brief biographical sketch and the page numbers on which they are quoted.

A

B

C

G

H

I

J

K

L

M

N

O

P

R

S

T

U

V

W

Y

Many blessings on your journey.
—Denise Bissonnette

All twenty-one of the original poems in this book are recited by Denise Bissonnette on the CD, *Poems for the Wholehearted Journey*.

"We sat down last night after dinner and allowed ourselves to be totally captured by the beauty of your poetry and its exquisite delivery!!! Oh, we can think of so many who would thoroughly enjoy it!"

360